Paradoxes of Modernity

*Culture and Conduct in the Theory
of Max Weber*

Paradoxes of Modernity

Culture and Conduct in the Theory of Max Weber

Wolfgang Schluchter

TRANSLATED BY
Neil Solomon

Stanford University Press
Stanford, California «» 1996

Stanford University Press
Stanford, California
© 1996 by the Board of Trustees of the
Leland Stanford Junior University
Printed in the United States of America

CIP data are at the end of the book

Stanford University Press publications are distributed
exclusively by Stanford University Press within the United
States, Canada, Mexico, and Central America; they are
distributed exclusively by Cambridge University Press
throughout the rest of the world.

Preface

This book is an attempt to spell out Max Weber's lasting contribution to a philosophical and sociological understanding of the Western trajectory and its consequences. All chapters were originally written in German; Neil Solomon provided the translations. I am very grateful to him for his unceasing effort to render the original as accurately as possible in English. However, I decided to free myself from my own German and revise the English, even to rewrite longer passages, especially in Chapter 2. Therefore, the texts published here differ considerably in length from the German originals and partly also in content.

I appreciate the help Guenther Roth gave me with this revision, as well as the suggestions made by Guy Oakes. A stay at the Center for Advanced Study in Berlin provided the time needed to finish the project. Thanks are due Grant Barnes, now Director Emeritus of Stanford University Press, who offered his good services. I would also like to thank Jan Spauschus Johnson at Stanford University Press and Ken Plax for excellent work in preparing the manuscript for typesetting. Now responsibility rests with me, and any mistakes are mine.

Quotations from Weber's texts are based on the extant English-language editions cited in the Notes and Bibliography but have been substantially modified. In case readers might want to consult the original, a reference to the German-language edition is also included.

W.S.

Contents

Table and Figures

Paradoxes of Modernity

*Culture and Conduct in the Theory
of Max Weber*

Introduction

In a letter to Hannah Arendt of October 4, 1964, Karl Jaspers mentions a conversation he once had with Heinrich Rickert, his colleague and competitor in philosophy at Heidelberg University during the days of the Weimar Republic. It revolved around Max Weber and what it means to be a philosopher today. Jaspers quotes Rickert as having said, "That you turn Max Weber into a philosophy is your indisputable right. That you call him a philosopher is nonsense."[1] Indeed, Weber never claimed to be a philosopher in any technical sense of the term. Although he was well acquainted with the philosophical discourse of the time and to an extent also took part in it, he refrained from crossing this boundary professionally, unlike his friend Georg Simmel. Weber regarded economics and sociology as his domain, not philosophy.

Although Rickert was right, he missed Jaspers's crucial point. When Jaspers, immediately after Weber's death and subsequently,[2] called Weber a philosopher, he identified him not as a member of an academic discipline but as a person who, like Nietzsche and Kierkegaard, advocated intellectual honesty and, unlike them, also lived up to its demands. To Jaspers, Weber was the embodiment of an idealized modern man who resolutely exposes himself to intellectual risks and lives through existential tensions passionately without accepting final resolutions. He saw Weber moved not so much by Nietzsche's dead God as by the God of the Old Testament, whom he experienced as both good and evil. According to Jaspers, Weber was dedicated to science and politics, but with the awareness that even living for them could never be ultimately fulfilling. This tension explains why, Jaspers concludes, Weber posed the question of meaning in the modern world radically, that is, philosophically.[3]

We need not accept Jaspers's philosophical Weber. Jaspers's contention that there is a philosophical dimension to Weber's work, however, is sound. In the first two chapters of this book I make an attempt to spell out at least some facets of this dimension. My focal points are value theory and ethics, both conceived as integral parts of Weber's theory of history and weltanschauung.

Weber not only struggled with the problem of meaning in the modern world; he was also driven by the question of how this world came about. Step-by-step he broadened and deepened his comparative and developmental perspectives. In the last two chapters I try to formulate what I regard as Weber's theory and history of the Western trajectory.

Like *Max Weber's Vision of History*, which I wrote with Guenther Roth,[4] this book is about matters left unfinished by Weber. In fact, it returns to issues partly dealt with in that book, especially the problem of ethics. I hope the solution I can now offer proves to be superior to the position I took almost fifteen years ago. This remark also holds for the reconstruction of Weber's view of the course of Western history that is offered in this book, which has its prelude in two other English-language books of mine, *The Rise of Western Rationalism*,[5] and *Rationalism, Religion, and Domination*.[6] Here I complement these studies and expand on the ideas expressed in them.

As is well known, Weber intended to extend his studies on the economic ethics of the major religions beyond those published in the *Archiv für Sozialwissenschaft und Sozialpolitik* (Archive for social science and social policy) from 1915 to 1920. These new studies would have included an investigation of Islam. In Chapter 3 I attempt to capture his intentions on the basis of the scattered remarks that we find in his writings. Although the picture that emerges from these passages may be sketchy and biased, perhaps we should remember that they were part of an encompassing and multifarious project, and not an effort to demonstrate the existence of a *homo islamicus* or the superiority of the West to the East. Such ill-considered enterprises were neither the purpose nor the result of Weber's comparative and developmental endeavors. Rather, they aimed at a better understanding of alternative modes of conduct caused by constellations of cultural traditions, by institutional arrangements, and by the material as well as the ideal interests of the social strata that were the cultural carriers of these traditions. The remarks on Islam should be read in this light. Chapter 3 supplements similar efforts already undertaken in *Rationalism, Religion, and Domination*, where studies on Confucianism and Taoism, Hinduism and Buddhism, ancient Judaism and early Christianity are assembled.

Weber wanted to conclude his studies of the major religions with an account of the distinctive features and developmental tendencies of Western Christianity. To trace the outline of this unwritten study has been a challenge to any interpreter of Weber's work. In Chapter 4 I try to meet it. I also attempt to put *The Protestant Ethic (Die protestantische Ethik und der Geist des Kapitalismus)* in proper context, something that has still not been achieved in most of the secondary literature.[7] Chapter 3 emphasizes the comparative perspective, Chapter 4 the developmental. Read together, they should convey a relatively coherent picture of the Western trajectory from a Weberian point of view.

Truth, Power, and Ethics

Max Weber's Political-Philosophical Profile

Activity and Renunciation

Max Weber on Science and Politics as Vocations

Allem Leben, allem Tun, aller Kunst muß das Hand-
werk vorausgehen, welches nur in der Beschränkung
erworben wird. Eines recht wissen und ausüben gibt
höhere Bildung als Halbheit im Hundertfältigen.
—Goethe, *Wilhelm Meisters Wanderjahre*
(*Wilhelm Meister's Journeyman Years*)

Wie an dem Tag, der dich der Welt verliehen,
Die Sonne stand zum Gruße der Planeten,
Bist alsobald und fort und fort gediehen
Nach dem Gesetz, wonach du angetreten.
So mußt Du sein, dir kannst du nicht entfliehen,
So sagten schon Sibyllen, so Propheten;
Und keine Zeit und keine Macht zerstückelt
Geprägte Form, die lebend sich entwickelt.
—Goethe, "Urworte—Orphisch"
("Primal Words—Orphic")

The Character of Weber's Two Lectures "Science as a Vocation" and "Politics as a Vocation"

The two speeches "Science as a Vocation" ("Wissenschaft als
Beruf") and "Politics as a Vocation" ("Politik als Beruf") are key

texts in understanding the position Weber took on central questions of modern culture. Some scholars consider them to be foundational efforts at a rational declaration of faith that even today remain pathbreaking. In fact, Weber responds more directly here than elsewhere in a fundamental way to the intellectual and political situation of his time and to its questions of meaning. This directness is the intrinsic connection between the two speeches. There was, however, an extrinsic one as well. Both were given in a similar framework and addressed a similar audience. This similarity is the reason why they should be read together.[1] Contrary to the editions of these addresses prepared by Marianne Weber and Johannes Winckelmann, "Science as a Vocation" should not be incorporated into Weber's writings on the methodology of science (*Wissenschaftslehre*), nor should "Politics as a Vocation" be included in his writings on politics.

Both addresses differ in character from Weber's scholarly treatises or his academic lectures, and from his political articles or election speeches. They pursue a different goal. They are "philosophical" texts, intended to lead the listeners (and later, the readers) to recognize facts and to encourage self-reflection, to win them over for responsible efforts on behalf of a realistic cause. In Weber's view, the future both of the German nation and of modern Western culture depended on the readiness of individuals to engage in such labors of self-renunciation as part of the dialectic of dedication and detachment. These two futures were interrelated: apprehension about the state of the nation was the starting point for apprehension about the state of modern culture.[2]

Max Weber was, as Karl Jaspers put it, a "national German."[3] Nevertheless, Weber fought against those representatives of the German spirit who contrasted it as something "of its own, self-grown and superior" to the progressive, democratic individualism of Western Europe and America.[4] As a national German, he was cosmopolitan in outlook. Nonetheless, he waged battle against those representatives of a moralistic, international pacifism who denied the necessity of a German power state (*nationaler Machtstaat*) and the "responsibility in the face of history" it involves.[5] Even at the end of the First World War, as imperial Germany collapsed—due to the politics of emotion and vanity practiced by its feudal-conservative and bourgeois forces[6]—he hoped, in a paraphrase of an expression of Heinrick von Treitschke's, for Germany's third age of youth.[7] If one was going to take advantage of this opportunity, political action had to take up again a line of de-

velopment that had begun with the events of 1806–7 and 1848–
49. This action presupposed that politically, the bourgeoisie finally stood on its own two feet and combined its powers with
those of the labor movement on behalf of a politics pursuing realistic causes.[8] It further presupposed that academic youth actively
participated in this historical alliance. To do this, youth would
need to cast off its illusions that one can replace rational, scientifically determined knowledge with "direct experience" (*Erlebnis*)
and that a politics of conviction that calmly ignores the realities
not only of Germany but also of life in general is more authentic
than a rational, power-oriented politics of responsibility. Both
speeches were addressed to the German academic *and* democratic youth;[9] they were and are speeches about political *and* human self-determination under the conditions of modern Western
culture.

To make the audience (and later, the reader) aware of intellectual and political conditions, of "the state of the world in general,"[10] it was thus not sufficient to diagnose the fate that only
Germany faced.[11] A world-historical perspective was demanded.
Weber had obtained it by means of a cultural science that employed a comparative and developmental orientation. It encompassed the value-related but "nonevaluative" (*werturteilsfreie*) investigation of the distinct nature of each of the world's major
civilizations (*Kulturkreise*). Only against this backdrop were the
distinct character of modern Western civilization and its accompanying problems of life, as well as the problems of Germany's life,
put in proper perspective. Therefore, the lectures represented a
summation of Weber's most important scientific findings and of
his most important political convictions.

What led to these two addresses? Even though they go together,
they do not form a single entity. Not only do they treat different
topics, they also were conceived at different times. The addresses
were given over a year apart: "Science as a Vocation" was delivered
on November 7, 1917, and "Politics as a Vocation" on January 28,
1919.[12] In the time between them, imperial Germany had suffered
its final military defeat, and the November Revolution had occurred. Moreover, a host of developments in Weber's life and work
took place between these two dates: his return to those manuscripts abandoned at the beginning of the war, on the economy and
other societal orders and forces;[13] his revision and expansion of the
comparative studies of the economic ethics of the world religions,
the publication of which had meanwhile progressed up to ancient

Judaism; his continued interventions into foreign, and increasingly, domestic policy; and finally, his participation in the election campaign for the national assembly[14] and in the choice of candidates for it, in which he failed to get himself nominated. Let us therefore take a closer look at the genesis of the two speeches. The broader context of the addresses primarily encompasses the development of Weber's work from the time he left military service on September 30, 1915.[15] The narrower context involves above all his ties to the Bavarian Free Students Association (Bayerischen Landesverband der freien Studentenschaft) in Munich, which planned and carried out the lecture series "Intellectual Labor as a Vocation."[16]

The Broader Context of the Lectures: Weber's Emergence as a Political Orator and His Return to University Teaching

Before the outbreak of the First World War, Weber worked very intensively on his articles for the *Outline* (*Grundriß der Sozialökonomik*).[17] Even though he participated not only in the scholarly but also in the organizational side of periodicals such as the *Archiv für Sozialwissenschaft und Sozialpolitik*, and of organizations such as the Association for Social Policy and the German Sociological Association, after his breakdowns in 1898–99, his real field of activity was his writing desk. Even after regaining his admittedly precarious ability to work, Weber continued to try to keep his distance from public speaking and teaching activities.[18] He had developed strong psychological inhibitions regarding public obligations of this kind.[19]

With the onset of the First World War he left his desk, and with it, a series of well-advanced, but as yet incomplete, manuscripts. During the following year, he performed the time-consuming and monotonous activities of a military member of the Heidelberg Auxiliary Hospital Commission (Reservelazarettkommission Heidelberg).[20] After departing from this "service for the fatherland" he began to publish his essays on the economic ethics of world religions, the revision and expansion of which occupied him from the winter of 1915–16 onward. At the same time, he intervened in the foreign-policy debate, especially on the war goals, with his first political articles.[21] After leaving the military hospital administration, he initially hoped to be active politically. This hope was one of his reasons for going to Berlin in the middle of November 1915. However, although he kept his chances alive by staying there (with some interruptions) until the middle of 1916, little came of it. He participated in organizations of a more "private" nature, such as Friedrich Naumann's working committee on Central Europe and a committee of the Association for Social Policy; but aside from sporadic and informal contacts with high-level government officials, he never had the chance to influence the political decision-making process in a way satisfactory to him.[22] As a result, Weber made use of his time to work in the library on "Chinese and Indian matters."[23] One result of this intensive scholarly activity was soon forthcoming. In 1916–17, he published the study on Hinduism in three parts in the *Archiv für Sozialwissenschaft und Sozialpolitik* as the continuation of his study of Confucianism and on the basis of the abandoned manuscripts from 1914.[24]

After reinvestigating the "Chinese and Indian matters," he immersed himself for a second time in "matters Jewish" in the autumn of 1916. He dealt with the Old Testament, primarily analyzing "the Prophets, Psalms, and the Book of Job."[25] In particular, the pre-exilic prophets of doom—independent of both political authorities and the people, and oriented toward foreign affairs—made a great impression on him now. Were there not certain similarities between the international situation of ancient Israel and that of imperial Germany? And in view of this situation, did Weber not feel himself increasingly pushed into the role of the pre-exilic prophets of doom? In the impressive series on ancient Judaism, the first sequel of which appeared in 1917, he described these prophets, the first political demagogues in world history, in a historical treatment with contemporary relevance.[26] Thus, he appeared to move between the present and the most distant pasts. But those Chinese, Indian, and Jewish "matters" were not just the past; they were, in a manner of speaking, also alternative to the present.[27]

The year 1916 not only brought the revision and expansion of important scholarly texts and the first results of policy-oriented political journalism, it also witnessed the conquest of the public platform. Admittedly, Weber still avoided the lecture hall, for which, as he later once wrote, he was not born.[28] In his first political address since his illness, the Nuremberg speech of August 1, 1916, to the German National Committee for an Honorable Peace (Deutscher National-Ausschuß für einen ehrenvollen Frieden), he still moderated himself, "following official regulations."[29] But he took off his gloves in the great speech "Germany's Situation in World Politics" ("Deutschlands weltpolitische Lage") on October 27, 1916, in Munich.[30] Whereas in Nuremberg he had been restrained in his treatment of the advocates of "peace through victory," he now stopped being "diplomatic," especially in regard to the pan-Germans.

"The lion had gotten a taste of blood,"[31] and now he slipped into that role of political demagogue molded by the pre-exilic prophets of doom. Weber mercilessly took to task the rightists' politics of prestige; he indicated that the causes of the war were primarily political and not economic, the most important being the threat of Russia to a powerful German nation-state. For this reason alone, Germany's entry into war had been justified. However, Germany's successful self-assertion and the maintenance of its honor and military security required political reorganization, especially of Central Europe, but not annexation.[32] Germany's national power had to remain tied to the national cultural community. Only on this basis could there be a peace of mutual understanding that included Russia. The latter, however, would have to restrain its expansionist urges, which were intimately connected to czarism as a system. Later, after the February and October Revolutions, Weber repeatedly emphasized that Germany's achievement in this war had been the definitive discrediting of the czarist system. Its elimination removed an important hindrance to rational international relations in Europe. Nevertheless, a peace agreement was based on the willingness of the opponents to recognize Germany as a powerful nation-state with its own cultural tasks. Germany was not a small state (*Kleinstaat*), but a big state (*Großstaat*), not just a *Kulturstaat* but also a *Machtstaat*, and thus subject to the "vicissitudes of power." The Germans must accept this without conceit as their "responsibility in the face of history." Who fails to recognize this, from inside just as much as from outside Germany, is a "political idiot." Furthermore,

Posterity will not hold the Swiss, Danes, Dutch, or Norwegians responsible for shaping culture on earth. They would not be blamed if there was on the Western half of the planet nothing but Anglo-Saxon convention and Russian bureaucracy. That is only fair. The Swiss or the Dutch or the Danes could not have prevented that. But we could have. A nation of 70 million between such world powers had the *duty* to be a *Machtstaat*.[33]

Weber thus anticipated, still in the period of German military successes, that the war would result in a reorganization of Europe.

On the one hand, there would be those large and powerful nation-states that were capable of an alliance: England, France, Russia, Austria-Hungary, Italy, and Germany; on the other hand, there would be a multiplicity of small states. Even if some of these states were closely economically connected to a greater or lesser extent to large and powerful states, all would remain politically sovereign entities. Nevertheless, continuous German national self-assertiveness in the international arena had to be accompanied, as in the case of Russia, by domestic reforms. The longer the war lasted, the more intensively Weber analyzed the necessary reorganization of Germany in a reconstructed Europe. And the more he did this, the tougher his polemics became, first against the Right, and then against the Left as well. In this context he revived some of his prewar reflections, further developing them in terms of the constantly changing political constellations.

He still considered the strictly parliamentary monarchy the best form of government.[34] It was clear to him, however, that this form of government, given the well-entrenched hegemonic position of Prussia, could not be fully realized in the foreseeable future. His various recommendations for constitutional reform after 1917, in part based on a comparative theory of the modern state, can be understood as steps toward coming closer to this parliamentary ideal. Only when the Hohenzollern dynasty completely compromised itself through the flight of Wilhelm II, and only after a decent interval,[35] did Weber declare his support for a parliamentary republic as the only form of government now appropriate for Germany. In the interest of the selection of leaders, he checked pure parliamentarism with certain plebiscitary elements, and in the interests of unity, he checked pure federalism with certain unifying elements. In substance, however, this new German state was to be bourgeois and working class in character. By opting for this political orientation, Weber took a stance against the National Liberals (Nationalliberale) and all parties further to the right, and against the Independent Social Democrats (USPD) and all parties further to the left.

Weber's political orientation, which recognizably guided his foreign and domestic policy positions, has, however, another and deeper side to it. He held politics—like the economy, science, art, erotics, and religion—to be a sphere in its own right that must be exclusively defined neither in terms of class or status group interests nor in terms of brotherly ideals. The conceptual distinction in connection with politics is not useful versus harmful, nor is it true versus false or beautiful versus ugly, nor is it even good versus evil;

it is honorable versus disgraceful. Failure to satisfy a political duty does not provoke feelings of discontent or guilt as much as it does those of shame. Of course, only he who roots his action in ultimate values can fulfill his "responsibility in the face of history." Any purely power politics is ultimately damned to oblivion, inasmuch as it offers no other support. The politics of realism that Weber advocates, termed the *politics of responsibility* in "Politics as a Vocation," must not be confused with so-called *Realpolitik*.

However, political values are not primarily universalistic human values if one disregards those incorporated in human rights; they are particularistic cultural values. Thus, their reduction not only to economic values but also to ethical values destroys the possibility of politics in its own right. Certainly, if politics hopes to avoid degenerating into pure power politics, it must relate itself not only to cultural but also to ethical values. For that reason Weber focuses on the ever problematic relationship between politics and ethics in the second half of the speech "Politics as a Vocation." Nevertheless, just as those who engage in the politics of responsibility must relate it to ethics, they must also use power. However, those who accept power as a means, says Weber, make a pact with diabolic forces. Although personal communication might be pervaded by the spirit of love,[36] political communication is always pervaded by the spirit of war. This is not to say that Weber wanted to leave Germany's fate to the mightier of the battalions. As he had already put it in 1916 in connection with German war goals, "Let us not forget, *honor*, not changes in the map or in economic profits, is what the German war is about."[37]

Of course, he also did not want to leave Germany's fate to politicians of conviction, with their love of humanity. For Weber the war effort was about the national self-assertion of Germany, not the realization of good in the world. National honor and human good are certainly values equally bound up with ideal interests. This connection, however, does not make them identical. Whoever exclusively follows the imperatives of ethic fulfills the imperatives of politics only in those few cases where the self-preservation and expansion of the collectivity run strictly counter to the self-determination of the individual. In all the other cases, however, where a certain degree of outer freedom is granted to the individual by the collectivity, the conditions of inner and outer freedom do not coincide. This conviction also guided Weber in the hotly debated question of Germany's war guilt after its defeat. Anyone speaking of war guilt, and especially of sole German war guilt, Weber contended, moralized politics in a way that permanently damaged Germany's material as well as ideal interests, a major political mistake that would have to be paid for in the long run, both domestically and internationally.[38]

Weber's political orientation also possesses a foundation in value theory. This orientation penetrates both addresses. Although it is always part of his political statements, it is most clearly developed in other parts of his work, especially in the sociology of religion and in the famous "Intermediate Reflections" ("Zwischenbetrachtung") of 1915 (see the discussion in Chap. 2). In 1916–17, another important element is added to this value theory. It is found in the essay on value freedom, which Weber had originally written as a response to the so-called controversy on value-judgment, but which he then published in revised form at the beginning of 1917. There he added "very brief remarks . . . regarding the theory of value." They clearly conceptualize thoughts already guiding the "Intermediate Reflections": we find ourselves in value relations that are without a common denominator and cannot be mutually harmonized; this forces us to choose our own fate. As an "advocate of [the theory of] value collision," Weber sought to remind youth above all of this "disturbing but inescapable" insight.[39] He also wanted to remind them that their understandable desire for a harmonious life, insofar as it was not counterbalanced by a "disciplined dispassionateness" with which to view "the realities of life," had to collide with the tragic, strifetorn character of life and ultimately lead to adjustment to or to flight from the world.[40]

Thus, by 1916 Weber had recaptured the public platform. He intensified his activities in the public realm in 1917 and also spoke again on scholarly themes. On January 24, 1917, he lectured to the Social Science Association (Sozialwissenschaftlicher Verein) in Munich on "The Sociological Foundations of the Development of Judaism" ("Die soziologischen Grundlagen der Entwicklung des Judentums"),[41] reporting on his work in progress on ancient Israel.[42] On October 25, 1917, he addressed the Sociological Association (Soziologische Gesellschaft) in Vienna on "Problems of the Sociology of the State" ("Probleme der Staatssoziologie"); the focus here was on the sociology of domination, with its three pure types of legitimate domination and a fourth type based on the development of the city in the Occident.[43] Between the occasions of these two addresses, the two Lauenstein conferences on culture took place, the first from May 29 to May 31 and the second from

September 29 to October 3, 1917, both behind closed doors, and both with selected participants. In addition, Weber gave a political speech before the Progressive People's Association (Fortschritt-licher Volksverein) in Munich on June 8, speaking about the "de-mocratization of the life in our state."[44] Moreover, he may have spoken in Heppenheim in mid-September, in an adult education course on "State and Constitution" ("Staat und Verfassung").[45] The high point of these activities, however, came in November, when the Munich public was given the opportunity within the space of three days to listen to the man of politics and to the man of scholarship,[46] to hear both the fighter for the political self-determination of a Germany threatened internally and externally by war[47] and the fighter for the self-determination of the indi-vidual human being threatened internally and externally by the disenchantment of the world: On November 5 came his speech for a negotiated peace and against the pan-Germanic danger ("Gegen die alldeutsche Gefahr"),[48] and on November 7 came his lecture "Science as a Vocation."[49]

The return to the academic lecture hall, to a professorship, also came within reach in 1917. In Vienna, Weber was asked to succeed the late Eugen von Philippovich; Göttingen had also made efforts to get him, and in Munich and Heidelberg appointments were be-ing discussed. The offer from Vienna came in the summer, and Weber finally decided, in spite of serious reservations, not to reject it out of hand. At the end of October, he negotiated in Vienna and agreed, for the first time since his illness, to a "trial lecture course" in the summer semester of 1918.[50]

"Science as a Vocation" thus comes in a phase of Weber's life in which he immersed himself with ever-increasing determination in fields of activity partly postponed due to illness and partly new to him. It was a time during which he sought to make something of his regained energies not only as a researcher, but also as a poli-tician and as a teacher. In spite of his sobriety and detachment, something like optimism seems to have captured his mind.[51] As a researcher, he had made decisive headway with his large-scale and continually expanding project on the economic ethics of the world religions. With the lecture course in Vienna, which he announced as "Economy and Society (Positive Critique of the Materialist View of History)" ("Wirtschaft u. Gesellschaft. Positive Kritik der materialistischen Geschichtsauffassung"), the stage was set for more than just occasional work on the manuscripts he had aban-doned at the outset of the war.

With his articles and speeches, Weber the politician had taken an incisive stand on the domestic and foreign policy situation of imperial Germany; he called for a negotiated peace settlement and the parliamentary reform of the imperial constitution, as well as for the democratization of German political life. In view of the peace resolution of the majority parties in the German Reichstag on July 19, 1917, and the developments in Russia, a peace settlement appeared to be in reach; the quick changes in the imperial chancellorship from Theobald von Bethmann-Hollweg to Georg Michaelis and to Georg Graf von Hertling had increased the actual say of the parties in the choice of leaders, and decisive legal steps toward parliamentarization appeared to be only a matter of time.

As a teacher, however, Weber had reopened the dialogue with parts of academic youth. As Marianne Weber had so desired, he gave at least occasional lectures.[52] He no longer talked just at the famous Sunday afternoon gatherings at the house at Ziegelhäuser Landstraße 17,[53] but also at the exclusive meetings at Burg Lauenstein. Admittedly there he appeared to the youth present not so much as a scholar or teacher, but—perhaps because of his very detachment from matters and people, because of his passionate objectivity—as a possible leader in politics and of men.[54]

On November 7, 1917, during the presentation of "Science as a Vocation," he made this impression once again. Karl Löwith provides a vivid account of the effects of this address on a group of students deeply sensitized by their experiences of war. In his memoirs, written in exile,[55] he observes:

In [Weber's] statements the knowledge and experience of an entire life were concentrated; everything was taken directly from within and thought through with critical understanding, the authority of his personality providing them with a powerful urgency. His acuteness in formulating the question was matched by his renunciation of all easy solutions. Although he tore away the veils of all wishful thinking, anyone listening had to feel that at the heart of this clear reason lay a deeply earnest humaneness.[56]

A year later, "Politics as a Vocation," presented in the same series and in front of a similar audience, did not have the same effect. Löwith made short shrift of it: "A second lecture on 'Politics as a Vocation' did not have the same captivating verve."[57] Weber himself indirectly confirmed this impression. A few days before the address he wrote to Else Jaffé: "The lecture is going to be bad; something other than this 'calling' occupies my heart and soul."[58]

He had long hesitated to deliver the lecture, and it appears that something like political blackmail was necessary to get him to finally do it.[59] What had changed?

Weber's cautious optimism from 1917 had by now disappeared. He saw the Germans—largely due to their own failings—as having been made by the war into the "pariah people of the world."[60] The extreme right-wing "politics of vanity" in conjunction with the inability of the political leadership, first under Bethmann-Hollweg and then under Hertling, to make the military accept the primacy of politics had led to Germany's destruction as a powerful nation-state. Those foundations still capable of being built upon were now being razed by that "bloody carnival," the "revolution." The price paid for the ruinous submarine policy, demanded by the military in conjunction with the Right and opposed by Weber from the very beginning,[61] was ultimately the entrance of the United States into the war. The price paid for the military-dictated policy toward Russia was the failure to reach a reasonable separate peace with Russia at Brest-Litovsk that could have laid the foundation for a lasting general peace.

The revolution added yet new calamities to these two serious foreign policy mistakes of the old regime. For example, Kurt Eisner, who had succeeded in coming to power as the Bavarian governor, hoped, with the support of a "small crowd of leftist literati," to arouse sympathy from the Allies by publishing the "records of guilt." Weber was deeply embittered by these completely undignified politics of conviction.[62] Moreover, the constitutional developments these and similar groups wanted appeared to him to be inappropriate for strengthening Germany internally and especially for finally guiding Germans—in terms of their values—toward realistic politics, toward a politics of responsibility. At the time of "Politics as a Vocation" Weber considered Germany's complete loss of power, and—as in the time of Napoleon, even foreign rule—a distinct possibility. The political prospects had been dismal. Germany was faced by that "polar night of icy darkness and harshness" that, as he wrote at the end of "Politics as a Vocation," certainly "will only slowly fade."[63]

Moreover, Weber now had to come to terms with yet another setback: the return to teaching, which he had ever more seriously considered since 1917, would be connected with even greater personal sacrifices than he had feared. Admittedly, the lecture course in Vienna had been a truly sensational success. Many reports attest to this. Theodor Heuss, who attended some of these lectures, summarized his impressions: "He had become the sensation of the university, one had to have seen and heard him at least once. In this way, he landed in the largest auditorium, where an irreverent curiosity kept the doors in continual motion. I was filled with righteous indignation, especially since I noticed how this pained him, and I told him so. I have never forgotten his reply: 'You are right, it certainly is not possible to roar the word 'asceticism' into such a room.'"[64] Nonetheless, it was not so much these adverse external conditions as the self-imposed obligation to keep the lectern and the public platform separate that caused him such difficulty. After his first lecture hours, he wrote, "My God, is that a strain! Ten speeches are nothing compared to two hours of lecturing. Simply being bound to the plan, to the ability of the people to take notes, and so on."[65] And then: "Nothing, but absolutely nothing has changed from twenty years ago."[66]

From the point of view of husbanding one's energies, the Vienna experience showed that the lecture hall was a much harder lot than the public platform or the writing desk. The course completely exhausted Weber, "dulling his senses" and prompting a "leaden tiredness." In this state of body and mind, he returned to Heidelberg at the end of July. In 1918, shortly after he turned down the Viennese offer in the midst of the semester, he wrote to Mina Tobler: "Naturally, it is very painful—more than I had expected—to become so distressingly aware of the limits of one's own *capabilities*. But—that is nothing new, and 'the view from the other bank,' with its isolation from all of those of good health, even those closest to one, is something I am indeed very familiar with."[67]

Of course, Weber did not turn down the appointment in Vienna because the burdensome nature of this experience had convinced him to permanently refrain from teaching. He wanted to stay in Germany for political reasons, and in the meantime more favorable professional opportunities had arisen there. One possibility was to succeed Lujo Brentano in Munich, the city with which, outside of Heidelberg, he was probably most closely connected, especially after the developments from 1916 to 1918.[68] By the time Weber delivered "Politics as a Vocation" it was clear that he would return to teaching in some form in the foreseeable future, if not in Munich, then in Bonn. If only for economic reasons, it was practically unavoidable. The war had not only destroyed Germany's position as a great power, it had also severely undermined Weber's life as a rentier. Weber could no longer afford to live purely for his work; he had to live from it, too. As much as he desired to earn a steady income solely with the pen or as a freelance lecturer, he had no illusions that this method would work. Only his return as a professor could guarantee in the long term his material existence. A return of this kind, however, as the trial lecture course had demonstrated, would in any case be bound up with sacrifices. Shortly before giving "Politics as a Vocation" Weber wrote to Else Jaffé that he was aware that "in terms of health, I will naturally have to pay for taking on a teaching position by *taking leave* of all 'politics,' since I am not able to do both."[69] Thus, for some time, the stage had been set for the inner and outer calling of scholarship, not of politics.

In March 1919, Weber accepted the appointment to the University of Munich, in spite of more attractive offers elsewhere. After the brief interlude of Versailles, where he prepared, together with others, a document on Germany's war guilt, he actually did pay for the acceptance by departing from all politics, which, as he once put it, was his secret love. This departure has been seen as a direct or indirect confession of political failure, the increased concentration on scholarly work as an escape, and the form in which it was carried out as the continuation of the political struggle with other means.[70] As plausible as such interpretations appear at first glance, one should not overlook one decisive point. Since the end of the war it had become ever more unavoidable for Weber, regardless of the momentary political constellation, to choose between his commitments to scholarship and to politics. Admittedly, the political development after the November Revolution and his manner of involvement in it may have made it easier for him to leave the political arena. There is little evidence that his choice would have been different had he had greater success in everyday politics, however, for although Weber was eminently political, given his public evaluation of political events, he was basically not a politician, at least not a party politician who could ever have made a living from politics. He simply made too many tactical mistakes,[71] and his desire to maintain his independence from political authorities and from the voters was too great.[72] His decisive contribution to German politics in no way consisted of his rather sporadic political actions.[73] It lay instead in his political thought, with which he sought first to make possible political action deserving of the name. In this context also belongs "Politics as a Vocation." In that lecture he deliberately abstained from taking any direct positions on political questions of the day.[74] Instead, he provided a contribution toward a theory of politics, or in his terminology, toward a *sociology of the state*.[75] As such, the lecture (which he subsequently revised into a treatise for publication) has become "a document of the state of democratic thought in that critical moment of German history," as Immanuel Birnbaum fittingly put it in retrospect.[76]

Weber's decision to return to the university and forgo all politics was motivated not only from without but also by serious concerns from within. Despite his numerous political speeches, extensive political journalism, and increasing activities in the politics of the day, even from 1916 until the beginning of 1919 he remained primarily a man of scholarship. The essays on the economic ethics of the world religions continued to be published throughout this period. It is highly likely, indeed practically certain, that the versions of these essays as we know them today, with the exception of the "Introduction" ("Einleitung"), the essay on Confucianism ("Konfusianismus"), and the essay titled "Intermediate Reflections" first came into being in the winter of 1915–16, and thereafter as revisions of older manuscripts.[77] These essays, however, represent only the visible results of an enormous theoretical and historical project. Although its broad outlines were already visible before the war, from the time of Weber's departure from the military hospital administration onward its focus became ever sharper. Emphases were changed, sections were shortened, others were expanded. As early as 1915, Weber anticipated that in addition to *Economy and Society*, already far advanced when the war began, an economic ethics of the major religions (*Kulturreligionen*) with a revised *Protestant Ethic* would exist in book form in the not-too-distant future. By the time Weber decided to return to the university and abstain from politics, the work on this double project was already well advanced. There had long been opposition and even conflict in Weber's life between the *vita contemplativa* (contemplative life) required for the completion of this scholarly work and the *vita activa* (active life) of current political activities.[78] Even though lecturing was agonizing, in contrast to the public platform it was directly useful for his program. Thus, the retreat from politics made Weber's life easier in this sense.[79] Indeed, he had only accepted the appointment to Munich under the condition that he would be allowed to lecture on sociology and the theory of the state instead of on economics.[80] The written and spoken word were supposed to coincide as closely as possible. In Vienna, he had already lectured from his handbook article, his contribution to the *Outline*, on his sociology of religion and domination; in the summer semester of 1919, his first semester in Munich, his lectures provided the basic conceptual introduction for it, "The Most General Categories of the Science of Society" (*Gesellschaftswissenschaft*).[81]

Thus, in the spring of 1919, Weber left the public platform that he had won back in 1916 in order to concentrate all his energies on writing and to find a way to cope once again with lecturing. In spite of the immense scholarly labors he had already performed, an enormous amount of work still lay before him, the core of which was found in the two large-scale projects "The Economy and the Societal Orders and Powers" ("Die Wirtschaft und die gesellschaftlichen Ordnungen und Mächte") and the "Collected Essays on the Sociology of Religion" ("Gesammelte Aufsätze zur Religionssoziologie"). The former was presumably supposed to consist of several parts, and the latter of four volumes.[82] In addition, Weber had apparently wanted to continue to work on the sociological studies on music, art, architecture, and literature that he had begun in 1910 and had always come back to, but ultimately was never to finish. From 1912 until 1918, Georg Lukács was perhaps his most important partner in scholarly dialogues in this field of interest.[83] As Weber prepared the speeches from November 1917 and January 1919 for print, speeches marked by different moods but by the same life experience, he aimed at grounding an interpretive sociology that, as a theory of action, order, and culture, was located between psychology and legal doctrine. In counterpoint to the "dilettante achievements of ingenious philosophers," his perspective was developed in a "strictly objective and scholarly" manner, in the service of historical understanding, and thus, at the same time, for the sake of understanding the present and its developmental tendencies.[84] The theoretical and historical dimensions of such a science of reality (*Erfahrungswissenschaft*) have the task of promoting knowledge of the facts and self-knowledge; in general, that science should impart clarity and intellectual honesty, a sense of perspective and responsibility, detachment, and dignity to a passionate and resolute academic youth. It should also serve the fatherland insofar as its happier future remains dependent on the practice of these virtues, and on a "steadfastness of heart" that "can brave even the crumbling of all hopes."[85]

In fact, Weber increasingly placed his hopes for Germany in the reform of government, and above all in the attitude of academic youth. In the speech on Germany's restoration on January 2, 1919, he pointed out that "the fatherland is not the land of the *fathers*, but the land of the *children*."[86] Above all, one could add, youth had to learn what it means to conduct or lead one's own life, to shape one's own personality. If one follows Weber's sociology, these lessons presuppose not only forms or institutional arrangements but also a "spirit" (*Geist*). In an instructive letter to Otto Crusius, professor of classical philology in Munich and participant at the Lauenstein conferences, Weber wrote as early as November 24, 1918, before throwing himself into the election campaign, that the resolution of present cultural problems involved above all the regaining of moral "decency." In order to cope with this formidable didactic task, the only form possible was "the American: the 'club'—and *exclusive* associations, i.e., associations of every kind based upon the *selection* of persons, starting in childhood and youth, *regardless* of their purpose; first signs of it [are seen] in the Free German Youth" (Freideutsche Jugend). As "spirit" however, there remained only objectivity and the "rejection of all spiritual narcotics of every kind, from mysticism all the way to 'expressionism.'" Only in this way could a true sense of shame arise, the sole source of a political and human "posture" "against the disgusting exhibitionism of those inwardly broken."[87] This statement shows how much Weber linked this hope for Germany to the Free German Youth, part of which he apparently considered to be the Free Students Association (Freie Studentenschaft). It also shows the great extent to which his two speeches before the Munich Free Students Association are to be seen in this context. This context leads us to ask how Weber's relationship to the Free German Youth, and especially to the Free Students Association, developed, and thus to the question of the narrower context of the genesis of "Science as a Vocation" and "Politics as a Vocation."

The Narrower Context of the Lectures: Weber's Relationship to the Youth and Student Movements

During his three semesters as a student of law and political economy at the University of Heidelberg, starting in the summer semester of 1882, Max Weber joined the student fraternity Allemannia, of Heidelberg. He approved of their code of honor that revolved around proof of honor through dueling (*Satisfaktion, Mensur*). As a young scholar, though, he had already raised doubts about the educational value of the reserve officers' patent and student dueling societies in his analyses of the authoritarian deformation of the German bourgeoisie. Moreover, as years went by, he distanced himself ever more clearly from these institutions of military and student "morality" and "honor."[88] Nevertheless, he remained a member of the fraternity until after the November Revolution, probably giving up his alumni membership on November 17, 1918, in the context of a public dispute about the symbolic value of wearing fraternity colors.[89] First, in a public meeting, Weber had termed the tradition of wearing colors feudal nonsense no longer suitable to the times and useful to no one. Then, in his letter of resignation, he denied both the right to existence of this form of student life in a reorganized Germany and its ability to reform itself. In the address "Students and Politics" ("Student und Politik"), delivered to a student audience on March 13, 1919, shortly before he accepted the appointment to the University of Munich,[90] Weber made it clear that the politically disturbing character of the system of fraternity colors resulted from its "exclusivity on the basis of the qualification for dueling."[91] This type of exclusivity made democratization impossible. It supported a false understanding of the special position of the student and graduate. Clearly, in Weber's opinion, this position should no longer be founded on the pretensions of an academic status group. Instead, it had to be individually earned by conducting one's life in the manner of an aristocracy of the *spirit*, by means of self-determined conduct that spurns all reminders of "feudalism" and does not close itself off from those not attending the university.

Thus, Weber radically and publicly rejected the color-bearing student fraternities after the November Revolution. He considered them incompatible with the future form of government he sought for Germany: a modern democratic parliamentary republic. His rejection, however, also extended to parts of the student body not organized in these fraternities. The account of the address makes this clear as well. Weber criticized "phenomena known from the free youth movement that basically amount to an emancipation from authority and have bred those literati against whom, in the interest of spiritual health, effective war must be waged." Even though no names were named, there can be hardly any doubt that Weber meant, among others, Gustav Wyneken and his followers,[92] whom he had rejected at Burg Lauenstein. His sympathy clearly belonged only to those student groups that, like the Free Students, were oriented around the idea of the university as an institution for scholarly education and self-development. Such students would believe in an education toward self-directed activity and autonomy through specialized scholarship and abstain in their university politics from all artificial forms of separate student politics.[93]

In fact, the Free Students Association deserves a special place in the history of German student life from the end of the nineteenth century until the reorganization of Germany after the First World War. It was of great importance in historical development. Its opponents alternately defamed and fought against it as Jewish, socialist, rationalistic, pacifist, collectivist, or even subjectivist, but it was in modern times "the first decisive bearer of ambitious social efforts aimed at the welfare of all financially weak students." Moreover, "through its emphasis on the student university community and on the necessity of general student committees, it paved the way for the large-scale student unity movement that [reached] its goal in 1919 by establishing the German Student Association."[94] Its struggle was directed above all at the privileged position of student societies and fraternities, which were most intimately connected with the very structure of imperial Germany. The free student movement, originally begun under the name Finkenschaftsbewegung,[95] can be understood as an umbrella movement for those student efforts directed against student fraternities and societies at the beginning of the century. The goal is given concise expression in a resolution adopted at the Weimar Free Student Conference in 1906. Here is one passage from it:

The ultimate and highest goal of the Free Student movement is the reestablishment of the old *civitas academica*, the unification of all students into one self-contained, autonomous body, which is officially recognized as one unit at every university, and alongside of the teaching staff as the totality of lecturers, and equal to the latter. The organization should build an essential component of the university body with its own constitution. The student body cannot receive its representation through a partial committee that includes members of only certain parties; it can do this solely by means of a committee for all students, resting on a parliamentary basis, in which every group of academic youth finds appropriate representation. Students must share equally in the burdens and advantages, and no part of the student body can withdraw from it, even if it waives its right to its representation.[96]

Thus, the Free Student movement was, as a collective movement of the "nonincorporated" (as it was expressed in the language of the time), pluralistic from the very beginning. It advocated a principle of tolerance and neutrality, valued independent convictions, and limited its political activities to purely academic matters.[97] In this way it was able to unify under one roof students of the most diverse world views and political orientations. It also demonstrated marked differences from university to university. In particular, the Munich Free Student Association, which invited Weber to give the two lectures, had its own distinctive image.[98] Of course, all groups were united in their dedication to the classical idea of the German university, above all, to the idea of education through scholarship and to academic freedom as freedom in teaching and studies.[99] For this very reason, one of the moot questions was how these ideas should be interpreted and how they were to be realized in a university system whose student population figures had dramatically risen since the establishment of the German Empire,[100] and whose structure had undergone far-reaching changes under the pressure of growing specialization of the academic disciplines, especially in the natural sciences. Weber reacted to these discussions: he took up these developments in detail in "Science as a Vocation."

The Free Student movement reached its high point before the First World War, as did the Free German movement, which initially has to be distinguished from the former movement. In contrast to the Free Student movement, the Free German movement arose out of the merger of several associations from the youth movement in October 1913 at a meeting atop the Hohen Meißner near Kassel. The most important of the student associations represented was the German Free Academic Youth,[101] which, although it opposed corporate student life as much as the Free Student Association, also initially opposed that group. There were fissures in the Free German movement from its very beginning in 1913. Open conflict soon arose between participating associations, especially between those to whom this youth movement was primarily a cultural movement and those to whom it was above all a community movement. In spite of their differences, which soon led to splinter groups, the associations were initially linked by their common emotive nationalism.[102] Especially among the Free Academic Youth, pacifist trends gained acceptance with the continuance of the war. This facilitated a rapprochement with the Free Students Association, which had meanwhile largely lost its old, admittedly never very secure "unity."[103] It also experienced the spread of pacifist thought in its ranks after the onset of the war.

The increasing importance of just this tendency in this part of the student body is made clear by the Foerster case. Friedrich Wilhelm Foerster, professor of philosophy and education at the University of Munich, had long advocated, in print and in speech, a Christian pacifism.[104] In 1917, he came out in his lectures for an immediate peace of mutual understanding. In order to counteract his supposedly defeatist influence, "A committee was formed among Munich students that protested against Foerster's propaganda and organized disturbances of his lectures. A countercommittee came to the defense of the lively preacher of peace."[105] The countercommittee was also supported by the Munich Free Students Association. Other Free Student Associations, such as those in Breslau and Königsberg, but also the Free Academic Youth, defended Foerster in public declarations.[106] In both speeches, Weber took a position on the Foerster case so fiercely discussed by the Munich Free Students. In "Science as a Vocation" it served to help him explain the logical principle of the freedom from value judgments, and its institutional correlate, the freedom of teaching and learning. In this way, he was able to make statements on the task of the university and the role of university instruction. In "Politics as a Vocation," the case facilitated his depiction of Christian pacificism as an ethic of conviction with a supposedly illusionist perspective and a lack of a sense of reality.

This reference to the Foerster case alone shows that despite the sympathies that Weber clearly manifested for the Free Students Association, in contrast to his feelings for the fraternities, he also noted that it "moves in the wrong direction." Thus, many of his arguments in both speeches must have provoked members of this circle and were certainly intended to be provocative. This intention held for Weber's *principled* antipacifism that, then as now, shocked many. It held even more for his diagnosis of the "illness" of academic youth that had also befallen parts of the Free Students Association. Most of all, however, it held for his prescribed therapy. Weber saw this "illness" manifested in the longing of academic youth for a liberation from scientific rationalism by means of "direct experience," in its "fashionable 'cult of the personality,'" and in general in its "extremely pronounced disposition to overestimate its own importance."[107] Where, as in the case of Foerster, the teacher lay claim to the role of leader or, even worse, where colleagues with less honorable convictions carried on a "professional type of prophecy,"[108] this destructive tenor, instead of being challenged, was only strengthened. In fact, "Science as a

Vocation"—with its sharp attacks against "direct experience," the primary idol of academic youth, and its restrictive view of the task of the university and the role of the teaching academician— brought forth a coalition between two otherwise warring camps of the Munich Free Students: between the Friends of *Bildung* ("Bildungs"-Freunde) and the Enthusiasts for the "Scientific Use of the Mind" (Schwärmer für den "wissenschaftlichen Verstandesgebrauch"). Immanuel Birnbaum wrote to Weber that after the "Science as a Vocation" lecture only a small circle adopted his position without qualifications. It was made up primarily of those who had been "prepared by Prof. Husserl's essay in *Logos* ('Philosophy as a Pure Science') and by the historians' *Methodenstreit* [debate on methods] and the economists' debate on value judgment."[109]

It was in fact the case that with his understanding of science and politics and with his view of the tasks and educational value of the university, Weber could reckon with undivided agreement from neither the students nor his fellow professors. Given the trends of the time, his was a minority position. As shown in Birnbaum's remarks, it was a position deeply interwoven with the histories of science and politics in imperial Germany. Husserl's critique of naturalism and the Methodenstreit and the debate on value judgment did in fact form part of the background to this position.[110] As I mentioned earlier, even before Weber gave the lecture "Science as a Vocation" he had his revised report on the value-judgment debate published in *Logos*. The report contains arguments brought forth in the two speeches, especially in "Science as a Vocation." It is thus worthwhile to pay some attention to this text. It will also provide us with more insight into the negative reactions to the position of Weber that Birnbaum had described.

In the essay on freedom from value judgments, Weber conceives of "value freedom" as a logical principle and as a maxim of action (in university politics). As a logical principle it refers to the heterogeneity of the spheres of cognition and evaluation (*Wertungssphäre*). It is thus positioned in the context of a radical critique of naturalism. Weber did battle against the naturalization of consciousness and against the naturalization of ideas and ideals, and consequently, against the naturalization of the sphere of evaluation. An act providing meaning cannot be equated to a physical phenomenon, he argued, nor can validity be equated to success. Where these equations occur, naturalistic self-deceptions are unavoidable. On this score, Weber finds himself in agreement not only with Rickert, Simmel, and many others, but with Husserl as well.[111] In order to defend his own antinaturalistic claims, Weber followed a value theory with three premises: the heterogeneity of the spheres of cognition and evaluation, the enlargement of the evaluative sphere to include nonethical values, and the collision of values irresolvable by scientific means.[112]

Weber thus demanded from the university teacher that for reasons of principle he keep two things separate: the objectivity of judgments of fact, on the one hand, and the subjectivity and objectifiability of value judgments, on the other. Only one who is aware of the heterogeneous quality of these two problems, and makes this quality clear, will not miseducate his audience "to confuse these different spheres with one another." Only that person avoids the danger of handling the establishment of fact and the adoption of a stance on the great issues of life "with the same cool dispassionateness."[113] It is the task of university teachers to handle and present questions of scientific knowledge in an unbiased, sober, and objective manner. They have qualified themselves to fulfill this duty. Whether they should also treat the second category of problems in their role as teacher is for Weber himself a practical question. The position one takes on this question therefore sheds light on the educational value one attributes to the university. Only by presupposing the comprehensive educational value of the university can one expect the university to take up the latter problem as one of its tasks. This position can be defended without internal contradiction as long as one recognizes the heterogeneity of the spheres of cognition and evaluation. In this case, one decides that university teachers, on the strength of their qualifications, are still allowed to lay claim to "the universal role of moulding human beings, of inculcating political, ethical, aesthetic, cultural, or other attitudes."[114] One could add that the founders of Berlin University had thought something to this effect. If one rejects this position—and according to Weber, the premises upon which the classic ideal of the German university rested have crumbled under the increasing weight of subjectivism in modern culture[115]—then it only remains to limit university education to "specialized training by specially qualified persons."[116] Weber expressly states that this is his standpoint.[117] The task of the university in his time is, accordingly, clearly no longer to educate students to become self-cultivated generalists (*Kulturmenschen*), but to become only specialists (*Fachmenschen*).[118]

By relating these reflections to the negative reactions described by Birnbaum, one suddenly sees clearly why the "Friends of *Bildung*" were not able to adopt Weber's line of argument. They obviously considered the university an institution of learning in the classical sense. What in contrast is less clear is why the "Enthusiasts for the 'Scientific Use of the Mind'" also rejected his position. Only by further studying the latter group does this rejection become less of a mystery.

Without doubt, Weber viewed the university as a place primarily for specialized training. This view, however, does not imply that he, presumably like those enthusiasts, spoke out in favor of a naive, unreflective world of specialists. He had already made critical remarks about this world of specialists in his famous study of ascetic Protestantism. There he used the expression of Nietzsche's Zarathustra to characterize those who do not see the inner limits of modern specialists as the last of mankind, as those who had invented happiness. For them, he chose the formulation "specialists without spirit, sensualists without heart."[119] Specialized training should definitely take place, but only in a way that produced intellectual honesty and, above all, a simultaneous consciousness of one's limitations. Such specialized training is, however, specialized education and cultivation (*Bildung*) in the true sense of the words. It sharpens the awareness of the limits of the world of specialists as such, and of the fact that life's problems of meaning cannot be resolved by specialized training alone.[120]

Weber hence no longer considered the universities capable of bringing forth generalists in the old style. Here, too, the ideal of "full and beautiful humanity," on which German classicism had rested, was irretrievably lost.[121] But he also sought to prevent students from becoming narrow-minded specialists, from becoming specialists without spirit. He desired the cultivated specialist, who had learned three things:

First . . . to content himself with the humble fulfillment of a given task; second, to first recognize facts—even, and especially, those that he finds personally inconvenient—and then distinguish between stating those facts and taking up an evaluative position toward them; and third, to subordinate his own personality to the matter in hand and so, above all, to suppress the need to display his personal tastes and other feelings where that is not called for.[122]

Weber wanted a cultivated specialist who, in addition, has ideals that he freely and openly advocates. The university should mold self-determined human beings committed to a cause. In order to do this, it needs teachers who know the connection between activity and renunciation and practice it credibly in their own lives before students.

When Weber vigorously insists on distinguishing the role of the university teacher who speaks to his students as a scientific specialist from the role of the citizen who addresses himself to the general public, it reminds one of Kant's essay on the Enlightenment.[123] As in Kant, these roles belong to institutions that differ in their respective control mechanisms and criteria of rationality. In contrast to the public meeting and address, the lecture hall and lecture stand under the "privilege of freedom from supervision."[124] This privilege, however, makes misuse possible. This danger cannot be averted by the "intrusion of the public, for instance in the form of the press,"[125] but only by the self-limitation of the university teacher, by his refraining from all propaganda on the behalf of his personal convictions. Such self-limitation caused great difficulties for Weber himself, as described earlier. Nevertheless, it was his aim in the lecture hall. Perhaps for this reason, the sober rationality that he achieved in visible struggle with his own passions had all the more effect on some of his listeners.[126]

To see the facts, even personally displeasurable ones, and to recognize them; to place oneself completely in the service of a given cause and to meet its daily demands; and to think clearly and soberly and to feel responsible: this is what a teacher is to educate a student to do. These are unspectacular, "everyday" virtues, not "extraordinary" ones. The one who succeeds in managing everyday life without simply conforming is also a "hero." Weber repeatedly praised the virtues of "normality" in this sense to his students. Such praise could apparently hardly enthuse many of the young persons agitated by war and revolution. They sought not the common, but the extraordinary; not the sober teacher, but the hero or prophet; and not a scientific rationalism incapable of providing meaning, but a substantive morality or a religious *unio mystica* (unification with the holy) admittedly often only pseudoreligious. Weber took a stand against both substantialism and romanticism. Until today, many have been more irritated by the former opposition than by the latter one. Werner Mahrholz, who, like Immanuel Birnbaum, held one of the leading positions in the Munich Free Students Association, and in conjunction with him helped organize the two public addresses, presumably voiced the innermost thoughts of many when he commented on "Science as a Vocation" in November 1919: "Distressing is the stance of pre-cisely those natural leaders among the professors: for more and more of them, scholarship has become a form of respectable sui-cide, a way to die in stoic heroism."[127]

Nevertheless, there was also a small circle of those who were convinced by Weber's defense of the ideal of an innerworldly as-ceticism freed from its religious foundations and for whom he played the role of a leader precisely because of his sober manner of teaching. This circle certainly included Karl Löwith.[128] Other names could also be cited.[129] Many of these people appear to have been of Jewish or Protestant origin and politically leftist-liberal or social-democratic, some even socialist. One who fits the picture especially well is Immanuel Birnbaum. It is primarily to his credit that the two addresses were given before the Free Students Asso-ciation and were then published in revised form in its name.

Birnbaum had begun his studies in Freiburg under Gerhart Schulze-Gaevernitz, Heinrich Rickert, and Friedrich Meinecke. Coming via Königsberg, where he joined the Free Students Asso-ciation, to Munich, Birnbaum was attracted chiefly by the teach-ing activities of Lujo Brentano and Heinrich Wölfflin. These are all figures who belong to the intellectual context of Weber's life. Birnbaum probably first met Weber later, during political discus-sions at the house of Lujo Brentano.[130] After first sympathizing with leftist-liberal groups, he joined the Social Democrats in 1917.[131] Birnbaum had reached the top of the Munich Free Stu-dents Association in 1913–14. Even after receiving his Ph.D. he participated decisively in its work up until the establishment of the General Student Committee (Allgemeiner Studentenaus-schuss) in Munich in the course of the revolution. In summer 1919 he was elected as one of the three presidents of the General Stu-dent Committee.[132] He thus contributed in turning those goals that the Free Student movement had set for itself into reality. At the end of its development stood the legally constituted stu-dent body.

"Science as a Vocation" and "Politics as a Vocation" were parts of a lecture series that the Munich Free Students had presumably planned since the summer of 1917. It was entitled "Intellectual Labor as a Vocation." It was provoked by the essay "Vocation and Youth" by Franz Xaver Schwab (most likely a pen name for Alex-ander Schwab), published in the monthly journal *Die weissen Blätter* on May 15, 1917.[133] In the essay Schwab termed the "vo-cation" (or profession) the idol that had to be smashed: it was the idol of the day's West European–American bourgeois world: it formed the core around which everything revolved; it had come between the basic forces of existence, between the (physical) life and the spirit, even though it was "completely alien to these primeval powers in their pure divinity."[134] Only alienation could come of this situation, the alienation of life from the spirit, and thus of each from its true essence. To produce their reconciliation represented the necessity of the times, and this could succeed only where the dominion of vocation and its accompanying world of specialists had been broken. Like the "Greeks at their time of prosperity," the youth of the day could also reach full and beautiful humanity once they had recognized the dangers for the soul that vocation represented. This recognition would force the youth into radical opposition to the bourgeois world, which was indivisibly connected to the ideology that made a moral virtue out of the necessity of enslaving vocational labors.[135]

It is unlikely that Schwab's romantic anticapitalism caused much excitement among the Munich Free Students. Such tendencies were not unusual among various youth and student movements of the period. What must have caused some agitation was Schwab's remark that none of the appropriate youth and student groups had as yet treated the problem of vocation seriously, and this included the Free Students.[136] At the same time, Schwab pointed to a way out of this regrettable situation: one should have a good look at the works of Max and Alfred Weber, because "the only persons in our time who have said something important about vocation in a conspicuous way are the brothers Max and Alfred Weber in Heidelberg."[137]

We do not know when Birnbaum or another member of the Bavarian Free Students Association first approached Weber with the request that he speak, in the framework of a lecture series planned in response to Schwab's provocation, on "Science as a Vocation" and then on "Politics as a Vocation."[138] What is of interest here, however, is not the external course of events, but the controversies on the level of ideas. And it is in this context that we note that in "Science as a Vocation" Weber at least indirectly takes a stand on Schwab's provocation. Weber mercilessly destroys the myth of full and beautiful humanity to which Schwab subscribed.[139] He also shows that vocation and a life with meaning are not necessarily opposed. Admittedly, everything depends on a proper understanding of the connection of the two. The two are linked not by removing the limits of vocational work, but by the very limitation of this work that Schwab finds so deplorable. It holds not only for scholarship that "a really definitive and good accomplishment is today always a specialized accomplishment."[140] Only those who are in the position to surrender themselves completely and continually to a limited subject and to meet the daily demands that arise out of it can grasp "the only part of [the] meaning [of calling] which still remains genuinely significant today."[141]

Now such a "sense of vocation" may appear to be plausible for the scholar and university teacher. Is it also plausible for the politician? Does not the latter have to provide answers to the great collective problems of life, answers unobtainable by either specialized training or specialized education and cultivation? Admittedly, according to Weber, modern democracy, which certainly does not give politicians the "privilege of freedom from supervision," is subject to bureaucratization in large states. It is a "bureaucratized democracy."[142] In such a system one has to reckon with the "necessity of specialized training of many years, ever increasing specialization, and direction by a corps of specialized officials trained in such a way."[143] This bureaucratization does not mean, however, that this trained corps of specialized officials, as indispensable as it is, should also be entrusted with political leadership. The modern "large-state democracy" as a mass democracy also needs political *leaders*. And for Weber, they represent in practice the counterpoint not only to those officials but to scholars as well.[144]

Admittedly, just as there are different conceptions of scholars and university teachers, there are also different conceptions of political leaders. Weber discussed them in his second public address, "Politics as a Vocation," drawing up a picture of the "responsible" politician, in contradistinction to the "principled" politician on the one hand and the power-obsessed politician on the other. The responsible politician must be able to formulate political positions capable of winning approval and be willing to advocate them at his own risk. He also must get involved with the "infernal powers" that lie in wait for him in every form of force, even the legitimate control and use of it,[145] and withstand their corrupting influence. He has to serve a given cause passionately, take responsibility for it, and practice a "disciplined dispassionateness" when viewing "the realities of life."[146] One can follow such a leader. One does this not out of "romantic sensations"[147] or out of the "worship of power,"[148] but out of educated conviction or, when the leader's exalted passions are an expression of his charismatic gift, out of a spontaneous "awakening."

The scholar as self-critical specialist and the politician as leader, in the sense of acting on an ethic of responsibility, thus appear to stand irreconcilably opposed to one another. Here we have sober recognition of the facts, there, the passionate profession of taking a stand; here, the demonstration of the possible, there, in addition, the effort to attain the apparently impossible.[149] Nevertheless, it quickly turns out that this is not Weber's final word on the matter. Although they display differences, both figures also have traits in common.

It should not be overlooked that Weber put forth an argument in "Politics as a Vocation" (as indeed in "Science as a Vocation") that was capable of creating a coalition between two otherwise antagonistic camps—analogously, to paraphrase Birnbaum: between the "friends of a politics of conviction" and the "enthusiasts for the use of pure power." Weber severely took to task those politicians of conviction and their followers among the Free Students who "intoxicate themselves with romantic sensations,"[150] thus deluding themselves. The most serious delusion of all is represented by the belief that any serious and important political activity could ever take place that does *not* entangle the political actor in the vicissitudes of power. Weber saw such self-delusion chiefly in pacifists, syndicalists, and in Spartacists at work; above all, however, he found it among the political literati who had gathered in Kurt Eisner's revolutionary government. (Indeed, Eisner himself was temporarily considered by radical members of the Free Students as speaker for the address on "Politics as a Vocation."[151]) All these groups tended in Weber's view either to deny the inescapable reality of all politics, namely, force with an inner logic all its own, or to call for the use of force "for the *last* time, so as to bring about a situation in which *all* violence will be abolished."[152] In this faith in the creative power of force, however, they come close to the "enthusiasts for the use of pure power" for whom power is a value in itself. Admittedly, these "pure 'power politicians'" are unable to commit themselves to a cause beyond the personal. They thus act in a "meaningless void,"[153] whereas self-deluding politicians of conviction, at least those of the radical Left, are guided by the hope of a liberation that can be produced by direct actions.[154]

Just as he abhorred pure specialists, Weber also found those advocating pure power loathsome. They embodied all the qualities he detested in politics: lack of objectivity, irresponsibility, and vanity. He considered them the play-actors of politics, whose "inner weakness and impotence is concealed behind their ostentatious but totally empty posturing."[155] This posturing is not the case with the "principled" politicians who serve a cause beyond the personal. They seek an inner point of orientation, an inner support. Admittedly, they all too seldom stand up to the realities of life. Nevertheless, wherever they are able to prove objectively the value of their "mission" and to cope with the entanglement in power relations, Weber is willing to recognize their vocation for politics, for they are aware of "the tragic element with which all action, but especially political action, is in fact intertwined."[156] They are thus also aware of the limitations of political action, and that it demands a specific type of self-limitation.

This awareness of the tragic nature of political action is also characteristic of the "responsible" politician. But in contrast to the "principled politician," he draws from that tragic nature a further-reaching consequence. He does not content himself with taking on the responsibility for the convictional value of his political action, but instead extends this responsibility to cover that action's foreseeable effects. However, he can do justice to this broadened responsibility only if he possesses those virtues that Weber says students should learn from their teachers in the lecture hall. These are the virtues cited earlier: to content oneself with the fulfillment of a given task, to recognize personally displeasurable facts, and to subordinate one's own personality to the matter at hand.[157]

The Key Terms: Vocational Duty, Self-Limitation, and Personality

Both times Weber addressed the Munich Free Students, he advocated the same basic idea: that one robs vocation of all meaning "if there [is] no exercise of that specific form of self-restraint which it demands."[158] Although the kind of self-limitation required differs, it is required in both scholarship and politics. Weber's message to the Free Students is that intellectual labor as a vocation means a life full of renunciation, not of reconciliation; it means "confining oneself to specialized work," not "Faustian omnicompetence."[159] Many did not want to hear this insistence on an ascetic basis of action. "Politics as a Vocation," just like "Science as a Vocation" before it, generally prompted feelings of uneasiness among the Free Students. This uneasiness was certainly not only because Weber made judgments, for example, of Foerster, Eisner, and the soldier and worker councils, with, as one participant put it, "calm disrespect."[160] It was much more because Weber brutally confronted the idealism of politicians of conviction with the entanglement of all political action in questions of power, and thus gave the impression that political action had nothing to do with values. There is no doubt that Weber did not argue this way. But one had to listen in an unbiased manner in order to grasp the complex mesh of relations among power, ethics, and truth in which he placed the form of politics that he undoubtedly advocated, the politics of responsibility.

Vocation and self-limitation, vocation *as* self-limitation, this is Weber's message to academic youth. He who seeks to give meaning to intellectual labor as a vocation, who—unlike Schwab—does not simply consider it an economic necessity, must affirm this ascetic basis of action. For Weber, vocation belonged from the very beginning to the bourgeois mode of conduct. And if conduct is to avoid degenerating into a mere technique of managing life, it cannot be allowed to simply disappear. Undeniably, the Christian spirit that once gave it inner support has long since given way. Weber had already demonstrated this in his studies on ascetic Protestantism. For this reason, this mode of action can no longer be valued on the basis of religious faith; a secular foundation must be established for it. This is precisely what takes place in Weber's two speeches.

In order to provide this foundation, Weber places the two concepts of vocation and self-limitation in an intrinsic relation to a third concept, that of personality. First the term is divested of all "romantic" implications. Early on, in his critique of Knies and the problem of irrationality, Weber had come out against that romantic-*naturalistic* concept of personality that "seeks the real sanctuary of the personal in the diffuse, undifferentiated, vegetative 'underground' of personal life."[161] In the two speeches, he directed his opposition against a romantic-*aestheticist* concept of personality that discovers this sacred core in direct experience or even in the effort of shaping one's life into a work of art.[162] Neither the naturalist nor the aesthetic variant captures what is crucial for Weber, namely "the constant and *intrinsic* relation to certain ultimate 'values' and 'meanings' of life"[163] that a person achieves in the unfolding of his fate, a process that at the same time is one of *Bildung*. Ascetic, humanistic individualism represents the closest approximation to the concept of personality: ascetic, because continuous *action* in the service of a cause is demanded; humanistic, because this cause presupposes the constant commitment to

ultimate *values*; and individualistic, because this constant commitment has to be *chosen* through a series of ultimate decisions.
Where these conditions are satisfied, a person has become a personality without necessarily intending to. He has, in the concluding words of "Science as a Vocation," found his daemon and
learned to obey him by satisfying the demands of the day that this
daemon makes.

It is certainly not a coincidence that two of Weber's most important texts, the *Protestant Ethic* and "Science as a Vocation,"
end with allusions to the later works of Goethe. The latter provides a preliminary formulation of the concept of personality
Weber had in mind. In spite of some tendencies toward an aesthetic and cosmological humanism in Goethe's work, which Weber certainly viewed coolly, he did consider *Wilhelm Meister's
Journeyman Years (Wilhelm Meisters Wanderjahre)*, subtitled *or,
the Renunciants (oder die Entsagenden)*, and *Faust II* to have va-
lidly developed the meaning of an ascetic basis of conduct not
founded on Christian religion. Moreover, he found in Goethe's
"Primal Words" ("Urworte") that it is made clear in describing the
interplay of a person's daemon (i.e., one's individuality or character) and the "world" that the only way to avoid the danger of losing
what is one's own to the merely accidental, of losing the intrinsic
to the extrinsic, is by means of self-limitation. It would certainly
be unfair to Weber if one interpreted his adoption of the concept of
daemon in an elitist fashion, something the George follower Friedrich Gundolf did in his book on Goethe. Gundolf argued that only
great men, geniuses, are capable of having a daemon and thus their
own fate, whereas the normal person is only capable of "mere
qualities, opinions, preoccupations, and experiences, conditioned
from without, not formed from within."[164] In contrast, Weber
strove for an aristocracy of the spirit, not a form of elitism.[165] All
people can find their daemons, become personalities, and determine their own lives, if only they serve with total sacrifice a self-
chosen cause going beyond the personal. Naturally, this presupposes that the ideas and images of the world, in terms of which
one interprets one's own life, and the societal orders in which one
is forced to live do not totally obstruct the ascetic basis of conduct.
However, it presupposes above all that the coming generation is
made aware—especially in times of crisis and radical change,
when hopes and desires are great—of the interrelations among vocational activity, the self-limitation expected from without and
that accepted from within, and the formation of personality.[166] Ul-

timately, both speeches serve this purpose of making the coming generation aware. Thus, at their core, they follow "philosophical" intentions, providing both a declaration of belief and challenge to action.

The Role of Science in the Modern World: A Controversy

After Max Weber had given the second of his two addresses, Immanuel Birnbaum arranged to have them both published as soon as possible, in one volume. Although he would have liked to have included the other addresses from the series, these had not yet been presented, and it did not appear that this would happen soon. However, the publisher subsequently decided against publication in one volume and published the two speeches as independent brochures.[167] This decision was apparently the result of commercial considerations. As can be inferred from the different number of copies printed, the publisher clearly expected "Politics as a Vocation" to be more successful. We can only guess if this in fact was the case.

What we do know is that immediately following its appearance in print, "Science as a Vocation" aroused more reaction than "Politics as a Vocation." Initiated early with a short piece by Ernst Robert Curtius in August 1919,[168] discussion continued in longer essays by Erich von Kahler[169] and Arthur Salz.[170] The latter two were friends and members of the Stefan George circle. Salz, who also belonged to the Weber circle, considered this paper a critique of Kahler's and aimed to defend Weber's standpoint against some of Kahler's charges. Ultimately, Ernst Troeltsch[171] and Max Scheler[172] also intervened in the controversy. In contrast, "Politics as a Vocation" initially drew no response.[173] Thus, in both its oral and written form, "Science as a Vocation" had the greater impact of the two addresses, a disparity that has basically continued to this day.[174]

What was the focus of this first debate? Even though the contending parties advocated radically different viewpoints, they were united by a common source of doubt: Were the limitations Weber placed on modern science and scholarship of a compelling nature in a historical, and especially, in a systematic sense? Is modern scholarship, as Weber claimed, merely "a 'vocation' organized in special disciplines in the service of self-clarification and knowledge of interrelated facts"? Or is it "the gift of grace or seers and prophets dispensing sacred values and revelations . . . partaking of the contemplation of sages and philosophers about the meaning of the universe" after all?[175] Can experience and cognition, life and knowledge in fact be ascribed to different functions in the cognitive process, as Weber implies, or is it rather the case, as Curtius puts it, that they are so closely interrelated that one practically has to demand that the scholar fulfill his "experiential obligations"?[176] And what is the status of the value presuppositions that Weber refers to in order to resist the notion that modern science is without presuppositions? Do they turn out to be merely subjective, or must they be philosophically developed from a "universally founded philosophy of life of existential values and their relative rankings"?[177]

Nevertheless, although the disputing parties were united in their common doubts concerning Weber's restrictive view of the possibilities of modern science, their respective counterproposals greatly differed from one another. Erich von Kahler went the furthest, demanding nothing less than a completely new science. By doing so, he gave voice to the sentiments of a generation marked by the war experience and a weariness of civilization. In fact, his frontal attack on Weber's position calls to mind Schwab's frontal attack on misguided West European–American humanity.

For Kahler, Weber is a representative of old science in whom "its greatest potential" is realized. This means at the same time that Weber's indisputable ethos is in the service of a "lost cause":[178] the self-liberation of reason, which started with Kant. Like Kant, he pursues an anti-Platonic course that destroys "the intuitive, deeply visionary element, indeed, the visionary element per se, the simple prior claim of cosmic unity and metaphysical substance." What remains is "purely immaterial reason."[179] Because Weber follows this misguided course of the Enlightenment, his conception of a resurrected Hellenistic polytheism, of a battle of the gods that characterizes the existential plight of modern man, shares nothing with the polytheism of ancient man. Whereas the latter involves the specification of the recognizable and definitive "good life" in accordance with time and place, the former revolves around the choice between different lives, outside of place and time, that are of equal merit. This absence of unity, however, would imply in practice relativism, something that is simply the philosophical expression of a conflicted and fragmented inner life.[180]

In Kahler's view, in "Science as a Vocation" Weber offers an apologetics for this conflicted and fragmented life, an apology for the separation of thought and emotion, of knowledge and action, of scholarship and leadership. This apology proves that the basic way of thought and method of the old science is already in decline, for Weber's rationalism, cut off from all that is visionary, is so consequential that he is forced to show the only way out of these divisions: the return to wholeness. In Kahler's view there is nothing accidental about the fact that such a radical diagnosis could be made in Germany: as with others before him—one is reminded of the young Marx—Germany appears to him as the location of the most radical deprivation and thus, as the very place where the most radical revolution, the revolution of science, can and must start.[181]

It is thus the calling of the Germans to acquire this new science for Europe, and indeed, for all of humanity. Although it retains the old science, the new gives the old the lower ranking it deserves.[182] The new science is based on the reversal of the purely empirical labors performed since Kant; it is based on the reestablishment of the true ranking of idea and concept, of knowledge and fact, of basic foundation and cause, and on the foundational role of contemplation vis-à-vis analysis. Furthermore, it is based on passion in the sense of Platonic mania, not in the sense of mere devotion to a cause which itself is only subjectively binding, such as in the restrictive rationalism of Weberian science. The new knowledge thus exists in contemplative, "organic works of imagery," and not, as in the old knowledge, "in [isolated] shreds of facts and calculations."[183] Nevertheless, the new knowledge is also knowledge, and not faith or art.[184] However, because this new knowledge presents a vision (*Zusammenschauen*) of "the living in its core, in its unity and uniqueness and according to its laws," it also resolves the value problem Weber found unresolvable.[185]

Thus, Kahler does not want merely to improve upon old science but to radically divorce himself from it. He seeks, as Ernst Troeltsch had already correctly observed, a revolution against the revolution brought about by the Enlightenment; in other words, his aim is a counter-Enlightenment. At the same time, he is "contemporary" enough to shy away from simply calling for the return to the humanity of antiquity. Its mode of conduct is gone forever. One must to aim to reach both before and beyond the Enlightenment. Thus, the counter-Enlightenment also appears to be a post-Enlightenment.[186]

In this respect, Kahler's position is symptomatic. It is part of the pursuit of "commitment [*Bindung*] and unity, dogma and law in spiritual life" that started long before the First World War and was directed not only against naturalism and its tendency toward intellectualism, but also against historicism and its tendency toward relativism.[187] Kahler's "revolutionary pamphlet,"[188] with its antinaturalistic and antihistoricist turn, is admittedly only a facet within this current of thought. Nevertheless, his countercritique makes clear that "Science as a Vocation" was perceived even by contemporaries as a defense of the continuation of the Enlightenment and as a manifesto against the new value syntheses.[189]

Arthur Salz clearly also perceived Kahler's attack on Weber this way. For him, Kahler's "revolution of the spirit" was a neoromantic rejection of modern European rationalism, and above all of the specific German contribution to it, Kant's transcendental philosophy, and accordingly of its political correlate, the French Revolution.[190] Kahler and the other neoromanticists sought to dissolve the bond between the scientific thought of the Enlightenment and republican constitutionalism. Their widespread anti-intellectual and antibourgeois stance required not only the seer instead of the scholar and the sage instead of the specialist, but it also demanded the circle with esoteric knowledge grouped around the genius who was ultimately outside of any external monitoring.[191] As much as Salz sympathized with Kahler's demand to fundamentally renew modern science after its age of routinization (he placed its charismatic age in the Renaissance and not in Greece), he did not accept Kahler's solution of how to do this. In the confrontation between the undemocratic elitism of a Friedrich Nietzsche and a Stefan George and the aristocracy of the spirit of a Max Weber that was capable of being democratized, Weber's position ultimately retained his favor.[192]

Ernst Troeltsch acutely observed in regard to the controversy that the younger disputants tended to assess the history of the German spirit "from Luther to Nietzsche and George," whereas the older participants viewed it as stretching "from Luther to Goethe and Helmholtz."[193] For Troeltsch this difference explains why there is generally a more favorable estimation of the positive sciences to be found in the older than in the younger authors' writings. What Weber says about these sciences in "Science as a Vocation" is in Troeltsch's view "in its clarity and virility the only truth" possible.[194] To recognize this, however, does not imply that one is in agreement with his conception of philosophy. For

Troeltsch, even those who reject[195] the visionary human sciences with their pursuit of the cognitive sensuality practiced in the George circle and elsewhere, who follow neither a new Platonism nor a new Catholicism regarding the problem of value, are not committed to Weber's highly restricted concept of philosophy. In this regard, he even ascribes some merit to Kahler's yearning for unity. It comes closer to the truth "than Weber's skepticism, which I, too, find impossible, and his heroism that forcibly affirms the values."[196] Curtius had already made similar remarks. For him, "Science as a Vocation" was a "symptom of the value anarchy" of recent Western European culture.[197]

Arguments in this direction can also be found in Max Scheler. Even though he largely shares Weber's characterization of the positive sciences, he views Weber's combination of ascetic science and an antifoundational weltanschauung as the "shocking document of an entire era."[198] Weber's position suffers from the fact that it no longer possesses a "substantive metaphysics" or a "substantive cognition of the objective hierarchy of value," a deplorable state of affairs that can ultimately be traced back to Kant and can be remedied only by means of an anti-Kantian position[199] (which in reality is a pre-Kantian one). Scheler continues to say that even the Southwest German neo-Kantians, with whom Weber philosophically sympathized, were only capable of a formal doctrine of cognition and norms. However, Weber and his entire school, in which Scheler includes Karl Jaspers and Gustav Radbruch, transform even these formal remnants into a descriptive doctrine of weltanschauung. Thus, what Scheler ultimately criticizes is Weber's supposed abstention from philosophy in any real sense, and "not just the contemporary state of the art but as an *essential cognitive position* of man per se."[200]

Scheler's harsh judgment of Weber as a philosopher is hardly an isolated assessment. It is basically shared by Curtius and Troeltsch, and not only they: even Heinrich Rickert, whose logic of historical concept formation initially helped Weber develop his own position, found his position on philosophy in retrospect "negatively dogmatic."[201] In Rickert's view, Weber "formed a somewhat one-sided opinion about scientific philosophy and its contemporary potential." Ultimately, he only considered logic but not the effort at a comprehensive value philosophy to be scientific philosophy.[202] Moreover, for Rickert, in "Science as a Vocation" Weber unduly exaggerates this difference between past and present, between the Platonic and the modern idea of truth, for modern scientific philosophy, which is more than just logic, does not just demystify, it also brings "the 'mystery' of life into full consciousness for the first time." And this is because "that which is *clear* about existence, nature, art, happiness, God [is] still in principle accessible to science today."[203]

Thus, even one who shared Weber's antinaturalism and antiromanticism, who affirms this concept of rational and empirical sciences,[204] in no way necessarily agrees with his answer to the value question. Quite the opposite: the reported reactions to "Science as a Vocation" show that Weber's thesis of objectified polytheism, of the battle of the gods, was the real cause of philosophical controversy. In an age in which the most different philosophical orientations all sought commitment and unity, dogma and law in spiritual life, Weber's remarks had to appear as unphilosophical and as the expression of a simplistic relativism. Here Troeltsch's cultural Protestantism, Scheler's Catholicism, and Rickert's crypto-Platonism all seem to be in agreement. The desire for a new value synthesis was everywhere. One no longer was willing to live without it. The fact that one has to live without it, if one wants to be honest with oneself, was what Weber had taught in "Science as a Vocation."[205]

Of course, Weber never claimed to be a philosopher. Even during the time in which he intensively took up the methodological questions of the social sciences and studied modern logicians, he repeatedly emphasized that he studied logic not for its own sake, but only to test the utility of the insights of modern logicians, especially Rickert, for the solution of the problems of his own discipline. He conceived of himself more as a patient who was conscious of his symptoms than as a physician who knew how to cure them. His attitude toward the question of value in "Science as a Vocation" can be similarly characterized. He described the illness; he also named the remedies that had already failed or that, being mere narcotics, would ultimately fail. He showed how one can continue living in this incurable situation, but he did not present himself as the physician who knew the redeeming therapy. At most, he presented physicians, especially the theological and philosophical ones, with a difficult problem.

If one seeks to grasp the existential character of this problem that so moved Weber, one must first rid oneself of the conception that Weber advocates a simplistic relativism in "Science as a Vocation." This we can see more clearly today than was possible immediately following its publication in an atmosphere in which new value syntheses flourished.[206] Nevertheless, this character really was not a question of universalism or relativism but of how Weber formulated the question of value and, more important, how he lived it. This seems to have been first and most clearly recognized by Karl Jaspers. In his commemorative speech of 1920, Jaspers commented that Weber, the scholar and politician, appeared to many as a philosopher, though admittedly not "in a sense realized prior to him." Instead, through his very existence, through the fragmentary character *and* the spirit of unity and coherence that it symbolized, he had given the idea of philosophy a presence and thus a new fulfillment. In this sense, he had lived a philosophical existence. For the "essence of a philosophical existence is . . . the consciousness of the absolute and conduct guided in its unconditionality by the living earnestness of the absolute. This is what was singular in Max Weber, that he radiated such an essence without concretely recognizing and presenting the absolute."[207]

The initial debate in the wake of the publication of "Science as a Vocation" has been largely forgotten today. The academic philosophies that opposed Weber's restrictive conception of modern science have also disappeared. However, the philosophical vitality that Karl Jaspers sensed in Max Weber's work, and especially in his two addresses, remains. In this sense they are indeed "philosophical" texts: in addition to rational insight and rational conviction, they also give expression to a philosophical existence.

Excursus: The Controversy Surrounding the Dating of the Two Speeches

There has long been a controversy in the literature on the dating of the speech "Science as a Vocation." The assumption that it took place in the winter of 1918–19 can presumably be traced back to a statement made by Marianne Weber in her biography of her husband. It declares that both "Science as a Vocation" and "Politics as a Vocation" were given in 1918 and published in 1919 (Marianne Weber 1975, 664). This claim is surprising insofar as Marianne Weber specifically instructed Frithjof Noack to check the dating for her while she was writing her book. She was thus informed that "Science as a Vocation" had "already" been given at the "beginning of November 1917," and "Politics as a Vocation" "one and a half years later in Febr[uary] o[r] March 1919" (Frithjof Noack to Marianne Weber, October 24, 1924, Max-Weber-Archiv, Munich). Johannes Winckelmann adopted Marianne Weber's winter 1918–19 dating of "Science as a Vocation" when he reprinted this text (see Max Weber 1951) and Eduard Baumgarten also held onto the notion in his book that both speeches were close in time, placing them in January–February 1919 (see Baumgarten 1964, 715).

In the years thereafter a controversy developed, prompted by a query by Winckelmann (see his letter to Immanuel Birnbaum, July 8, 1970, Max-Weber-Archiv, Munich), between Immanuel Birnbaum and Eduard Baumgarten. Whereas Birnbaum, who at this point was an editor at the *Süddeutsche Zeitung*, believed himself able to remember an interval of "several months" between "Science as a Vocation" and "Politics as a Vocation," Baumgarten, on the basis of his good knowledge of Max Weber's correspondence and personal circumstances, believed he was able to say precisely that "Science as a Vocation" was delivered on January 16, 1919, and "Politics as a Vocation" on January 28, 1919 (see Baumgarten's arguments in "On the Question of Dating Weber's Speeches," Max-Weber-Archiv, Munich, typescript).

On the basis of accounts given in the Munich daily press, others ultimately succeeded in definitively ascertaining that the public address "Science as a Vocation" was delivered in November 1917 (see Mommsen 1974, 289–90, n. 292; and Schluchter 1979, 113–16; and Schluchter 1980, 236–39, n. 2). Nevertheless, the possibility that Weber could have presented "Science as a Vocation" a second time in the winter of 1918–19 was still discussed. Birnbaum, who was asked about this topic again in 1979, termed this "highly unlikely" (see his letter to Martin Riesebrodt, January 17, 1979, Max-Weber-Archiv, Munich).

However, the old conception of the close temporal proximity of "Science as a Vocation" and "Politics as a Vocation" or the thesis of the second enactment of "Science as a Vocation" received new life from an account written by Karl Löwith in Japan in 1940 and published in 1986. Löwith claims to have heard both speeches in the winter of 1918–19 (see Löwith 1986, 16–17). However, Löwith's dates are extremely vague. For example, he started studying in Munich in the winter semester of 1917–18 (according to information in the University Archives of Munich as of July 5, 1989) and not, as is stated in his book (14), in the summer semester of 1918. As a result, it is quite possible that he could have been present at Weber's address on November 7, 1917. It follows from his relatively correct description of the course of Weber's speech that he was in fact present. He emphasizes that Weber had spoken extemporaneously and that his address was taken down in short-hand. If Löwith did not hear him speak on November 7, 1917, Weber would have had to have spoken twice in the same auditorium, in an event organized by the same persons, in front of the same audience, with his extemporaneous address taken down in shorthand for the second time. There is, however, no support for this assumption in the correspondence of the Free Students Association, or from the publishers, Duncker & Humblot, who published both "Science as a Vocation" and "Politics as a Vocation" as texts, or in the recollections of Birnbaum. Nor can Baumgarten's statement that he could prove on the basis of Max Weber's correspondence that the speech on "Science as a Vocation" took place on January 16, 1919, stand up to investigation. The "addresses before students" mentioned in the correspondence to which Baumgarten refers are not speeches Weber held in front of the Free Students Association, but instead the speeches "Occidental Bourgeoisie" ("Abendländisches Bürgertum") and "Students and Politics" ("Student und Politik"), which were organized by the Social Science Association of the University of Munich and the Political Association of German Students (Politischer Bund deutscher Studenten [Bund deutsch-nationaler Studenten]), and which, after several postponements, took place on March 12 and 13, 1919 (see Weber 1988:482ff., 557–58).

CHAPTER 2

Conviction and Responsibility
Max Weber on Ethics

> In a sense, successful political action is always the "art of the possible." Nonetheless, the possible is often reached only by striving to attain the impossible that lies beyond it. . . . I, for my part, will not try to dissuade the nation from the view that action is to be judged not merely by its success value [*Erfolgswert*] but by its convictional value [*Gesinnungswert*] as well. In any case, the failure to recognize this fact impedes our understanding of reality.
> —Max Weber, "The Meaning of 'Ethical Neutrality'"

The Polemical Use of the Distinction Between an Ethic of Conviction and an Ethic of Responsibility

Max Weber's distinction between an ethic of conviction and an ethic of responsibility has regained some currency in recent political debates, especially in Germany. It is noteworthy, however, that the distinction serves primarily polemical purposes. It is often used to split the political world into two parts: good and bad. Good are the adherents to an ethic of responsibility; bad, those who cling to an ethic of conviction, which is regarded not only as old-fashioned but also as politically dangerous. There is a preference for an ethic of responsibility, relatively independent of one's political standpoint, whereas the ethic of conviction is given little respect. It is almost used as a term of abuse. On the one hand, we have the naive adherent to the ethic of conviction, the sincerity of whose motives no one doubts but whose blindness to reality leads to politically irresponsible conduct. On the other hand, we have the thoughtful adherent to an ethic of responsibility, guided by reason and experience, who anticipates the consequences of his action and responsibly orients his conduct accordingly. True enough, if these were the alternatives, who would not place himself on the side of reason and experience in spite of the danger of being reproached by adherents to an ethic of conviction as being a mere realpolitiker?

Admittedly, even Weber did not always resist the tendency to oversimplify the distinction for polemical purposes. Especially in those passages in "Politics as a Vocation" where he took a political stance on the situation of Germany after the November Revolution of 1918, he tended—as Guenther Roth has pointed out—to "equate enmity to capitalism with the incapability to bear the ethical irrationality of the world" and to "force Christian pacifists and socialist revolutionaries . . . under the same rubric," that of adherence to an ethic of conviction. The political devaluation that goes with this classification is obvious.[1]

As soon as we take a closer look at Weber's texts however, we immediately realize that matters can not be that simple, for he himself emphasized that the ethic of conviction must not be equated with irresponsibility nor the ethic of responsibility with mere realpolitik.[2] A proper demarcation of the two ethics obviously rests on a specification of the *kind* of responsibility connected with them, that is, on the answer to the questions *to whom* and *for what* one is responsible.[3] This demarcation calls for a more comprehensive analysis. Only by reconstructing the overall theoretical context in Weber's work of which the distinction is a part can the distinction be secured against precipitate misuse— whether at Weber's own hands or at those of his "followers."

In order not to fall prey to polemical simplification from the very outset, we must remember that Weber's distinction is made in the context of a theory of values and of the *limits* of ethics. Ethical values are not the only ones that carry claims of validity. They also cannot always offer unequivocal directives for solving practical problems. This is especially true for political problems, where ethical and cultural values often compete. In certain circumstances, cultural values can even be realized only by those who "take ethical 'guilt' upon themselves."[4] Thus, the distinction is part of the characterization of different worldviews and different modes of conduct. It has also a historical-sociological and a normative-axiological side to it. The former is primarily taken up in the sociology of religion. The latter, however, which is related to Weber's own value position, has never been fully worked out.[5] By combining Weber's sociology of religion with certain of his political writings, we can uncover a typology of ethics that in part guides his research. This is the context in which the distinction between the ethics of responsibility and conviction plays a *diagnostic* role. Weber's own value position, his own "philosophy of life," can be culled from his scattered remarks on value theory. Indeed, in some of his scholarly writings he openly admitted to having such a philosophy. He called himself, for example, an advocate of the idea of value collision who at the same time considered the designation as relativist the "crudest [imaginable] misunderstanding" of his position. Relativism, Weber wrote, denotes "a philosophy of life that is based on a view of the interrelations of the value-spheres that is diametrically opposite [to that of the advocates of the theory of value collision], and that can be held with consistency only if it is based on a very special type of ('organic') metaphysics."[6] Thus it is only in terms of Weber's philosophy of life, in terms of his view of the interrelation of the value spheres, that the normative stance he connected to the distinction can fully be appreciated. This is where it plays a *therapeutic* role. Only after both of these aspects—the diagnostic and the therapeutic—have been investigated can one claim to have presented a full view of the status of this conceptual dichotomy.

I will, however, confine my analysis to the diagnostic aspect, touching on the therapeutic only occasionally. In concentrating on the first aspect, I want to improve on a typology of ethics that underlies Weber's historical and sociological analyses. This improvement will enable me to elaborate the distinction between an ethic of conviction and an ethic of responsibility and to continue as well as to correct earlier analyses of mine.[7]

The Career of a Distinction: Key Themes from the Three Phases of Weber's Work

The First Phase: The Inaugural Lecture at Freiburg

Weber did not initially make use of the distinction between an ethic of conviction and an ethic of responsibility in his writings.

It appears fully formulated only after 1910, and thus in the third phase of his work.[8] Both concepts have predecessors with which they are combined or which they replace. This raises the question whether this is merely a terminological matter or substantive changes are involved.

To answer this question adequately, it is useful to assemble the key themes related to the "problem of ethics" in Weber. This also serves to prepare the grounds for a more sophisticated typology of ethics than can be found in the secondary literature. We will begin with key themes from the first phase of Weber's work and then move to the themes of the following two periods.

In the winter semester of 1894–95, Weber assumed a chair in economics (*Nationalökonomie*) at the University of Freiburg. In his inaugural lecture (*Antrittsvorlesung*) in May 1895, entitled "The Nation State and Economic Policy" ("Der Nationalstaat und die Volkswirtschaftspolitik"), he took the opportunity to address the basic problems in his discipline, presenting his own viewpoint, something still expected today on such occasions. These problems arose in the dispute between the historical and theoretical approaches. The proper relation between theory and history and between theory and practice was controversial.[9] German economists considered their field not only a theoretical and historical discipline, but—in the form of national economic policy—a practical art obliged to offer policy directives. The evaluative standard of national economic policy was the young professor's concern. As he stressed in a prefatory remark to the published text of the speech, he wanted to offer a frank "presentation and account of his personal and in this sense 'subjective' standpoint in the *evaluation* of phenomena of economic policy."[10] He thus formulated his normative standpoint, his value position. It is true that he first gave an analysis and explanation of the social and economic dislocations caused by the capitalization of agriculture in eastern Germany, an analysis based on his investigations of the conditions of agricultural workers in the countryside east of the Elbe. However, he followed this analysis with a discussion of the evaluative standard of economic policy prevalent among his colleagues and the standard he himself advocated. The latter, which was in opposition to ruling doctrine, resulted in the well-known accusation that Weber was a German nationalist, even an imperialist.[11] This charge is certainly justified, even if one takes into account the changes in value and practical cultural problems that have occurred between 1895 and today.[12] Weber emphatically called on his fellow economists, especially those with a historical approach, to become economic nationalists and to disavow their partly eudaemonist, partly ethical standards for the well-being of the people, for "what we are to provide our descendants with for their journeys is not peace and human prosperity, but the *eternal struggle* for the maintenance and cultivation of our national character."[13]

Nevertheless, the decisive point is not this glorification of the German national *Machtstaat* (praise combined, incidentally, with an unusually critical diagnosis of the political weakness of the empire and its most important classes, including the bourgeoisie); it is the attempt to morally neutralize economic policy in order to *politicize* it. Weber struggled against a set of conflations: against the identification of political with ethical ideals and of political *or* ethical ideals with happiness. He fought even harder the "naturalistic fallacy": "As if, thanks to the work of economic science, not only *knowledge* of the basis of human communities had been powerfully extended, but also the *standard* by which we ultimately *evaluate* the phenomena had become a completely new one, as if political economy could derive distinctive ideals from its own material."[14] Instead of relying on (what was later termed) "naturalistic monism," economics has "to cooperate in the *political* education of our nation." This means taking Germany's "responsibility *in the face of history*" seriously,[15] and—given the unification of the country under Bismarck—creating social unity and national democracy in order to secure subsequent generations with the "elbow room" necessary for fulfilling the cultural tasks. This contribution to the political education of the nation, however, can only be accomplished by those economists, regardless of approach, who practice conscious self-control, who strictly separate analysis from evaluation, and who always remember that, in evaluation, there are "*no* distinctive and independently gained ideals, but only the *old, general types of human ideals*, which we too bring into the materials of our science."[16] Moreover, one must never forget that politics is a field in its own right, not to be reduced to economics or to ethics. Only those qualify as political leaders who can responsibly secure the continuing economic, political, and cultural interests of a nation, and its continued existence and expansion in the circle of nations.[17]

Thus, in his inaugural lecture, Weber formulated (though, as he later confessed, in an admittedly completely unsatisfactory manner) a twofold thesis: the thesis of the heterogeneity of "is" and "ought," and the thesis of the various "laws governing the ought" (*Sollensgesetze*).[18] Not everything that is valid is ethical, and not everything that seeks such validity is in accordance with the pursuit of happiness. In the terminology of neo-Kantianism—of which there is no trace either in the inaugural lecture or in the "early economic writings" in general—the twofold thesis reflects the transition from the contrast between the "is" and the "ought" to that between the "factual" and the "valid." On the one hand, this means that while things "exist," values carry claims; on the other hand, it implies that "though every 'ought' refers to a value, it is not the case that every value grounds an 'ought.'"[19]

Thus, Weber rejects economics as an ethical science. In the words of the second phase of his work, he did this because this "attitude sought to deprive ethical norms of their formal character," thus obliterating "the particular autonomy of the ethical imperative."[20] Even as late as in the debate on value-neutrality,[21] that is, in the third phase of his work, Weber attacked Gustav Schmoller, the leading representative of the (new) Historical School of economics, because he had fallen prey to "the grave but widespread misunderstanding" that "'formal' propositions, for example, those in Kantian ethics, contain no material directives," and furthermore, that one could equate ethical imperatives with cultural values.[22] He also combated Ethical Culture, a movement that in his view, aside from its political illusions, fell prey to errors similar to those of ethical economics. Above all, however, he waged war against eudaemonism, the doctrine that happiness or spiritual joy has to be seen as the ultimate or highest goal of human action. In other words, he contested *pre-Kantian* positions in ethics, whether they tended toward egoistical (individual) happiness or toward altruistic eudaemonism, that is, the greatest happiness of the greatest number.[23] In ethics, as in epistemology, Weber's approach was, as far as the normative-axiological aspect is concerned, based on Kant's critical turn.[24] Whoever espouses eudaemonist ideals in ethics reduces ethics—in Kant's terms—to a doctrine of prudence, or—in Weber's terms—naturalizes ethics.

The Second Phase: The Bourgeois Revolution in Russia and the Sexual Revolution in Germany

This rejection of all forms of eudaemonism in ethics finds clear expression in the key themes arising in the second phase of

Weber's work. In this period, he found himself confronted by two "revolutionary" processes: the political revolution in Russia and the sexual-erotic revolution in his own circle of friends and acquaintances. Whereas the former once again involved the relationship between ethics and politics, the latter concerned the relationship between ethics and a nonrational value sphere. It presented a challenge to Weber's own view and forced him to take a stand.[25]

In 1905, the "bourgeois" revolution took place in Russia. It appeared that the old autocratic system of czarism had reached its end and that Russia had been placed on the same course of development as that of the rest of Europe. Weber followed the paths of Russia's liberal democrats with fascination. He learned Russian in order to be able to keep up with events, and he wrote "chronicle-like notes" for the readers of the *Archiv für Sozialwissenschaft und Sozialpolitik*, a periodical that he had edited along with Edgar Jaffé and Werner Sombart since 1904. As a whole, these notes took on the size of an imposing book. For Weber, this bourgeois revolution represented a process of universal cultural significance involving nothing less than liberalism's political mission. The latter was confronted with not only the task of helping overcome the autocratic system, but also that of "opposing both bureaucratic and Jacobinic *centralism* equally and . . . seeking to spread among the masses the old individualist principle of 'inalienable human rights,' which to us in Western Europe seems as 'trivial' as black bread is to the man who has enough to eat."[26]

There were basically two alternatives to autocratic rule: constitutional and radical democracy.[27] Their representatives ultimately agreed in the demand for general, free, direct elections using secret ballots. Nevertheless, they differed on the means by which this demand was to be realized given the illiteracy, political inexperience, and lack of education of the masses. In this context, Weber formulated the following passage of importance for our topic:

I know Russian Democrats who have something of this viewpoint: "Fiat justitia, pereat mundus. Let the masses reject or destroy all cultural progress. We can only ask what is just, and we have done our duty when we grant them the right to vote and thus provide them with the responsibility for their own actions." At most they add: "Even the most extreme form of mob rule cannot sink to the level of the 'Black Hundreds' hired by those officials whose positions of power were threatened. But regardless of that, it is better to suffer generations of cultural darkness than to do political injustice. And perhaps sometime in the future, the educational power of the right to vote will in fact do its part."

And continuing, now in an analytical vein:

The absolute rejection of a "success-oriented ethic" even in the political field here means: only the unconditional ethical imperative holds at all as a possible guide to positive action. There is only the possibility of the struggle for what is right *or* of "holy" self-abnegation. Once what is recognized as positive "duty" is accomplished, and since *all other* values outside the ethical have been eliminated—that biblical principle goes unconsciously into effect that is most deeply rooted in the soul not only of Tolstoy, but of the Russian people as a whole: "Resist not evil." The abrupt fluctuation between headstrong will to action and surrender to the situation results from the nonrecognition of the existence or at least the possible "value" of the ethically indifferent, a nonrecognition just as inherent in the panmoralism of Solovievan "holiness" as in purely ethically oriented democracy.[28]

In my view, three points in this passage are important: (1) "It is better to suffer generations of cultural darkness than to do political injustice. And perhaps sometime in the future, the educational power of the right to vote will in fact do its part." This statement represents the conscious rejection of responsibility for the foreseeable consequences of one's action recognized as a duty and amounts to a trust that the "good" will win out in the end. What is decisive here is not that one could not foresee the consequences of a given action, but that one ought not to draw upon foresight to justify action. ("We can only demand what is just," and, one should add, we must then do what is recognized as one's positive 'duty' regardless of consequences.) Weber later characterized this position with the words: "The Christian acts rightly and leaves the consequences of his action to God." This position expresses unconditional faith in God, or in secular terms, unconditional trust in the ultimate victory of good in the world.[29] (2) This position is clearly not problematic in a purely ethical sense. However, by disputing the autonomy of politics vis-à-vis ethics, it rejects the justification of an ethical action (or the refraining from that action) in terms of its foreseeable political consequences. This, however, also means that in politics one must follow unconditionally the ethical imperative and accept negative consequences as an expression of the irrationality of the world, or as a test of the firmness of one's own faith or convictions. (3) This stance is based on a worldview in which only ethical values can be recognized as principles guiding action and in which this state of affairs holds for *each and every* realm of life. It is for this reason that Weber termed it "panmoralism." Thus, this ethical vision of the world either totally negates all nonethical values or devaluates them vis-à-vis ethical values. In this sense, it knows no limits to ethics; only ethics can claim validity.

Thus, Weber contrasts panmoralism and success-oriented ethics.[30] Panmoralism recognizes only the *ethical* imperative as a possible guide to positive action. It is *unconditional* and *unequivocal*, and because it has to be *fully* realized, it demands one's willingness to engage in a constant "struggle for what is right," for justice. If this (revolutionary) struggle is rejected, for example because the ethically required love and good disregarding the orders of the world (*Akosmismus*) is incompatible with the use of force, one's only alternative is self-denial. This alternative means the forgoing of political action, Tolstoy in his later years being a case in point.[31] In contrast, a success-oriented ethic invokes a different relationship to the world, as can be inferred from the text.

An adherent to a success-oriented ethic accepts both nonethical and ethical values as possible guides to positive action. This acceptance does not mean that the former *take the place* of ethical values. As implied by Weber's very concept of a success-oriented *ethic*, a balancing of ethical and nonethical imperatives is apparently at stake. Thus, the focus here is on the *problematic* relationship between ethics and politics. Even though Weber had not yet fully defined this concept in this manner, one should not reduce it to mere realpolitik, because Weber not only contrasted the politics of the panmoralists (whom he also termed "political romanticists") with that of adherents to a success-oriented ethic, he also distinguished both from the type of self-preservation by police action practiced by the regime. He offered a devastating critique of the latter (as well as, incidentally, of German practitioners of realpolitik):

The horrendous objective senselessness of this goal, the complete impossibility of deluding oneself that this regime embodies even the most modest of "moral" or "cultural values" does in fact provide the doings of these power holders and the "vocational labors" of these servants of the state—especially the most "proficient" among them—with precisely that haunting quality that Tolstoy's apolitical position in his "Resurrection" knew so astoundingly well how to convey.[32]

That for Weber *no* position that preaches simple adjustment to the realities of life—be they political or otherwise—deserves to be termed ethical can also be inferred from his reaction to the other revolution, the sexual-erotic one, that occurred around 1907 in his very own circle of friends and acquaintances. This "liberation movement," in part a generational phenomenon, played an important role in shaking up accepted ethical conceptions, especially in academic circles. It provoked reflection on "questions of principle in sexual ethics."[33] However, this movement involved more than recognition of a sexual-erotic sphere of life heterogeneous vis-à-vis all ethics, a sphere with its own inherent dignity. At least in parts of this movement, a new weltanschauung and a new ethic emerged. In his business report to the 1910 German Convention of Sociologists (Deutscher Soziologentag) in Frankfurt, Weber used this movement as an example, in connection with a proposal to survey associational life. He spoke of a sect oriented around Freud's theories that propagated a life free of inhibitions by means of which a "human free of complexes can be created and sustained."[34] As coeditor of the *Archiv*, he had already had professional (as well as private) contact with this side of the "liberation movement." In his public remarks Weber's allusion had been to Otto Gross, who had offered the periodical an essay for publication in which he advocated, in Weber's sarcastic words, a psychiatric "ethic," an ethic of a "thoroughly banal show-off of mental health."[35] Weber rejected publication with a long explanation, which is of much interest for our purposes.

The target of Weber's polemic was not merely, as was so often the case, the inflation of the perspective of a scholarly discipline (in this case psychiatry) into a weltanschauung. His real target was much more a particular understanding of ethics that relativized moral demands in terms of "natural" needs and thus turned their justification and the adherence to them into a question of psychic costs. This relativization, however, subverts the absolute nature of the claim characteristically made by all authentic ethics, and sacrifice and responsibility are struck from ethical reasoning. Weber too distinguished different types of ethics according to the degree to which they accommodate human nature. But for him an ethic in the strict sense of the word (what he termed an "idealistic ethic") was unthinkable without the belief in absolute values and without the continuous inner compulsion to self-transcendence, the suppression of "natural" needs. Every authentic ethic has an imperative character; it causes us—in Kant's words—to undergo duress at odds with our inclinations. It demands sacrifice, placing responsibility for one's own moral character at the center of one's effort. In anticipation of a later distinction between the ethics of the virtuosi and of the masses in his sociology of religion, Weber formulated:

One can divide all "ethics," regardless of their substantive contents, into two large groups. One set makes demands of principle on human beings, which they are generally *not* able to meet, except at the great high points of their lives. They give direction to their *pursuits* as destinations on an unreachable horizon. These are "heroic ethics." The other set contents itself with the acceptance of common human "nature" as the maximum limit of demands. These are "everyday or average ethics" [*Durchschnitts-ethik*]. It appears to me that only the first category, "heroic ethics," can call itself "idealism." It subsumes both the ethic of *early*, "authentic" Christianity as well as that of Kant. Both—in terms of their respective ideals—start from such a pessimistic evaluation of the "nature" of the average individual that the Freudian discoveries in the realm of the un-conscious have—God knows—*nothing* more "terrible" to add.[36]

This reaction to psychiatric "ethics" confirms what was al-ready visible in the inaugural lecture at Freiburg: Weber rejects every form of eudaemonism in ethics, regardless of how it is grounded. In Weber as in Kant, there is always tension between the ethically imperative and the pursuit of happiness; moreover, the moralization of the person is always kept separate from the culti-vation or civilizing of that person.[37] This separation implies the idea of an ethical, and more generally, an axiological turn. Human beings, although subject to the laws of nature, move beyond their "natural state" (*Naturalität*) by binding themselves to values. This "idealism" necessarily produces tension and even conflict between the natural state and the "cultural state" (*Kulturalität*).[38] Which values an individual takes as binding is for Weber a ques-tion of faith or of reason, not of scientific cognition. Nevertheless, this value commitment, if properly understood, requires—regard-less of its specific content—an openness toward scientific cri-tique. In an instructive letter to Ferdinand Tönnies from the same period as his confrontation with psychiatric ethics, Weber defined the limits and the possibilities of science in relation to the prob-lem of value, or more specifically, in relation to the problem of ethics, in the following way:

Certainly I am also of the opinion (perhaps even more decidedly than you, in any case just as decidedly) that, *if* someone recognizes at all the neces-sity of orienting his personal action in terms of "values," "value judg-ments," or whatever you want to call them, and if he is not "insensitive" in this regard, then it can be demonstrated that all the consequences of the Kantian imperative (whether modernized or not—it remains the same thing) *necessarily* hold for him. To prove this dialectically (or more accurately: to take up this problem) *is* a question of ethics as a science—a science that proceeds just as dialectically, by means of "immanent" critique, by uncovering that which is logically implicit or "assumed" in a thesis—as does logic. But this never provides more than proof of *formal* characteristics of moral *conviction*. Never can a system of social, suprapersonal structures be proven to be *ethically obligatory [ethisch gesollt]* by means of this purely formal critique of conviction. Metaphysical dogmas always play a part here . . . and *the individual may affirm them but he should never believe that he is permitted to present them as science.*[39]

In addition, however, Weber's reaction to psychiatric "ethics" can also be taken to show that for him, a success-oriented ethic could be neither an ethic of happiness nor an everyday or average ethic. It could not be an ethic of happiness because it presupposes belief in absolute ethical values; it could not be an everyday ethic because it raises unconditional demands. If Weber had wanted to characterize this ethic not only negatively, as he had largely done up until then, but positively, he could have attempted to distinguish it from the ethic of early Christianity as well as from the Kantian ethic, as another type of heroic or virtuosi ethic. This would have been congruent with the idea of the limits of ethics already implicit in the inaugural lecture at Freiburg.

In my view, this is in fact the path Weber took. Step by step, he defined more precisely the idea of the internal and external limits of ethics: whereas the former involve the nature of ethical values themselves, the latter concern their relationship to nonethical values, termed cultural values up until now. This distinction, however, also requires a value theory that—proceeding from the givenness of values—at least permits the typological characterization of the different kinds of values or spheres of value. The insight that this typology had to encompass more than just political values had already been gained in the confrontation with the sexual-erotic "liberation movement."[40] Hence, Weber followed with ever-increasing interest the debates on value theory in the philosophy of culture that involved contemporaries inspired by neo-Kantianism or vitalist philosophy.[41] He presented to the public his own value theory—in fairly developed form as compared to his Freiburg inaugural lecture—for the first time in that version of the "Intermediate Reflections" appearing at the end of December 1915. Here, the main focus was placed on the historical-sociological dimension.[42]

The Third Phase: From the "Intermediate Reflections" to "Politics as a Vocation"

In the "Intermediate Reflections," the ethics of conviction and responsibility are distinguished in the same way as in Weber's final writings. (This is the case even though the adjectival form of the ethic of conviction [*gesinnungsethisch*] finds use as a term, but not the corresponding form of the ethic of responsibility [*verantwortungsethisch*].) This distinction is part of the analysis of the tensions to which a (religious) ethic of brotherhood (as found in the writings on Russia and in the critique of the psychiatric ethic) must fall prey vis-à-vis the world. These tensions exist first of all between the ethic of brotherhood and the other, nonreligious value spheres. However, they also exist within the (religious) ethic of brotherhood insofar as it aims to realize its ideal in the world, for this ethic finds itself confronted by the question of what is sufficient in order to justify an action (or the refraining from an action) as ethical: (good) conviction or the foreseeable consequence(s) of the action.[43]

In 1917, Weber revised his 1913 contribution to the debate over value-neutrality in the Association for Social Policy. In a new passage that explicitly discusses the limits of ethics, he provides, in my view, the definitive formulation:

But even in the field of personal action there are quite specific ethical problems that ethics cannot settle on the basis of its own presuppositions. These include above all, the basic questions: (a) whether the intrinsic value of an ethical action—the "pure will" or the "conviction" in customary terms—is sufficient for its justification, following the maxim of the Christian moralists: "The Christian acts rightly and leaves the consequences of his action to God"; or (b) whether the responsibility for the foreseeable *consequences* of the action is to be taken into consideration. All radical revolutionary political attitudes, particularly revolutionary "syndicalism," have their point of departure in the first postulate; all *Realpolitik* in the latter. Both invoke ethical maxims. But these maxims are in eternal conflict—a conflict that cannot be resolved by means of ethics alone.[44]

To this Weber adds: these maxims possess a strictly formal character, and "in this they resemble the well-known axioms of the *Critique of Practical Reason*."[45] Finally, in "Politics as a Vocation" and thus at the end of Weber's life, one maxim is called—as previously—"*gesinnungsethisch*," whereas the other maxim is for the first time labeled "*verantwortungsethisch*."[46]

What can be learned from this third phase of Weber's work for our purposes? In my view, three points are important: (1) The ethic that Weber had described in the writings on Russia as panmoralism was now termed the "ethic of conviction." He maintained the subdivision of this ethic into an active and passive variant (revolutionary radicalism versus Tolstoyan love that disregards the orders of the world). They are confronted by an "ethic of responsibility" of equal status. This latter concept had replaced that of a success-oriented ethic. The ethic of responsibility is—just as the ethic of conviction—an ethic of virtuosi, but it makes possible an ethically grounded realpolitik, a "politics of responsibility." In this way, the latter is now also terminologically distinguished from pure power politics.[47] (2) Weber explicitly speaks of the convictional value and the success value of an ethical action (or the refraining from an action). A convictional value is illustrated—as in Kant (and in Fichte)—in terms of the pure or good will.[48] A success value is portrayed in terms of its foreseeable consequences. For this reason the distinction does not represent a strict either/or. The maxim of an ethic of responsibility does not require that the responsibility for the foreseeable consequences of an action should be taken into account instead of the responsibility for the purity of the will. Rather, the former responsibility must be taken into account alongside of, or better, in addition to, the latter one. Consequently, there is no such thing as a moral action without convictional value. It is, however, possible to have a moral action without success value, without its losing its ethical status in this way. (3) The two maxims have strictly formal character and are thus independent of the particular contents of any given ethic. This implies that they can only be adopted where the convictional value of an action is already determined.

By reflecting back on our initial question, we now see clearly that these terminological changes are also connected to substantive ones. Certainly the stage had already been set in the second phase of Weber's work for the distinction to be made between an ethic of conviction and an ethic of responsibility. Nevertheless, two distinctions had not yet been made in a manner barring all misunderstanding: between a success-oriented ethic and a mere "ethic" of adjustment to the possible,[49] and between a politics of responsibility and power politics. Moreover, the ethics of conviction and responsibility had not yet been presented as maxims of strictly formal character. However, precisely because Weber increasingly did just this, a problem arose in the third phase of his work that had not appeared previously: the two concepts were used to characterize, on the one hand, alternate rules or principles, a way to connect the convictional value to other values, especially to success values, and, on the other, different types of ethics. This is a crucial ambiguity, one we have to resolve.

Admittedly, in his studies in the sociology of religion Weber used the concept of an ethic of conviction mostly to denote a specific type of ethic. The ethic of responsibility does not show up in this context at all. This, however, could owe to the latter's being a very late conceptual formulation; its treatment as a specific type of ethic took place largely within Weber's political writings. Be that as it may, one thing is clear for me: *both* concepts possess the twofold relevance just described. Both are thus also employed to characterize different types of ethics that have played and still play a culturally significant role. They are both part of a typology of ethics. The question is, what does this typology look like?

The Typology of Ethics

Ethics and Doctrines of Prudence

As a way of introducing the typology of ethics, which, in my view, underlies the comparative sociology of religion, I would like to return to three key themes developed earlier. They involve the distinctions between heroic ethics and everyday ethics, between ethical values and cultural values (especially political values), and, finally, between ethics and happiness.

As mentioned before, Weber took up the distinction between heroic and everyday ethics in his comparative sociology of religion, but systematically transformed these concepts into the ethics or religiosity of virtuosi and of the masses. This is seen in the first version of the "Introduction" to the comparative essays on the economic ethics of the world religions, initially published in October 1915, which was then supplemented with commentary in the 1920 edition (in part in regard to this very aspect). Here Weber pointed to the intrinsic connection between heroism and virtuosity and to the fact that one has to remove from the concept of virtuosity "any and all evaluative connotations still adhering to it today."[50] The distinction refers exclusively to the fact of unequal religious or ethical qualification, and of unequal interest in such qualifications. Thus, the "masses" here are neither necessarily the socially underprivileged nor the "all-too-many" of the "herd." The "masses" comprise those "unattuned" (*unmusikal-isch*) to religious or ethical matters. For this reason, the opposition between virtuosi and masses finds more or less sharp expression in all differentiated configurations of order. It is the expression of religious, more generally, cultural stratification; it can be congruent as well as at odds with economic stratification.[51] As an instrument for making cultural distinctions, this cultural stratification is relatively independent of a specific type of ethic. For this reason, the distinction between virtuosi and the masses remains of subordinate importance for the typology.

This is not the case with the two remaining aforementioned distinctions. By juxtaposing ethical and cultural values, Weber emphasized the special status of ethical vis-à-vis other kinds of values. An ethic imposes unconditional imperatives on the conscience of the individual. It thus affects practical conduct, as it were, from within. This impelling force is the reason why the sociology of religion deals above all with the effects of different types of ethical conceptions of duty.[52] These arise from value commitments and require action for its own sake. If action is rational, this results in value-rational action. This type of action is to be distinguished strictly from success-oriented action; here, if action is rational, instrumental or means-ends rational action (*zweckrationales Handeln*) results. Weber explicitly defined purpose as the conception of success that becomes the cause of an action. In analogous fashion, value could be defined as the conception of validity that becomes the cause of an action.[53] Some of these conceptions are connected with the conception of *duty*. But not every conception of duty directs unconditional imperatives to the conscience of the individual.

In terms of the key themes that define the relationship between ethics and politics (as delineated earlier), we might distinguish between two conceptions of duty. Whereas ethical values are tied to absolute conceptions of duty, political values are connected to historical conceptions of duty. The object of reference for ethical values is the individual, for political values the "collectivity." Consequently, an ethical value is the conception of an absolute validity related to the individual that becomes the cause of an action. A political value, however, is the conception of a *historical* validity related to the collectivity that becomes the cause of an action.[54] What Weber had already described in his inaugural lecture as *our* responsibility before history—having to fulfill the cultural tasks of a *Machtstaat* in the center of Europe—he later explicitly termed a historical duty. This historical duty resulted from the founding of the Reich under Bismarck, and it was thus the result not of a geographical, economic, or political necessity, but of a political decision.[55] Clearly, the decision could have been made against the establishment of the Reich. However, once Bismarck and his generation had created the German *Machtstaat,* "the distinct character of the culture of the future," as Weber put it, was placed "at the disposal" of his generation. In his view this was the historical demand they were not permitted to disavow.[56] Such duties, however, apply not to the individual as such, but to the individual as a member of a *particular* collectivity. Thus, the specificity of the relationship between ethics and politics emerges from the tension involved between different conceptions of duty.

The third distinction—between ethics and happiness—is connected to this last one, for conceptions of duty regardless of their status are always different from conceptions of happiness. It is generally known that Weber spoke of ideal and material interests, of interests from within and from without. Conceptions of duty fall under ideal interests, whether from within, such as salvational interests, or from without, such as the interest in individual or collective honor. The division between the pursuit of happiness (health, wealth, longevity, and so on), or more generally, the pursuit of success and the pursuit of value obligations, pervades Weber's entire sociology. With regard to action orientations, the division finds expression in the distinction made between success orientation and value orientation. With regard to social relations, it finds expression in two types of coordination: one in terms of interest constellations, in which the participants behave according to the calculations of loss and gain; the other in terms of conceptions of the validity of an order, in which duties play a role. The fulfillment of these duties is guaranteed by sanctions, whether primarily from within or from without.[57] This basic dichotomy, however, is found once again in the sociology of domination, in the distinction between domination by virtue of interest constellation and domination by virtue of authority.[58] I would like to propose that it is formed in analogy to Kant's distinction between hypothetical and categorical imperatives. Success-oriented action ultimately follows technical or pragmatic imperatives, rules of skill or prudence. As Weber put it his Stammler essay, it follows utilitarian maxims motivated by material interests. In contrast, value-oriented action follows categorical imperatives, normative maxims propelled by ideal interests.[59] Such imperatives are carried out for their own sake, out of respect for the duty so formulated, and completely independently of success.[60] Following Kant's practical philosophy, one can further divide such duties into legal duties and duties of virtue, into legal imperatives and moral imperatives.

What is more important, though, is that success-oriented action falls within the realm of technical-practical action, in Weber's words, within the realm of utilitarian maxims; value-oriented action falls within the realm of normative-practical action, in Weber's terms, within the realm of ethical maxims and maxims of fair play.[61] In the former realm, our discretion is limited by "natural laws" of more or less strict character. If we do not adhere to technical or pragmatic rules (Weber sometimes calls them "teleological rules"), which are derived by applying intersubjectively valid, nomological knowledge, we act unskillfully and imprudently and do harm to our happiness and well-being. In the latter realm, our discretion is limited by "normative laws" enforced by more or less strict sanctions. By transgressing against moral rules, for example, we are not necessarily acting ineptly or imprudently, nor do we necessarily harm our material interests. We are, however, forgetful of our duty, and we endanger self-regard in addition to the regard of others.[62] As with Durkheim's distinction between technical and moral rules, one has to view Weber's distinction between success-oriented and value-oriented action, between means-ends rational and value-rational action, against the backdrop of Kant's system of reason. Neither Durkheim nor Weber employs Kant's arguments, but both have adapted his architectonics for sociological purposes, with admittedly different intentions and different results.[63]

Kant's distinction between the sphere of natural concepts and the sphere of concepts of freedom also provided the background for Weber's thesis that the rationalization of success-oriented action, and thus means-ends rationalization, need not develop in the same direction (*gleichsinnig*) as the rationalization of value-oriented action, and thus value rationalization. The two forms of rationalization belong to heterogeneous spheres. Means-ends rationalization falls within the cognitive sphere, value rationalization within the "evaluative sphere" (*Wertungssphäre*), a term that one should distinguish from "value sphere" (*Wertsphäre*), even though Weber employed them largely interchangeably.[64] Means-ends rationalization depends upon our nomological knowledge. The better this is, the more comprehensive the possibilities of a technical critique of success-oriented action. This is feasible because technical and pragmatic rules are the simple reversals of causal relations. Undoubtedly, the methodically controlled improvement of our nomological knowledge through modern science—a knowledge of the behavior "of objects of the external world and of other humans"[65]—does not make superfluous the distinction between subjective and objective means-ends rationalization (the latter also called *Richtigkeitsrationalisierung*).[66] However, in the realm of success-oriented action, objective progress takes place; that is, there is a gradual replacement of subjective means-ends rationality by the rationality of objective correctness (*Richtigkeitsrationalität*). This is not the case with value rationalization. It falls within the evaluative sphere, a realm heterogeneous vis-à-vis the cognitive sphere. Though knowledge also exists here, it does not arise in a conceptual ordering of reality.[67]

Value rationalization is connected to the fact that we are forced to take a stance toward the world and to provide this world with meaning. We know, for example, that we can take a critical stance to the world and to the technical progress in it. We also know that such a critique is not purely technical and that the knowledge informing such a critique is not limited to empirical or even philosophical knowledge of the cognitive sphere. It is much more a knowledge of the validity of value. It is thus not knowledge in the sense customarily understood, but more a "possession" in the way that Weber applied this term to religious knowledge. Correctly understood, however, this has to be said of all knowledge of values.[68] In analogy to Kant, one can formulate that the objects of the cognitive sphere are given to us (*gegeben*), whereas those of the evaluative sphere are posited (*aufgegeben*);[69] the objective reality of the cognitive sphere can be proved, whereas that of the evaluative sphere can only be defended. Admittedly, just as we can scientifically scrutinize subjective means-ends rationalization, we can do the same to subjective value rationalization. We can subject an obligation that has been taken on, a value commitment, to a formal critique, as Weber argued in his letter to Tönnies. But such a critique is not capable of turning subjective into objective rationalization, as is the case with means-ends rationality. A value decision can only be objectified (*objektiviert*) by means of such a critique. This, however, points also to the fact that, in spite of the "unbridgeable difference" between the cognitive and evaluative spheres, a transfer of knowledge is not only possible between them, it is also required.[70] For Weber, there is a truth-relatedness of practical *and* a praxis-relatedness of theoretical-historical issues. Of course, these relationships have to be correctly conceived. Theoretical-historical questions that fall into the cognitive sphere have to be relevant, they have to arouse our interest. This requires a theoretical relation to values. Practical questions that fall in the evaluative sphere require evaluations. They are capable of being discussed and even need to be discussed. Out of such discussions participants gain increasing clarity as to their value commitments vis-à-vis the value commitments of others. But although this implies cognition, there is no necessary connection in the evaluative sphere, in contrast to the cognitive sphere, between cognition and recognition.[71]

Consequently, one does not find the gradual replacement of subjective by objective rationalization in the evaluative sphere. One could even say that the reverse takes place. The transformation of the world into a causal mechanism through the cognitive sphere is connected to the subjectification of the evaluative sphere. To the extent that this subjectification occurs, the once seemingly "objective" foundations of values disintegrate.[72] But regardless of shifting historical circumstances Weber presupposes a *fundamental* tension between technical and normative rules, between success values and convictional values. For this reason, there are no *unequivocal* connections between means-ends rationalization, in the sense of technical progress, and value rationalization, in the sense of moral or cultural progress. Neither determines the other, even though objective means-ends rationalization certainly creates restrictive conditions for value rationalization. (For an overview, see Figure 1.)[73]

Value	Theoretical	Ethical	Extra-ethical
Faculties	What one is able to do	What one ought to do	What one wants to do
Action	Technical-practical	Moral-practical	Cultural
		Normative-practical	
Process	Technicalization on the basis of success values	Moralization on the basis of convictional values	Cultivation on the basis of cultural values
Rationalization	Instrumental rationalization	Value rationalization	

Figure 1. Conceptual scheme of values.

The distinction between technical-practical and moral-practical action, between prudence and ethics, appropriated from the Kantian tradition, is central to Weber's approach. This can already be seen clearly in the first version of the never-completed study "The Protestant Ethic and the 'Spirit' of Capitalism."[74] In this attempt from 1904–5 to uncover the religious roots of the conceptions of modern vocational duty (*Berufspflicht*) and thus of one of the most vivid elements of modern culture, Weber had precisely this Kantian distinction in mind. It is no accident that he accentuated this very point in the revised version of this study by launching a countercritique to objections raised by Werner Sombart and Lujo Brentano to his historical account.[75]

The point of departure of Weber's analysis was the question, Who was the spiritual father of the "spirit of modern capitalism"? In his search for the answer, Weber first cited the "spirit" of Benjamin Franklin as reflected in his advice on commercial life. This was to serve as a provisional portrayal of this complex "historical individual."[76] His thesis was that Franklin's suggestions reflect an orientation toward the "ideal of the honest man of recognized credit, and above all the idea of a duty of the individual toward the increase of his capital, which is assumed as an end in itself." If one compares, as Weber notes, Franklin's statements with those statements of Jakob Fugger that Sombart took as exemplifying the spirit of modern capitalism and with which he prefaced his analysis of the genesis of modern capitalism, one can see "what in [Fugger's] case was an expression of commercial daring and a personal inclination morally neutral, in [Franklin's] case takes on the character of an ethically colored maxim for the conduct of life."[77] In the second edition of 1920, Weber expanded on this thesis: "Truly what is here preached is not simply a means of making one's way in the world, but a peculiar ethic. The infraction of its rules is treated not as foolishness but as forgetfulness of duty. That is the essence of the matter. It is not mere business astuteness, that sort of thing is common enough, it is an ethos. *This* is the quality which interests us."[78]

Doctrines of prudence and success orientation versus ethics and value orientation comprise the key contrasts. The infraction of technical or pragmatic rules is foolishness; that of moral rules is irresponsible neglect of duty. In reality, admittedly, success orientation and value orientation are found in combination. Moreover, even in the first version of *The Protestant Ethic*, Weber had already placed emphasis on the utilitarian undertone to Franklin's moral requirements. Utilitarianism did in fact in part replace ascetic Protestantism.[79] The turning point came as early as the eighteenth century. This shift also represented the beginning of the move from ethics to doctrines of prudence. Thus, the transformation of the "bourgeois" conduct that had already occurred with Franklin is due not only to secularization, but also to the replacement of ethical by nonethical, especially success, values. This is why Weber pointed out at the end of his study that in the age of advanced capitalism the idea of vocational duty moves about in our lives as the *ghost* of formerly religious values.[80] By the beginning of the "iron age" in the nineteenth century the capitalist "spirit" had already lost any ethical foundations; vocational duty was replaced by mere striving for success. Where economic activity meant more than the adjustment to strict economic constraints, where it also claimed to be fulfilling, it no longer took moral rules as its point of reference. They were replaced by technical and pragmatic rules. As it had with Jacob Fugger, economic activity once again took on the character of a personal and morally indifferent inclination. It permitted a lifestyle rather than conduct.[81] Just as Leon Battista Alberti provided a precapitalist economy with a doctrine of prudence, so marginal utility theory does the same for advanced capitalism.[82] Clearly, a modern doctrine of prudence is distinguished from Alberti's by its foundation in science, but it promotes a purely technological relationship to the world. Moreover, if unchecked by other ideals, it ultimately promotes a way of life of (formally rational) adjustment to the world by elevating rationality based on scientific verifiability to the status of sole guide for positive action.

Thus, the first task of a typology of ethics is to distinguish ethics from mere doctrines of prudence. As the preceding discussion has shown, this can be done in terms of rules, in terms of interests or motivation, and in terms of sanctions. In comparison with doctrines of prudence, an ethic formulates normative, not technical, rules. It relies on ideal, not material, interests, and it addresses feelings of duty, not inclination. Finally, it sanctions by withdrawing the respect of others and, above all, self-respect, and by mobilizing feelings of sin and guilt, not by means of gains and losses.

Magic, Ethics of Norms, and Ethics of Principles

The distinction between ethics and doctrines of prudence is important not only in a typological but also in a developmental perspective. The differentiation between the realms of success orientation and value orientation was an unusually protracted and complex process in history. One crucial step in this process was taken in the civilizations of the Axial Age two and a half millennia ago. The symbiosis between success orientation and value orientation, between conceptions of utility and of duty that had held up until then was definitely dissolved.[83] This step also plays an important role in Weber's sociology of religion. This role can be seen in his reflections on the gradual emergence of religious ethics out of the world of magic. Regardless of how tortuous the actual historical paths were, one generalization can be made: Only with the transition from taboos to religious laws, from coercion and bribery to worship and service of the divine, from a fraternization guaranteed by taboos to one guaranteed by one's "conscience," was the equation of useful versus harmful with good versus evil rejected and faith in the power of demons and gods and in their mediators made relatively independent of their contribution to the (material) success of the faithful.[84]

For this reason, a magical "ethic" is not an ethic in the strict sense of the word. It lacks the clear distinction between a technical and a normative rule. It also lacks the conception that divine benevolence can be gained neither by coerced subordination nor by bribery but only by voluntary obedience and devotion. Admittedly, most religious ethics remain pervaded by taboos and magical practices, just as many normative rules are encumbered by utilitarian motives. However, in typological terms, an ethic has to be strictly distinguished conceptually not only from scientific technologies but also from magic, which can be regarded as a technique based on subjective means-ends relationships. In sum, the development of a religious ethic, indeed of every ethic in the strict sense of the word, presupposes the axiological turn and the strict distinction between the natural and the cultural state, between action and norm.[85]

Thus, in his sociology of religion, Weber employed the concept of religious ethic as a genetic class concept, contraposed to scientific technologies on the one hand and to magical "techniques" on the other. Both "counterconcepts" play an important role in his analysis of religious action in its different social and cultural milieus because, as elsewhere, action in accordance with an ethic (here of a religious nature) is more the exception than the rule, and where such action is pursued, it always mixes with other orientations. As we have seen, only minorities live the life of religious virtuosi. How they live depends, alongside external conditions—exhaustively treated by Weber in his sociology of religion—on the character of the religious ethic to which they adhere. Although a religious ethic must be clearly distinguished from doctrines of prudence and from magic, it seems, however, that not every religious ethic is an ethic of conviction. Therefore the question arises, What can be learned from Weber's sociology of religion in order to differentiate the concept of religious ethics?

Weber treats three types of religious ethics in addition to magic: ritualistic ethics, legal ethics, and ethics of conviction. The effects of the first two are similar to those of magic: they tend to stereotype conventional and legal norms by making them sacred, that is, by giving them religious sanctification. Therefore, they represent not two types, but two subtypes of one type. Both produce a religious base for "the entire realm of legal institutions and social conventions." They help create a situation in which ceremonial and ritual norms are to be treated in exactly the same way as legal and ethical prescriptions.[86] Moral, legal, and conventional rules remain amalgamated, and these rules are primarily secured by external guarantees. Law in particular is elevated into sacred law in this way and thus is largely protected from secularization. Legal obligations are regarded as obligations of virtue, and vice versa; in Weber's terminology: legality (*Rechtlichkeit*) determines the conduct of the individual.

This changes only with the transition to a religious ethic of conviction. At this point, ethical norms are separated from legal norms. Moreover, ethical norms are systematized and internalized. Obligatory action can now become action done out of a sense of duty; cultural prescriptions subdivide into the spheres of outer and inner freedom, legality, and morality. Whereas convention and law previously ruled the day, conviction now enters the picture. In Weber's research in the comparative sociology of religion, this is the central aspect of his analysis of the inner conditions of conduct. In contrast to the sacralized typification of convention and law in ritualistic and legal-ethical religions, a religion with an ethic of conviction creates an essentially different internal situation by means of

a systematization of religious obligations guided by principles. It breaks through the typification of individual norms in order to relate all conduct to the goal of religious salvation. Moreover, an ethic of conviction does not recognize any sacred law, but only "sacred conviction" that may sanction different maxims of conduct in different situations, and which is thus elastic and susceptible to accommodation. It may, depending on the conduct it engenders, produce revolutionary consequences from within, instead of exerting a stereotyping effect. But it acquires this ability to revolutionize at the price of also acquiring a whole complex of problems that becomes greatly intensified and internalized. The inherent conflict between the religious postulate and the realities of the world does not diminish, but rather increases.[87]

This passage contains a formulation of systematic significance, namely, that the religious ethic of conviction arises from a systematization of obligation based on principles. Individual norms previously largely fragmented are placed, as it were, into groups, and put on different levels. But more important, there is a linkage of at least all ethical norms, because now they are all directed to the religious goal of salvation, an ultimate, internally consistent religious value axiom that serves as a common point of reference. In other words, the norms are all subject to a process of cognitive abstraction. In a different context, Weber described this process in the following way: it is an "operation that begins with particular evaluations and the analysis of their meaning. It then continually advances to an ever more principled evaluation."[88] Out of the value axioms thus uncovered, practical postulates can then be derived. As a result, a religious ethic of conviction possesses not only a principle of normative integration, but one of norm generation as well. In contrast to ritualistic and legal ethics that are based on stereotyped (and thus largely unchangeable) and disconnected individual norms, the ethic of conviction is an ethic of principles. It presupposes logical and speculative labors, performed either by religious intellectuals, including theologians,[89] or by lay intellectuals.[90]

Moreover, a second formulation from the quote is also important, namely, that an ethic of conviction sanctifies an individual's conviction that "may sanction different maxims of conduct in different situations, and which is thus elastic and susceptible to accommodation." Thus, a religious ethic of conviction is already an ethic of individuality (Persönlichkeitsethik) in the strict sense of the term, that is, it requires an autonomous individual with the capacity for practical judgment. As Karl Jaspers formulated it in view of Kant, an adherent of an ethic of conviction would act immorally if he "irresponsibly" considered that "the absoluteness of abstractions of the supposedly good, correct or sacred" were to be found "in the one-dimensional obedience" to such abstractions.[91] Adherence to unconditional principles in no way excludes their flexible application. Whether in fact an autonomous but rigid "type of conscience" rather than an autonomous but flexible one tends to be connected with an ethic of conviction is, of course, a historical and empirical question. In any case, the passage cited earlier demonstrates that for Weber an autonomous "type of conscience" can develop from a religious ethic of conviction.[92]

Thus, if one wants to distinguish typologically a religious ethic of principles (ethic of conviction) from a religious ethic of norms (ritualistic and legal ethic), one can again take recourse to the three aspects chosen above: (1) in terms of rules, moral rules instead of conventional or legal rules; (2) in terms of motivation, obedience out of a sense of duty instead of obligatory obedience, or ideal interest from within instead of ideal interests from without; (3) in terms of sanctions, guilt and shame instead of disapproval or punishment.

The transition from a religious ethic of norms to a religious ethic of principles thus implies value rationalization: from the typification of single norms to unifying principles, from legality to morality. In terms of rules, this is a process of systematization; in terms of motivation, it is a process of individuation; and in terms of sanctions, it is a process of the replacement, or at least the supplementation, of external by internal sanctions, of physical by psychic ones, and of control by others through self-control and self-censorship.[93]

Where, however, do nonreligious ethics fit in? And above all, what is the place of the ethic of responsibility in this typology? These are the two questions that now need to be addressed. The answers to these questions will not only take us beyond the two-part typology of religious ethics already developed, but beyond the sociology of religion as well.

Ethics of Reflexive Principle: Formal Ethic of Conviction

The question of nonreligious ethics in Weber can be clarified by considering his scattered remarks on Kant's ethics. They can be interpreted in two ways: as remarks describing a specific type of ethic, and as remarks meant to mark Weber's own value position vis-à-vis Kant. Even more than in our previous discussion, both aspects are intertwined. Keeping this in mind, we will find Weber's debate with Gustav Schmoller on the formal character of Kantian ethics especially instructive as a point of departure.

Weber contested Schmoller's claim that Kant's formalism in ethics is devoid of any substantive directives.[94] He provided an example aimed at showing just the opposite. He started by translating the following sentence into the language of Kant's ethics: "At the beginning our relationship to one another was only a passion, now it is a value." In Kant's language it would read: "At the beginning we were *only means* for one another; and we may add: now we are *ends* for one another."[95] Even without the second half of the sentence in Kant's language (which he chose not to consider), Weber took the first part to be a "thoroughly brilliant formulation of an immeasurable variety of ethical states of affairs." Why? The complete sentence describes the transition from a nonmoral or morally indifferent relationship to a moral or at least a morally colored one. It thus distinguishes between nonethical and ethical states of affairs. In a basic sense, those states of affairs are nonethical in which I treat any other person as a means to an end, be this my own end or the end of others, be it individual or general. As long as this is true, I am conducting myself toward another in a success-oriented manner. Only when I treat the other person as an end in himself or herself, when I recognize in that person an intelligible character capable of rational self-determination, do I honor the community of rational beings in the other person, and in this way, in myself. But in this case, I cannot conduct myself toward another in a success-oriented manner. Instead, my relationship to him or her takes on a significance in moral-practical terms. It becomes *our* relationship through the common recognition of an (ethical) value.

Admittedly, Weber's skepticism was directed precisely at this positive version of the ethical states of affairs resulting from the addition of the second half of the sentence, and we shall see why. He let the matter rest with the interpretation of the first part. The negative version of the formulation satisfied him by establishing what ethical states of affairs can never be. In it alone, in the allegedly substantive emptiness of Kant's ethics, he found displayed three important implications for a theory of value: "(1) the recognition of autonomous, nonethical spheres, (2) the delimitation of the ethical sphere from these, and finally, (3) the determination of the sense in which different degrees of ethical status may be imputed to activity oriented towards nonethical values."[96]

Thus, Weber started by defending the formalism of Kant's ethics. He attempted to show that the recognition of "'formal' ethical truths" in the sense of *The Critique of Practical Reason* is in no sense without consequence for a theory of value and for the place of ethics within it.[97] This type of formal ethic, however, is also an ethic of principles. And it also appeals to a feeling of duty. Precisely the "cool matter-of-factness" of Kant's ethic,[98] in Fichte's terms, the "cool approbation" with which Kant motivationally underpins the ethical imperative, underscores the unique dignity of ethical imperatives and the distinctiveness of principle that they display vis-à-vis cultural ideals. The latter are as a rule linked not merely to cool approbation, to a feeling of the evident character of the true and certain, but to (pleasurable) enthusiasm.[99] For there is and always will be, according to Weber, "an unbridgeable distinction . . . [in the evaluative sphere between] (1) those arguments that appeal to our feeling and our capacity to become enthusiastic about concrete practical aims or cultural forms and values, [and] (2) those arguments in which, once it is a question of the validity of ethical norms, the appeal is directed to our conscience."[100] Admittedly, for Kant, too, the respect for moral law is a feeling the will requires in order to carry out that which reasoned self-determination concludes should be. However, it is an ideal sentiment, a feeling that first arises in the execution of the given duty.

Here, too, of course, Weber avoided the adoption of Kant's *philosophical* construction of a "feeling . . . *self-produced* by a rational concept" based on a dualism posited between pure reason and pathological sensibility, between duty and inclination.[101] Weber did, however, adopt what Kant emphasized as the special position of ethics in the concert of values in regard to rules and motivation. For him, too, a formal ethic formulates unconditional, absolute imperatives and mobilizes "ideal" feelings, namely, inner ideal interests that are linked to the conscience.[102] Moreover, as for Kant, there also exists for Weber an ethic of principles outside of religions. The more formal it is, the less the danger that it will conflate ethical imperatives and cultural values (as religion sometimes does). "Objectivity" ("Die 'Objektivität' sozialwissenschaftlicher und sozialpolitischer Erkenntnis") already contains the following interesting formulation:

Whatever the interpretation of basis and nature of the validity of ethical imperatives, it is certain that from these norms for the concretely conditioned action of the *individual cultural values* cannot be unambiguously derived as being normatively desirable; and even less so the more inclusive the content concerned is. Only positive religions—or more precisely expressed, dogmatically bound *sects*—are able to confer on the content of *cultural values* the status of unconditionally valid *ethical* imperatives. Outside these sects, cultural ideals that the individual wishes to realize, and ethical obligations that he *should* fulfill do not, in principle, share the same status.[103]

If one follows the indications given up until now, it appears that Weber did not suspect Kant's formal ethic of panmoralism. He did, however, consider it an ethic of virtuosi, formulating absolute, unconditional duties. In our terminology, it must be categorized, therefore, as an ethic of principles. As such, however, it is distinct from a religious ethic of principles. This seems to be due to the grounding of its imperative. The principles of positive religions are "revealed," whereas the principle of Kant's ethics is established by reason. Moreover, although established by reason, it is not a substantive principle that can be theoretically deduced and thus grounded. Instead, it is a formal principle by which one can examine the rational character, and thus the general lawfulness, of maxims and of rules that are held by individuals to be morally valid.[104] What the will seeks, its material, is always already given in the form of maxims originating from a concrete life-world, a definite social and cultural milieu. The question is, Can the object of the will's desires be recognized as moral? The only possible affirmative answer is, If it allows itself to be brought into a specific form. Only those maxims that can be desired as *universal* (practical) laws qualify themselves as moral. A maxim of which I desire that, though I act according to it, not all others do, can never earn the designation as moral. It cannot qualify as an unconditional imperative because it does not fulfill the condition of being able to be "recognized . . . as valid for the will of every rational being."[105] Resultantly, the basic law of pure practical reason reads: "So act that the maxim of your will could always hold at the same time as the principle of a universal legislation."[106] This basic principle (or basic law, *Grundgesetz*) links all rational beings. Consequently, as Albrecht Wellmer puts it, the "test of [the] generalizibility [of a maxim] is at the same time a test of [its] general ability to find approval." In this sense, the basic principle of pure practical reason can be interpreted as a universalizing principle.[107] Out of categorical imperatives there arises the "categorical imperative," out of ethical principles there arises a second-order principle or a metaprinciple. All unconditional moral duties "are subject" to this one principle. In the terminology of this volume, the principles are turned into one reflexive principle.[108]

Thus, Kant's ethic is not merely an ethic of principles but an ethic of a reflexive principle. Due to this, despite its incorporation of moral theology, Kant's ethic remains clearly distinct from the religious ethics of principles (or conviction). Moreover, in Kant, faith in revelation has to conform to the requirements of reason, and not the other way around, for "a religion that unhesitatingly declares war on reason will not survive against it in the long run."[109] In his writings, the relation between faith and reason took on a meaning different from that found in the religious ethics of norms or of principles. For the latter, the following sentence—ascribed to Tertullian and often quoted by Weber—ultimately holds true: *Credo quia absurdum* (I believe in it because it is absurd).[110] The sentence points less to the irrationality of faith than to the sense in which faith stands *beyond or above* reason (to its *Übervernünftigkeit*).[111] It reflects the claim that, in terms of the Occidental tradition, Jerusalem should possess priority over Athens. This relationship of superordination and subordination is dispensed with in Kant. Religion is placed within the limits of pure reason.

Although Kant reverses the relationship between faith and reason in this way, although he launches a pointed critique of religion's delusions, clericalism, and obsequiousness,[112] he does not envisage an unbridgeable opposition between faith and reason. In contrast to Weber, Kant does not necessarily force the individual adhering to a positive religion to perform the "sacrifice of the intellect."[113] In Kant, it is indeed possible for an individual with an enlightened mode of thinking to be a "believer in the church" without suffering inner contradiction. Yet, in spite of the potential of religion, specifically of Christian religion, to link itself to reason, Kant's ethic is, in typological terms, neither a religious ethic nor a nonreligious ethic of substantive principles. It is an ethic of formal or reflexive principle that interprets—on the basis of our rationality and freedom—the reciprocal relationship between the consciousness of freedom and the imperative character of moral law. It thus represents a type distinct from the religious ethic of conviction.[114] In comparison to all other ethics of norms or principles, it provides the "basis and nature of validity of ethical imperatives" with new meaning. Revealed or rationally deduced substantive norms and principles are replaced by a formal principle, the universalizing principle. This replacement implies at the same time a subdivision of the realm of morality. The sphere of concrete morality that still remains embedded in its specific social and cultural milieu, in its specific "life-world," is now joined by a sphere of abstract morality, in which the "culturalism" of this concrete morality is reflexively broken.[115] This holds true—although it is precisely Kant's ethics that demonstrate that abstract morality presupposes concrete morality, that the universalizing principle presupposes the "life-world"—because only the latter serves as the source for those maxims whose suitability as practical law is to be inspected.[116]

According to Jürgen Habermas, in this way Kant formulated one example of that kind of cognitivist ethic "that in one sense or another holds fast to the potential for ascertaining the truth (*Wahrheitsfähigkeit*) of practical questions."[117] This he accomplished not by subordinating practical laws to theoretical ones, laws of freedom to laws of nature. He did it by relating the use of both theoretical and practical reason to the unity of reason. This unity is at the same time the community of all rational beings who take part in a kingdom of ends. This kingdom is defined as the "systematic union of rational beings under common objective law."[118] Whenever I define my maxims in accordance with the universalizing principle, and whenever I, in accordance with the resulting practical compulsion or moral duty, then act out of respect for the law given within me, I act as a member of this realm and thus show myself as worthy of my membership. In this way, I am secure in the knowledge of being connected in solidarity with all other members. This worthiness falls only to those who obey no other law as the self-given and at the same time general law. It is, according to Kant, an inner value, distinct in principle from the external value, from the reward, that we confer for skillfulness and prudence. This worthiness, this virtue, is earned only by conviction that is morally good and not by our technical and pragmatic capabilities. Actions originating from such conviction remain virtuous, "even if they are not favored by success."[119] They are above every "reward." Only conviction is ultimately the guarantee that "practical reason [the will] may not merely administer an alien interest, but may simply manifest its own sovereign authority as the supreme maker of law."[120]

It is in this sense that one can interpret Kant's ethic as a formal ethic of conviction according to which the rational self-determination of the will is accomplished monologically and moral action stringently, without exceptions from the rule and largely without consideration of the special circumstances of situations of action (or, adopting Weber's words, *sine ira et studio* [impartially]).[121] Admittedly, the appropriateness of this characterization is a point of controversy surrounding Kant's ethic, and I side with those who tend to see this as a distorting view. First, Kant certainly did point to the necessity of changing perspectives in the rational determination of the will. In the *Critique of Judgment* we find the following description of an enlightened mode of thinking: "(1) thinking for oneself, (2) thinking from the positions of each and all others, (3) always thinking in harmony with oneself"[122] (or thinking consistently). This, however, includes rather than precludes "ideal role-taking" and "universal discourse," and thus the opening to dialogue advanced by Jürgen Habermas with reference to George Herbert Mead.[123] Moreover, Kant—knowledgeable of the ethical tradition—was completely aware of the problems connected with applying the moral law in the face of the "average defects of humans."[124] One need only to read *The Metaphysics of Morals* (*Die Metaphysik der Sitten*) and, above all, *Anthropology from a Pragmatic Point of View* (*Anthropologie in pragmatischer Hinsicht*) to be convinced of this. The fact that possible success must be completely disregarded in transforming a maxim into practical law certainly does not mean that this maxim has to be carried out without consideration of losses and by excluding all skillfulness and prudence.[125] Nevertheless, one can justify using this somewhat "distorted" characterization for typological purposes. In Kant we encounter a new type of ethic, an ethic of reflexive principle, which Weber himself obviously considered an ethic of conviction different from those ethics of conviction he dealt with in his comparative studies on the economic ethics of the world religions.

There is at least one passage in Weber that indicates that he indeed confronted a religious ethic of conviction with a Kantian ethic of conviction from a typological viewpoint. In "Intermediate Reflections" from the comparative essays, a distinction is drawn between a religious ethic of brotherliness and a priori rigorism in ethics, the latter undoubtedly a reference to Kant. This remark is of interest to us not only as a reference, but also because of the context in which it is found.[126] Weber did not confine his remarks to the two types of ethic, but extended them to art. He provided—at least implicitly—the analysis of a three-sided relation of tension centered around the problem of form versus content and its associated problems. Following his line of reasoning and combining it with some ideas of Kant, we can broaden our understanding of a formal ethic of conviction, especially with regard to the motives associated with it.

Let us start with Weber's observations. As art increasingly becomes an autonomous value sphere, he argues, aesthetic form per se becomes emphasized. The interest of both the creator and the interpreter of art is attached to form and not to content. This pursuit of beautiful form in art, Weber goes on, can easily arouse the suspicion of the religious ethics of brotherliness, inasmuch as the latter "have focused upon the meaning alone, not upon the form, of the things and actions relevant for salvation."[127] Especially in its mystical versions, the religious ethics of brotherliness is practically opposed to form as such. And this practical opposition to form holds true not just for its relationship to art, but also for its relationship to a priori ethical rigorism because the latter, in the moral realm analogous to autonomous art in its realm, subordinates content to form. One can add that a priori ethical rigorism itself stands in tension to autonomous art. The latter tends to violate boundaries by ignoring the differences between beauty and good, between aesthetic and moral definitions of form, between disinterested appreciation and respect for the law, between aesthetically reflexive and morally defined judgment. This violation of boundaries can lead to the aestheticization of ethical questions, which, Weber emphasized, is something to which an intellectualistic age, with its subjectivist needs and its narrow-minded prejudices, is especially prone.[128] Where this violation in fact occurs, consciousness of moral responsibility is lost. It then becomes common "to transform judgments of moral intent into judgments of taste ('in poor taste' instead of 'reprehensible'). Since the latter are inaccessible to appeal, discussion is excluded."[129]

Two aspects of these remarks by Weber on the relationship between ethics and aesthetics, between morals and art, deserve comment here. First, judgments of taste cannot raise the same claim to general validity that moral judgments can, and they are thus not open to discussion in the same sense. This is a renewed expression of his aforementioned view of the truth-relatedness of practical questions. Second, an ethic of a priori rigorism has difficulty defending its intrinsic and autonomous value vis-à-vis art or the religious ethics of brotherliness. This difficulty seems to be due to the very fact that such an ethic has to resort, like aesthetics, to form, not to content. Because it is an ethic, it can not rest its case with purely disinterested appreciation. Because it is a formal ethic, it can not turn to love and affection, as a religious ethics of brotherliness can.

How to associate the formal ethic with interests is indeed one of Kant's problems, for human nature does not of its own proper motion accord with the good, "but only by virtue of the dominion that reason exercises over sensibility."[130] Thus, in contrast to the beautiful aesthetic form, ethical form requires interested appreciation, but, in contrast to the ethics of brotherliness, this interested appreciation must be limited to a "pure and unconditioned intellectual appreciation."[131] Admittedly, the moral law awakens a feeling of respect. But this feeling is, to use Talcott Parsons's terms, "affectively neutral," and thus, in a psychological sense, a weak motivational impulse. It refers to a purely cognitive motivation, to an interest of reason in itself. It is thus the weak motivation by which reason becomes practical. Of course, it is true that affects, and thus feelings of pleasure and displeasure, can attach themselves to the moral law. Kant defined moral enthusiasm as the idea of good with affect.[132] Nevertheless, though the affects can enlarge the motivational basis for carrying out the moral law, they can also hinder free reflection and "cool approbation." They thus tend to do more harm than good and are not reliable supports for the ethically rational conduct of life in accordance with the formal moral principle.

Indeed, Kant eliminated everything from moral feeling that Durkheim, in his critique of Kant, named objects of desire morally worthy of being pursued.[133] The only "moral object of desire" to which Kant admitted is the law itself, and the only motivation in accordance with it is pure respect for this law. The religious ethic of brotherliness, by contrast, recognizes other sources of motivation.[134] True enough, even a religious ethic of conviction very generally demands respect for the divine laws. But this respect is not tied purely to the laws as such, but to the promises connected to following these laws, that is, to the goods of salvation. This however implies that, in typological terms, one should not categorize action performed out of a sense of duty solely in terms of Kant's model. Religious ethics of conviction, regardless of whether they tend toward an ethic of duty or an ethic of love, motivate respect for the law by means of the salvational goods that are themselves worth pursuing. This, however, would further imply that they do not contend themselves with cognitive or purely rational motives. Although moral feelings are connected to cognitive orientations, they also are related, to use another of Talcott Parsons's terms, to "cathected objects."[135]

In this manner we have gained the possibility of distinguishing typologically ethics of principles from ethics of reflexive principle, at least in terms of rules and motivation. We can contrast substantive, dogmatic moral principles to a formal, reflexive moral principle, that is, the universalizing principle (*Universalisierungsgrundsatz*); action performed out of a sense of duty due to the (salvational) goods promised by the fulfillment of duty can be contrasted to action performed out of a sense of duty due to (pure) respect for the formal moral principle. It is true that even Kant promises good will a good, this being his concept of the highest good. Nevertheless, this is not, as in the case of a religious ethics of conviction, conceived of as a basis of motivation.[136]

The question now arises, Can the distinction also be extended to the third aspect of the typology of ethics: to sanctions? And if so, how? In contrast to rules and motivation, I have treated the aspect of sanction in a fairly cursory manner up until now. Thus, certain basic conceptual considerations are in order. First, the concept of sanction is part of a wider context, that of the control of action. This can be divided into internal and external control, according to who carries it out. Moreover, sanctions can also be distinguished according to whether they reward or punish—whether they can be termed positive or negative sanctions. Especially in Weber's sociology of religion, positive sanctions play a decisive role in terms of the premiums connected to certain kinds of religious action. As Talcott Parsons above all has shown, the control agency can communicate sanctions by means of two channels: it can attempt by means of sanctions to influence either the actor's situation or his intentions. By combining the two types of control with the two channels of control, Parsons classified four types of control that can define the interaction between the control agency and the actor. He termed them "inducement" (positively related to the situation), "deterrence" (negatively related to the situation), "activation of commitments" (negatively related to intentions), and "persuasion" (positively related to intentions). He described these in the following way:

(1) Inducement is ego's attempt to get a favorable decision from alter by an offer of situational advantages contingent on [alter's] compliance with his suggestions. (2) Deterrence is ego's corresponding attempt to get compliance by invoking commitments in such a way that noncompliance exposes alter to a contingent threat of suffering a situational disadvantage. (3) Activation of commitments is ego's attempt to get compliance by of-

fering reasons why it would, from alter's own point of view, be "wrong" for him to refuse to act as ego wished. And, finally, (4) persuasion is ego's attempt to get compliance by offering reasons why it would, from alter's own point of view, independent of situational disadvantages, "be a good thing" for him to act as ego wished.[137]

I will apply these distinctions here in a modified fashion in order to clarify the aspect of sanction. The modification involves applying the four types of control to internal and to external control.[138] It is precisely the character and the interrelationship of these two agencies of control that change with the transition from an ethic of norms to an ethic of principles, as the previous analysis has implied. The first type of control, inducement (positively related to the situation), includes, in the case of external control, the provision of material stimuli of all kinds. In the case of internal control, it refers to self-discipline, with a resulting expansion of one's own physical and psychic capacities. The second type of control, deterrence (negatively related to the situation), means, in cases of external control, the threat of material damage and in its severest form, the (physical) exclusion from social organizations. In cases of internal control, it means self-discipline, with resulting "inhibition of instincts," and in its severest form, repression. The physical and mental techniques that play a role in a negative or positive sense in the process of self-discipline were studied by Weber in terms of the different ascetic and mystical techniques for reaching salvation. The third type of control, the activation of commitments (negatively related to intentions), is expressed in the case of external control in social disapproval; its severest form is social ostracism. In the case of internal control, it is expressed in the loss of self-respect and in feelings of shame and guilt. Finally, the fourth type of control, persuasion (positively related to intentions), expresses itself in the case of external control, in the granting of prestige or recognition. In the case of internal control, it expresses itself in terms of self-respect. (For an overview, see Figure 2.)

The transition from an ethic of norms to an ethic of principles is, according to my interpretation, connected to the increasing importance of internal control. This does not mean that internal control grows at the cost of external control. I will show in a moment that in terms of Weber's analysis of ascetic Protestantism, just the opposite can be the case. The contention here is that the control process no longer functions without ever more pervasive forms of

Control agency and type of sanction / Channel of control	External control		Internal control	
	Negative	Positive	Negative	Positive
Situational	Threat of material damages	Provision of material rewards	Self-disciplining as the inhibition and repression of drives	Self-disciplining as self-realization
Intentional	Social disapproval and ostracism	Social regard, attribution of social prestige	Mobilization of feelings of guilt and shame	Self-respect

Figure 2. Types of control of action.

internal control. The history of the salvation religions, and especially of the Asiatic ones, serves well to substantiate this point.[139] All ethics of principles demand, in comparison to ethics of norms, a greater degree of inner-directed action. In this way, they mark the transition from a heteronomous to an autonomous type of conscience, from an other-directed to an inner-directed personality. But this autonomous type of conscience still remains embedded in concrete forms of morality, something Weber demonstrated in terms of ascetic Protestantism. Here the inner compulsion to vigilant self-control, to methodical and rational discipline of one's conduct, was connected to increasing external control through the various forms of ecclesiastical organization. Internal control did not replace external control; rather, both were increased, and to an extent foreign to both Catholicism and Lutheranism. In the world of ascetic Protestantism depicted by Weber, the individual is never in the position to become master of—in Kant's words—his tendency toward evil[140] without the scourge of a sect-like church or a genuine sect. The believer has to get himself into a position where, by means of his own impulse and above all by means of situational self-control, he, with the support and under the control of his fellow congregants, can at least approximate the fulfillment of the demands of an ethic of principles.

At this point, an interesting difference between Weber and Kant comes into play. In Kant's theory, all use of this external punishment, of this scourge, is foregone. In contrast to the believing ascetic Protestant, the man of reason, a follower of the idea of good, is subject to no law of external constraint. It is true that Kant also constructs, in analogy to his theory of jurisprudence, a principle for unifying man solely in terms of laws of virtue. Just as it is an ethical commandment to move from the state of nature to a legal-civic state (to a political condition), it is also an ethical command-ment to leave the natural state of ethics, in which the individual is exposed to the "continuous attack of *evil*,"[141] and to establish, along with all well-disposed men, "an ethical community," a "general republic according to laws of virtue" that takes as its task the communitarian promotion of the highest good.[142] However, in contrast to the concept of the church and sect in ascetic Protes-tantism, Kant does not connect the idea of external control to his ethical community (it incorporates the citizens of the world, not just those of an individual state). In Kant's ethic, not only does internal control have priority over external control, but among the sanctions connected to internal control, those related to the inten-tions of action have priority over those connected to the situation of action.[143]

We are now in position to distinguish typologically an ethic of reflexive principle from an ethic of principles in terms of all three aspects: the former grounds moral rules with the help of a formal principle (the universalizing principle) and not with substantive principles; it motivates with the moral rule's worthiness of being pursued and not with moral goods; and it relies exclusively on in-ternal, intention-related sanctions and not on a combination of sanctions. This ethic of reflexive principle is, in typological terms, however, at least in Kant, an ethic of conviction. Nonetheless, it is qualitatively different from that religious ethic of conviction found in Weber's sociology of religion. The decisive difference is not, as one might think, the result of its "nonreligious" character, but of its formal character, of the fact that it, in contrast to a reli-gious or a nonreligious ethic of principles, is a formal ethic of con-viction. The distinction between religious and nonreligious is solely dependent on how moral rules are "produced": by revela-tion, by rational deduction, or, not to be overlooked, by one's own decision, one's own choice. Kant's ethic thus represents the ideal type of a formal ethic of conviction, an ethic of reflexive principle and, following Habermas, of the cognitivist variety.

In this way, the two-part typology is enlarged into a three-part one. This enlargement led to a differentiation of Weber's concept of an ethic of conviction. In my view, this differentiation is indispensable for the proper classification of his historical analyses and the adequate judgment of his theory of value. A glance at the secondary literature is enough to show that this is not always recognized. That this important distinction is as a rule overlooked may be connected to the fact that in his sociology of religion Weber is primarily occupied with the effects of substantive ethics of conviction on conduct. And even in those cases, such as in the sociology of law, where, in a developmental perspective, he explicitly presents the interplay between substantive and formal principles in natural law constructs, the accent is placed on substantive natural-law constructs, which are then contrasted to the formal qualities of modern positive law.[144] The sociology of law nevertheless clearly shows how important it is to make this distinction for any unabridged reconstruction of Weber's investigations in historical sociology. The same holds true for his theory of value, that is, for the axiological side of his theory. Weber often appears to "jump" from the religious ethic of conviction to modern moral indifference, or from substantive natural law to modern positive law, but one should watch for the usually concealed link. It is one of those elements of Weber's theory that only becomes intelligible by playing one part of the theory off against another.[145]

Nevertheless, in my view, it is only against the backdrop of this differentiation that Weber's concept of an ethic of responsibility can be defined in a systematically satisfactory way. The usual practice, that of merely contrasting the latter with a religious ethic of conviction or, more generally, with a substantive ethic of conviction based on revealed or deduced principles, is insufficient. It is also at odds with a formal ethic of conviction, for a variety of reasons. By taking the ethic of responsibility as an ideal type and evaluating it in terms of the aspects of rules and motivation, this becomes strikingly clear. Even though it is only cursorily described by Weber, in the terms of my argument an ethic of responsibility can be regarded as an ethic of reflexive principle, like Kant's formal ethic of conviction. But unlike the latter, it modifies the formal principle in a decisive way. Simultaneously, it offers a different interpretation of motivation, of moral feeling. Finally, it reopens several of the channels of sanction closed by Kant. For these reasons, an ethic of responsibility is not only linked to a formal ethic of conviction by means of their common opposition to a substantive ethic of conviction (the distinction between principles and a reflexive principle); it also represents an alternative to it.

Ethics of Reflexive Principle: Formal Ethic of Responsibility

Let us search for arguments that can support this thesis through a comparative discussion between a formal ethic of conviction of the Kantian type and the ethic of responsibility as described by Weber. Because he seems to accept the latter type as a viable ethical position for himself, their comparative presentation allows us to at least indirectly infer Weber's critical position on Kant. As a point of departure for this comparative discussion I pick up on the differences worked out between a substantive and a formal ethic of conviction. These differences also initially apply to the relationship between a substantive ethic of conviction and an ethic of responsibility, insofar as the latter, like a formal ethic of conviction, is based on a reflexive principle. In this sense, we treat Weber's ethic of responsibility from the outset as a formal ethic. This poses the question, How can this decision be justified?

If we want to answer this question, we have to clarify the concept of formality employed here. In order to do so, I would like to follow up on two key themes that were yielded by our previous passage through Weber's work: the ethic of responsibility entails a conviction; and a person acting in accordance with an ethic of responsibility has *also* to take into account what can be foreseen as consequences of his action. The combination of these two themes appears to imply that an action that aspires to moral status in terms of an ethic of responsibility has to satisfy two conditions. First, it has to result from moral conviction. Second, it has to reflect the fact that it is ensnared in the meshes of an ethically irrational world, and thus pay homage to the insight that evil can result from good.[146] In other words, such an action has to justify itself not only in terms of a moral conviction, but also in terms of an estimation of foreseeable consequences. In determining one's will, one cannot, as in Kant, abstract from all consequences; one has to draw them into account.[147]

Weber termed the first condition the "convictional value," the second condition the "success value," to which a moral action must be related, as is evident from the quote prefacing this chapter. Every moral actor has to face the conflict that is implied in this double relatedness. Even adherents of an ethic of brotherliness found themselves confronted by the inherent conflict between convictional values and success values, between good intention and the irrational effect of consistently realized good intention, as Weber's statement in the "Intermediate Reflections" suggests. That is to say, the more an ethic of brotherliness turns into an ethic of principles, the more it has to address the problem of how to relate convictional values to success values. And what holds true for an ethic of principles holds true for an ethic of reflexive principle. Both the substantive and the formal ethic of conviction come to terms with this task by denying success value ethical relevance.[148] In Fichte's terms, the following maxims hold for these types of ethics vis-à-vis this problem: Act solely according to your best conviction (*Überzeugung*) of your duty; or always act according to your best conviction of your duty; or simply, act according to your conscience,[149] and according to nothing else. This denial of ethical relevance to success value is not the case for an ethic of responsibility; rather, success values possess ethical relevance in terms of the ethic of responsibility. This does not mean that success values are ethical values, but it does mean that the demands arising from success values ought to be acknowledged. For this reason, the following maxim holds: Act according to your best conviction of your duty, and, beyond that, in such a way that you can also account for the (foreseeable) consequences of your action according to the best of your knowledge. Whereas the adherent of an ethic of conviction takes on, as it were, a single responsibility, namely, for the convictional value of his action, the adherent of an ethic of responsibility has to carry a double responsibility, namely, for the convictional value *and* for its relationship to other values, especially success values, in an ethically irrational "world." One could say that the maxims of an ethic of responsibility demand a careful weighing of alternative goods in ethical terms before any action is taken, something not required by the maxims of an ethic of conviction.

This provides us with the first distinction between a formal ethic of responsibility and a formal ethic of conviction. At the same time, it distinguishes the ethic of responsibility from every kind of ethic of conviction, be it formal or substantive, religious or nonreligious. This distinction lends precise meaning to what Weber must have had in mind when he termed the ethic of conviction and the ethic of responsibility opposing maxims of strictly formal character. He was thinking of bridging principles.[150] Convictional values, regardless of their status, are to be related to success values. In order to avoid terminological confusion, I suggest distinguishing between the "bridging principle of hierarchy" and the "bridging principle of balance." Either can be adopted by a moral actor who has to solve the problem of relating convictional values to success values.

One could simply leave the matter at that. This result, however, would hardly represent an exhaustive account of the ethic of responsibility as an alternative type to the formal ethic of conviction. Alternative bridging principles is one thing, alternative determinations of convictional value another. It is conceivable that a formal ethic of responsibility differs from a formal ethic of conviction not only with regard to the bridging principle used, but also with regard to the determination of the convictional value itself.

This is indeed the case. In order to bring this difference into the open, we have to return to Kant. In Kant's view, that will is good which is always able to define itself according to the general law of reason. The decisive qualities are self-determination and general law. Such a will, such a conviction, finds crucial support from an enlightened way of thinking. This way of thinking, as we saw earlier, demands thinking for oneself, thinking from the standpoint of everyone else, and always thinking consistently. This way of thinking has a "public" character; it rests on dialogue. That this need not be a real dialogue but can remain imaginary results from the nature of the general point of view: it is the same for all rational beings. Taking the standpoint of the other means taking the standpoint of reason. One is always able to reflect on the "subjective private conditions" of one's judgment[151] by taking the general point of view vis-à-vis oneself, by basing oneself upon one's own reason, which is at the same time the reason of all rational beings.

What is Weber's position toward this construct of a formal ethic of conviction? One has to be willing to speculate in order to give an answer here, because a systematic discussion of the Kantian ethic is lacking in his writings. Nevertheless, one of the key terms employed in this context provides us with an important lead. In the letter to Tönnies in which the possibility of a scientific ethic is discussed, Weber described the task of that ethic in the following manner: to demonstrate the formal qualities of a given moral conviction, to perform a formal critique of conviction. It does this by demonstrating to anyone who recognizes the necessity of orienting his or her personal action around values "*the unavoidable necessity* of [adhering to] all the consequences of the Kantian imperative (regardless in which more or less modernized form—it comes to the same thing)."[152]

As noted earlier, Weber distinguished between ethical and political duties and between ethical value judgments and judgments of taste. Ethical duties are absolute, whereas political duties are historical in character; ethical value judgments are subject to appeal and thus can be discussed, something that does not hold for judgments of taste, at least not in the same sense. These distinctions imply that ethical values raise claims to being absolute and generally valid and are directed toward our conscience. This is the case neither with cultural values (e.g., political values) nor with aesthetic values. In his letter to Tönnies, Weber discusses an orientation toward values or value judgments in general. Nevertheless, I consider it justified, and even appropriate, to read this comment on the Kantian imperative and its function as an "instrument" of a formal ethic of conviction against the background of the distinctions between ethical and nonethical values. What is at stake, as Weber himself puts it in the letter, is the judgment of moral conviction: unlike a political or other kind of conviction, it can be made subject to a formal critique with the help of the universalizing principle.

The universalizing principle of the formal ethic of conviction is thus for Weber thoroughly suitable for examining the moral character of a given conviction. In a fragment of Weber's writing, the date of which is uncertain—the assumption is that it was written in 1912—we read that "the Kantian imperatives [are] . . . valid analyses of certain of the simplest facts [Tatbestände] of the procedure [employed] in an ethical *judgment*." Beyond this, the logical possibility is at least left open that "as a result of this" they are also fit to serve a "function" in substantive decisions of an ethical nature.[153] If this is in fact the case, what precisely can the universalizing principle offer? What role does it play, in Weber's view, in determining convictional value?

As already mentioned, the universalizing principle provides a rule for examining, not a rule for producing, maxims. That which I am willing and able to recognize as a general law depends on my convictions. I have developed the latter as a participant in a definite social and cultural milieu, in a life-world, in complicated processes, or as Weber would say, by means of a string of ultimate decisions.[154] If one follows Albrecht Wellmer, the universalizing principle in the Kantian sense is, so to speak, a second-level principle. A first-level principle of universalization would imply only that I myself am always bound to those obligations that I recognize and that I demand of others. Such a principle, however, in no way implies "the possibility of a *rationally acceptable* 'ought' or a 'must.'" Although it is "a principle valid for all 'rational beings,' it is not a principle that necessarily favors certain universalistic norms instead of others."[155] Wellmer rightly points out that the first-level principle, representing one dimension of the Kantian, is in no way without consequences when I apply it to my own conviction. Such a principle means that I ought "to recognize the already recognized normative obligations *here and now and without self-deception in my own action.*" Furthermore:

The demand to act in terms of my own normative convictions does not however mean that I think out an appropriate justification for my actions on each occasion, and it does not mean that I ought to act in accordance with *that* which I can *claim* to be my normative conviction on a given occasion; what this demand actually implies is a *not easily* satisfiable demand that I not deceive myself about what I would expect from the *other* person *if* the roles were reversed.[156]

Weber, I propose, adopts the universalizing principle in this reduced sense. He deletes the second level and thus that part of Kant's theory that makes it, as he notes, into the archetype of a metaphysical theory of culture and personality.[157] As in Kant, the will has to take on a definite form in Weber. The way in which this form is determined, however, loses the character of constitutive universalism that it possesses in Kant. It is true that ethical values are connected to claims of absoluteness and general validity for Weber. This connection is what gives ethics its special position vis-à-vis other value spheres. For this reason, the good will can never settle for a narrow-minded particularism. Instead, it always has to define itself as if the possibility of a rationally acceptable "ought" existed. This can be termed "regulative" universalism. This at the same time means that the realization of (universalistic) practical reason is replaced by the realization of the (universalistic) imperative to be rational. Although the idea that my best conviction of my moral duty is also the right conviction can no longer be rationally grounded, it ultimately has now to be believed. Nevertheless, this faith, this possession (or holding of a conviction) is tied to the satisfaction of rational conditions.[158]

One of these conditions is to bind my moral claims to the enlightened way of thinking (as defined earlier). The imperatives of autonomy, change of perspective, and consistency also hold for Weber's ethics. Only that will can in fact be termed good that has subjected itself to the imperative to be rational. And only that will has in fact subjected itself to this imperative that does not blindly act, but instead follows a self-chosen law and thus can be counted upon to act in a certain way.[159] In analogy to the Kantian formulation one can say that for Weber, that will is good that is at all times capable of determining itself in terms of an individual law. The decisive qualities here are self-determination and individual law.[160] It is individual because the correctness of the convictional value held is a matter of faith. It is a law because that which I recognize I have to consistently satisfy at all times without self-deception. This points to something established long ago by Dieter Henrich—namely, that the imperative to be rational is ultimately an imperative to conscious conduct and to the cultivation of personality.[161]

Whoever seeks to satisfy—without self-deception—the law according to which they engage in action must have knowledge of their own "ultimate, interiorly 'consistent' value axioms" and of their consequences. This demands, using a term from Nietzsche, "intellectual honesty." It also demands, however, the readiness for real dialogue, an indispensable preliminary stage to real confrontation.[162] Weber repeatedly emphasized that ideals can only prove themselves in struggle with other ideals or perish if lacking the strength to prevail. However, before they can pass the test in real life, ideals must survive the relativizing effects of value discussions. Only in this way can they be capable of arousing conviction (*überzeugungsfähig*). Whereas in Kant, everyone can, in principle if not in fact, always take the general point of view, Weber's approach necessarily demands a formal critique of conviction in the framework of a value discussion. The institution of such discussions is—in addition to a theory of personality—at the center of his own standpoint in ethics.[163]

We can thus distinguish between two universalizing principles that can be inferred from Kant's ethics and from Weber's critique of the same. The former finds its classic formulation in the basic law of *The Critique of Practical Reason*: Act in such a way that the maxim of your will could always also hold as the principle of universal legislation. This also represents the basic law of an ethic of reflexive principle insofar as it advocates a constitutive universalism, that is, insofar as it conceives of the universalizing principle as a principle of justification (*Begründungsprinzip*). Analogously, the Weberian principle could be stated in the following way: Act as if the maxim of your will as the true expression of an individual law could always also hold as the principle of universal legislation. This also represents the basic law of an ethic of reflexive principle insofar as it represents a regulative universalism and thus conceives of the universalizing principle as a principle of critical examination (*kritische Prüfung*). Thus, the formal justification of conviction is contrasted to its formal critique. Both positions demand that one always think consistently. Moreover, both demand that one think from the standpoints of all others involved. However, whereas in the first case this can occur in an ideal dialogue that is actually a monologue, in the second case a real dialogue is indispensable. One way to express this is by modifying a maxim of Goethe's repeatedly cited by Weber: How can you get acquainted with your own conviction? Never through observation. Expose it to a value discussion, and you will quickly know what it can offer!

As I mentioned earlier, Jürgen Habermas terms all positions that in some manner maintain the potential for ascertaining the truth of moral-practical questions *cognitivistic*. The dispute that he stages between ethical cognitivists and ethical skeptics in the style of classical philosophical dialogues shows that he ultimately considers cognitivism a different expression for the rational procedure of justification in ethics.[164] If one understands cognitivism in this sense, then the formal ethic of responsibility—developed up until now primarily for typological purposes—is, in contrast to the formal ethic of conviction, not a cognitivist ethic. It admits the potential for ascertaining the truth of moral-practical questions in only a very limited sense. For this reason I have intentionally spoken of the truth-relatedness of moral-practical questions in Weber, but not of the potential for ascertaining the truth of such questions. One of the indispensable elements of Weber's position is the assertion that a convictional value can be criticized but not justified by reason. This position contrasts with that of Kant and those of other ethical cognitivists whom Habermas considers. They all hold fast to the justification claim in some form. In this sense, Weber belonged to the ethical skeptics and not to the ethical cognitivists. Thus, on the level of ethics of reflexive principle, he can be said to be a criticist rather than a cognitivist.

This serves to characterize the decisive difference between a formal ethic of Kant's type and a formal ethic of Weber's type in terms of the aspect of rules. This distinction involves the status of the universalizing principle. In one case, this principle is understood as a principle of justification, in the other, as a principle of critical examination. In one case, it is understood as being constitutive, in the other, as being regulative.

There are, however, two interesting consequences of this attempt to more sharply define the concepts of formal ethics in regard not only to alternate bridging principles, but also to alternate universalizing principles. One consequence concerns the universalizing principles directly, the other concerns the connection between these principles and bridging principles. The proposed distinction between a Kantian and a Weberian version of the universalizing principle implies that the latter calls for its dialogic application. The universalizing principle as a principle of critical examination requires an ethic of dialogue. The basic principle of such an ethic of dialogue can be formulated, in analogy to Kant's philosophy of religion, in the following manner: You ought to move from the ethical state of nature, where your conviction is continuously threatened by self-deception, to the state of concrete value discussions, because the latter are capable of producing self-clarification and a sense of responsibility,[165] both of which have to be pursued by anyone seeking to satisfy the imperative to be rational.

The second consequence concerns the relationship between the universalizing principles and the bridging principles. I have distinguished between these two sets of principles. This was appropriate because Weber sometimes used the concept of an ethic of responsibility (as well the concept of an ethic of conviction) to characterize a certain type of ethic and at other times to characterize the way in which a convictional value ought to be related to other values, especially success values. One of the purposes of the proposed reconstruction of the typology of ethics is the resolution of this systematically unsatisfying ambiguity. In my view, however, it is no coincidence that this ambivalence exists in Weber, for there are, in fact, intrinsic connections between universalizing principles and bridging principles. Kant's version of the universalizing principle demands that one abstract from consequences in determining the will. This rules out an elective affinity to the formal maxim of an ethic of responsibility, or, in our terminology, to the "bridging principle of balance." In contrast, Weber's version of the universalizing principle demands—in the face of the eternal struggle of the "gods," where ultimately fate and not science holds sway—that the foreseeable consequences of a convictional value consistently thought out and acted upon, be taken into consideration in *all* of their aspects in the determination of the will.[166] This involves an elective affinity with the formal maxims of an ethic of responsibility or the bridging principle of balance. For Weber, both the founding problem and the bridging problem should be addressed in a value discussion, because it can achieve the following: the working out of the ultimate, internally consistent value axioms; the deduction of the consequences entailed by the evaluative stances to given states of affairs; the establishment of the factual consequences of carrying out such stances; and the confrontation with value axioms not taken into account by the stance in question. In terms of all of these aspects, a real dialogue can help overcome narrow-minded "particularism" and destroy the illusions that one generally falls prey to vis-à-vis one's own moral conviction and that of one's opponent.[167]

Thus, in typological terms, in the case of formal ethics the real contrast is found between a monologic, cognitivist ethic of conviction and a dialogic, critical, ethic of responsibility. This is so because in both cases an intrinsic relation exists between the determination of the convictional value and the determination of the relationship between the convictional value and the success value. Of course, fundamentally, both of the opposing bridging principles can be combined with convictional values determined in different ways. This is the way in which I interpret Weber's statement that the formal maxim of the ethic of conviction and that of the ethic of responsibility "are in eternal conflict—a conflict which cannot be resolved by means of ethics alone."[168] This possibility of combination, however, also enables one to resolve the contradiction between this statement and one made by Weber in "Science as a Vocation" whereby the ethics of conviction and of responsibility are not absolutely contradictory but complementary to each other. This can be the case because a follower of the formal maxim of the ethic of responsibility can face circumstances in which, after careful weighing of the options, he or she finds no balance between convictional value and success value; here, convictional value has to be realized even when all the demands related to success values are violated. Thus, it can be said that the moral actor acted like an adherent of an ethic of conviction. Naturally, strictly speaking, this can still be understood as a consistent application of the bridging principle of an ethic of responsibility, the principle of balance.[169]

If one accepts Weber's remarks on the religious ethic of brotherliness in the "Intermediate Reflections," this conflict between the two formal maxims as bridging principles does not first arise at the level of ethics of reflexive principle. Ethics of principles are already confronted by it. In admitting this, one should not forgo the twofold meaning of the concepts of an ethic of conviction and an ethic of responsibility: that they sometimes refer to the way in which the convictional value is determined and other times refer to the way in which the relationship between convictional and success value is determined.[170]

This concludes the first step in distinguishing a formal ethic of responsibility and a formal ethic of conviction as types. This step involved the aspect of rules. The reconstruction, however, has yielded unexpected results. In distinguishing more sharply between universalizing principles for determining convictional values and bridging principles for determining the relationship between convictional values and success values, we were forced to look at the ethics of principles from a new angle. Under the assumption that founding principles, which are not confined to universalizing principles, of course, and bridging principles vary independently of each other, we have to extend our typology beyond the distinction between a formal ethic of conviction and a formal ethic of responsibility. There is not only a cognitivistic and a criticistic variant of each of these types, there is also a substantive ethic of conviction and a substantive ethic of responsibility. (For an overview, see Figure 3.)

Having established the distinction of a formal ethic of conviction and a formal ethic of responsibility with regard to rules, I must now treat motivation. Here, too, I would like to compare Weber with Kant. Kant admitted only an ideal sentiment, respect for the law, the interest of reason in itself. He kept moral motivation separate from affects and especially from passions. What can be learned from Weber on this question? Did he specify any motives that could correspond to the criticistic formal ethic of re-

Grounding principle / Bridging principle	Dogmatic (substantive)	Reflexive (formal)	
		Constitutive	Regulative
Hierarchization	Substantive ethic of conviction	Cognitivistic formal ethic of conviction	Criticistic formal ethic of conviction
Balancing	Substantive ethic of responsibility	Cognitivistic formal ethic of responsibility	Criticistic formal ethic of responsibility

Figure 3. Typology of ethics of conviction and ethics of responsibility.

sponsibility as a type in contrast to a cognitivistic formal ethic of conviction?

Wherever Weber made more extensive statements on the ethic of responsibility, one is confronted by concepts such as clarity, a sense of proportion, inner detachment from persons and things, passion, and a sense of responsibility. These terms name qualities those persons should have who seek to conduct their lives in a conscious fashion. In "Politics as a Vocation," these are the qualities that Weber demands from a politician of responsibility, in contrast to both a pure politician of power and a pure politician of conviction. Both cognitive and emotional qualities are involved here. Clarity and a sense of proportion belong to the cognitive realm, whereas passion and a sense of responsibility belong to the emotional realm. Inner detachment from persons and things, and from oneself, appears to be the overall attitude of mind, the general stance, one that combines all of these qualities. It is a stance in keeping with the imperative to be rational. This inner detachment, however, is but the reverse of the devotion to a cause or task. For Weber, everything is contingent upon that detachment because it alone is capable of providing action with an inner foothold, so to speak. This is of course the case only when the actor is passionately gripped by this devotion, not when he or she merely plays a "frivolous intellectual game" or he or she loses him- or herself in "sterile excitation." Persons of true moral conviction passionately devote themselves to a suprapersonal cause in which they have faith without losing themselves completely in the process.[171] This is so because this devotion, which not only allows but demands detachment, ultimately originates from a conscious decision. Dieter Henrich has been prominent in pointing out in Weber this relation between being rational and being passionate: "The living experience of a rational human being is passion." In the passion of a cause, according to Henrich, "The unity of a person who has emerged from the undifferentiated unity of living experience is established by the strength of reason." And finally, "Being a personality means being committed by virtue of passion."[172]

Now this concept of personality certainly cannot be reserved solely for the adherent of an ethic of responsibility. It also holds for adherents of an ethic of conviction whose ideals originate from a string of consciously made ultimate decisions. Here, too, personality is not merely what it seems to be in Kant, the individual modification of the general law. It is much more the creation of an individual law that can unfold exclusively out of the way one is (*dem So-Sein des Menschen*). Georg Simmel, who originated this contrast of two types of personality, of two types of individualism, spoke in another context of the terrible inner danger that a person exposes himself to by following the path of individual law. He demonstrated this in terms of two ways of saving the soul already found in Christianity.[173] In order to be able to follow what Simmel also termed the path of active individualism, those qualities are required of which Weber spoke with such emphasis in reference to the politician of responsibility. This is active individualism in its secular form. Admittedly, adherents of a formal ethic of conviction must also possess clarity, a sense of proportion, inner detachment, "passion in the sense of *matter-of-factness*," and a "feeling of objective responsibility."[174] But they apply these qualities solely to their convictional value. They are not practiced out of a sense of concern (*Sorge*) for the success of a conviction, in order to "smooth its path into reality."[175] Adherents of an ethic of responsibility are occupied by precisely this concern. In comparison to the adherents of the ethic of conviction, they are marked in emotional terms not only by passion for the cause but by an increased sense of responsibility.[176]

This makes it clear that the formal ethic of responsibility also distinguishes itself from the formal ethic of conviction in terms of the aspect of motivation. In the formal ethic of responsibility, moral sentiment is not solely limited to the cognitive component. As important as the latter is, it ultimately remains embedded in the emotional component, in the passion for the cause and in that increased sense of responsibility that arises from one's concerns regarding the consequences of one's actions. It is not an exaggeration to say that for Weber, the good will is never capable of carrying out its moral law solely on the basis of rational motivation. It is no coincidence that in his typology of action orientations he suggested an intrinsic proximity between affectual and value-rational orientations. A value-rational orientation also requires an ultimately passionate devotion to a cause. In this way, in contrast to Kant, new sources of motivation for moral action are incorporated. But these are not, as in substantive ethics of principles, linked to promised moral goods. Although a formal ethic of responsibility takes an "objective" turn in comparison to a formal ethic of conviction, a turn toward the "objects," this does not mean that it loses its formal character.[177]

The comparison between Kant and Weber is also useful for discovering differences between the formal ethics of conviction and of responsibility in terms of the third aspect, that of control or sanctions. These differences revolve primarily around the institution of the value discussion. Not only did Kant leave moral motivations underdefined, he did the same for the "ethical community" (*ethische gemeine Wesen*), the institutional side of moral action. This included the institutional side of moral dialogue. The departure from the natural state of ethics is for Kant very desirable. And a "general republic based on laws of virtue" even appears necessary in order to overcome a "*public* endangerment of the principles of virtue and a state of inner immorality."[178] Nevertheless, in spite of this, neither moral dialogue nor moral action may be placed under coercive laws (*Zwangsgesetze*). In this way, however, they are ultimately removed from all institutional regulation, because there are no institutions, in sociological terms, that do not also impose constraining laws. Institutions belong, in Kant's terms, in the sphere of law, in the sphere of external freedom. It is not by chance that Kant contradicted every effort to legally codify (*verrechtlichen*) the sphere of inner freedom. Clearly, legal duties should not conflict with duties of virtue, that is, the duties of the citizen of the state should not conflict with those of the citizen of the world. Nonetheless, for Kant, to functionalize morals in terms of the legal order, to functionalize the ethical community in terms of the legal-political community, is one of those widespread strategies that are counterproductive and ultimately lead to the disintegration of both the moral and the legal order.[179]

Finally, an important point of agreement between Kant and Weber should be mentioned: Just as for Kant the entrance into an ethical community has to be free of compulsion, so for Weber the entrance into a value discussion must be free of compulsion. According to Weber, science is only for those who seek truth. Analogously, the value discussion is only for those seeking to adhere to the imperative to be rational. Without this precondition, a value discussion cannot function.[180] Whoever clings to a closed mind cannot be helped by it. By entering into such a discussion, I recognize the obligation to subject my own conviction to the universalizing principle and thus to move from a restricted to an expanded way of thinking. This does not mean that the participants in a value discussion have for this reason found a general standpoint. What it does mean, however, is that the value discussion is premised not only on voluntary participation but also on universalism as a regulative idea. It also means that although this discus-

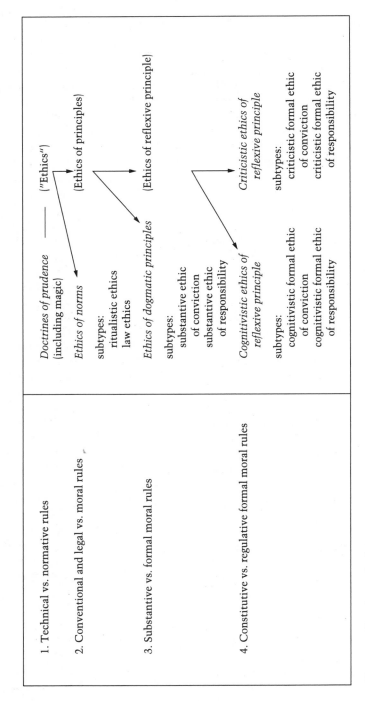

Figure 4. Typology of ethics.

sion cannot turn a particular standpoint into a general one, it can turn a narrow-minded one into an enlightened one.

In spite of the voluntary nature of entrance into value discussion, it is an institution for real dialogue. As such, it subjects its participants not only to a constraining law from within, but also from without. Of course, Weber treated in a rather implicit manner not only the normative premises, but also the institutional rules of value discussion, or in the terms of Jürgen Habermas, the "rules of discourse and its conventions."[181] In this sense, dialogue remained underdefined, normatively and institutionally, in Weber. Nevertheless, in contrast to Kant, in Weber individual abstract morality again took an institutional turn. One certainly must not interpret this as the return to concrete morality, to *Sittlichkeit*. Value discussion is an "artificial" institution, part of the culture of academic experts, removed from everyday institutions. This is true even though the convictions that are treated in it and by it originate from a concrete social and cultural milieu, from a life-world, as do Kant's maxims. In this sense, they are outside of and beyond science. With this institutional turn, however, in comparison to a formal ethic of conviction, processes of external control once again gain significance. Just as in the case of motivation, Weber's position goes beyond Kant's restrictions with regard to control or sanction.

This elaboration of the typology of ethics has led us from Weber's sociology of religion via Kant to Weber's partly hidden critique of Kant, from a two-part to a four-part typology. (For an overview, see Figure 4.) Although the diagnostic aspect has been the focus of attention, essential elements of Weber's own ethic, under the title of a criticistic formal ethic of responsibility, have also been treated. It turns out that the distinction between an ethic of conviction and an ethic of responsibility is much more elaborate than is usually admitted. It also turns out that Weber himself obviously adhered to an ethical position not only beyond fundamentalism, but also beyond naive relativism, which renders the widespread depiction of him as a moral agnostic hopelessly flawed.

Religion, Economy, and Politics

Max Weber's Historical-Sociological Profile

3

Hindrances to Modernity
Max Weber on Islam

> Industrialization was not impeded by Islam as the reli-
> gion of individuals . . . but by the religiously conditioned
> structure of the Islamic state formation, its officialdom,
> and its implementation of law.
> —Max Weber, *Economy and Society*

The Fate of Weber's Study of Islam

While working on his comparative and developmental analyses
of the major religions, on their relations to the nonreligious—especially the economic and political orders and powers—Max
Weber also took up Islam. It is one of the six major religions that
interested him most.[1] As in the case of these other religions, he
was especially attracted to its inception and early development:
the "birth" of Islam in Mecca and Yathrib (later Medina), its "heroic age" during the rule of the early caliphs (632–61) and the
Umayyads (661–750), and its "maturation" during the period of
the Abbasids (750–1258), generally regarded as the golden age of
Islam. This coming-of-age is reflected in the canonization of the
crucial religious sources, the consolidation of the most significant
orthodox and heterodox movements, and the establishment of religious stratification between the masses and the virtuosi. It also
found expression in a lessening of the dynamism characteristic of

its initial drive toward world conquest and in a subsequent religious, and above all political, polycentrism that stands in contrast to the originally unifying, national-Arabic movements. Of course, none of this is intended to deny the fact that important secondary movements followed in the wake of these primary ones. On the contrary, Weber clearly recognizes the effect of such secondary movements of "empire-building" power in the Ottoman and Mogul periods, without which Islam would be unimaginable. However, his comments remain rather scanty here, which, at least with regard to Indian Islam, is somewhat surprising given his thorough analysis of Hinduism and Buddhism. Admittedly, even in the case of early Arabic Islam, there exists no coherent text that could serve as the basis of interpretation. Before attempting such an interpretation, I think it is appropriate to say a few words about the fate of Weber's study of Islam, a study that certainly would have included not only Arabic and Persian, but also Turkish and Indian Islam.

Weber's interest in non-Christian religions and in the civilizations (*Kulturkreise*) influenced by them[2] appears to have intensified around 1910. It was presumably awakened earlier, not least of all in Eranos, the Heidelberg circle on religion in which interdisciplinary scholarship was writ large.[3] Religious scholarship of the time favored comparative studies of religion,[4] and Weber was a strong adherent of this approach.[5] Moreover, 1910 appears to be the beginning of a new phase in his work. In 1909, he had published his large and comprehensive study *The Agrarian Sociology of Ancient Civilizations* (*Agrarverhältnisse im Altertum*) (Weber 1924a, 1976) and completed publication of the series of essays "Psychophysics of Industrial Labor" ("Psychophysik der industriellen Arbeit") (Weber 1995). With the "Anticritical Last Word" ("Antikritisches Schlußwort") (Weber 1978d, 1978a), which appeared in 1910, he closed the debate in the wake of *The Protestant Ethic and the Spirit of Capitalism* (Weber 1921, vol. 1; 1958b).[6] The new phase was marked by a return to the sociology of religion (already implicit in the two countercritiques of Rachfahl) and by the planning and execution of the large-scale "Handbook on Political Economy" ("Handbuch der politischen Oekonomie," later "The Outline of Social Economics" ["Grundriss der Sozialökonomik"]). This is also confirmed by Marianne Weber in her biography (Marianne Weber 1926). There she wrote, in view of the conclusion of the essays on "Psychophysics," the last part of which appeared on September 30, 1909:

Now that all of this has been cleared up, Weber is returning to his studies in universal sociology, and in a twofold manner. He wants to continue the essays in the sociology of religion and is at the same time preparing, in response to the prompting of his publisher, Paul Siebeck, a major collective work: "The Outline of Social Economics." He is designing its plan, recruiting its coauthors, and has allotted to himself, in addition to the organizational work, the most important contributions. The writings in the sociology of religion draw in part from the same sources as this new work and are being brought along hand in hand with it.[7]

Apparently, in this new phase Weber initially follows the lead given by his previous findings. *Agrarian Sociology* contains an economic theory of the ancient world, a sort of economic and political sociology of ancient Mediterranean-European civilization and its development. It can be viewed as a preliminary stage to Weber's later sociology of economics and domination.[8] In the "Anticritical Last Word," Weber formulated the "truly most urgent questions"[9] for a sociology of religion:

1. The investigation of the different effects of the Calvinist, Baptist, and Pietist ethics on methodical conduct.
2. The investigation "of the beginnings of similar developments in the Middle Ages and in early Christianity."
3. The investigation of the economic side of the process or, in later formulations, the investigation of the other side of the causal chain—after the investigation of the conditioning of economic mentality by religion now the investigation of the conditioning of religion by the economy, especially by class constellations.[10]

This undertaking amounted to a sociology of the bourgeoisie (*Bürgertum*), a depiction of the elective affinities between bourgeois class constellations and religiously conditioned modes of conduct, affinities provided not only but certainly "most consistently by ascetic Protestantism."[11]

If the conclusion of *Agrarian Sociology* is read in conjunction with these programmatic statements, it appears that in this new phase Weber intended to clarify above all the historical preconditions of modern capitalism. These included both the "subjective" and the "objective," the motivational and the institutional ones.[12] This new phase also included the analysis of obstruction, indifference, or reinforcement among these preconditions.[13] This required the reconstruction of Occidental development from a necessarily one-sided viewpoint, based on a theoretical relation to values. It also required a comparative perspective, especially with regard to Judaism and Islam, because both contributed to this development.

Admittedly, Weber gave no indication of such an intention in his "Anticritical Last Word." He did, however, make plain his desire to show, by elaborating further upon the *Protestant Ethic* and *Agrarian Sociology*, to which preconditions modern capitalist development—in the interplay between form and spirit, subjective and objective, motivational and institutional factors—owes its existence. It is worth noting the parameters of Weber's solution in 1910, as formulated in the closing passages of the "Anticritical Last Word." Weber first distances himself from any purely technological explanation of modern and indeed of any capitalist development. His purpose, however, is not merely to reject monocausal approaches, but to reject as well those multicausal approaches that take only one side of the causal chain into account. He writes:

The capitalism of antiquity evolved *without* technical advances and in fact occurred simultaneously with the cessation of such advances. The technical progress of the Continental Middle Ages was surely of no little importance in creating the *possibility* for the development of modern capitalism, but certainly it constituted no decisive stimulus for development. Objective factors such as certain aspects of climate, which influence conduct and labor costs, count among the most significant prerequisites, along with the inland culture that shaped the political-social organization of medieval society and therefore the medieval city, particularly the continental city and its bourgeoisie. (See my previously cited article in the *Handwörterbuch der Staatswissenschaften.*) In addition, new forms of productive organization in, for example, cottage industries, were specific economic influences; although not entirely alien to ancient culture, they displayed a unique structure, diffusion, and importance.

The great process of development that lies between the highly unstable late medieval developments toward capitalism and the mechanization of technology, which is so decisive for capitalism in its present form, culminated in the creation of certain objective political and economic prerequisites that are so important for the emergence of the latter. It culminated particularly in the creation and diffusion of the rationalist and antitraditionalist spirit and the whole mentality that absorbed it. Major insights into this phenomenon may be furnished by the history of modern science and its recent practical relation to the economy and by the history of the modern *conduct of life* and its practical meaning for the economy.[14]

The developmental history of political and economic organization, and also of science and conduct, must be written in such a way that the writer does not hastily degrade one into a mere function or consequence of the other.[15] It needs to be written with a view to the qualitative transformations that occurred in antiquity, in the Middle Ages, and in the period between the late Middle Ages and modernity. This reconstruction of Western development, especially of capitalism, must be carried out not only in terms of a specific viewpoint; it must be "dissolved" into a series of partial developments that have to be continuously and repeatedly interrelated. This calls for a value-related, ideal-typical developmental construct as a prerequisite for the realization of this project. Indeed, Weber does not object to developmental constructions as such, but only to those that operate with models of complete and all-inclusive stages based on normative criteria that are then reified. That he subsequently repeatedly raised the question of why rational industrial capitalism arose only in the West, and that he responded to it with the constellation of conditions that existed only here, does not imply that other constellations could not also have produced such a result or that other civilizations that later followed the path to industrial capitalism had to pass through the same "stages" into which one can "dissect" Western development. For Weber, universal history dissolves into a plurality of developmental histories in and between civilizations.[16] However, this plurality does not imply that the dimensions one chooses for their reconstruction are arbitrary. The recourse to organizational forms, especially to economic ones, is never sufficient,[17] for these are only some of the important elements shaping conduct. Other important elements are normatively based conceptions of duty. They are, at least in precapitalist times, embedded in religious world views and ethics. Therefore, one needs to take into account not only economic but also cultural, especially religious, forces if one aims to reconstruct Western and non-Western developmental histories.[18]

It quickly becomes clear that this new phase of work coincides with a qualitative transformation of Weber's approach.[19] He made a discovery, and it too is documented in Marianne Weber's biography. Although its dating is unclear, its nature is not. It is the insight that the development of modern scientific rationalism demonstrates connections not only with economic but also with aesthetic developments, especially with the Western development of music.[20] Marianne Weber provided the following description:

The times hurl abuse at rationalism and many artists in particular consider it an inhibition of their creative powers. For this reason this discovery [of the connection between scientific and aesthetic development] especially excites Weber. He has now also planned a sociology of art, and sometime around 1910 undertook as a first attempt, in the midst of his

other studies, the investigation of the rational and sociological foundations of music. It led him into the most remote areas of ethnology and
into the most difficult investigations of tonal arithmetic [*Tonarithmetik*]
and symbolism. Nevertheless, as soon as this part was provisionally established, he forced himself to return to those writings promised and already in progress.[21]

The discovery did not only lead to "detours"; it was also of far-
reaching significance for Weber's twofold project. It motivated
him to broaden the scope of his analyses. Certainly, the distinctive
character and development of Occidental capitalism remained at
the center; however, this was now but one of several Western cultural phenomena of universal significance.[22] This broadened scope
meant that one cannot confine oneself to the investigation of religious and economic development. Analyses of domination and
law, of social organizations ranging from the family to the "state,"
have to be included as well. Moreover, if one seeks to define and
explain the distinctive character of the *whole* of Western culture
in terms of its rational-methodical conduct, its rational capitalist
enterprise, its rational *Anstaltsstaat*, its formally rational law, its
rational science, and its music of harmonic chords, it is necessary
to compare this civilization with others and to show why these
phenomena did not occur there. In order to do this, one needs criteria and concepts. These criteria and concepts are, as Weber emphasized with all the clarity one could ask for, based on the cultural values of the civilization to which he belonged. Although
this basis leads, in accordance with the postulate of theoretical
value relation, to a heuristic Eurocentrism, it does not entail normative Eurocentrism. To make these comparisons, one also needs
basic knowledge of other civilizations, especially of the religions
and the forms of economy, domination, and law that helped shape
them. This knowledge must go at least as far as is necessary to find
"the points of comparison" with Occidental development,[23] and
thus, at least far enough to work out the similarities and differences vis-à-vis Western development.

That rational industrial capitalism and other Occidental cultural phenomena arose only in the West, or more precisely, that
they occurred here for the first time, is a historical fact for Weber.
These phenomena do not necessarily interest everyone, nor does
everyone consider them the most important of phenomena; nevertheless, no one can deny their reality. But exactly because they
aroused Weber's interest, he was compelled to go beyond the limits of his own civilization and, not to be forgotten, beyond the lim-

its of his own scholarly discipline to investigate these phenomena.[24] There are three chief reasons for this: the clarification
of the problems of identification (demonstration of the unique features), the clarification of the problems of causal attribution (demonstration of the historical preconditions), and the clarification of
the problem of diagnosis (demonstration of the "sacrifices," of the
"lost" possibilities); for the comparison does not merely show the
unique features of the West and facilitate causal attributions, it
also makes clear what was, in contrast to other cultures, not realized here. Thus, in addition to theoretical and historical dimensions, cultural science also possesses a practical dimension.[25]
Weber apparently first took the step beyond the limits of his own
civilization in connection with his research on music, but this
step continued to have consequences. As his wife reported, "When
(sometime around 1911) he resumes his studies in the sociology of
religion, he is drawn to the Orient: to China, Japan, and India, and
then to Judaism and Islam."[26]

No later than 1911, Weber worked through those "sources" important for his twofold project. For non-Western civilizations,
these sources were largely secondary, to an even greater extent
than those he used to analyze Western development.[27] For Islam,
it appears that outside of his knowledge of the holy sources (Koran, Sunna, Sharia), presumably gathered from secondary literature, he based his analysis primarily on the work of German
Islamicists of the time, such as Carl Heinrich Becker, Julius
Wellhausen, Ignaz Goldziher, and Joseph Kohler, whose studies
have not lost their relevance even today. These were supplemented by the works of Christian Snouck Hurgronje and probably
one or another English or French author.[28] This accords with the
impression one gains of Weber's analysis of other civilizations. His
comparative studies reflect above all the contemporaneous German scholarship in sinology, Indology, Semitics, Egyptology, and
Islamic studies, as well as in Protestant theology insofar as it
was oriented toward comparative religion (*Religionswissenschaft*).
Differences that do arise here depend on the extent to which
Weber approached the monographic presentation of his findings.

How then did the two projects develop, in which Islam—alongside Confucianism, Hinduism, Buddhism, Judaism, and Christianity (and its "internal" subdivisions)—plays an important role? By
the end of 1913, Weber had apparently brought to paper large parts
of *both* projects. In the meantime, the one project had been entitled "The Economic Ethics of the World Religions" ("Die Wirt-

schaftsethik der Weltreligionen"), whereas the other was called "The Economy and the Societal Orders and Powers" ("Die Wirtschaft und die gesellschaftlichen Ordnungen und Mächte"). As Marianne Weber's comment shows, the sources tapped during this new phase of work were used for both projects. As Weber himself later put it, the two projects—at least in terms of the parts on the sociology of religion—serve mutually to interpret and supplement each other and were meant to be published simultaneously.[29] Let us look at two letters that yield a relatively clear picture of the state and substance of the two manuscripts at the end of 1913. On December 30, 1913, Weber wrote to his publisher Siebeck of "The Economy and the Societal Orders and Powers" that he had

worked out a complete theory and exposition that relates the major forms of social groupings to the economy: from the family and household to the enterprise, the kin group, the ethnic community, religion (encompassing all the major religions of the world: a sociology of salvation doctrines and religious ethics—what Troeltsch did, now for *all* religions, only much more concise), finally a comprehensive sociological theory of the state and domination. I can claim that nothing of the kind has ever been written, not even as a precursor.[30]

On June 22, 1915, Weber offered Siebeck a series of essays, "Economic Ethics of the World Religions," for publication in the *Archiv für Sozialwissenschaft und Sozialpolitik*. He said he had had them "since the beginning of the war" and that they encompassed "Confucianism (China), Hinduism and Buddhism (India), Judaism, Islam [and] Christianity," and furthermore represented the successful "generalization and realization of the method" proposed in the *Protestant Ethic*. He went on to say that four essays were involved, of four to five press sheets each, "preliminary studies toward, and commentaries on, the systematic sociology of religion" for the "Outline of Social Economics," and thus for that manuscript spoken of in the letter of December 30, 1913. The essays—according to Weber—could at some point, along with others and in revised form, be published on their own. In this way, he anticipated the *Collected Essays in the Sociology of Religion* (*Gesammelte Aufsätze zur Religionssoziologie*) (Weber 1921). They did in fact start appearing in 1920, with a first volume that Weber himself had prepared for print.[31] At least a part of this series, however, must have dated from 1913 rather than the beginning of the war. This follows from the footnote that Weber added to the publication of the first article. The latter appeared, along with an "Introduction" to the complete series, on October 14, 1915. This note stated that the subsequent essays were being published "unchanged" in the manner "in which they were written down two years ago and were read aloud to friends."[32] Thus, one can infer that by the end of 1913, at the latest by the beginning of the war, voluminous manuscripts existed on both projects, and Islam was included in their analyses.

One of these manuscripts, entitled "The Economy and the Societal Orders and Powers," was not published during Weber's lifetime. It was part of his literary estate and was published after his death (along with a later manuscript that he himself had completed for publication) as parts 2 and 3 (later only part 2) of *Economy and Society*. The latter included—from the time of the second edition of this highly problematic "book construct" created by the editors[33]—four texts in which Islamic civilization is discussed: those on the sociologies of religion, domination, law, and the city. Although the other of the two manuscripts was published by Weber himself under the title "The Economic Ethics of the World Religions" (Weber 1921), it was published only in part and (after the printing of the "Introduction," the first two articles on Confucianism, and the "Intermediate Reflections") in a version different from the one to which the letter of June 22, 1915, gives witness. Weber revised the articles on Hinduism prior to first publication. This was also true of the articles on Buddhism and ancient Judaism.[34] More important, though, the series of articles reaching fruition by January 1920 did not go beyond ancient Judaism. Weber never managed to publish the parts on Islam and Christianity mentioned in the letter.

This provokes two questions: Did Weber still want to publish these articles? And what became of that part of the "Economic Ethics" manuscript dealing with Islam and Christianity? An unequivocal answer can be given to the first question: there can be no doubt that Weber intended to incorporate studies of Islam and Christianity (though no longer into the *Archiv* series) into the "Collected Essays on the Sociology of Religion." This is not only confirmed in the second version of the "Introduction" of 1920,[35] but above all in the announcement that Weber himself wrote in September 1919. Here he presented the public with the contents of the planned four-volume "Collected Essays on the Sociology of Religion" (cf. Weber 1921). He commented that two of these volumes were in press. These would include a revision of those essays on the sociology of religion already published, that is, the essays on ascetic Protestantism, Confucianism and Taoism, Hinduism and Buddhism, and Judaism, to be supplemented by analyses not yet published of Egyptian, Mesopotamian, and Zoroastrian religious ethics and of "the development of the European bourgeoisie in antiquity and the Middle Ages." These would then be followed by two further volumes consisting solely of unpublished studies (and, one must add, of studies largely not yet written): a third volume treating "early Christianity, talmudic Judaism, Islam, and Oriental Christianity," then a "concluding volume" on "Christianity of the Occident."[36] In my view, this announcement makes two things clear: First, the treatment of Islam would definitely have been shorter than that of Confucianism, Hinduism, or ancient Judaism. Second, it presumably would have been twofold in purpose, pursuing developmental and typological aims, for similar to Judaism, Islam belonged to the context of the historical "preconditions" of Western development and at the same time represented a development of historical significance in its own right vis-à-vis that of the West.[37] This is also implied by the placement of Islam in the project: within the context of both its historical predecessors and its most important rivals.

In contrast, it is not as easy to supply an unambiguous answer to the second question, which concerns the manuscript. An indirect approach is required, unless one simply answers that Weber never had a manuscript on Islam and that his remarks to the contrary can only be understood as a projection. In fact, if the statement in the letter of June 22, 1915, were accurate, would there not have to be a manuscript among his posthumous papers? Furthermore, does not the fact that the *General Economic History*, which some like to see as Weber's "last words,"[38] contains no lengthy passages on Islam imply that it no longer interested him after the war began? It can hardly be denied that no manuscript entitled "Islam" was found in the literary estate or that Weber no longer intensively dealt with Islam after the war broke out. But I still consider the statement made in the June 1915 letter truthful. What manuscript is Weber then referring to in this letter? I will offer a confessedly speculative solution to this riddle.

In my view, the only manuscript that could be considered is found today in the sociology of religion section of *Economy and Society*. In chapter 6, it is entitled "*XV*. The Great Religions and the World" (Weber 1978b: 611–34; in German: "Die Kulturreligionen und die 'Welt'"). It is preceded by the text (chap. 6: *XII–XIV*; Weber 1978b: 576–610) that Weber refined into his famous "Intermediate Reflections." In another essay I have shown that *Economy and Society* and "The Collected Essays in the Sociology of Religion" are shaped by an increasing division of labor.[39] Just as parts *XII–XIV* were used in the "Economic Ethics of the World Religions," so too was part *XV*. Whereas parts *XII–XIV* remained as they were in *Economy and Society*, a section of part *XV* is missing. An indication of this is its beginning. It is not the direct continuation of *XIV*, but instead that of a text or part of a text that is no longer found in the sociology of religion section of *Economy and Society*. It is that text or part of a text, I claim, that Weber incorporated in the revision of the studies of Confucianism and Hinduism. The beginning of part *XV* in *Economy and Society* reads:

Judaism, in its postexilic and particularly its talmudic form (the only forms we are interested in here), is the *third* of those religions that are in some sense accommodated to the world. Judaism is at least oriented to the world in the sense that it does not reject the world as such but only rejects the prevailing social rank order in the world.

We have already made some observations concerning the sociological classification of Judaism.[40]

After this opening sentence, the religiously motivated relation to the world of talmudic Judaism is described and compared to that of the Catholics, the Puritans, and the early Christians. This is then followed by a description of Islam. It is classified as the fourth world-accommodating religion. The analysis then turns to the relations to the world of world-rejecting religions. Here, early Buddhism and early Christianity are treated. At this point the manuscript breaks off. It was intended to be continued. But much more important is that its beginning, which apparently once existed, is missing. Moreover, the remaining manuscript contains sketches of all religions mentioned in the letter except Confucianism and Hinduism. As is known, Weber considered Confucianism, but also parts of Hinduism (at least before 1915) as "religions that are in some sense accommodated to the world." This missing section, however, could mean that not only were the first parts of the manuscript "The Great Religions and the World" in fact used for the "Economic Ethics," but the remaining truncated portion would have served as the basis of the continuation of the series. It is in any case not improbable that Weber was also thinking about this manuscript when he offered his publisher a series of essays in 1915. And it is just as probable that he would have made use of other parts of the sociology of religion for the "Economic Ethics." Thus, after 1915 at the latest, he probably considered the manuscript in the edited posthumous form in which we have it today to be only a preliminary version of the sociology of religion.[41]

What can be concluded from the fate of the Islam study? Four points can be made:

1. By the beginning of the First World War, Weber had attained a basic knowledge of Islamic civilization, which he had chiefly made use of in the context of the sociologies of religion, domination, and law. However, this research did not result in a monographic essay. His intention was to write this essay in the framework of the "Economic Ethics of the World Religions," initially for inclusion in the *Archiv* series, later for the "Collected Essays in the Sociology of Religion."

2. Although Weber intended to do so, he evidently did not deal intensively with Islamic civilization from the outbreak of the war until his death. The remarks found in his work about Islam basically rest on preliminary work done from 1911 until 1914 at the latest, terminologically also reflecting Weber's approach of this period.

3. The monographic essay envisioned would hardly have equalled the size of the studies of Confucianism and Taoism, Hinduism and Buddhism, or ancient Judaism. Without a doubt, Islam belonged to the same extended context of historical prerequisites of Western development as talmudic Judaism, early Christianity, and oriental Christianity—prerequisites that Weber apparently hoped to treat as a whole in the concluding volume of his "Collected Essays in the Sociology of Religion." However, Islam, as a "comparatively late product . . . in which Old Testament and Jewish-Christian elements played a very important role," could hardly have the same genetic significance for Weber as ancient Judaism or ancient or medieval Christianity.[42]

4. Weber's real interest in Islam is typological. As will be shown, it demonstrates similarities with ascetic Protestantism and especially with Calvinism—similarities, however, of a purely external character. Weber would certainly have centered the essay around this thesis.

Thus, if one seeks to reconstruct the basic outlines of Weber's study of Islam, attention has first to be directed to the manuscript entitled "The Economy and the Societal Orders and Powers" and especially to the discussions in the sections on religion, domination, law, and the city. Insofar as the later version of the sociology of domination, which Weber himself was still able to submit to publication in 1920, builds upon the earlier version, there are also references to Islam. The latter, however, do not represent an advance over 1913–14. The same holds for the second version of the *Protestant Ethic* and for the *General Economic History*, in which scattered remarks on Islam are also found.

An Outline of Weber's Analysis of Islam
Methodological Considerations

How can Weber's remarks on Islam be tied together, how can a relatively coherent overall picture be derived from them? Some preliminary methodological considerations, starting from a thought already presented, are useful here. Weber's comparative studies are subject to a *heuristic* Eurocentrism and they are not *comprehensive* cultural analyses. What interested him were Western cultural phenomena—their distinct character, and the "combination of circumstances" that brought them about.[43] The clarification of the questions of identification and causal attribution raised in this context is the ultimate purpose of the comparison. For this reason, all comparisons for Weber were governed by the goal of uncovering the contrasts (the points of opposition or difference) to those cultural phenomena that held his interest. These interests can range over a variety of areas; to establish this range is a theoretical task.

As the letter of June 22, 1915, points out, the comparative essays on the "Economic Ethics of the World Religions" are intended to generalize the method found in the *Protestant Ethic*. Thus, the religious conditioning of economic attitudes is doubtlessly involved. Yet, the class conditioning of religion must also play a part. This class question, however, is at the same time a question of the "structure of society."[44] In other words, more is involved than just economy and religion; the analysis also takes up domination (including law), and it concerns all these orders and their interrelations. This is the widening of scope that resulted from the discovery that ushered in a new phase of work: that Western culture is not only distinct from other civilizations in its economic development, but also in its scientific and artistic development, and above all in its political and legal development. In short, its configuration of order is different from others in its most important features. Accordingly, in the "Economics Ethics of World Religions" both sides of the causal chain are treated despite its repeatedly emphasized limited objective; moreover, attention is brought not only to differences in religion, but also to differences in domination and law, and, in the cases of India and China even, at least in passing, in science.[45]

Weber provides not only a typological classification, but also a genetic reconstruction of Western cultural phenomena. These are linked in a series of causal relations, the recognition of which presupposes the subclassification of overall development into partial developments and developmental phases. I cannot retrace Weber's complex analysis of Occidental cultural development here.[46] However, this development clearly "culminates" in the elective affinity between rational capitalism and the rational *Anstaltsstaat*.

For Weber rational capitalism is (still!) the more fateful of the two forces. What definition of rational capitalism does he provide? From the first version of the *Protestant Ethic* to the economic sociology in the second version of *Economy and Society* (chapter 2), Weber uses many definitions that are not completely identical but have a common core. It is first of all important to separate the definitions referring to the *individual enterprise* from those referring to the *economic system*. A rational-capitalist enterprise, for example, can be distinguished from a large-scale household (*oikos*), a large workshop (*ergasterion*), and a craft shop through the combination of four characteristics: it is a profit-oriented enterprise, it is a factory enterprise, it is independent of the household, and it controls its economic activity by means of double-entry bookkeeping. The other three units lack at least one of these features. The craft shop comes the closest to the rational-capitalist enterprise, but it lacks mechanized technology and fixed capital. In order for an individual enterprise to rationally calculate its activity, however, a legal order guaranteeing free property and contractual freedom is presupposed, for rational calculation presupposes that the material means of production (*Beschaffungsmittel*) are appropriated as "free property by autonomous, private, profit-oriented enterprises" and that market freedom exists in the labor market (formally free labor!) and in the commodity and capital markets. Moreover, decisions of justice and administration must be predictable. This presupposes the priority of procedural rationality, of legal security, before substantive rationality, before "justice."[47] Of course, all of this does not suffice to establish a capitalist economic system. This exists only when numerous such enterprises produce mass goods for expanded markets—goods that serve to fulfill everyday needs—and when this is the dominant mode of want satisfaction. Admittedly, the rational-capitalist mode of want satisfaction never exists to the exclusion of all other modes. Nonetheless, one can speak of a capitalist epoch only "if want satisfaction is primarily capitalist; if we think away this kind of organization, want satisfaction as such would collapse."[48]

This makes two things clear. First, rational profit-oriented enterprises in expanded markets can exist without capitalist want satisfaction predominating. In this case, this mode competes with others, such as craft shops or manors, and is constantly in danger of "death by suffocation" if markets shrink. Second, there are attitudinal as well as political and legal presuppositions for this mode of capitalist want satisfaction that are *not* required by other modes of capitalist want satisfaction, such as trading, tax farming, lease and sale of offices, plantations and colonial enterprises, provisioning of the state, and the financing of wars. Under certain circumstances, these modes can flourish with traditional economic attitudes and ethics.[49] For Weber, this kind of ultimately politically oriented capitalism has existed throughout the world. Not its historical prerequisites but rather those of rational capitalism as an economic system are of interest.

These historical preconditions were already fully described by Weber in his "Anticritical Last Word" of September 1910. This can be seen by comparing it with later formulations, such as that of the *General Economic History*, which in any case, given its complicated textual status, always has to be taken with a grain of salt. Nevertheless, the formulation reported in this connection is too similar to others to be a distortion of Weber's conception. It is of special interest because here the step mentioned previously is at least implicitly taken from a purely typological to a more genetic treatment of distinctly Western cultural phenomena. Weber first describes the distinct character of Western capitalism in terms similar to those mentioned earlier; then he "explains" why it emerged only in the West. To do this, he names "certain features of its general cultural development":

Only the Occident knows the *state in the modern sense*, with a constitution (*gesatzter Verfassung*), specialized officialdom, and the concept of citizenship. Beginnings of this institution in antiquity and in the Orient were never able to develop fully. Only the Occident knows *rational law*, made by jurists and rationally interpreted and applied, and only in the Occident is found the concept of *citizen* (*civis Romanus, citoyen, bour-*

geois) because only in the Occident does the *city* exist in the specific sense of the word. Furthermore, only the Occident possesses *science in the present-day sense of the word*. Theology, philosophy, and reflection on the ultimate problems of life were known to the Chinese and the Hindu, perhaps even of a depth unreached by the European; but a rational science and in connection with it a *rational technology* remained unknown to those civilizations. Finally, Western civilization is further distinguished from every other by the presence of men with a *rational ethos for the conduct of life*. Magic and religion are found everywhere; but a religious basis for conduct that, when consistently followed, had to lead to a specific form of rationalism is again peculiar to Western civilization alone.[50]

State, city, law, science, and methodical conduct provide both the key terms and the "points of comparison" for the "Economic Ethics." It is contingent upon these cultural phenomena whether the developments toward rational capitalism—the beginnings of which indeed exist in all civilizations—meet resistance or not.[51] The structures of political domination and law are decisive for the extent of external resistance, whereas the religiously anchored conceptions of duty and the modes of conduct associated with them are decisive for the extent of inner resistance. Just as in the case of the other studies, Weber's essay on Islam would have concentrated above all on these.

In fact, Weber's scattered remarks on Islam can be organized around these points of comparison: the type of religious ethic—world mastery as world conquest and world adjustment; the type of political domination—Oriental prebendal feudalism; the type of city—Oriental urban anarchy; the type of law—theocratic and patrimonial *Kadi*-justice; and the interrelation of these orders and powers (their mode of "integration")—"centralism." Science is the only key term about which nothing can be found in these remarks. In the other studies, too, it is largely neglected, as is art. This neglect, however, is certainly not an oversight but is connected to the limited aim of the studies. Admittedly, this is a failing if one adheres to Weber's own theoretical approach as presented in the "Intermediate Reflections," which distinguishes religious, economic, political, aesthetic, erotic, and intellectual spheres, or as presented in the "Author's Introduction" to the "Collected Essays in the Sociology of Religion," which lists the distinct Western cultural phenomena according to spheres, or even as presented in the aforementioned quotes from the "Anti-critical Last Word" or the *General Economic History*. In accordance with this theoretical approach, the development of science in particular belongs to those factors constitutive of each and every cultural development.

The Religious Ethic: World Mastery Between World Conquest and World Adjustment

One side of the causal chain of development toward rational capitalism concerns the relationship between religious ethics and conduct, something that had intrigued Weber since the turn of the century at the very latest and that remained undiminished thereafter. He had pursued this interest in the comparative framework of "The Protestant Ethic and the 'Spirit' of Capitalism" (1904–5), although he admittedly limited it to pre- and post-Reformation Christian movements. Here Weber established that the relationship between religious ethics and conduct is, to begin with, an internal one. Even though this internal relationship can be supported, distracted, or obstructed by its external aspects, it is to be analyzed independently of the latter.[52] The "ability and disposition of men to adopt certain types of practical rational *conduct*"— so Weber's thesis—is also dependent upon the belief in the exemplary status of duties formulated in religious-ethical terms. This in any case holds true for a "precapitalist era" in which religion was still a force in life.[53] But orientation to values, especially to ethical values, is to be regarded as a general feature of human beings. A person acts not only according to purposes, but also according to values. Whereas a purpose is the conception of success that becomes the cause of an action, a value is the conception of validity that becomes the cause.[54] Admittedly, human action is undoubtedly determined over large stretches by utilitarian motives and supported by doctrines of prudence. Human beings are also moral beings, however, and therefore capable of making the axiological turn.[55]

This was the educational achievement of the great religions: that they affected—with different degrees of radicalness—this axiological turn among their respective followers. This, for example, distinguishes them from magic in all its expressions. Of course, the axiological turn can not only vary in degree of radicality, it can also differ in *direction*. This decides which stance to the world a religion supports. In a different context I have shown how Weber's comparative sociology of religion leads to a typology of religiously motivated stances toward the world and to related modes of conduct.[56] His study of Islam also would have focused on this line of thought.

In order to conceive of Islam as precisely as possible and to "bring . . . out the points of comparison with our Occidental religions as well as possible,"[57] it is reasonable to start with Christianity and with its most important representative in terms of Weber's central question, Calvinism. It is well known that Weber also regarded his quickly famous historical study of ascetic Protestantism as a contribution "to the understanding of the general manner in which ideas become effective forces in history."[58] Because of this he justified its publication in the *Archiv*, which "generally did *not* [involve itself] with purely historical work."[59] Interestingly enough, Weber explicitly distances himself in this context from two explanatory approaches, one that attributes the creation of ideas exclusively to economic situations and another that attributes the development of created ideas exclusively to inborn forces. For an idea such as the duty of calling, constitutive as it is for the "spirit" of rational capitalism, to be selected at all and to be able to function as a superstructure, however, "it had to originate somewhere, and not in isolated individuals, but as a way of looking at things [that is] common to whole *groups*";[60] for it to become an effective historical force, it had to "fight its way to supremacy against a whole world of hostile forces," a struggle that in no way always ends with the "best" surviving.[61] Here the twofold significance of Weber's later frequently used concept of autonomy (*Eigengesetzlichkeit*) comes into view: ideas and worldviews (*Weltbilder*) do not always originate as functions or results of material interest constellations, and in some circumstances they survive by struggle, even when they have become "dysfunctional." The foe, however, against which the spirit of rational capitalism was created and which it had to overcome, was the spirit of traditionalism. To oust the latter, a truly "revolutionary force" from within was necessary.[62] Weber's claim was that this could not have been achieved by a doctrine of prudence (*Klugheitslehre*), no matter how elaborate. It required a *religious* ethic and a group of individuals with *heightened* interest in salvation for whom this ethic offered a convincing doctrinal basis.

Ideas must work their way through the minds and hearts of actors. Two different relations have to be kept separate in order to understand the way this process works: the subjective appropriation of such ideas can be weak or strong, passive or active; and ideas do not always come to match interests, they can provoke "practical entanglements of interest."[63] The more active the appropriation and the greater the discrepancy between ideas and interests, the greater the practical psychological tensions ensuing from the ideas. The greater the tensions, the greater the tendency that such practical entanglements or conflicts of interests will be provoked, in the wake of which the meaning of the subjective appropriation is altered. It is for this reason that Weber always emphasized that one must distinguish strictly between the dogmatic and the pragmatic-psychological effects of a given ethic when the relation between ethics and conduct is taken up for study. The logical and the pragmatic-psychological consequences following from the doctrinal basis of a given ethic need not point in the same direction, because as a rule they are two different things. This has sometimes been interpreted as if the substance of the doctrinal justification, the doctrine in itself, were immaterial. This is not the case. Just because two processes are not identical does not mean they are unrelated to each other.

In spite of the distinction, basic to his entire approach, between the logical and pragmatic-psychological consequences arising from the doctrinal basis of a given ethic, Weber emphasized the following point in the context of an instructive criticism of William James: the latter's pragmatic approach failed to take up the significance of the substance of thought in its own right, which "captures and moulds the immediate experience of religion in its own way."[64] Anyone who on principle classifies ideas according to the way in which they prove themselves in life ultimately proceeds in a reductionist manner. He can offer no explanation whatsoever as to why practical entanglements of interests arise. They can in fact mean two different things: that religious interests "capture" religious ideas for their own purposes (instead of vice versa), or that religious interests are captured by other interests—salvational interests being put into the service of social honor, political power, or material wealth.

For Weber, the doctrine of election by grace belongs to the foundations of Calvinism. It is not the only dogma, and not even the most important, but it is the one—when actively appropriated—that most heightens those psychological tensions ensuing from Calvinism. Were a religiously motivated person to believe unconditionally in this dogma and in it alone, that person would be compelled to fatalism. The pragmatic-psychological effect of Calvinism, however, was just the opposite, namely, unceasing activity.

One reason for this is that the notion of predestination does not stand alone. Rather, it is connected to the notion of proving oneself, of justifying faith, according to which the believers have to prove themselves and their actions before God by adhering to His commandments. This idea is more important than that of the doctrine of election by grace.[65] Instead of lessening the tension, however, this combination heightens it, for it prevents the believer from taking two well-traveled and natural paths to salvation. It negates both the mystical solution, the unification with God, and the "traditional" solution, the fulfillment of duty in the expectation of reciprocity. The very principles of this doctrine prevent good works from being the source of salvation. Such works must be done simply for their own sake, or more accurately, solely for the glorification of God, that being the purpose of the world. Moreover, such works do not "count" in themselves, but only as part of the overall way one conducts one's life. "The God of Calvinism demanded of his believers not single good works, but a course of good works transformed into a *system* of life."[66] He further demanded the continuous and persistent transformation of one's entire being, an overall methodological way of conducting one's life from within toward without, confident and self-disciplined.

However, as much as the idea of proof provides practical instruction, setting the basis for activity, it is constantly upset, in psychological terms, by the doctrine of election by grace, with its unchangeable and unknowable wisdom of God. This instability provides the second reason why Calvinism impels its followers toward unceasing activity. The theory of predestination produces in every believer enormous insecurity about the fate of his salvation, and this creates fear. The logical need of the dogmatist is confronted in stark and unreconcilable fashion by the apprehensive believer's need for security. This would ultimately have resulted in inhibition of action, in fatalism, if this need for security, for *ceritudo salutis*, were not satisfied in some manner. Thus, precisely at this point a practical entanglement of interests arises. The interest in the certainty of salvation captures, as it were, the dogma. In addition to its manifest meaning, the idea of proof is attributed a latent one. Although the idea is thus left in its dogmatic framework, it is in fact partly reinterpreted. The good works performed by the individual, with which he increases God's glory and not his own, must continue to hold their validity as not only willed by God but ultimately effected by God. Nevertheless, they are simultaneously reinterpreted to be signs of election.

Weber uses a certain type of theological literature that could be named "response literature"[67] as evidence that this practical entanglement of interests did in fact exist and have dogmatic repercussions. By reproducing the decisive theological responses to the need of the faithful for salvational certainty, these sources provide a striking display of the "process of mutual adjustment" between ideas and interests. Their choice as an object of analysis thus also allows one to follow the course by which ideas make their way into life. Decisive for Weber is the mutual and reciprocal quality of this process of alignment. Ideas and interests tend to work upon each other. Neither a reductionism of ideas nor of interests is supported. This is the exact meaning of the famous later formulation according to which material and ideal interests directly determine man's action, but ideationally defined worldviews very often, like switchmen, determine along which tracks "action has been pushed by the dynamic of interest."[68] Without the combination of the ideas of predestination and proof and without the maintenance of the dogmatic core of this combination even after its reinterpretation, the "collapse into a purely utilitarian doctrine of good works with a solely inner-worldly orientation" would have been probable.[69] Without this combination the tension produced by the linkage with one's fate beyond would largely be lacking, a tension that was the occasion for the "greatest possible systematic focusing of the ethic of conviction imaginable."[70] Because reinterpretation does not do away with the original dogmatic foundations, because success in action as the sign of election is the means "not of purchasing salvation but of getting rid of the fear of damnation,"[71] it results in the pervasive Christianization of all of life, producing self-certain saints in the form of the "Puritan merchant men of steel of that heroic age of capitalism."[72] These were men for whom otherworldly salvation and not thisworldly prosperity was important.

The fact that the idea of proving oneself before God for His greater glory concretized itself as the "idea of methodically proving oneself in one's vocation in economic life"[73] also has dogmatic grounds. According to the Calvinist doctrine, the field of proof is, strictly speaking, the whole world created by God. This follows for Weber from the objective impersonal conception of the idea of love of one's neighbor such that the fulfillment of "the vocational tasks resulting from the *lex naturae* [law of nature]" can be decisive for action willed by God and pleasing to His sight.[74] Admittedly, such a concretization of religious duty as vocational duty is in accordance with the nonreligious ideal and material interests of a rising bourgeois stratum. Moreover, the connection of these nonreligious interests with the religious ones and the worldview that serves to interpret the latter is important for an appropriate sociological understanding of the process of dissemination, whereby the idea of vocational duty proves itself in its struggle with other ideas. Nevertheless, this connection is not primary and also not decisive for understanding the inner or intrinsic relation between the religious ethic and the mode of conduct. Interests in themselves are in any case blind, and nonreligious interests in precapitalist eras do not produce any forces that radically transform life from within.

Weber thus shows with regard to Calvinism the factors that play a decisive role in the relationship between religious ethics and conduct: the religious foundations or substance of ideas on the one hand, and the need for consistency in dogma and the need of assurance of one's salvation on the other. The latter could also be termed the need for religious legitimation. Weber links it with the nonreligious need for legitimation, interconnected but nonetheless not identical with the religious need; this nonreligious need is related to the justification of the distribution of worldly goods such as power, social honor, and wealth.[75]

Against the backdrop of this analysis and the thesis of the possible difference between the logical and pragmatic-psychological effects of religious foundations, two interesting patterns emerge. On the one hand, thoroughly similar psychological effects could occur on the basis of differing religious foundations, and on the other, the psychological effects could be different given similar religious foundations. The first case is exemplified by the Baptists, the second by the Islamic religious ethic. The religious ethic of the Baptists—even without a doctrine of predestination—had psychological consequences similar to those of Calvinism, whereas Islam, though it possessed such a doctrine, produced psychological effects in contrast to those of Calvinism.[76]

In order not to misconstrue this first main thesis of Weber's analysis of Islam from the very start, it must be emphasized in just what way the religious foundations of Calvinism and Islam are not essentially different, namely, in the way in which the unconditionally transcendent character (*Überweltlichkeit*) of the *one and only* God of creation is maintained.[77] In contradistinction not only to all Asiatic religions but also to all religions of antiquity with the exception of Judaism, God is here "endowed with [the traits of] absolute unchangeableness, omnipotence, and omniscience—

that is to say, with an absolutely transcendental character."[78] He is "a transcendental unitary God who is universal," whose powers are immeasurable.[79] This makes unbridgeable the gap between God and humans. In terms of the question of individual salvation, such a conception of God limits the significance of all mediators, be they personal or institutional in nature. Mohammed is a prophet, the *last* of the prophets through whom God, Allah, proclaims his will to man for the final time. He is "an instrument for proclamation, who on the strength of the mission given him demands obedience as an ethical duty"; in short, he is the prototype of an ethical prophet.

He is, however, neither the son of God nor one who dies sacrificially for the sake of the salvation of a humanity burdened by original sin.[80] Thus, the idea of the church as an institution of sacramental grace administering salvation always remained totally foreign to Islam. It is a creation of the Christianity of late antiquity and the Middle Ages. Calvinism also limits the salvational significance of all mediators: Jesus died only for the chosen, and the idea of salvation via ecclesiastical sacrament falls under the suspicion of magic.[81] In fact, the conception of God and the idea of predestination are most intimately connected. The more radically the transcendence of God is conceived, the more the individual's salvational fate tends to appear to be predestined; the more consistently the faithful are followers of the idea of predestination, the greater the tensions between God and man. In view of ancient Judaism (Job), early Islam, and early Calvinism, Weber described this general relationship in the following manner:

Belief in providence is the consistent rationalization of magical divination, to which it is related, and which for that very reason it seeks to devaluate as completely as possible, as a matter of principle. No other view of the religious relationship could possibly be as radically opposed to all magic, both in theory and in practice, as this belief in providence which was dominant in the great theistic religions of Asia Minor and the Occident. No other so emphatically affirms the nature of the divine to be an essentially dynamic activity manifested in God's personal, providential rule over the world. Moreover, there is no view of the religious relationship which holds such firm views regarding God's discretionary grace and the human creature's need of it, regarding the tremendous distance between God and all his creatures, and consequently regarding the reprehensibility of any deification of "things of the flesh" as a sacrilege against the sovereign God. For the very reason that this religion provides not rational solution of the problem of theodicy, it conceals the greatest tensions between the world and God, between the actually existent and the ideal.[82]

As in Calvinism, so too in Islam do Old Testament and Judeo-Christian motifs continue to play an important role, especially in the conception of God.[83] As in Calvinism, the belief in providence perhaps initially provided a rational solution to the theoretical but not the practical problem of theodicy. As we saw, in Calvinism this was made possible by means of the idea of proof and its two-fold interpretation. What does the process of mutual "adjustment" look like in early Islam?

To determine Weber's answer to this question, one must risk conjecture. Nevertheless, Weber did provide indications of the direction in which the answer is to be sought. In the 1920 version of the *Protestant Ethic*, two passages are found that make positive reference to F. Ulrich's Heidelberg dissertation in theology. Moreover, in the systematic sociology of religion, a short comparison is made between Calvinist and Islamic predestination and their respective consequences.[84] These indications do provide an orientation, yielding a relatively clear picture once they are elaborated on.

Let us begin with Ulrich's dissertation. It starts by making two distinctions, between destination and predestination and between determination and predetermination. Which of these concepts is chosen to describe the religious foundations of belief is contingent on whether omnipotence and absolute dominion (*Allwirksamkeit*) (determination) or absolute goodness and mercy (destination) predominate and whether God's acts of will are consigned to primeval or prehistorical times (representing predetermination and predestination, respectively, in each of the two alternatives). The concepts of God in both Islam and Calvinism arise from similar sources: in both cases the accent tends to fall more on the God of the Old rather than the New Testament. In the Christian tradition, however, the God of the New Testament, of redemption and mercy, is never totally sacrificed to the God of the Old Testament, the omnipotent God. This holds even for Calvinism, whose concept of God is perhaps the closest of all religions within the Christian tradition to that of ancient Judaism and Islam. Weber too had already pointed to the tension in Calvinism's conception of God in the first version of the *Protestant Ethic*. It knew a double God, "the gracious and kindly Father of the New Testament . . . and behind him the *Deus absconditus* [the hidden God] as an arbitrary despot" of the Old Testament.[85]

Islam lacked this tension. God's most outstanding feature here is His omnipotence and, linked to it, His benevolence and bestowal of favor, not, however, His granting of a "sin-pardoning grace."[86] This whole realm of thought—encompassing as it does ideas such as original sin, life in its entirety beset by guilt, the incapability of being good, and saving grace—remained peripheral to Islam. Metaphysical, cosmological, and teleological interpretations of God's effectiveness, and not ethical and soteriological ones, occupy the foreground of this religion. In its worldview, cognitive components are generally given priority over evaluative ones. The relationship between faith and reason is much less problematic in Islam than in Christianity. Admittedly, Islam recognizes the ethical relation between God and man. It also recognizes sin and final judgment. But sin is not original sin and final judgment is not the site of a grace that pardons sins. No one is incapable of being good, and final judgment functions in a certain sense according to the principles of bookkeeping. The ethical relation, similar to that of Judaism, has a legal-moral orientation, with works being ultimately conceived of as the basis for salvation. Of course, whether one is saved or not is determined by God—"*God guides* whom he pleases," as one sura reads, but he guides those "who show themselves open to his revelations and adopt them in faith."[87] Those who do not do so, who are unrepentant and unmoved, take upon themselves guilt for which they are accountable. To err is the result of one's own activity, and God punishes this fault. But He does not punish without warning. Concepts such as error and offense, just punishment, and obedience on the basis of understanding, not those of (original) sin, saving grace, and love, are the focus of thought. It was apparently with these facts in mind that Weber wrote: "The ethical concept of salvation is actually alien to Islam. Its God is one of unlimited power but also of mercy, and the fulfillment of his commandments is certainly not beyond the powers of humans."[88]

Thus, the God of Islam is above all one of absolute power, whereas the God of Christianity is above all one of absolute benevolence and mercy. These different accents affect the belief in providence. In Islam, where it is one of the most important dogmas, according to Ulrich,[89] this belief undergoes a cosmological and teleological turn rather than a soteriological one; it tends more toward predetermination than toward a doctrine of predestination. But, more important, neither in the Sunna nor in the Koran is the doctrine developed consistently and conclusively. Instead, two lines of thought appear with little connection made between them: on the one hand, the absolute power of God that can also bring about evil, and on the other, the self-determination and responsibility of man for his own salvation. The theoretical development never reaches the conclusiveness and consistency of Calvinism. Weber views this similarly when he writes: "Islamic predestination knew nothing of the 'double decree'; it did not dare attribute to Allah the predestination of some people to hell, but only attributed to Him the withdrawal of His grace from some people, a belief that admitted man's inadequacy and thus His inevitable transgression."[90]

Thus, in Islam, as compared to Calvinism, the belief in providence not only has a deterministic bias, but it also never attains the same rational coherence as in the latter. Moreover, it is not linked to the idea of proof. The relationship of man to God is one of subject to lord, a relation of submission and of worship from a position of subordination. It provides support for faith in Allah and the prophets and for obedient adherence to divine law, but not for setting the proof of one's ethic of conviction in terms of overall conduct as the "central and constant quality of personality."[91] The contrasts between dutiful fulfillment of the law and its fulfillment out of a sense of duty, between fulfillment as the real foundation (Realgrund) and as the mere indication (Erkenntnisgrund) of grace appear to be the most important typological distinctions between the Islamic and the Calvinist religious ethics. They are rooted in the respective contents of their faiths. In spite of the Islamic providentialism, the basic beliefs did not contribute to the religious undergirding of innerworldly vocational calling. Thus, as in lay Catholicism or Lutheranism, though of course for other reasons,[92] no systematization of salvation by works emerges in Islam. Instead, it suffers, as do the others, from the constant threat of collapsing into an unsystematic and utilitarian salvation by works.

The matter could have rested there. However, Weber's analysis goes beyond an interpretation compatible with Ulrich's comparative remarks.[93] Weber is convinced that the belief in providence also had *special* consequences in Islam—consequences that one can conceptualize only by looking into the tensions precipitated by the doctrine and the practical "solutions" arising from them. The idea of predestination, as we have seen, is actually one of predetermination, and it is not linked to any idea of proof. This undoubtedly weakens the ethical character of the doctrine and lessens the compulsion to systematize life that is inherent in Calvinism. Nevertheless, even in this weakened form, it is able to bring about the "complete obliviousness to self in the fighter for the faith in his allegiance to the religious commandment of the holy war for the conquest of the world."[94] Why is this so?

Weber claims the following: in Islam, predestination, or better, predetermination, is ultimately related above all to one's fate not in the world beyond but in this world: "The prevailing conception was that predestination determined, not the fate of the individual in the world beyond, but rather his singular fate in this world, the question, for example (and above all), whether the warrior for the faith falls in battle or not."[95] In contrast, one's fate in the beyond is secured by observing the five pillars of faith: belief in Allah and the prophets, prayer five times daily, the month of fasting (Ramadan), the pilgrimage to Mecca, and the giving of alms (*tauhid, salat, sawm, zakat,* and *haj*). Not least because of the largely unconnected juxtaposition of deterministic and nondeterministic lines of thought in the Koran and the Sunna, but also because of the simplicity, even the parsimony of the early Islamic vision,[96] Muslims were not confronted with the problem of the certainty of salvation, of the *certitudo salutis,* to as radical a degree as were the Calvinists. The belief in providence did not produce the same measure of uncertainty and fear. Admittedly, fear of death is involved in both cases; however, in one case it is the fear of death in the face of the beyond, whereas in the other it is fear of death in the face of battle. In this context, deterministically interpreted providence—due to its fatalistic bias—is an interpretation that actually impedes rather than produces fear, for it provides the warrior for the faith the certainty that he will only experience that which Allah has predetermined for him. It is precisely this certainty about one's fate in the beyond that transforms the faithful Islamic warrior's fear of death into a proud, thisworldly spirit. It is this basic deterministic feature of the dogma that represents a motivational source of his invincibility and equips him with world-conquering military discipline.[97] In the later version of the *Protestant Ethic* Weber summarizes this first major thesis in a pointed fashion. He discovers that in Islam the fatalistic consequences of the belief in providence, which were never completely eradicated in Calvinism either, have actually come into force. He asks why and then responds:

Because the Islamic idea was that of predetermination, not predestination, and was applied to fate in this world, not in the next. In consequence the most important thing, the proof of the believer in predestination, played no part in Islam. Thus only the fearlessness of the warrior (as in the case of *moira* [personal destiny]) could result, but there were no consequences for the rationalization of life, for there was no religious reward for them.[98]

Thus, we find that in Islam religious interest "confiscates" religious doctrine in such a way that it brings forth logical consequences that the doctrine itself does not draw on its own. It is a kind of "practical entanglement of interests" that provides these consequences with both an active and a passive accent, so to speak. In no way does the doctrine lead to a renunciation of activity. What it does instead is to give fearlessness in war a religious foundation. Conversely, in those situations involving one's fate in the everyday life of this world and not extraordinary circumstances such as war, the "complete obliviousness to self" is repressed in favor of an unsystematic, utilitarian salvation of works or even in favor of "lightly fatalistic characteristics (*kismet*)."[99] This is for Weber, incidentally, also the reason why Islam (similar to most religions), despite its basically antimagical orientation, did not completely eradicate magic in the religiosity of the masses.[100] Hence, Weber presents an image both divided and cyclical of the psychological effects of the Islamic doctrine. In extraordinary situations it works to unify and discipline, whereas in everyday situations it loses this influence on conduct.[101]

Prerequisites for the "confiscation" of religious foundations for the sake of an innerworldly hero and warrior ethic were naturally also found in the doctrine: in the concept of the holy war (jihad) and in the division of the world into the house of Islam and the house of war (*dar al-Islam, dar al-Harb*). Another prerequisite also existed in the nonreligious legitimation interests of those strata that appropriated the doctrine. These interests, however, are only at the very beginning similar to those so important for Calvinism:

In the first Meccan period of Islam, the eschatological religion of Mohammed developed in pietistic urban conventicles which displayed a tendency to withdraw from the world. But in the subsequent developments in Medina and in the evolution of the early Islamic communities, the religion was transformed into a national Arabic warrior religion, and even above all into a status-oriented warrior religion. Those followers whose conversion to Islam made possible the decisive success of the Prophet were consistently members of powerful families.[102]

A warrior aristocracy with its feelings of knightly status has no sense for a worldview marked by concepts such as sin, humility, and redemption.[103] Moreover, a member is far removed from the

ideal of innerworldly vocational asceticism. At most he is capable
of developing "the asceticism of the military camp or of a martial
order of knights, not that of monks, and certainly not the bourgeois, ascetic systematization of conduct. Moreover, this ascetism
was truly predominant only periodically, and was always disposed
toward turning into fatalism."[104] The Sufism of the petty bourgeoisie was even further from developing inner-worldly asceticism. Instead, it moved along contemplative and mystical paths
and "under the leadership of plebeian technicians of orgiastics."[105]

Similar conceptions of God and doctrinal foundations are thus
found in Calvinism and Islam. Nevertheless, the psychological effects of these similar religious sources are radically distinct. They
make possible, on the one hand innerworldly vocational asceticism, and on the other self-sacrifice in extraordinary situations, a
heroism that disintegrates into thisworldly utilitarianism during
routinization, that is, in the transition from war to everyday life.
Calvinism increases the inner tension between salvational doctrine and salvational interest to an inhuman extent, and thus un-
leashes the motivation for constant world mastery; in contrast,
Islam does not involve believers in such unbearable tension.
Although it motivates them in this way to temporary world mastery as world conquest, it prevents, especially because of the marginal position of original sin and redemption, long-term world
rejection.[106]

For this reason, Islam also does not revolutionize economic
mentality. It remains feudal or petty bourgeois or booty capitalist.
As are all world religions, Islam is compatible with all forms of
traditional economic activity, including the politically oriented
mode of capitalism. But it does not provide a force to transform
life from within and thus to overcome the spirit of traditionalism
in economic or other areas of life. Despite its antimagical and activist tendencies, in spite of its intellectual rationalism, Islam
(along with Judaism, Catholicism, and Lutheranism) failed to
achieve that which ascetic Protestantism alone among all the
most important religions achieved, namely, the breeding of those
steely merchants and entrepreneurs who did not act as economic
supermen letting their acquisitional urge run free, but instead
tempered this urge rationally, compelling it to take the form of a
vocational duty, and in this way objectivated and objectified it.

Weber thus sees a double psychological effect of the Islamic religious ethic: it motivates its followers to world mastery, in the
sense of world conquest, but also to world adjustment. He also

discovers a cycle between these stances toward the world and the modes of conduct associated with them. It is a cycle that moves between extraordinary and everyday situations, between struggles of faith and "bourgeoisification."[107] Following Ibn Khaldun, others have diagnosed Islamic regimes in terms of a distinctive cycle of stability and instability on the basis of the cooperation and conflict between monocentric imperial politics and polycentric tribal politics, exacerbated by the cooperation and conflict between the ethical monotheism of high religion and the ritual polytheism of tribal religion.[108] What they apply to domination, Weber appears to espouse for the religiously conditioned mode of conduct in Islam. The fact that this cycle arises, that Islam in contrast to Calvinism does not cultivate "a systematic rational ordering of the moral life as a whole,"[109] means that, though it perhaps does not directly obstruct the "development of an *economically* rational mode of conduct,"[110] it certainly does not encourage it. There are, as we saw above, intrinsic reasons for this. The doctrinal foundations in their relation to the religious interests of the believers are decisive. They lead, in spite of a similar conception of God and a theory of predestination, to a result "divergent" from that of Calvinism. The often claimed "puritanism" of Islam is but superficially similar to Puritanism as Weber conceives it.

Although indispensable, the analysis of the internal relationship between the religious ethic and conduct is only the first step in working out the contrasts between the Islamic and Occidental civilizations in terms of their respective positions toward rational capitalism as an economic system. The investigation of the internal relations has to be followed by a study of the external ones, that is, by the study of the class-conditioned character of religion. This other aspect of the causal chain has already been touched upon in the context of the mutual "adjustment" between religious and nonreligious legitimation interests. The fact that Calvinism and with it all of ascetic Protestantism, and even beyond that, Christianity and Judaism, were specifically bourgeois religions (*bürgerliche Religionen*) from the very beginning and remained so, whereas Islam, like Asiatic religions, ultimately came into being as a religion of the ruling stratum (*Herrenreligion*), is of utmost importance here. However, the external relations encompass more than social stratification. They also involve orders and organizations. Whereas in the case of the concept of order the emphasis is on rules, in the case of the concept of organization it is on the administrative staff in charge of applying sanctions in order to enforce these rules.

Weber insists on the two aspects of the causal chain, because, in my view, he makes a claim for a double-sided relationship between motives and institutions. There is just as much an institutionally formative power of motives or interests as there is a motivationally formative power of institutions.[111] For this reason the analysis must proceed both from within toward without and from without toward within until that point is reached where the linkage between the two sides becomes visible. Every analysis that seeks to satisfy the premises of an interpretive sociology understood as a theory of action and order has to proceed in *both* ways in the analysis of those "historical individuals" selected and constituted by means of the theoretical value relation ("individuals" that can represent single persons or entire cultures).[112] Thus, "explanations" in Weber are never purely motivational or purely institutional. This insight, which in a methodological sense renders the contrast between materialism and idealism obsolete, is nothing new in Weber.[113] It marked the first version of the *Protestant Ethic* of 1904–5. This insight is seen not only in Weber's envisioned supplemented and extended project at the conclusion of this study or in his methodological foundation of cultural science of 1903–4; it is above all given witness to by the well-known closing lines of this historical study itself:

For although modern man is on the whole usually incapable, even with the best of will, of conceiving the true importance which religious beliefs have had for conduct, culture, and national character, it nevertheless cannot be our intention to substitute for a one-sidedly "materialist" interpretation an equally one-sidedly "spiritualist" interpretation. Both are equally possible, but both are of equally little service to the interests of historical truth if they claim to be not preliminaries to enquiry, but its conclusion.[114]

A nonreductionist approach can never derive the "spirit" from the "form" nor the "form" from the "spirit," even though there are certainly historical situations in which one of these "factors" loses its relative independence vis-à-vis the other. This, however, is not a methodological statement; it is a statement about a historical pattern, where the form "produces" the spirit or the spirit the form. It is therefore important to sharply distinguish two different cases: the case of a one-sided and the case of a mutually favorable relationship. Furthermore, there are also the relations of indifference and obstruction. Which of these relations holds is a historical question. In routinized long-term formations, one-sided relations are especially frequent. Here, as a rule, form produces its corresponding spirit, as is said of modern capitalism in its "iron age." Here, the relations sometime prevail that are generally postulated by naive historical materialists and Darwinists. But this approach is unsuitable for explaining the genesis of modern capitalism. Here, Weber argues, we are faced with a case of a mutually favorable relationship, of an elective affinity between a religio-ethically motivated conduct and the early capitalist institutions, which originated in European inland cities.

External relations do not exist only between religio-ethically generated motivation and economic or political institutions. They already exist within the religious sphere. In the *Protestant Ethic*, with special clarity in the later version, Weber draws attention to the independent importance of "church organization" (*Kirchenverfassung*)[115] vis-à-vis doctrinal foundations, devoting a separate essay, "The Protestant Sects and the Spirit of Capitalism" ("Die protestantischen Sekten und der Geist des Kapitalismus"), to this aspect.[116] Here the postulated two-sided relationship between motive and institution can be shown especially clearly. For psychological reasons, the doctrine of predestination and proof was joined to organization efforts "to separate regenerate from unregenerate Christians, those who were from those who were not prepared for the sacramental order of life."[117] This led to a system of external control imposed on the believer. It provided support for the idea of proof, by demanding from him "that he holds his own in the circle of his associates."[118] The psychological effect of this external control supporting the idea of proof could be so strong that the organization was able to replace the doctrine of predestination, that is, an important element of the internal relation in Calvinism.[119] This holds true for the Baptists mentioned earlier.

No such organizational force shaped Islam, according to Weber. Admittedly, a kind of hierocracy exists, centered on the Koran, the Sunna, and above all, the Shari'a, the divine law. A kind of priesthood also exists, if one understands by this a "bearer of the systematization and rationalization of religious ethics."[120] Nevertheless, these "priests" (*ulema*) are, like rabbis, not cultic priests; moreover, they are closer to legal scholars than to theologians. Above all, they are not the heads of a church in the Christian sense. The Islamic hierocracy is not a charismatic institution of grace, as was the medieval Catholic Church. Neither is it an instrument of discipline, as were the churches and sects of ascetic Protestantism. Although Islam, like the other world religions, distinguishes between religious virtuosi and the religious masses and between believers and nonbelievers, the former distinction is without salvational importance and the latter is linked to the stratification of status groups, with the "economic privileging" of the adherents of Islam.[121] Islamic religious organization also offers nothing that would work in the direction of ascetic proof in everyday life. Weber is even of the opinion that early Islam, despite its strict monotheism and its conception of a transcendent creator God, like Judaism "directly repudiated asceticism, whereas the unique character of Dervish religiosity stemmed from (mystic, ecstatic) sources quite different from the relation to a transcendent God and was intrinsically quite remote from Occidental asceticism."[122] Finally, one can add that the *umma*, the Islamic community, the "best community," as it was first realized in Medina, served—on the supralocal level, in its intermediary position between religion and politics, and between particularism and universalism—more to secure a certain degree of cultural unity in the face of growing internal differentiation than to comprehensively and effectively regulate all aspects of everyday life.

Even early Islam, by the time of its codification and canonization, was not left untouched by tensions and even conflicts between religion and politics. This was the case despite its pursuit of a kind of organic unity between religion and politics and in spite of the interconnecting of religious and political functions starting with Mohammed and continuing under the early caliphs. By the time of the Umayyads this conflict had erupted openly. The tension is apparently also reflected in the Shari'a. As Patricia Crone writes, "By the 750s . . . Islam had already acquired its classical shape as an all-embracing holy law characterized by a profound hostility to settled states."[123] From this point onward, at the latest, the accusation of worldliness is used as a weapon against political rulers. Admittedly, despite this conflict between religion and politics, a separation between political and hierocratic power was never effected as it was in the West. Nor did it ever come to a long-term strictly theocratic solution, much less to a purely caesaropapist solution, even though the tendency to theocracy, especially in Shiite Islam, always existed.

Internal and external conditions can thus always be one-sidedly or mutually favorable, indifferent, or obstructive. Such relations, however, can also exist solely among internal conditions (just as they can solely among external ones). The unifying force of the Calvinist religious ethic, so strongly emphasized by Weber, indeed consists in gathering the various internal relationships in which the believer is involved under one effective principle. On the basis of this "greatest possible systematic focusing of the ethic of conviction imaginable," religiously motivated action had effects on all areas of life.[124] What can be said about motives can also be said about institutions. They too are involved in one-sidedly or mutually favorable, indifferent, or obstructive relationships with one another. Especially in the later version of the sociology of domination, Weber treats not only the relationship of the political structure to economic mentality but also to economic structures. The question always raised there is which constellations of conditions were favorable for the rise and development of rational capitalism and which were not. Emerging and developing rational capitalism is dependent not only on intrinsic conditions but also on extrinsic ones. It can run into institutional resistance just as much as it can be obstructed by mentality. In this context political domination and law are particularly interesting. Naturally, they too have their internal aspects. But after having proceeded from within toward without, I will now proceed in the opposite direction.

Political Domination: Oriental Patrimonialism, the Oriental City, and Sacred Law

Oriental Patrimonialism and Occidental Feudalism

Islam arose from a twofold movement, both religious and political in character. Decisive in its emergence was the "novel" combination of these two components found here. Mohammed was both an ethical prophet and a charismatic politico-military leader. He overcame tribal particularism by surpassing its polytheism and ritualism with monotheism and a legal ethic, and by transforming feuding tribes into a national-Arabic movement of conquest. In contrast to the ancient Jewish prophets, and above all to Jesus, Mohammed was, from the moment of the Hegira of 622 onwards, not a marginalized prophet of doom, and certainly not a wandering charismatic preacher; instead, he was a religio-political leader who knew how to realize his intentions step by step, especially through the skillful use of the time-honored tribal practices of the creation and resolution of conflict. Presumably following Ignaz Goldziher and Julius Wellhausen, Weber makes a clear distinction between the first Meccan period and the time in Medina: with the departure from Mecca and the successful "reception" in Medina, the transformation of Islam from an eschatological religiosity into a political religion—into a religion of national-Arabic warriors—was inaugurated.[125]

The course of Mohammed's career—his initial failure in Mecca, his "departure" for Medina, his success there, his victorious return to Mecca, and the beginning of "world conquest"—has often been recounted. The images remain basically the same. In contrast to the research of the life of Jesus, research of the life of Mohammed is impeded not only by religious reservations but also by the state of available sources. Neither the application of the methods of criticism of biblical sources to Islamic sources, already initiated by Wellhausen, nor the application of formal biblical criticism to these sources, as carried out by Noth, have had results comparable to those for the Bible.[126] Carl Heinrich Becker once spoke of the "wild chaos of rampant religious growth and conflict"[127] in Islamic studies, while Patricia Crone speaks today of a sort of rubble heap lacking in characteristic structures.[128] This holds for the oral tradition, the Sunna. By comparison, the Koran stands as firm as bedrock. The picture of the Prophet results from both, but above all from the Sunna, which represents Mohammed's sayings and actions (*Hadith*). Their authorization rests not on their contents, but on the constructed genealogy of the transmitters of the tradition reaching back to the Prophet. This tradition was not merely oral, it was also characterized by an atomistic quality and rapid transformations. The individual sayings and actions were handed down nearly free of context, and were used as ammunition in the religious struggle. The Sunna is a compilation that reflects these conflicts. It is more the "theology" of its compilers and their "parties" than the history of Mohammed.

This open horizon toward the past was quickly closed, however. The rapid fixation of the constructed tradition corresponded to the destruction of the sources. In the frozen form of six collections, the tradition became monolithic. By the ninth century, the canon was already largely established and consecrated.[129] This situation satisfies dogmatic needs, but not historical ones. As Patricia Crone puts it: "There is of course no doubt that Muhammed lived in the 620s and 630s A.D., that he fought in wars, and that he had followers some of whose names are likely to have been preserved. But the precise when, what, and who, on which our interpretations stand and fall, bear all the marks of having been through the mill of rabbinic arguments and subsequently tidied up."[130]

Nevertheless, regardless how "theologically biased" the tradition might be, two presuppositions contained in Weber's statement appear to be historically "correct": that the transition from Mecca to Medina represents a decisive point in the course of Mohammed's life, and that his ethical prophecy is a decisive precondition of his political effectiveness. Subsequent to his "departure" Mohammed moved, as Wellhausen puts it, from preacher to ruler, but the model of rulership is not human kingship (*Mulk*), but rather the monarchical prophet of late Judaism:

The authority to rule is not a private possession for the usufruct of its holder. The realm belongs rather to God; his plenipotentiary, however, who knows and carries out His will, is the prophet. The prophet is not just the proclaimer of the truth, but also the sole rightful ruler on earth. Outside of him, there is place for no king, and no other prophet either: at any one time there is but one.[131]

The realization of this model necessitates the satisfaction of both external and internal preconditions. Let us first turn to the former. Medina offered an incomparably more favorable terrain than Mecca for Mohammed's pursuit of religio-political power. Mecca was at the Arabic religious, political, and economic center, a kind of city of the royal lineage, and in any case, firmly under the control of lineages skilled in imposing their will. They guaranteed the city's peace. It was a rich city whose profit was not unconnected to the host of religious festivities encouraged under polytheism and the trade fair linked to them. In these circumstances, Mohammed's radical monotheism must have appeared to be bad for business. The rejection of his message in Mecca was thus in part economically motivated. At the time of the Prophet's first appearance, Mecca found itself in neither a religious, political, nor economic crisis. A situation of inner and outer need that, according to Weber, opens the horizon for charismatic movements did not exist. In Medina, the situation was different. Jathrib, as it was called at the time of the Hegira, was a city on the margin, under Greco-Roman and Christian-Aramaic influence, with a strong Jewish community; from the Arabic point of view, it was, if not the periphery, at least the semiperiphery. The peace of the city had been laid low. Feuds between rival tribes predominated, in a situation similar to that of some southern European medieval cities. At the very least there was a political crisis situation with economic consequences, a situation of external need. It was a situation open to an arbitrator but also to an interpretation that—with the help of an order-giving "central power"—transcended the family and tribal particularism responsible for the strife.[132]

Mohammed, supported by the followers he had won in Mecca, mostly "friends, relatives, and slaves,"[133] established the umma in the place of the rule of families and tribes. Admittedly, he did this in accordance with the established pattern for arbitrating tribal feuds, in W. Montgomery Watt's words, as "the head of the clan of *Emigrants.*"[134] Nevertheless, the "community" took the place of relatives and tribe. Here, too, Jewish and Christian examples appear to have played a role. The transition to the "community" represented at the same time a transition to the peace of the land as the peace of God. Because there is only one God and all believe in Him, the law of the feud as defined by membership in lineage, tribe, or clan no longer retained validity among members of the community. Corresponding to the duty of internal peace is the duty of war. The duty of revenge in pre-Islamic law was no longer incumbent upon one "brother for another, but upon one believer for another." As Wellhausen observes, war becomes a military operation.[135] In addition, it becomes a holy war.

However, the communitarian principle did not totally replace the tribal principle. Associations, not individuals, joined the umma. Similar to the ancient polis, the gentes association lost significance in relation to the "cultic" and military association, but kinship (sib) solidarity was not completely broken. As Weber puts it in view of later development, "Islam . . . never really overcame the divisiveness of Arab tribal and clan ties, as is shown by the history of internal conflicts of the early caliphate; in its early period it remained the religion of a conquering army of tribes and clans."[136] Admittedly, just on the basis of this radical monotheism and the strict otherworldliness of the universal God, there was no possibility of distinct "cults of the gentes" existing in subordination to the "community," as they did in the ancient polis. Pre-Islamic Arab polytheism was consistently eliminated. But neither is the umma an oath-bound brotherhood in the pattern of Christian medieval urban communities. This was ever less the case the farther the Islamic religious and military association went beyond the city limits of Medina.

The umma did not initially exclude all outside it and treat all equally within it in the sense of radically excluding all heathens, Jews, or members of certain status groups. Even after the rise of Mohammed in Medina, the old relations, now pacified, remained largely the same. Similar to the Jewish communities at the time of Christ, the Medina umma was apparently also acquainted with different degrees of membership, probably a reflection of the ancient Arabic distinction between those with full rights ("first-class citizens") and co-inhabitants ("second-class citizens" [Beisassen]),[137] and more generally, a reflection of the way in which guest tribes became incorporated in larger organization throughout the ancient Orient. But Mohammed's relationship to the Jewish community in Medina changed dramatically when he realized that they did not recognize his claim to messianic prophecy. Only thereafter did he turn away from and indeed militate against Judaism. It is likely that changes in the direction of prayer, from Jerusalem toward Mecca, along with other symbolic acts, are connected to this.[138] Regardless of the actual historical facts of the situation, this shows a process of autonomization and the creation of identity on the symbolic level vis-à-vis the other two monotheistic and ethical religions of revelation, redemption, and the book, whose superiority over Arabic polytheism and ritualism obviously deeply impressed Mohammed. It also shows an important step along the road toward an Arabization of monotheism, toward defining the new doctrine as a "national-Arabic" religion.[139]

The mission of Islam that Mohammed began to develop in Mecca and that made it possible for him to create a new form of war and peace grew out of the tension caused by the cultural chasm separating the world of the Jewish and Christian transcendental and universal God and the world of the Arabic functional and local gods with their commercialized cultic sites and sacredmundane festivities. Arab gods had permanent places of worship if for no other reason than that immense stones were usually part and parcel of their arrangement. As Wellhausen put it, as a rule, Arabic tribes wandered but their shrines did not. Along with stones, trees and water were also objects of worship at the cultic sites. The stone served as the sacrificial altar and as the representation of divinity. Originally, cults were probably without images—images being a secondary development.[140] As I mentioned earlier, the place of worship served both functional and local gods and as a commercial center. Some of these were places of pilgrimage and in this way additionally economically privileged. Mecca also possessed such a place of worship of "nationwide" importance, the Ka'ba. As a Meccan, Mohammed was perfectly well acquainted with it.[141] He established his doctrine around it and not around unknown or newly invented shrines. Here he also formed a link with ancient Arab traditions. These he transformed in the light of monotheism by means of the cleansing, standardization, and centralization of heathen rituals. Functional and local gods were done away with, and the various places of worship were organized in terms of the Ka'ba—made, so to speak, into branches of it.[142]

Mohammed thus related two already existing "worlds": the world of ancient Arab tradition and the world of monotheism, one connected to nomadic and urban tribal particularism, the other, to world empires, or at least to the prospect of a world empire, ruled by a powerful universal God by means of his instrument on earth. Without a doubt Mohammed is an Arabic prophet from the very beginning. The language of revelation is Arabic, the translation of the Koran into other languages being frowned upon even today. Mohammed sought to overcome Arabic particularism. Initially, however, he intended to do this in conjunction with rather than in opposition to Judaism and Christianity. They served him as "reference religions."[143] Even though he apparently was not well acquainted with them, they appeared to offer him a way out of the "regulated anarchy" of Arabic conditions. Thus, he probably originally understood himself not as a prophet superior to Moses and Jesus, but as one equal to them.[144] In Medina, this all changed. With the turn against Judaism as well as Christianity, in symbol and in fact, Islam was no longer placed in the Judeo-Christian tradition but above it, at the same time taking a place in the overall context of the Arabic history of religion that now began with Abraham's establishment of religion at the Ka'ba.[145]

The doctrine of a transcendental, omnipotent, universal God must have appeared as an alien element in the ancient Arabic conceptual universe. It signified a radical break. To legitimize his message, Mohammed was unable to cite Arabic traditions, not even in the sense that pre-exilic Jewish prophets could in reminding the people of the commitment they had taken upon themselves, and thus of something that was part of their past. Mohammed was left with only the break with tradition and the charismatic legitimation of his new mission. What is reported of the times gives indications confirming this. They fit Weber's specifications of charismatic leadership: the conversion experience; "rebirth" in a situation close to "bourgeois satiety," and, at around forty years of age, the pathological states and stances that are then rationally worked through; the break with Mecca; and finally, the proof of supernatural powers in the battle of Badr. Yet, what we have here is a rather moderate form of charisma. There is no radical break with the family ties and economic life. In this way, too, Mohammed, in comparison to Jesus, represents an intermediate position. Although he transforms the old into the new, he does not completely break with the old. Instead, the latter is "raised in value": "monotheism with a tribal face."[146]

Mohammed died after he had conquered Mecca and largely unified Arabia. His fortunes in war were admittedly mixed after Badr, and apostasy, the *ridda*, already arose during his lifetime. However, as in all forms of charismatic leadership the greatest obstacle it left behind was the unresolved question of succession. The search for a solution split Islam into the Sunni and Shiite movements and traditionalized it quickly under the rule of Sunniism, which remained predominant outside of Persia. As Weber observed:

> The structure of Islam has been decisively affected by the fact that Mohammed died without male heirs and that his followers did not found the Caliphate on hereditary charisma, and indeed during the Omayyad period developed it in an outright anti-theocratic manner. It is largely owing to such differences about the ruler's qualification that Shiism, which recognizes the hereditary charisma of Ali's family and hence accepts the infallible doctrinal authority of an imam, is so antagonistic to orthodox Sunna, which is based on tradition and *idshma* (*consensus ecclesiae*).[147]

The earlier caliphate, in which the leaders were recruited from the circle of Mohammed's followers—from the circle of "disciples"— still kept the religious and the politico-military function unified. It employed the Arabic tribes, largely unified under Mohammed, for the purpose of world conquest. In this way, the "urban rule" in Medina developed in less than thirty years into a territorial rule of considerable scope (Syria, Iraq, Mesopotamia, Egypt, and Iran). Under the rule of the Umayyads, further areas were added (Carthage, the Indus Valley, Spain).

The incredible thrust of this movement was tied to the interconnection of politics and religion. The battle for God brings both paradise in heaven and booty on earth. Allah in his power to control and move all, in his transcendence, is suitable as the God of war of battle-experienced nomads. Thus, in a holy war the dissemination of doctrine is tied from the very beginning to the subjection and economic exploitation of unbelievers. The ideal and material interests of the holy warriors are so intimately connected that religious ends merge with politico-economic ones. Interestingly enough, this has a moderating influence. One would expect from a basically universalist ethical salvation religion, which Islam in fact represents—in conjunction with Judaism and Christianity and in contrast to the remaining major religions, that a holy war would serve either to force unbelievers to convert or to eradicate them. This certainly was a consequence of certain versions of the vision of the Christian Crusades, a consequence that did not, according to Weber, occur in Islam. The "elevation" of the believers through the "subjugation of the unbelievers to [their] political authority and economic domination [via taxation]" suffices.[148] In the interest of this "elevation," which naturally has primarily politico-economic effects, the protection of the subjugated is even required. In this manner, political and economic interests push themselves ever more into the foreground in the battle on behalf of the faith. At stake is not converting or missionizing the unbelievers, and certainly not saving their souls; what is involved are revenues, and in this way religion becomes a defining characteristic of status group stratification.[149] This led, however, to the ethical and salvational aspects receding in the face of its political aspects: "Those religious elements of ancient Islam which had the character of an ethical religion of salvation largely receded into the background as long as Islam remained essentially a religion of warriors."[150]

Along with the areas where they resided, unbelievers had not only to be conquered but also administered. The farther the area of domination expanded, the greater number of peoples brought under the rule of Allah, and the more poignantly was Islam confronted with the basic organizational problem of charismatically and traditionally legitimated authority: the problem of centralization and decentralization.[151] This universal problem of traditional configurations of order was only intensified in this particular case inasmuch as Allah's elite troops were originally tribes of nomadic tenders of herds, who, unlike settled peasants, for example, were not accustomed to a continuous territorial power to which they were to submit. They did not easily accept the constraints of this system, even as its rulers. The problem of religious, and above all, political unity, had to be resolved, however. This required both institutional differentiation and the establishment of military and

civilian administrative staffs, without which a central power cannot successfully rule over large geographical areas.

The institutional differentiation involves above all the relative
autonomization of religious and political functions, of hierocratic
and political powers, and the separation of powers between and
within them. The establishment of administrative staffs primarily
involves the military troops and the organization of officials, both
in structure and in spirit. According to Weber, the Arab, tribally
organized, theocratic levy had already dissolved in the ninth century the "'booty-happy' religious zeal [that] had carried the great
conquests."[152] The caliphate, too, separated itself from the sultanate under the Abbasids in a kind of division of labor between spiritual and worldly tasks, both admittedly—at least according to the
intent of the canon taking shape—subject to a single religious law.
In comparison with the situation in Medina and then under the
early caliphates, however, this represents a new structural constellation. We must turn to this constellation if we want to fully
understand the relationship of the "Islamic Orient" and the "Islamic states" to rational capitalism—a relationship that was not
merely unfavorable, but rather one of obstruction and resistance.[153]

Weber employs different terms to characterize this new constellation in relation to political domination: "arbitrary patrimonialism," "sultanism," "prebendal feudalism," and even "free prebendal feudalism."[154] This is initially surprising insofar as in
arbitrary patrimonialism (under which sultanism can be classified) the lord has a wide realm of discretionary powers, and thus
his powers are hardly stereotyped. In contrast, feudalism represents "a marginal case of patrimonialism" because the stereotyping of relations of domination is relatively far advanced.[155] For this
reason, a developed feudal system is "at least an approximation of
a *Rechtsstaat*."[156] It thus limits the ruler's discretion (*Eigenrecht
der Herrenmacht*) through a regulated division of authority (*Her-
rengewalten*). Such a "rule of law" is of course not based on an
objective legal order, but on "subjective" rights, on privileges. It
protects the rights of individuals and, in certain circumstances,
those of associations (as a kind of *Ständestaat*) as well as the resulting mode of distribution. By contrast, in patrimonialism the
individual right of the ruler is increased vis-à-vis other sources of
power, and the more arbitrary political domination, the greater
the discretion of the ruler. This individual right is a "right to intervene" that does not spare the vested rights of others and the
associated mode of distribution. Again, the more arbitrary the pat-

rimonial formation, the more they are compromised. What patrimonialism and feudalism do share is the necessity for the central power to come to terms with the other powers. Both are territorial forms of domination that have to regulate relations of domination, in nonpatrimonial as well as patrimonial domains. They are distinguished by *how* they regulate these relations. It thus logically follows that a formation cannot be both sultanistic and feudalistic at the same time.

Now this terminological indeterminacy could simply be the result of the history of *Economy and Society*. We know that Weber wrote two versions of the sociology of domination, and that although the second one built upon the first, it was more stringently formulated and more conceptually precise. In the latter version, the Islamic Near East and the Mughal empire are classified under fiscally conditioned prebendal feudalism, not under sultanism. The latter is also described, as in the original version, in conjunction with the greatest possible power of the ruler in patrimonialism; however, it is but briefly described and characterized as a marginal and historically fairly improbable phenomenon.[157] There could also be substantive reasons for the terminological indecisiveness. Islamic state formations were perhaps both sultanistic and prebendal-feudal, depending on the object of one's attention.

In the first version of the sociology of domination (and thus in that text which, as part of "The Economy and the Societal Orders and Powers," most directly reflects his study of Islam) Weber treats Islamic feudalism in comparison with its Occidental counterpart. Once again his aim is to show that Western medieval feudalism represents a special historical case that is one of the general cultural prerequisites for the rise and development of rational capitalism. The comparison encompasses equally form and spirit, structure and ethic. Let us go briefly through this comparison.

A general consideration is helpful here. The feudal relation has in fact a highly stereotyped and legalized form in comparison to the purely patrimonial relation. In typological terms, it is both patrimonial and charismatic in origin. The patrimonial origin is connected to two facts: a ruling power requires an administrative staff in order to militarily defend and administer a territory, and this administrative staff can appropriate political rights of rule and economic opportunities, and thus take possession of military and administrative means. The administrative staff develops an autonomy (*Eigenrecht*) that it secures economically: the *beneficium*. The charismatic origin is tied to the fact that the lord is a war hero who gathers around himself followers who believe in his heroism. It is a relation of nonmaterial, purely ideal devotion. Even if this relation becomes routinized, it maintains its ideal character. A specific relation of loyalty arises between the lord and his administrative staff: one of *homagium*. In the feudal relation, both of these components, the material and the ideal, the beneficium and the homagium, become interconnected, and in such a way that "a revenue-based right to rule" is "exchanged" for a personal commitment of loyalty. This occurs by way of a contract that, strictly speaking, presupposes "free" contractual parties. A fiefholder is not a patrimonial subject, he is a freeman. On the basis of such contractual relationships—"a *revenue-bearing* complex of rights the possession of which [makes possible] a *lordly* existence" in exchange for personal fealty, especially in war—a complex system can develop, a hierarchy of fiefs with intermediary strata. This is particularly the case where such a system spans large territories. More important, though, the feudal formation has, in addition to its economic, material, and "patrimonial" character, an ideal, ethical, and "charismatic" side. The authority relation (*Herrschaftsbeziehung*) is regulated by a "very demanding code of duties and honor"—by means of a specific mentality and a corresponding mode of conduct, more specifically, by means of a chivalrous mode of conduct.[158]

There are thus internal and external aspects to the feudal relation. It requires a special ethic, a feudal ethic, centered on the concepts of fealty and honor. It is important to make clear that this ethic was more than one of filial piety. The appeal "to honor and personal fealty, freely assumed and maintained" is constitutive for the mode of conduct associated with these virtues.[159] This is connected to a specific feeling of dignity and the "permeation of the most important relationships of life with very personal bonds."[160] Weber points out the educational significance of the game for this chivalrous mode of conduct and the affinity that exists between it and an artistic mode.[161] Even a patrimonial relation—for example, in the form of a prebendal relation—has its "inner" aspect, its "ethic." It, too, is built upon the idea of loyalty. However, "filial piety," the model of which is provided by the authoritarian relationship between father and child, differs from vassal fealty. Even though the former can also be status group–oriented, emphasizing "being" over "function," it nevertheless lacks that basic aristocratic trait of vassal fealty that is born in the playful shaping of a heroically oriented life. It also lacks the legal structure upon which the feudal relation is ultimately based: the "free" contract.

A formation of patrimonial domination can thus undergo both prebendal and feudal modifications. Which kind of modification is involved is solely a legal and ethical question, not an economic one. In both cases, patrimonialism becomes *ständisch*, with powers being divided through the appropriation of rights of rule and economic opportunities by the administrative staffs. The staffs are no longer separable from the material means of administration, whether they be military or civilian in nature. This aspect is crucial for the clarification of the structural question. As we know, in this way Weber applies Marx's thesis on the centrality of the relation to the means of production to all areas of life and to all periods in history. Now the division of lordly power and the limitation of the discretion (*Eigenrecht*) associated with it serves the purpose of maintaining the undivided domain of domination, the unity of the empire. This unity is constantly threatened by the manner in which this goal is to be reached. The relatively autonomous regional powers can become opposing powers. This potential forces the central authority to take countermeasures that aim at eliminating or at least "taming" the independence of the administrative staffs, which portends, however, the expansion (or at least the "protection") of the autonomous rights of the central authority and thus the return to patrimonialism, the extreme form of which is sultanism.

According to Weber, in a typological sense, the West came to terms with this central problem of all traditional political formations in three steps: with the help of fief-based feudalism, with the help of the *Ständestaat* that represents a kind of corporate form of fief-based feudalism, and with the help of a rational bureaucratic patrimonial state that arose out of the *Ständestaat*. All these formations were characterized by rule of law (*Rechtsstaatlichkeit*), which admittedly reached full maturity only in the modern *Anstaltsstaat*. The idea of contract is joined by that of the *Anstalt* to form the core of this "rule of law." The notion of the *Anstalt* was never limited to the sphere of political territorial power, but also included the hierocratic power, the church, and the urban powers. An important aspect of Occidental political development thus involves the fact that here corporate territorial bodies arose, in part autonomously and in part out of fief-based feudalism, which came into fierce conflict with one another because each stood on its own feet. This conflict promoted decentralization and structural pluralism and made possible a hierarchy of legal and de facto autonomous units. In this way, the center of power gravitated, so to speak, toward the intermediate level, supported by a strong tendency to subject the internal and external relations of domination to the constraints of law.[162] This represents a relatively early tendency toward a rational constitution (*Satzung*), not least of all because the West was already acquainted in the Middle Ages both with a clear division—as compared to other legal systems—between sacred (canonic) and profane (Roman and Germanic) law and with a relatively formal sacred law. Ever since the Investiture Struggle, this legal demarcation between church and "state" received, moreover, support from political motives.[163]

Thus, since the Middle Ages, the West has basically ceased to employ patrimonial, much less sultanistic, strategies in coming to terms with the "problem of unity." Instead, its strategy aimed at a *ständisch* division of powers among structurally heterogenous units and their legal fixation by means of statutes. If one views the Islamic state formations in this regard, two institutions above all stand out: the army of purchased slaves and the fiscally conditioned military prebendalism. Both are connected to the "warrior" origin of the Islamic movement. In Weber's view, the Islamic state formations are first of all "military states," for the structural characterization of which the analysis of the military organization is especially important.

"Slaves on horses" as a system is apparently peculiar to Islamic state formations.[164] Of course, and this must be equally emphasized, there is no religious foundation for this system in Islam.[165] But as we shall see momentarily, it helps to understand why these states posed structural obstacles to any form of rational capitalism.

The system of "slaves on horses" appears to have already arisen in the early ninth century.[166] In any case it defined the structure of political domination at the time of the Abbasids. As Weber observes: "The Abbasids bought and militarily trained Turkish slaves who, as tribal aliens, appeared wholly tied to the ruler's domination; thus the dynasty became independent of the national levy and its loose peacetime discipline and created a disciplined army."[167] The national levy was the levy of Arab tribes that had succeeded at Islamic world conquest. The holy warriors, marked in part by the religious ethic, had proved themselves as heroes through the conquest of ever new areas and peoples. However, with the pacification of the realm, the time was over for both discipline and tribal cooperation. The tribes became—in the transition from the extraordinary situation of war to the everyday situation of peace—subject to the cyclic movement between readiness to self-oblivious sacrifice and bourgeoisification. For this reason they were not a suitable administrative staff for securing the central power's domination of the empire. By creating a troop of purchased slaves out of tribal aliens, the central power crafted itself an instrument that freed it from dependency on the tribes and, above all, from the maelstrom of their centrifugal, anticentralistic tendencies. The administrative staff was recruited nonpatrimonially, and employed patrimonially, indeed, sultanistically. This did not prevent the dissolution of the empire, which had already occurred under the Abbasids in the ninth century. What the military slave system did provide, however, was a powerful instrument for reestablishing imperial unity after periods of breakdown into regional empires. Admittedly, this came about because Islam as a religion held alive the idea of unity: "The religious unity of the caliphate did not prevent the disintegration of the purely secular sultanate, a creation of the slave generals, into sub-empires. But the unity of the well-disciplined slave armies in turn favored the indivisibility of these sub-empires once they were established; partly for that reason hereditary division never became customary in the Islamic Orient."[168]

A large slave troop, nonpatrimonially recruited and sultanistically employed, and for this reason necessarily freed from all forms of civilian labor, cannot be provisioned by the royal household. Other arrangements have to be made. In this context, Carl Heinrich Becker put forth the thesis (in an essay that apparently deeply impressed Weber) that Oriental feudalism, the decisive development of which he placed in the time of the Crusades, arose out of tax farming. The slave generals increasingly functioned as tax collectors on their own behalf. In addition to payment for their military service they were originally provided with taxable units for which they acted as tax guarantors vis-à-vis the central authority. In exchange for the discontinuation of the service payments and in addition to the entrepreneurial profits made in tax collection, they came to appropriate the taxes for themselves. The fact of monetary payment was connected to the relatively highly developed monetary economy. In contrast, Occidental feudalism was initially based on a natural economy.[169] Weber adopts this idea but immediately links it to another: "The extraordinary legal insecurity of the taxpaying population in the face of the arbitrariness of the troops to whom their tax capacity was mortgaged could paralyze commerce and hence the money economy; indeed, since the period of the Seljuks the Oriental economy declined or stagnated to a very great extent because of these circumstances."[170]

Thus the two institutions, the military slave system and the military fief for fiscal purposes, extended the realm of arbitrary discretion, in comparison to Western fief-based feudalism. That realm lessened the calculability of the administrative process. According to Weber this had an interesting economic consequence: the artificial immobilization of wealth, especially by means of pious foundations (*wakfs*), in order to evade arbitrary seizure by patrimonial authorities. Once again following Becker, Weber views the transfer of wealth into the restrictiveness of the *wakfs* as a reaction against the unpredictability of patrimonial domination that was conducive to an "increase of the realm bound by sacred law."[171] This transfer could also keep wealth from possibly being used for capitalist purposes. Weber views the function of the *wakfs* as similar to that of the "entailed estate" (*fidei commissum*). Support of the latter, especially in Prussia, had provoked his opposition in the strongest terms possible due to its "anticapitalistic consequences."[172]

However, the military fief for financial purposes is not a fief, strictly speaking. Even Becker had already pointed out that what is given here is a *beneficium* but not a *feudum* because *homagium*, vassalage, is lacking. Originally, the granting of the beneficium was not linked to military service in any way. The military, according to Becker, had forced itself "improperly and after the fact into the existing system of benefices."[173] This basic pattern is seen in ethics and in the mode of conduct attendant to it. This "base" ultimately does not permit a feudal ethic with a chivalrous mode of conduct, as Western feudalism does. Only in phases of religious war does a knighthood of the faithful emerge that approximates Occidental knighthood but without the game-like character of the latter. As Weber points out: "In the age of the Crusades, Oriental prebendal feudalism sustained a sense of knightly status, but on the whole its character remained defined by the patriarchal character of domination."[174]

Weber thus identifies three points of comparison between Oriental, especially Islamic, prebendal feudalism, and Occidental feudalism that turn out to represent three points of contrast: the economic foundation of military organization, its social carriers, and the ethic encompassing this structure. In terms of the economic foundation, prebends that were originally usurped stand in contrast to fiefs that were originally contracted. The prebends are utilized solely for fiscal purposes; of interest are strictly the taxes, more precisely, the monetary taxes, and not the land. The predominance of this monetary orientation is possible only because of a monetary economy that is more developed in comparison to that of the West. Becker points out that there was an intensive development of limited partnership and cooperatives and that checks and bills of exchange were used for fiscal and economic purposes.[175] In terms of the social carriers, purchased slaves stand in contrast to freemen. The army of purchased slaves is a disciplined mass army, the feudal army one of knights geared toward individual heroic battle. The army of purchased slaves tends to sustain plebeian traits; the knightly army, aristocratic ones. Admittedly, even the slave troops—if sufficiently pervaded by the conceptual universe of Islam—can become an army of "noble warriors of the faith."[176] Nevertheless, a difference remains in terms of the third point of contrast, the ethic and respective mode of conduct. Here, what is ultimately an ethic of submissive piety stands in contrast to a feudal ethic. Oriental feudalism is not a feudalism of fealty, as are its Occidental (and Japanese) counterparts. In Weber's comparative typology, Oriental feudalism lacks fealty, Japanese feudalism lacks a patrimonial foundation, and only Occidental feudalism combines both—and this is what defines its singular historical character.[177]

Thus, Oriental feudalism is less "typified" than is its Occidental counterpart. It is also less decentralized. It is furthermore lacking the idea of contract in the Western sense and the concept of the *Anstalt*. The combination of the two is important for the development of Occidental feudalism into the *Ständestaat*. This leads to differences in the manner of, and especially the predictability of administrative action. One could ask, however, Are these differences so decisive in answering the questions whether and in what way the form and spirit of political domination influence the developmental prospects for rational capitalism? Is it not in fact the case, moreover, that regardless of whether there is more or less arbitrary patrimonialism, prebendal or fief-based feudalism, do they not all deprive industrial capitalism of a breeding ground? For what is at stake are the developmental prospects for productive capital, not those for commercial capital. The formation of the latter, as Weber repeatedly emphasizes, "is feasible under almost all conditions of domination, especially under patrimonialism."[178] The commercial enterprise repeatedly arises under the conditions of traditional political domination in varying frequencies. At issue, however, is not commercial capital or some subsidiary modes of market production, but the capitalist economy as a system. At stake are the developmental prospects for a new structural principle: the meeting of everyday needs on the basis of industrial capitalism.[179] It involves the replacement of the principle of the household through the market principle, the replacement of a power amenable to tradition with one thoroughly antagonistic to it.[180]

Indeed, it would be a mistake in my opinion to take Weber's comparative analysis as a direct explanation of the external aspects that favored rational capitalism in the West. Within a traditional framework, administration, taxation, and as we will see, the administration of justice are nowhere so organized as to fully offer the predictability of governmental action so indispensable for the formation and utilization of industrial capital. The feudal ethic, so highly developed in the West compared to in the Islamic Orient, can, like all status group–oriented ethics, be considered an anticapitalist force par excellence. Nothing is so distant from capitalist business morals, from a vocational ethic defined in terms of functions performed, as a heroic ethic that is deeply hostile to all means-ends rationality.[181] Of course, the form and spirit of traditional political domination can be so constituted that they develop toward the predictability of governmental action when additional conditions are met. This, however, was the case only in the West and not in the Islamic Orient. In my view, we have here Weber's second thesis.

Occidental feudalism contains within it, for example, two of the elements that "permit further development" but are missing in Oriental prebendal feudalism: the decentralization of political domination by means of a feudal hierarchy, which is a form of estate-type division of powers that, through compromise, makes possible a predictable distribution of burdens;[182] and the feudal contract. Both were influential in the further political development of the Occident. Otherwise, however, in its relation to rational capitalism, Occidental feudalism is not different from traditional political domination in general. The latter favors politically oriented, not economically oriented capitalism. In a refinement of the first version, Weber provided a particularly concise formulation for the exception to this rule in the later version of the sociology of domination:

The situation is fundamentally different only in cases where a patrimonial ruler, in the interest of his own power and financial provision, develops a rational system of administration with technically specialized officials. For this to happen, it is necessary (1) that technical training should be available; (2) that there is a sufficiently powerful incentive to embark on such a policy—usually the sharp competition between a plurality of patrimonial powers within the same cultural area; (3) that a very special factor is present, namely, the participation of urban communes as a financial support in the competition of the patrimonial units.[183]

One way to summarize our analysis of external conditions is to say that in Islam the second aspect cited in the quote is but weakly developed. In Islamic civilization the political cycle of unification and disintegration does exist, but neither the continuous conflict between relatively independent territorial units nor the sharp competition of several powers within the framework of a *ständisch* division of powers, with a legal superstructure as in the West, does. This holds both for the relationship between the lord and his administrative staffs and for that between political hierocratic domination. Despite tendencies toward autonomy that are also intrinsic to prebendal feudalism, the former relationship is centralistic in the Islamic Orient, thus lessening competition; the latter relationship is conflict-ridden, but Islam lacks the church as a bureaucratic apparatus of power.[184] The first and third aspects from the quote, however, direct attention to further potential points of differences. These will be my last subjects.

Oriental and Occidental Cities

Let us begin with the third point from the passage quoted earlier, the role of urban communal organizations. Weber proceeds in the same way in the case of the city as he did in the case of feudalism. He makes a typological comparison between the Occidental city—or more precisely, the medieval, northern European, continental, city—and the Oriental city. Interestingly enough, Mecca at the time of Mohammed and thereafter serves him as an example of the latter.[185] It is not possible for me to give a full account of Weber's comparative analysis of the city here—an analysis that is of central importance in his explanation of the rise and development of rational capitalism in the West.[186] I will cite only those ideas important in our context. The first question involves Weber's claim that the Oriental city tends to obstruct rather than favor the developmental prospects of rational capitalism, even though it also possesses the following characteristics: it is generally the site of markets attracting trade and craft; it accommodates merchant and artisan guilds with autonomous "statutes"; it has a city patron or lord, and its pattern of social stratification diverges from that of nonurban regions; and it possesses, especially under

Islamic influence, religious associations to which religious inhabitants belong independently of their social position.

Weber classifies cities in part according to which social stratum rules in them (the patrician or princely city versus the plebeian city); which economic functions they primarily fulfill (the consumer or rentier city versus the producer city—or city of trade and industry); how they are geographically situated, and connected to this, which ways and means of transportation they favor (maritime versus inland cities); and which primary orientation they possess (the politically oriented versus the economically oriented city). Thus, many cities of Occidental antiquity are patrician, consumer, maritime, and politically oriented cities; in contrast, many medieval Occidental cities are plebeian, producer, inland, and economically oriented cities. One could also classify the Oriental city in this way. It would then more closely approximate the city of Occidental antiquity than that of the Western Middle Ages. But one can quickly see that this procedure does not lead very far. Weber makes his comparison on a more sophisticated basis.

First of all, Weber strictly distinguishes the economic concept of the city from the politico-administrative and legal one; these are two different things.[187] Moreover, in purely economic terms it is sometimes difficult to distinguish cleanly between city (or town) and village. Both can be the sites where traders and businessmen settle; both can possess a market for meeting everyday needs; both can act as landowning economic associations, as economic units with revenues and expenses, and as associations regulating the economy. But even in terms of politico-administrative criteria, the distinction is not always easy to make. Villages, like cities, can possess their own territory, their own authorities, or even their own fortress, or they can belong to a fortress with garrison; moreover, both a village (always) and a city (usually) are part of a greater political association. There is one thing that villages have not developed, however: political, administrative, military, and legal autonomy and autocephaly. Admittedly, not all cities did this either. A city with fully developed autonomy and autocephaly is a special historical case. The one that especially interests Weber is found in the Occidental Middle Ages and represents but a "historical interlude."[188] One sees that here, too, he unfolds his comparative analysis from the special Occidental case, which then furnishes him with points of comparison with which he can analyze Islamic cities.

Urban autonomy and autocephaly are by themselves characterizations without specific contents. Both hold for some of the ancient poleis, especially for those that were the starting point for "great power formations."[189] Thus, it is not autonomy and autocephaly as such that are important but the manner in which they are legitimated and organized—in short, the structural principle on which they are based. In these terms the city that preoccupies Weber is the corporate urban commune. The invention and realization of this structural principle was a *"revolutionary* innovation which differentiated the medieval Oriental cities from all others."[190] This structural principle breaks with the prebendally or feudally appropriated manorial, ecclesiastical, and urban powers. Because of this usurpatory aspect of medieval Occidental urban development, Weber entitled his analysis of the city "Nonlegitimate Domination: A Typology of Cities" ("Die nichtlegitime Herschaft. Typologie der Städte") in his manuscript "The Economy and the Societal Orders and Powers." This is not to be understood as if urban domination in general and that of the medieval West in particular is always nonlegitimate domination. What this title actually refers to is this: Weber's comparative analysis of the city is organized around the particular Occidental case. Here and only here did this new structural principle make a breakthrough of historical consequence. Only infrequently did this breakthrough involve a consciously illegitimate and revolutionary act.[191] In the majority of cases, usurpation occurred gradually or not at all. Above all, most cities arose out of completely different conditions. The usurpation theory is not a theory of the genesis of the medieval city. In addition, only a few medieval cities were able to attain complete autonomy, and those that succeeded were soon once again subject to restrictions. The interlude was sufficient, however, to create three important historical "prerequisites" for later capitalist development: the democratic principle of legitimation; the organizational principle of the corporate urban commune; and the market-oriented bourgeoisie.[192]

Thus, in Weber's view the medieval city is a "special developmental case." This becomes comprehensible only if one focuses on "the general position of the city within the framework of the medieval political and status-group organizations."[193] As important as the economic aspect is, analysis must not be restricted to it alone. Instead, it must also take into account the aspect of politics and domination, subdivided into form and spirit. It is not by chance that Weber subsumes the comparative analysis of the city under the sociology of domination and not the sociology of the

economy. Political domination and the question of its relationship
to the economy are the main issues here.

The medieval Western city is thus in its "full development" a
corporate communal body, legitimated on the basis of the will of
the governed; its burghers are politically "revolutionary" and oriented toward economic acquisition. Such a formation is not found
in Occidental antiquity, despite certain lines of continuity between ancient and medieval democracy, and it is certainly not
found in the Islamic world. Here urban development did not lead
to a break with the prerogatives of patrimonial rule. It also did
not lead to the formation of urban communes as civic communes, with politico-administrative, legal, and (under some circumstances) military autonomy directed outside the commune
and fraternization directed within.

This kind of civic commune no longer followed the lines of
nonurban or preurban constituted organizations, but rather those
of a "freely" constituted burgher organization that one joined as
an individual and that was based upon some idea of legal equality.
This is what is decisive about the "fully developed" Western city:
It replaces the traditional principle of the person (*Personalprinzip*)
with that of the institution (*Anstaltsprinzip*) and in this way replaces the traditional statuses of lord and subject with membership status. This legal development finds support in religious
convictions, for this profane legal equality has, so to speak, a sym-
bolical substructure in the Eucharistic community of Christianity.[194] This is not to say that "the law of the land" did not continue
to have effects on "the law of the town" (town charters), nor that
this legal equality is incommensurable with division according to
status group. It certainly does mean, however, that the urban commune as an institutional body (*Anstalt*) radically transforms the
personal legal situation of the burgher vis-à-vis that of the rural
inhabitant.[195] It also means that the fraternity of burghers stands
above the solidarity of relatives, neighbors, and colleagues and
that the solidarity with the overall urban organization stands
above the solidarity with larger territorial units of which it is a
part.

The special developmental case of the medieval Occidental city
is further illuminated by a comparison with Arab cities, particularly Mecca. Weber follows here the description of Snouk Hurgronje, who had already dedicated a study to this city before the
turn of the century.[196] As discussed earlier, Mecca was at the time
of Mohammed a kind of clan city, or more precisely, a "clan settle-

ment"[197] located in a rural territory and not legally distinguishable from it. Essentially, this remained so. Divisions according to organizations of gentes (*Gentilverbände*), tribes, and clans also remained intact; as at the time of Mohammed, they were the social carriers of military organization. Admittedly, other organizations also existed, such as the guilds. But they never attained town rule. This was in part because the competing town-resident clans later also took advantage of the institution of purchased slaves, in this case Negro troops, who here really were "the private armies of their master and his family."[198] Although the Arab city served as the location of powerful economic interests that were influential well beyond city limits, it was never a communal organization. The religious community, the *umma*, would not have obstructed such a development. But it alone was too weak to cause a break with the importance of tribal and clan bonds at the level of the city and beyond. The decisive legal institution for doing this was lacking, the concept of the corporation (*Anstalt*).

Thus, in Islamic states, city domination is an extension of territorial domination. The same principles of legitimation and organization were employed for both. It was not the case, however, as in India and in part in China that magical sib bonds prevented urban fraternity and an urban commune attendant to it. These bonds had been broken by Islam. What was actually obstructive was the mode of military organization, the prebendal feudalism connected to it, and military prebendalism: its "centralism" prevented autonomous urban development and thus also the development of a production-oriented capitalist bourgeoisie. Weber formulated the generalization: "Thus, the more unified the organization of the [larger] political association, the less the development of the political autonomy of the cities."[199]

Weber speaks of the "distinctive anarchy of the city of Mecca." But, he adds, this anarchy was not a specific trait of Islamic or Arab cities. Rather, it was a condition found throughout the world, in Occidental antiquity and even in medieval Occidental cities, especially in southern European ones. The anarchy consisted in the fact that here "numerous claims stand side by side, overlapping and often conflicting with each other."[200] The city was perhaps a more convenient location than the countryside for pursuing economic interests, but it was not yet an independent social organization. It became one in the West, however, beginning in antiquity, just as the church would later develop into one. That neither the city nor the church rose as a corporate body in the Orient had the consequence that no heterogeneous counterforces were available to challenge Islamic patrimonialism. Of course, Islamic patrimonialism struggled continuously with the disintegration of the unity of the realm. Disintegration, however, only brought forth repeatedly the same institutions and orientations. The unity of the empire was made up of homogeneous units, and when it broke up, it broke up into homogeneous subunits. The structural heterogeneity, the structural pluralism that marks the medieval West, was lacking. In this way, however, the historical preconditions arising from it, prerequisites for the genesis and development of rational capitalism, were also missing. Thus, as opposed to the West, both in terms of form and spirit the overall constellation of political domination in the Islamic state formations was ultimately a hindrance to the developmental prospects of rational industrial capitalism.

The Role of Law

A further aspect must be considered to understand the constellation of political domination as an impediment to rational capitalism: the development of law. In the passage cited earlier, Weber emphasized that an exception to the normal effect of traditional political domination could be expected only in cases where a patrimonial ruler, due to considerations of power and finance, turns to the use of a rational system of administration with technically specialized officials. This administrative staff has to be technically, commercially, and legally trained and oriented toward a functional ethic, that is, a vocational ethic understood in terms of an ethic of performance (*Leistungsethik*).[201] Such a "secular" administrative staff was available rather early on in the West. Important contributing factors here were the "relatively clear dualism" of sacred and profane law and the development of each of these two kinds of law in accordance with their "own inner logic."[202] This dualism also had its effects on university development, which was initially under ecclesiastical influence. The patrimonial state in the West was able to take recourse to this potential source of technical specialists in the age of absolute princely power. It was able to use it for its fiscally conditioned alliance with those bourgeois capitalist strata supported by the development of the city.[203] According to Weber, this potential administrative resource did not exist to the same extent in the Islamic state formations. Admittedly, like China, Islam had universities that resembled those of the West, but "a rational and systematic pursuit of science, with trained specialists, has only existed in the West in a sense at all approaching its present dominant place in our culture."[204] This distinctive development leads us to our last question: Why did this not occur in Islam?

We pointed out earlier that no comprehensive comparative analysis of scientific and university development exists in Weber. Although comments are repeatedly found on education and educational institutions, they satisfy to only a very limited extent the theoretical requirements of his approach.[205] The comparative analysis of law and legal development is the text that comes closest to satisfying them. One object of Weber's analysis there is to arrive at the types of law and legal thought and their social carriers. This requires a short characterization of legal training. He includes here all the civilizations that interest him in his analysis: the Chinese, Indian, Jewish, Christian, and Islamic realms. Insofar as the focus is on the early developmental phases in these civilizations, special attention is paid to sacred law and its relationship to profane law. Even this specialized investigation is centered on the West's distinctive development, for, as has already been emphasized, Christian sacred law is distinguished from other examples of sacred law by its relatively clear separation of the sacred and profane spheres. In this way it works against the growth of theocratic hybrid structures: "The Canon Law of *Christendom* differed at least in degree from all other systems of sacred law."[206]

Weber distinguishes three kinds of legal training: the empirical-practical, the theoretical-formal, and the theocratic. The first type of legal training treats the empirical order from the perspective of practical problems as a craft; the second seeks to work up these problems in doctrinal terms, and thus to systematize them rationally in a legally immanent manner; in contrast, the third does not limit itself to this, instead taking recourse to norms "that represent mere idealistic religious-ethical demands on human beings or on the legal order," and that are thus based on substantive presuppositions from outside.[207] These presuppositions originate from sacred and usually fixed traditions. Thus, here too systematization takes place but, from the perspective of juridical doctrine, in an informal manner. This is characteristic of all types of sacred law: although they are the products of rationalizing doctrines, the orientation of the latter is legally transcendent rather than legally immanent. The systematization reached by such a doctrine is thus not formal-juridical, but substantive-theological in nature, for the purpose that law serves here is not primarily profane.

According to Weber, Islamic law is sacred law in this sense. It is the product of the speculative rational labors of law schools, "specifically a 'jurists' law'"[208] performed on the basis of the Koran and Sunna and by making use of the consensus among legal scholars (*ijma*) and of argumentation by means of analogy (*qiyas*) and conceptual work (*ijtihad*). Lawmaking "in a great measure even today, [has] rested in the hands of the theologian jurists responding to concrete questions."[209] They are specialists in sacred law (*mufti*), who issue opinions (*fetwa*) on valid doctrine, in distinction to judges (*kadi*), who administer justice. The lawmakers were initially legal prophets, thereafter only commentators of the law. The transformation occurred with the end of the prophetic and charismatic age.[210] Pure casuistry began to replace the creation of law, and disputes of interpretation move into the foreground. In Weber's view, the great jurists of the four law schools definitely continued to be legal prophets. They extended and elaborated the law and legal scholarship (*fiqh*) in a creative way on the basis of the holy scriptures and the oral tradition, the Koran and the Sunna, and by means of independent interpretation and the *tacitus consensus omnium*. Nevertheless, with the sacred tradition having become fixed, this charismatic source of law dried up. Legal development was paralyzed. The result is a "stereotyped 'jurists' law'"—a jurists' law, moreover, that opposes secularization with all the means available to it.[211]

These three processes—paralysis, stereotypification, and resistance to secularization—are mutually supportive of one another, however. They permit systematization, but of an ultimately substantive-theological and not formal-juridical nature. More important, because sacred law organizes the Moslem's entire life, the real and the ideally required orders of life distance themselves from each other to an ever greater extent. As a result, the de facto validity of sacred law is limited to "certain fundamental institutions." The remaining institutions are left to profane law—a law, however, that is not guaranteed "by statutes or stable principles of a rational legal system." The gulf between sacred and profane law is "overcome" by circumventing strategies (*hijal*) and "disputatious casuistry," and thus in a largely opportunistic manner.[212] Weber views this as "paradigmatic for the way in which sacred law operates in a scriptural religion that has genuinely prophetic origin." Sacred law can consistently be neither implemented nor eliminated.[213]

If one accepts this diagnosis, it can be linked to three points relevant to our concerns. First of all, sacred law is an effective weapon in the hands of those who administer it. This is paradoxically true because it cannot be strictly implemented. The real order never corresponds to the ideal one. This brings the social bearers of the sacred law tradition into a critical position vis-à-vis the carriers of the real order, especially vis-à-vis the political rulers. Even in the early phase of Islam, the *ulemas* were not integrated into the caliphate.[214] Second, sacred law is a decisive impediment to the establishment of a unified legal system. This is paradoxically true because, although the validity claim of sacred law as a doctrine of religious duties is unconditional for Moslems, its realm of validity is restricted to "status-group law."[215] The result, as Weber observes, was that the "legal particularism" of the subjugated peoples continued to exist "in all of its forms" and in a precarious relationship to the law of the Moslems. This made the creation of a *lex terrae* impossible.[216] Third and finally, sacred law is also a decisive impediment to the establishment of a predictable legal procedure. This is paradoxically true because, as a doctrine of religious duties that makes no distinction between law, ethics, ritual, and etiquette, sacred law did not sufficiently realize this unity in practice. In this way it promoted the dualism between the spiritual and worldly administration of justice, without, however, allowing for a formal juridical systematization of the profane side. Neither spiritual nor worldly adjudication followed an abstract logic immanent to the law; both were instead oriented toward substantive justice, toward concrete considerations of equity.[217]

This means, however, that because the separation of spheres between sacred and profane law, and between the spiritual and worldly administration of justice de facto existed, but remained normatively hierarchized, and because sacred lawmaking changed from legal creation to legal interpretation and became paralyzed in this way, profane law proliferated, so to speak, without guidance. It did not receive direction from sacred law, nor was it self-directing. Neither of the two modes of law developed into juridical formalization—sacred law, because it was rooted in presuppositions lying outside of law; and profane law, because it remained dominated by sacred law.

It is for this reason that, in typological terms, Islamic justice is theocratic and patrimonial "kadi justice."[218] This is due less to its individual norms than to its overall spirit. It is the spirit of material justice, based on nonlegal postulates. The social carriers correspond to this spirit. They are not "profane" specialists, but

rather military prebendaries and patrimonial officials with profane status-group ethics, on the one hand, and theological jurists
with sacred status-group ethics on the other. This spirit generally
prevented a "logical systematization of law in terms of formal juridical concepts."[219] Weber's view of the practical effects of Islamic
law, therefore, can be summarized in this paradoxical formulation:
Because stereotypification of Islamic sacred law increased rather
than diminished, sacred law intensified the already low level of
stereotypification of Oriental patrimonialism. Thus, once again
the points of comparison to Western development represent points
of difference.

Let us summarize these points once more. We have spoken of
the fact that the differentiation between sacred and profane law in
the West was not simply de facto, but enjoyed a normative foundation. Naturally, it also required constructs bridging the two
spheres. This was not primarily accomplished, however, as in Islam, by means of "circumventing strategies,"[220] but on a natural-
law basis originating in the Stoic tradition.[221] Moreover, the separation between the spheres was also reflected in teaching: "The
structure of the Occidental medieval university separated the
teaching of both theology and secular law from that of canon law
and thus prevented the growth of such theocratic hybrid structures as they developed everywhere else."[222] Above all, however,
canon law was not hindered in its development through the fixed-
ness of the sacred tradition, and profane law stood on its own very
early in terms of both its legal tradition and its social carrier stratum. Unlike Islam and Judaism, whose legal traditions resemble
each other, the Occidental medieval church never fell back on responses to specific legal questions as the sole path of legal development. It had instead "created for itself organs of rational lawmaking in the Councils, the bureaucracies of the dioceses, and the
Curia, and, quite particularly, in the papal powers of jurisdiction
and infallible exposition of doctrine. No other of the great religions has ever possessed such institutions."[223] Moreover, the development of profane law had the Roman and Germanic legal
traditions available as guides, and its social bearers were neither
clerics, theological jurists, or prebendaries, but instead legal *honoratiores* in the form of Italian notaries, English attorneys, and
"Occidental medieval empirical jurists of the northern European
continent."[224] This autonomous development of a profane system
of law was closely connected to medieval Occidental urban development. Once again, one sees how important Weber's thesis of the

structural heterogeneity or pluralism of the Occidental configuration of order was for his analysis of the singularity of Occidental development.

Thus, in the West there are relative autonomous developments of sacred and profane law that follow their own inner logic. These developments tend to be more mutually supportive than impeding of each other. These are developments that lead away from charismatic creation and judgment in law toward an orientation around formal juridical techniques for which Roman law, equally influential in both sacred and profane legal development, served as a precursor. This produces a spirit even in the social carriers of sacred law that promotes the formation of a juridically formal doctrine of law. Moreover, Roman and even Germanic law provide legal institutions that are totally alien to the Islamic legal realm. Here Weber is not thinking primarily of private or commercial law, as has been repeatedly claimed. What he has in mind is public law, for it was the Islamic legal realm that developed institutions of commercial law favorable to rational capitalism. It was from there that they made their way to the West. However—and here I follow Joseph Schacht—it is the legal institutions of the *Anstalt* that are foreign to Islamic law. In a presentation of Islamic law that follows Weber's sociology of law, although criticizing its treatment of Islamic law in points of detail, Schacht writes: "The concept of the juristic person that arose from the problem of organizations . . . is just as unknown in Islamic law as are corporate organization and the concept of the *Anstalt*. The only 'corporation' recognized by the Sharia is the sib (*aqila*) taken from ancient Arab tribal organization, which in most cases is obligated to pay blood money."[225]

As important as these points of contrast are, what was said in the comparison of Oriental prebendal feudalism with Occidental feudalism also holds here: The claims for the relatively special position of canon law among the types of sacred law and for the relatively autonomous development of profane law do not provide a direct explanation as to why rational capitalism was favored in the West. Here, too, we are dealing at most with elements that permit development and are missing in the Islamic state formations. Although they increased the predictability of administrative and legal procedures, as did feudalism and the *Ständestaat*, they still remained traditionally defined. All modes of sacred law have the tendency, as in Islam, to treat ethical, legal, ritual, and ceremonial norms "along the same lines," and like Islam, all of them have restricted the autonomy of profane legal development. All of them were also compelled to resort to circumventing strategies in order de facto to annul normatively imperative regulations, or more accurately, to be able to tolerate their being disregarded, for example, in the Occidental church's prohibition of usury.[226] But according to Weber, such "impractical" single-case regulations never hindered rational-capitalist economic activity.

The overall effect of a given normative complex, its spirit, was always decisive. This, however, was similar in all hierocracies. Like traditional political domination, traditional hierocratic domination is fundamentally anticapitalist in orientation, however. Its animosity is directed not at politically, but at economically oriented capitalism, where capitalism represents a rational, yet unethical economic system. In spite of "fundamentally different beginnings" and "different developmental destinies," after the conclusion of their "charismatically heroic ages" religions are similar in their effects on economic life. They favor traditional economic activity, the traditional economic spirit, and the traditional form of the economy. This holds for Islam just as much as it holds for the Roman Catholic Church. The most important exception to this rule is ascetic Protestantism and its "spirit of objectification" (Versachlichung).

This closes the reconstruction of Weber's analysis of Islam. It turned out to be a difficult puzzle to complete. Nevertheless, the pieces of the puzzle could be found and arranged in such a way that the basic features of a picture emerge. The main connecting thread was provided by Weber's analysis of Occidental development. It names the points of comparison that guide the analysis of Islam and of other cultural realms. These points of comparison represent above all points of difference. They come sharply into view as long as the typological comparative aspect is in the foreground. But the points of difference obtained in this way can also be considered in terms of their genesis. If Weber had still been able to write his projected study of Islam, this aspect certainly would have moved more into the foreground.

The reconstruction of Weber's analysis of Islam is not the only puzzle. His explanation of why rational capitalism only "succeeded" in the West and not in Islamic civilization is equally enigmatic. Here, too, many pieces, termed historical "prerequisites," were used in putting the puzzle together. They could arise only in the West—according to Weber's thesis—due to a chain of circumstances. Of course, a historical agent was required to put all these pieces together. This was the achievement of the methodical conduct of ascetic Protestantism, its rationalism of self- and world-mastery, something that was ultimately lacking not only in Islam but also in Lutheranism, Catholicism, early Christianity, Judaism, and in all Asiatic religions.

Weber's sociology of religion, indeed his sociology as a whole, thus culminates in a sociology and typology of worldviews and related modes of conduct. One could also term it a sociology and typology of axiological turns and the types of personality connected to them. For the sociology of religion this is demonstrated very clearly by the "Author's Introduction" and "The Intermediate Reflections"—and also in the "Conclusions" to the study of Confucianism, the end of the study of Hinduism, and the final paragraphs of the section on religion in *Economy and Society*.

The catalogue of traits that is included in the comparative typology is unusually complex. Its complexity is especially visible in those places where the analysis switches from the comparison between Asian religions and Near Eastern–Occidental religions to the comparison among the different Near Eastern–Occidental religions themselves. The treatment of Islam provides a good example of this. Its similarity especially with Calvinism makes a detailed discussion of commonalities and differences necessary. This means bringing together the most important traits of this catalogue and examining whether the characterizations of the Near Eastern–Occidental religions really allow them to be finely demarcated. Of these religions, all of which continually appear in the manuscript "The Economy and the Societal Orders and Powers," Weber succeeded in treating only two in monographic form in the course of his lifetime—ascetic Protestantism and ancient Israelite ethics in its transition to Judaism. Nevertheless, he planned to make such monographic presentations to the very end. Thus, by compiling this catalogue of traits, one can also examine whether the most important constitutive elements for the unwritten studies were in fact all present in 1920, at the time of Weber's death. My conclusion confirms Marianne Weber's statement: The preliminary work for the studies of talmudic Judaism, ancient and medieval Christianity, and Islam were completed long before 1920 (for an overview, see Table 1).

The Critique of Weber's Approach to Islam

Max Weber's analysis of Islam has not evoked much response in the literature of Islamic or sociological scholarship. The essay by

TABLE I

A Comparison of Early Judaism, Early Christianity, Early Islam, and Ascetic Protestantism (Calvinism), According to the Original Version of Economy and Society

(All these religions are salvational, revelational, ethical, monotheistic, and theocentric, and all are scriptural religions with more or less strongly marked activistic and antimagical tendencies.)

Religious ideas	Early Judaism	Early Christianity	Early Islam	Calvinism
1. Social carrier of the "revelation"	Ethical prophets as prophets of salvation and esp. as prophets of doom with political intentions (pre-exilic prophecy)	Ethical prophets as prophets of salvation without political intentions (John and Jesus)	An ethical prophet with a political intention (Mohammed)	Recourse to Old Testament prophecy
2. Social carrier of the systematization of the "revelation"	Priests, then scriptural and legal scholars Prototype: rabbis	Theologians and bishops Prototype: church fathers	Legal and religious scholars (jurists and theologians) Prototype: ulemas	Theologians Prototype: reformers
3. Religious "canons"	Torah and the interpreting tradition, as well as supplementary oral tradition, later recorded (Talmud) Relatively closed	Old and esp. New Testament and interpreting tradition, as well as supplementary church tradition (Concilia, etc.) Relatively open	Koran and the interpreting tradition, as well as oral tradition, later recorded (Sunna) Closed	Old and New Testament Closed
4. Concept of God	Yahweh as transcendental god of "wrath" Absolute power	God as merciful and gracious heavenly father Absolute goodness and mercy	Allah as transcendental "great" God Absolute power and greatness	Double god: God of Old and New Testament

5. Relationship between God and man	Contractual (covenantal) relationship (Reciprocal)	Relationship of mercy and love (Reciprocal)	Relationship of submission (One-sided)	Relationship of proof (One-sided)
6. Theodicy	Messianic eschatology	Theodicy of suffering	Divine providence as predetermination	Divine providence as predestination

Structuring of religious interests

1. Means and paths to salvation	No asceticism	Otherworldly asceticism	No asceticism	Thisworldly asceticism
	Knowledge (studying) and ritual activities of worship without magical significance	Faith and ritual activities of worship with magical significance (sacraments)	Faith and knowledge (cognition) as well as ritual activities of worship without magical significance	Faith and ritual activities of worship without magical significance
	Animosity to magic	Involvement in magic (sublimated magic)	Indifference to magic	Radicalized animosity to magic
2. Goals and goods of salvation	The coming of God's kingdom on earth and collective salvation on the basis of present collective suffering	Individual salvation in the hereafter due to God's goodness and mercy	Individual happiness in the hereafter (paradise) on the basis of faith and bravery	Individual salvation in the hereafter on the basis of God's free will
	"Retribution"	"Forgiveness"	"Honor/Veneration" (*Verehrung*)	"Chosenness"
3. *Certitudo salutis*	Strict adherence to religious law	Adherence to God's commandments out of faith and trust	Strict adherence to religious law	Strict adherence to God's commandments for the glory of God
	Action as the factual basis of salvation	Action as the expression of promised salvation	Action as the factual basis of happiness	Action as the cognitive basis of salvation
	Strict reciprocity	Mitigated reciprocity	Strict reciprocity	No reciprocity

TABLE I
Continued

	Early Judaism	Early Christianity	Early Islam	Calvinism
4. Religious ethical orientation	"Sacred law" Principle of legality Legal ethic	"Sacred conviction" Principle of morality Ethic of conviction (Ethic of love)	"Sacred law" Principle of legality Legal ethic	"Sacred conviction" Principle of morality Ethic of conviction (Ethic of duty)
5. Scope of religious message	Religious traits tied to ethnic stratification	No connection between religious and nonreligious traits—religious stratification	Religious traits tied to stratification—status group stratification	No connection between religious and nonreligious traits—religious stratification
	Dualism of the chosen people and all others	Dualism of believer and unbelievers	Dualism of believers (conquerors) and unbelievers (conquered), House of Islam and House of War	Dualism of chosen (*electi*) and damned (*reprobati*)
	Weak missionizing impulse	Strong missionizing impulse	Strong impulse to conquest, resulting in mass conversion	Weak missionizing impulse
	Nonreligious particularism	Religious universalism	Nonreligious particularism	Religious particularism
Religious organization				
1. Internal relation: hierocratic power	Community with sermon, prayer, song, scriptural reading, and interpretation, under religious guidance but without priests	Church as an institution of grace with priests as dispensers of grace Orders as ecclesiastically recognized special organizations ("sect")	Community (*umma*) on the basis of the five pillars" under the guidance of legal and religious scholars as well as of religious leaders (imam, mullahs) for public prayer and sermon	Church as disciplinary institution with priests as proclaimers of the word (of the Holy Scriptures) and administrators of the divine "reason of state" Church as "sect"

2. External relation: relationship of the hierocratic power to political power	Separation of powers in an independent polity but with a tendency toward theocracy; if dependent, an externally closed confessional organization (paria religiosity)	Separation of powers with a tendency toward theocracy	Unified, all functions as expressions of a religious law, but with a tendency toward separation of powers (caliphate and sultanate)	Theocratic with a tendency toward separation
Carrier strata	Plebeian strata residing in cities	Plebeian strata residing in cities	Military ruling strata	Urban entrepreneurs and merchants
Results				
1. Religiously conditioned relationship to the world	Indifference to the world	Fluctuation between world indifference and world transcendence	Fluctuation between world mastery (as world conquest) and world adjustment	World mastery
2. Religious ideal of life	Scriptural scholar well-versed in the law, "intellectual"	Virtuoso of faith	"Hero," especially the war hero	Professional man of expertise

[a] Bearing witness to Allah and Mohammed, praying five times a day, fasting during Ramadan, giving alms, and making a pilgrimage to Mecca.

Joseph Schacht dedicated to the study of Islamic law represents an early exception. Schacht orients himself along the basic lines of Weber's sociology of law—he speaks of similar ways of viewing things—but criticizes both the all-too-easy application of concepts taken from the Occidental history of law to Islamic legal conditions and the lack of periodization of Islamic legal history. Certain individual statements he also considers false. For these reasons, he corrects Weber's short discussion of Islamic law in several places. Nevertheless, in his overall sociological view of Islamic law, he arrives at conclusions similar to Weber's. He points to the lack of differentiation of substantive realms of law, to the priority of substantive rationality over procedural rationality, to the succession of legal revelation by traditionalization, to the opening and closure of the canon, to the importance of the strategy of circumvention in "assimilating" the practices of the law of custom into the Sharia, to the hybrid character of sacred law and the restriction of its realm of validity, and to its claim to supremacy and its tendency to permeate profane law such that the latter develops along nonformal lines. Finally, he emphasizes the lack of legal concepts, such as the juristic person, the corporation, and the *Anstalt*, central to Occidental legal development. He also evaluates the role of the Islamic communal principle vis-à-vis the ancient Arab tribal principle in a manner similar to Weber. Schacht emphasizes that the ancient Arab law of custom continues to exist within the Sharia, but is "corrected" by the Islamic communal principle: "[P]recisely the tribal organization at the basis of those legal relationships with its civil and criminal law solidarity [is] repressed." Nonetheless, the effects of the Islamic communal principle remained limited; indeed, due to "the patriarchal character of political patrimonialism, a character established for good with the Abbasids," it even "worked *against* the corporate organization."[227]

The lack of response to Weber's analysis of Islam is not surprising. Considerable effort is required to piece together its fundamental characteristics on the basis of his scattered remarks, as this chapter demonstrates. Nevertheless, aside from a number of thematically specialized evaluations similar to Schacht's, there are two monographs that analyze Weber's general approach in connection with Islam. Both, one more generally and the other more specifically, are based on a reconstruction of Weber's view of Islam from his works. Both are critical and written from a modified Marxian perspective. One comes from Maxime Rodinson, the other from Bryan S. Turner.[228] Let me turn briefly to each of these two works.

Rodinson raises the question of why the Islamic world, in contrast to the West, did not give rise to a capitalist economic formation, and thus to a condition in which not just the majority of enterprises produce on the basis of free labor and for the sake of profit, but in which the economic system is dominated by the capitalist sector, which in turn dominates all other sectors of society. He thus poses Weber's question, even if he does so in Marxian terms. Indeed, on this point he sees—and this is certainly correct—no opposition between Weber and Marx.[229]

The differences first arise in their respective responses to the same question, for here Weber makes recourse, in contrast to a properly understood Marx, to ideas as factors obstructing or favoring development. He thus gives what in Rodinson's view is an ultimately "ideological" explanation, and this in two senses of the word. On the one hand, Rodinson claims that ideology, in the case of Islam and Koranic and post-Koranic "ideology," has a decisive influence upon economic development. On the other hand, this explanatory approach is itself an ideology. It is an ideology of the higher rationality of the West, especially of an activist and anti-magical religious ethic that is missing in Islam. Although Weber also emphasizes the importance of state and law, here too, the same Western bias prevails.[230] Rodinson goes on to say that if, however, one examines the thesis of the low level of rationality of non-Western cultures, and thus also of Islamic culture, which follows from the claim of the "specific rationality of the European"[231] (and if one does this scientifically and, so to speak, positivistically),[232] one quickly sees that this thesis cannot be upheld, neither in terms of method nor in terms of substance. In terms of method it rests on a circular argument, and substantively, it rests on an underestimation of the level of rationality of Islamic "ideology" and Islamic institutions.

The thesis is circular inasmuch as it offers examples of the higher rationality of the West that originate from an epoch that comes after that age "in which Occidental Europe very decisively placed itself on the path of modern capitalism." The asserted rational characteristic, however, can "just as well be owed to the economic development on the capitalist path, or they could have arisen in the interplay with this development and together with it have arisen from a common cause."[233] Conversely, the thesis is substantively false because Islam in no way represents an anti-activist and magic-bound "ideology." Just the opposite is the case: If one compares the Koran, for example, with the Old and New Testaments, one can even speak of the higher rationality of the

Koran: "It thus appears as if the Koranic ideology allows rational thought, rationality, to intervene to a greater degree than do the ideologies reflected in the Old and New Testaments; as if it grants the idea of predestination about the same importance as do the two other holy scriptures, but that it unambiguously exhorts one to an active orientation in individual and social life; and finally, as if it subordinates magical technique to divine will, just as the other two revelatory scriptures do, in this way maintaining the human potential for counteracting this technique regardless of how easy it is to employ."[234]

The objection to method can be disposed of quickly. It has nothing to do with the question of whether ideas can be effective in history as obstructive or favorable factors. Without doubt, circular arguments do not provide explanations. One cannot explain something in terms of something else that occurred subsequent to it, and one must always examine whether any given correlation might be based upon a third factor. These are elementary preconditions of valid explanations that Weber was assuredly acquainted with. He possessed a much more developed understanding of the problems of causal attribution than this objection insinuates.[235]

One aim of the foregoing analysis has been to show that Weber actually pays attention to these elementary preconditions of historical explanation in his substantive investigations. Weber's difficulties are located in a completely different area. They are connected to the logic of concept formation in the cultural sciences as he adopted it from Rickert, to the simultaneity of the selection and constitution of "historical individuals," and to the ensuing question of whether he is able to stringently separate defining and explanatory conditions.[236] Such problems arise, of course, only for those who consider neither dialectical concept formation nor a "positivist orientation" as an appropriate solution to the problem of historical explanations. Weber was neither a dialectician nor a positivist.

Thus, Rodinson's methodological objections miss the point. Unfortunately, this is true for the substantive objections as well. First of all, he seems to have overlooked the fact that in his typological comparative investigations Weber does not distinguish between levels of rationality, but between types of rationalism. It is well known that his entire sociology of religion is conceived of as a contribution to a sociology and typology of religiously conditioned rationalism.[237] Then, in his discussion of the Islamic system of belief, Rodinson does not take into account the distinction between logical and psychological consequences. He also lacks the entire conceptual apparatus to do so. In the end he comes to conclusions largely in accord with those of Weber—except that he does not know it.

Weber had also underscored the "relaxed" relationship between faith and reason in Islam, the activist potential of the Islamic doctrine of predestination, and the basic antimagical character of this prophetic scriptural religion. Of course there are many details in Rodinson's analysis that could help supplement and indeed improve Weber's study. But this would in no way affect Weber's first main thesis on the traditional character of Islamic economic ethics and mentality and the economic mode of conduct connected to it. It would also in no way affect his second main thesis that the institutional conditions that prevailed in the Islamic states were favorable for commercial capitalism but not for industrial capitalism as an economic system, and that fiscally conditioned prebendal feudalism, the lack of urban autonomy, and the relationship between sacred and profane law in part caused this. One can certainly disagree as to whether Weber identified all of the important internal and external conditions and, above all, whether they add up to a convincing explanation. In Rodinson, however, one looks for such an explanation in vain. He does offer statements such as this: "Since a certain number of structural conditions and conditioning events were given, a corresponding capitalist economic formation was able to develop in Europe."[238] However, the only thing that is certain for him, and is often reiterated, is this: Whatever these structural conditions and conditioning events may in fact have been, religion and ideology were not among them.

This is actually the decisive point of difference vis-à-vis Weber. It is not a question of method or substance, but one of theory. Despite interesting modifications of the orthodox Marxist approach, especially in regard to the theory of evolution and the variable relationship between the type of appropriation (the mode of property) and the type of exploitation (the mode of extracting the surplus product), Rodinson proceeds as a materialist in terms of method and theory. For him, only the external conditions (the "base") ultimately count, not the internal ones (the "superstructure"). Religion is a reflex, an echo: an ideology. It is therefore also not independent and cannot have any independent consequences. It is, in accordance with the *German Ideology*, like all dominant thought, "nothing more than the ideal expression of the prevailing

material conditions."[239] Any explanation that does not conceive
of them as such is itself ideological.

As we have shown, Weber rejects this base-superstructure
model from the outset. Ideas—world views—may sometimes be
the ideal expression of material conditions, but this is not always
true. This is the basis of Weber's crucial distance from all Marxist perspectives, regardless of how "moderate" they may be. He
sought instead to go beyond these approaches, and the *Protestant
Ethic* is the first demonstration that it is possible and of how it
can be achieved. Rodinson simply did not understand this crucial
point of the Weber thesis he cites so often. More generally, he operates against an author with whom he is at best only superficially
acquainted. In his introduction to the new German edition of Rodinson's book, Bassam Tibi complains about the remnants of the
base-superstructure model in Rodinson's approach. Nevertheless,
Tibi emphasizes at the same time that this affects neither the
"monumental results of research" nor Rodinson's judgment of
Weber, in that the study of Weber's work gives proof that Weber
"lacked the knowledge of the subject both in regard to the doctrine
and the history of Islam that is necessary in order to be able to
make a sound judgment of it."[240] The latter may be true of Weber's
knowledge of Islam, but it is all the more true of Rodinson's
knowledge of Weber!

The same cannot be said about Bryan S. Turner. He was the first
to make a serious attempt to reconstruct Weber's view of Islam
from the remarks scattered in Weber's work. In my view, however,
he started from a false premise. He distinguishes two theses that
Weber supposedly put forth in the context of his comparative studies: the Protestant Ethic thesis (PE), of which there are two versions, and the Weber thesis (W). Turner claims that the first thesis
was formulated in the well-known essay on the Protestant ethic of
1904–5 and then repeated in revised form in 1920, whereas the
second thesis defined Weber's sociological investigation of the
most important distinctions between Occidental and Oriental
civilizations. In Turner's view, whereas the former places religion
at the center of analysis, in the latter it plays at best a secondary
role. Obtained in part by expanding the first thesis and in part independently of it, the second thesis, the real Weber thesis, moves
institutional conditions into the forefront. Turner views the second thesis as the sociologically more productive and more mature
one.[241] He claims that this is in part because Weber moved closer

to Marx and Engels in this way. This is supposedly shown precisely in terms of Weber's treatment of Islam:

When Weber came to analyze Islam, he focused on the political, military and economic nature of Islamic society as a patrimonial form of domination. He treated the role of values as secondary and dependent on Islamic social conditions. Insofar as Weber did adhere to that position, his analysis was not far removed from Marx and Engels, who claimed that the Asiatic mode of production, characteristic of India, China and Turkey, produced an enduring social order which was incompatible with capitalism.[242]

As I have tried to show elsewhere,[243] in Weber's view spiritual conditions naturally also make up some of the stabilizing conditions of the Chinese and Indian orders. But much more important, the contrast of the two theses is itself inappropriate. There are simply no PE thesis and a W thesis that can be distinguished from it. They are only two sides of the same approach. The fact that Weber later also treats the other side, which he had deliberately neglected in the *Protestant Ethic*, implies neither the abandonment of the "first" side nor a "later discovery or recognition" of the other. As was shown earlier, the *Protestant Ethic* itself already makes points of transition from one side to the other visible. The extension in the range of his approach found in the two manuscripts "The Economy and the Societal Orders and Powers" and "The Economic Ethics of the World Religions" is substantive and theoretical, not methodological in nature. It is false to believe that Weber's approach drew nearer to that of Marx.

Turner's reconstruction of Weber's analysis of Islam thus serves above all the purpose of demonstrating the subordinate importance of ethics vis-à-vis the social structure.[244] This leads him to an interesting discussion of the institutional factors, with Weber's scattered remarks serving as the guiding thread. It is a discussion that is in many respects congruent with the analysis presented in this chapter. Moreover, the relation between religious ethic and conduct is also treated in substantive terms. Here the thesis is that this side of the Weber thesis, in comparison with the institutional side, is substantively weaker, for Weber's assertion that the Islamic religious ethic is "confiscated" for the sake of the ideal and material interests of the warriors for the faith and transformed into a warrior ethic is untenable. For Islam "was, and continued to be, an urban religion of merchants and state officials; many of its key concepts reflect the urban life of a mercantile society in opposition to the values of the desert and of the warrior. The warrior ethic described by Weber was simply one religious perspective which was regarded with suspicion and hostility by the orthodox."[245]

This may be so, but the statement is not at odds with Weber's analysis. Above all, as is shown in Weber's comparative studies, the material and ideal interests of traders and officials do not create, even in the Christian tradition, methodical conduct and the rationalism of world mastery. The effects of religious sources are never the result simply of the interests of its social bearers; they are also always dependent on the contents of the sources. This aspect of Weber's approach is completely lost in Turner's analysis. Indeed, it has to be lost if one hopes to maintain the convergence thesis of Weber and Marx.

This thesis of the subordinate, secondary importance of ethics vis-à-vis the social structure, of motivational factors vis-à-vis institutional ones, makes the decisive point of the whole story: for the sake of "reconciliation" with Marx, the central point of Weber's approach is interpreted away. Weber never spoke of primary and secondary factors, only of causally important ones. These include internal factors just as much as external ones. The fact that it is difficult or even impossible to quantify their relative weight does not speak against his approach; as he wrote in his dispute with Rachfahl: "The fact that in historical attribution no distribution ratio can be put into numbers is not my fault."[246]

There are undoubtedly gaps in Weber's analysis of Islam, which is guided by a central question the relevance of which can and must be the subject of controversy. This pertains also to concept formation. Whoever does not share the assumed value will criticize these concepts and construct others in their stead. This is thoroughly in the spirit of Weber's methodology, for the "greatest advances in the sphere of the social sciences are *substantively* tied up with the shift in practical cultural problems and take the *form* of a critique of concept formation."[247] This does not alter Weber's basic insight that any sociological analysis interested in promoting historical truth has to take into account both sides of the causal chain.

The Emergence of Modernity
Max Weber on Western Christianity

All in all, the specific roots of Occidental culture must be sought in the tension between and peculiar balance of, on the one hand, office charisma and monasticism, and on the other the contractual character of the feudal state and the rational bureaucratic character of the hierarchy.　—Max Weber, *Economy and Society*

The elimination of all ritual barriers of birth for the community of the Eucharists as realized in Antioch, was also, in terms of its religious preconditions, the hour of conception for the Occidental "citizenry," even if the latter was first to be born more than a thousand years later in the revolutionary "coniuratio" of medieval cities.　—Max Weber, *India*

Ascetism is *bourgeois virtue.*
—Eduard Bernstein, *Geschichte des Sozialismus in Einzeldarstellungen*

Themes and Questions

Max Weber began his long series of publications with an essay on the history of trading enterprises in the Middle Ages.[1] In it, he pursued the "conditions of sociation"[2] (*Vergesellschaftung*) out of which the modern partnerships of limited and unlimited liability arose.[3] He did this from a genetic and comparative perspective (which later would probably have been termed a "developmental-historical perspective"). As the title indicates, the analysis is aimed primarily at medieval legal conditions; however, it also makes recourse both to antiquity and to the present. Its focus is on the "genesis of legal principles"[4] or, put in another way, on the invention of an institution that allows for a spatial and above all legal separation between the private and the business spheres. On the one hand Weber compared the legal form of the Roman *societas* and the Germanic household with medieval societies of Italy in particular, and on the other he compared the *societas maris* of the medieval Italian coastal town with the *societas terrae* of the medieval Italian inland town.[5] His interest already centered on differences; for example, he demonstrated that the credit basis of the modern, unlimited partnership is fundamentally different from that of the limited partnership, and that the two owe their existence to different historical roots.[6] In addition, he considered the separation a process of far-reaching historical significance. This, in any case, is the impression made by later passages in which he repeatedly refers to his first work.

An especially interesting statement is found in the first version of his *Protestant Ethic*. Summarizing its most important findings, he points out that the conception of the Puritan entrepreneur who has a special obligation toward the possessions entrusted to him can "be traced back, in some of its roots, like so many aspects of the modern spirit of capitalism, to the Middle Ages," in this case to the conception of business as a "mystical entity" (*corpus mysticum*).[7] It found institutional support in the legal inventions that Weber analyzes in his study of medieval trading enterprises: in the firm, in the consideration of business wealth as a special form of wealth, and in the concomitant notion of limited joint liability.[8] But although the institutional separation between private and business matters, between the private household and the business firm, between private and business wealth was advanced in the Middle Ages and in this way promoted the idea of the economic service of an impersonal "cause," it was only ascetic Protestantism that first created this institutional separation's ultimately "coherent ethical foundations."[9] This ethical foundation did not originate in the Middle Ages, but in the post-Reformation period, especially in the seventeenth century.

When one considers the long line of publications building on the dissertation, it is striking that the study of the medieval trading enterprises already addresses one of the ever recurring themes of Weber's work. This theme can be transformed into two questions: What constitutes the distinctive economic and social character of the West? How is it to be explained? As the dissertation shows, the focus of attention is initially on distinctive *institutional* arrangements and their causes; however, by the studies on Protestantism at the very latest, this focus also includes the distinctive *mentalities* found in the West. Weber gets increasingly interested in the nature of the *connections* between the distinctive economic and social features of the West and the development of its religious ethic. In September 1919, after readying his 1904–5 studies of Protestantism for print within the framework of his *Collected Essays in the Sociology of Religion*, this is what he terms his cognitive interest, at least for that part of his work dedicated to the comparative studies on the economic ethics of the great religions in history.

Even in the first version of the *Protestant Ethic* he had claimed that there was a connection between developments in religious ethics and the economy that holds not only for the post-Reformation period, but for the pre-Reformation period as well. At the end of these studies, he expressly maintained that "of course, the period of capitalist development which preceded that considered in our study was everywhere influenced by Christianity, which both retarded and advanced it."[10] As a result, in 1904–5 he planned to expand these studies both forward, and, above all, backward in time. The more intensively he dealt with the economic ethics of non-Christian religions in order to divest the studies on Protestantism of their isolated character, the more urgent it became to place the latter studies in the more general framework of a study of Western Christianity. Only in this way could they be placed "in the context of overall cultural development," and that was the stated purpose, as can be gathered from the revised version of these studies.[11] In fact, as we know from an announcement of the contents of his *Collected Essays on the Sociology of Religion* in September 1919, Weber intended to write such a study. In the projected four-volume collection, the entire final volume was reserved for this study of Western Christianity.[12]

Owing to Weber's death in June 1920 this plan was never realized, as is true of his writings on early Christianity, talmudic Judaism, Islam, and Eastern Christianity, which were supposed to appear in the third volume. Nevertheless, to take up a remark by Marianne Weber, the necessary preliminary studies for these monographs had long been completed.[13] Unlike the monographs planned for the third volume, however, the preliminary studies for Western Christianity were not primarily undertaken from 1910 until the beginning of the First World War. Rather, Weber could draw on studies from the first and second phase of his work.[14] In addition to the dissertation and the studies on Protestantism, there was the lecture course on general ("theoretical") economics, given several times before 1900, in which antique, medieval, and modern Western economic development had been dealt with. These lectures were meant to provide the basis for a textbook.[15]

In the third phase of Weber's work, however, his interest was not limited, since it was evidently still there, to Western economic development alone; instead, it now encompassed Western development more generally, including developments in political domination, law, religion, science, and art. Moreover, the focus was no longer on Western development per se, but on its singularity (*Sonderentwicklung*). Weber established the fact that the very foundations of Mediterranean-Occidental civilization differ from those of other civilizations in his comparative studies on religion and economy. Even though the study of Western Christianity—like all the other studies—would have emphasized this specific relationship, like these other studies, it certainly would not have been limited to that relationship. I suspect it would have also aimed at showing the singularity of Western development in the linkage of external and internal transformations—of revolutions in institutions and revolutions in mentalities—and this in view of "the tension and peculiar balance" (*Ausgleich*) among the religious, economic, political, and social orders. It would have included the analysis of the distinct character of the subjectivist culture of the modern West; of its rational capitalism, with its scientifically defined technology; of its *Anstaltstaat*, with its formal-rational law; of its non-state associations, based on *Vergemeinschaftung* and *Vergesellschaftung*; of its system of "acquired" inequality, with its commercial classes and occupational status groups.[16]

With this analysis, Weber did not simply want to repeat Ernst Troeltsch's pathbreaking study, *The Social Teaching of Christian Churches and Groups* (*Die Soziallehren der christlichen Kirchen und Gruppen*).[17] This monograph, which he held in the highest possible regard, motivated him to put off for the time being the continuation of his studies of Protestantism as originally planned and to turn to the economic ethics of the world religions.[18] Admittedly, Troeltsch primarily dealt with the teachings, not the practical effects of Western Christianity. This certainly left Weber room for analysis even within Troeltsch's domain of investigation.[19] The studies of the economic ethics, however, required that the analysis oriented around the practical effects of the religiously conditioned character of the economy be supplemented by an analysis of the "class-conditioned" character of religion. Moreover, it required this two-pronged analysis for all important societal orders and their interrelations.[20]

That this is not mere conjecture is indicated not only by those monographs on the economic ethics of the world religions actually written, but also by the aforementioned announcement, especially if the latter is read in connection with a statement Weber made in a letter from the same period. In September 1919, Weber sent the revised version of the *Protestant Ethic* to his publisher, Siebeck. In the covering letter, he announced his essay on the Protestant sects. Thereafter, he let it be known, he intended to prepare his studies of China and India for republication and then insert an essay that he had finished in his head, but which he still needed to put to paper. It would deal with "the general foundations of the singular development of the West." This study would be followed by the study of Judaism, which would go beyond the period already covered in the published articles.[21] When one compares this statement to the announcement formulated just days later, it appears that the mentally completed essay had in the meantime become "a sketch devoted to the rise of the social distinctiveness of the West [depicting] the development of the European bourgeoisie in antiquity and the Middle Ages."[22] In any case, the temporal proximity of the two statements suggests such an interpretation.

Admittedly, the essay anticipated in the announcement appears to be thematically more narrow in scope than the essay anticipated in the covering letter. Nevertheless, in my view it is more significant that the function to be fulfilled in each case was identical. With an essay of this kind, a transition was to be effected from the Chinese and Indian religions to the Near East–Occidental religions. This transition was at the same time linked to a change in perspective. Whereas the analysis of the Chinese and Indian religions went only as far "as is necessary to find points of comparison with a Western development that is then to be further analyzed,"[23] the study of ancient Israelite and Jewish religious development marks the beginning of the depiction of Mediterranean-Occidental cultural development. That Weber intended to expand the latter to include a "short depiction of the Egyptian and Mesopotamian, and the Zoroastrian religious ethics" (in the words of the announcement) is in accordance with Weber's aim of genetic reconstruction and is nothing new. He had intentionally left this short exposition out of the initial publication of the first part of *Ancient Judaism* (*Das antike Judentum*) (Weber 1952).[24] Presumably, the change in perspective was to be accomplished by inserting the aforementioned essay.

A shift had to be made from a comparative perspective that emphasizes the contrasts between the Asiatic and Mediterranean-Occidental world to a developmental perspective that focuses on continuities within the Mediterranean-Occidental world. Without doubt, the focal points of analysis identified by means of the comparative perspective remain important in the treatment of Western development. They serve, as it were, to organize the latter. However, questions of historical preconditions and causal attribution now move to the fore. In his major study of the economic and social history of antiquity, "Agrarian Sociology," written at the end of the second phase of his work, Weber already pointed to this shift in his "somewhat pointed remarks" on urban development in antiquity and the Middle Ages.[25] Here he writes that

one might take these anomalies and exceptions as yet another demonstration that "there is nothing new under the sun," and that all or nearly all distinctions are simply matters of degree. The latter is true enough, of course; but the former notion annuls any historical study. One must, instead, lay the emphasis on the divergences, despite all parallels, and use the similarities of two societies to highlight the singularity [*Eigenart*] of each.[26]

Divergences, however, occurred not only between antiquity and the Middle Ages, but also between the latter and modernity. Admittedly, even though Weber expressly emphasized divergences, he also spoke of the "continuities of Mediterranean-European cultural development" in the same study. Although there is no "one-directional, linear development," there are also no closed cycles that would be completely discontinuous with one another.[27]

The projected essay on the singular development of the West thus would have had a double function to fulfill: it had to characterize the distinctiveness of Mediterranean-Occidental civilization vis-à-vis the Chinese and Indian civilizations, and, at the same time, it had to produce a developmental perspective on the basis of which the combination of circumstances that led to modern Western culture could be made plausible.[28] The conclusion of the study of Hinduism and Buddhism and the first part of the study of ancient Judaism, both first published in the *Archiv*, already contained the major clues. In *The Religion of India* (*Hinduismus und Buddhismus*), although the essay was not more than "an extremely superficial . . . survey of the Asian cultural world,"[29] Weber insisted that one decisive element of the Western economy was lacking in Asia: "The curtailment of this instinctive avarice, its transformation into a rational pursuit of gain and its integration into a system of rational, inner-worldly ethics of action—that achievement of Protestant 'inner-worldly asceticism' which had had a few genuine predecessors."[30] And, he goes on to say, this specifically "bourgeois" mode of conduct owes its existence to the emergence of prophets and thinkers who arose against the backdrop, not of economic problems, but "of political problems of a social structure alien to Asian culture—namely, the political citizenry, without which neither Judaism nor Christianity nor the development of Greek thought could be conceived."[31]

In the study of ancient Judaism Weber begins by noting that without "the creation of the Old Testament" and an adherence to it by the Pauline mission (that was certainly both selective as well as transformative), there never would have been a (universalistic) Christian church and a (universalistic) Christian ethic of the everyday world. Because of these "world-historical consequences" of Jewish religious development, one finds oneself "at a turning point of the whole cultural development of the West and the Middle East." Of similar "historical significance was the development of Hellenic intellectual culture; for Western Europe, the development of Roman law and of the Roman Catholic Church resting on the Roman concept of office; the medieval order of estates; and finally, in the field of religion, Protestantism. It transmuted the older medieval institutions."[32]

It would be tempting to search for additional passages in which Weber comments on the general foundations of the singular development of the West or on the developmental history of the citizenry in antiquity and the Middle Ages. Such statements could put the link between the analyses of the Asiatic religions and that of the Mediterranean-Occidental religions in sharper relief. This will not be done here.[33] For these general foundations, the reader can follow above all the "Anticritical Last Word" and the *General Economic History*; for the developmental history of the citizenry, one can follow the concluding passages of "Agrarian Sociology" and, above all, the posthumous manuscript "The City."[34]

Admittedly, at the time Weber conveyed his further plans for the two major projects to his publisher, Siebeck, in September 1919, "The City"—the manuscript certainly best fitting the announcement's account—almost certainly had been in his desk drawer for some time. There are many indications that it is relatively old, at least in part, and that in the form handed down, it was connected to the development of the sociology of domination since 1910. Possibly, Weber would have ultimately used it as a basis for both major projects, which is in accordance with his procedure that was increasingly based on the division of labor. Regardless of how one assesses this question, one thing is clear: the projected essay's location following the revised studies of Protestantism and preceding the studies of ancient Judaism, Islam, Eastern Christianity, and Western Christianity. This location implies, however, that the analysis of Western Christianity did not become superfluous after the studies on ascetic Protestantism were revised, nor would this depiction have limited itself to the characterization of the general foundations of the singular development of the West or solely to a developmental history of citizenry.

Weber—and one cannot emphasize this point enough—used the opportunity to revise the studies of Protestantism neither to enlarge the scope of the carefully limited original project nor to alter his original thesis.[35] Further accounts of the latter are given in the revised text, but it is neither rescinded nor modified, or even given new accents. Thus, the study of Western Christianity also would not have changed any part of the thesis that only the ethic of ascetic Protestantism, apart from some anticipations, provided one of the constitutive elements of the modern capitalist ethos and vocational culture. Rather, just the opposite would have occurred: it would have more clearly defined this thesis by expanding the intra-Christian scope of comparison and by integrating Judaism (and possibly Islam) into the analysis. Moreover, the study would have expanded the horizon for causal attributions. This, however, required an investigation that transformed the general foundations of the singular development of the West into historical preconditions. This transformation can already be witnessed in the study of ancient Judaism, where one such general foundation, the Old Testament, is put in a developmental perspective.[36]

In view of this and other statements, one could have expected in the envisioned concluding volume analyses of Christian salvation movements and their organizations; Western territorial and urban associations; Western sacred and profane law; Western science and technology; Western organizational forms in trade and industry, supplemented by those of banks and exchanges; as well as of "the tension and peculiar balance" existing above all between the hierocratic and political powers, including the urban ones. As part of the study of the economic ethics of world religions, the analysis of Western Christianity could no longer limit itself to one side of the causal chain, to the practical effects of a certain religious ethic on conduct. As already envisioned in the original version of the *Protestant Ethic*, the analysis also had to trace the "influence of economic development on the destiny of systems of religious ideas"[37] and reconstruct the practical effects of religious institutions on conduct as well;[38] above all, however, it had to show religion as an internal and external power in life, and in its tension-filled relation not simply to the economy, but also to political domination. Of course, it could do all of this in a "division of labor" with the second version of *Economy and Society*.[39]

If we accept this diagnosis of the status and the outline of the planned study of Western Christianity, then it seems reasonable to take the older version of *Economy and Society*, especially its chapters on the sociologies of religion, law, and domination, as a primary point of orientation in the reconstruction of those explanations necessitated for the "other side of the causal chain." Special attention must be given in this context to the development of the city, to the "rise of the Western bourgeoisie and its singularity."[40] This development would have formed one of the axes of the analysis, just as the rise and singularity of the Chinese patrimonial bureaucracy did in the study of China, and the rise and singularity of the Indian caste system did in the study of India.[41] As I mentioned earlier, however, in this case, there are—in contrast to the cases of the other never written studies—additional reference points beyond the older version of *Economy and Society*. Preceding it in time are above all the works on antiquity and the Middle Ages; following it is the *General Economic History*, in which Weber sketched an outline of a social and economic history of the West. Although he included a chapter on the cultural history of the West,[42] we are largely left—for the conceptions of duty anchored in religious ethics and its concomitant motivational forces, with the exception of a few passages in the chapter on religion in *Economy and Society*—with the two versions of the *Protestant Ethic*. A comparison of these two versions shows that the later one contains several references to the projected study of Western Christianity.

What topics would Weber have dealt with that go beyond the studies of Protestantism? Five are prominent. First of all, he intended to discuss the distinctiveness of Christianity in general within the history of religion. He attributed that distinctiveness, in spite of varying dogmatic foundations, to the "insertion of the decisive interest in proof" of one's salvation,[43] which provided Christianity in general with a tendency toward activism. Second, he wanted to furnish a more detailed depiction of pre-Reformation Catholicism. Provoked by Werner Sombart,[44] he had in mind here, not merely Thomism, which he had already touched upon in the first version, but also the differing "economic ethic of the Scotists, and especially of certain mendicant theologians of the fourteenth century," authors such as John Duns Scotus, Bernardine of Siena, and Anthony of Florence, and this in connection with the "discussion of the economic ethics of Catholicism in its positive relations to capitalism."[45] Third, he planned to deal with the few predecessors of ascetic Protestantism, with the monastic ethic, "the sects and . . . the ethics of Wyclif and Hus."[46] Fourth, he wanted to analyze post-Reformation and Counter Reformation Catholicism— for example, the Jesuits—as well as the "fundamental position of Port Royal and Jansenism on 'vocation.'"[47] Finally, again at the provocation of Sombart, he wanted to address the role of the Jews in economic life, something that, aside from the second version, can be inferred from the sociology of religion in *Economy and Society*[48] and from the *General Economic History*.[49] He wanted to do all this not in order to alter the Protestant Ethic thesis, but to supply the broader context in which it should be read.[50]

Thus, Weber would not have contented himself simply with the characterization of the distinctive features and singular developments of Mediterranean-Occidental civilization. He would have had to explain it, for the mere establishment of interconnections did not suffice here. A telling remark on this is found in the second version of the *Protestant Ethic*. There is nothing novel, Weber states, about the claim of a more or less "strong" relation between the different tendencies within ascetic Protestantism and the (modern) spirit of capitalism; this was something contemporaries were already well-acquainted with. The attempt "to explain the relation,"[51] however, is novel. And this claim is maintained throughout. In the "Author's Introduction" we read that "it once again is our first concern to recognize the special peculiarity of Western rationalism, and within this complex, its modern form, and to explain it."[52] Thus, the explanatory effort is paramount.

Admittedly, the singularity of this rationalism, which penetrates not only the economic but also the other important spheres and provides them with its own specific "hue," must, as the quote indicates, first be established. This is above all the task of comparative research, and even here we find a parting of the ways, as Weber's dispute with Marx on the one hand, and with the most important of his contemporary rivals—Georg Simmel, Lujo Brentano, and Werner Sombart—on the other, goes to show.[53] But regardless of what one holds to be the unique feature of modern capitalism—and according to Weber, this is not independent of one's own theoretical value relations—it has to be explained. This is premised on the separability of defining and conditioning properties.[54]

Thus, in the study of Western Christianity, as was already the case in the studies of Protestantism, Weber's first concern would have been to provide an explanation. In my view, this is shown unambiguously not least of all by the "Author's Introduction" that serves as the linchpin connecting the revised studies of Protestantism with the studies on the economic ethics. The attempted explanation would have been dedicated to answering: why it is only in the modern West that, aside from the kinds of capitalism prevalent everywhere, there exists "a very different form of capitalism which has appeared nowhere else: the rational capitalistic organization of (formally) free labour."[55] This was part of a further question, Why "did not the scientific, the artistic, the political, or the economic development [in China and India] enter upon that path of rationalization, which is singular to the West?"[56] The "rationalism specific to Western culture" is a rationalism of world mastery, something I have sought to demonstrate in a variety of contexts.[57] It appears in the economic realm in a specific form— in the utilization of capital on the market in the framework of rational business organization based on formally free labor—and in a specific spirit, one of innerworldly active asceticism on the basis of the idea of vocational calling. From the very beginning, in one way or another, as the reference to the dissertation has shown, Weber's thoughts revolved above all around these two cultural phenomena of universal significance. But only the study of Western Christianity would have "unified" in one explanatory approach both the topics and questions connected to these phenomena and the answers discovered after a long course of investigation.

What can be said about this explanatory approach? In other

words, What was Weber's "last theory" of modern Western capitalism? Formulated differently, the question is, How did Weber explain the singular development of the West?

Explaining the Western Trajectory: Three Great Transformations and Their Legacies

Historical Preconditions and Historical Epochs

Before I attempt to provide a sketch of the explanatory model of development in the West, a few remarks on Weber's mode of analysis need to be made. Here, not only his writings on method but also his practiced method has to be taken into account.[58]

I would like to begin with a piece of practiced method. At the very latest with the *Protestant Ethic*, and even more pointedly in the "Anticritiques," Weber distinguishes between the *spirit* of capitalism and capitalism as an economic *system*. The latter he sometimes terms its form or organization, or even its organizational form.[59] This distinction matches that between subjective and objective conditions, and is thus not limited to the economic sphere.[60] Capitalism stands for a certain spirit and a certain form that one can conceive of in either relative-general or relative-specific terms.[61] If one conceives of it in relative-general terms, ideal types of a general character—ideal-typical class concepts (*idealtypische Gattungsbegriffe*)—are formed that "distill that which is permanently the same, in conceptual purity" out of capitalism. If one conceives of it in relative-specific terms, ideal types of an individual character are formed that underscore those traits characteristic "for a definite epoch in contrast to other epochs," whereby "that which generally exists . . . is also presupposed as given and known of."[62] For example, when one contrasts an economic act in a capitalist economy to one in a household economy, one would stress that it is motivated by the pursuit of profitability; that it employs formally peaceful opportunities of exchange for this; and that it makes use of capital accounting, that is, of "the comparison of estimated monetary incomes with estimated monetary expenses, no matter how primitive the form."[63] Weber expressly states that, in the sense of this ideal-typical class concept, capitalism "even with a fair degree of capital accounting, has existed in all civilized countries of the earth, as far back as economic documents permit us to judge."[64] Nevertheless, as important as the precise formulation of such ideal-typical class concepts are—and it is the purpose of the sociology of the economy in the second version of *Economy and Society* to do just that—ultimately, it is not those "kinds, forms, and directions of capitalism" found in all the civilized countries that are of interest, but rather those brought forth only in the modern West. To achieve this formulation, the specific features have to be named that are singular to this modern capitalism in terms of spirit and form.

Spirit and form or system, however, are relatively independent from one another. Accordingly, different degrees of elective affinity can exist between them. The spirit can, as Weber expressly puts it, be more or less (or not at all) "adequate" to the form.[65] This is the case because neither do they necessarily share a common origin, nor is one necessarily derivable from the other. Any position that makes either of these two claims is to be considered reductionist. The respective transformations of institutions and mentalities, the revolutions from without and from within, are rarely synchronized in historical reality.[66] This is also the reason why the historical preconditions of the rise of a given capitalist economic system should initially be studied separately from the historical preconditions of the rise of a given capitalist spirit. Only after each "unit" has been analyzed on its own, can one then examine to what degree an elective affinity exists, whether spirit and form or system are one-sidedly or reciprocally favorably related, unrelated (indifferent), or even obstructive to one another. Moreover, this last analysis must be related to a specific epoch and a specific developmental realm.

According to Weber's own testimony, by 1910—and thus at the time he entered into the third phase of his work—he had written primarily two historical studies on capitalism: "Agrarian Sociology," to cover "the 'capitalism' of antiquity as an economic system," and the studies of Protestantism, to cover "what I sought to term the 'spirit' of modern capitalism."[67] Thus, in "Agrarian Sociology," by making recourse in part to some of his older writings, he rounds out his view of the economic and social, but not religious history of antiquity. In contrast, in the studies of Protestantism, mentality and motivation were placed in the foreground. These latter studies were not meant as a conclusion, but as a beginning. Their initial goals were "to trace the course of the factors arising out of the period of the Reformation," and then to go beyond that period and to the other side of the causal chain.[68]

The time of Reformation, or more precisely, the period following the Reformation, especially the seventeenth century, is important for Weber because it brings about a transformation—from within. This transformation adds a new thread to the pattern of Western development. In doing so, it creates one of the historical preconditions for modern cultural development. This is not the only one, not even for the modern spirit of capitalism.[69] It does, however, provide the capitalist spirit with a pattern "specifically different from that of the Middle Ages and Antiquity."[70] This is the reason why ascetic Protestantism is of historical significance. The latter has itself historical preconditions, internal and external, subjective and objective. To identify them and interweave such historical preconditions according to their spheres and epochs is the mode of analysis that Weber employs already in the studies of Protestantism, although in a deliberately one-sided manner. He changes this mode in the series on the economic ethics of the world religions,[71] where he performs a two-sided analysis throughout. Accordingly, the developmental history of Mediterranean-Occidental civilization would have been a history of epoch-related motivational and institutional transformations. Put another way, it would have been a history of motivational and institutional inventions, their interconnections, and their preservation as historical legacies.[72]

The thesis that historical preconditions have to be related to specific epochs may appear surprising. After all, did Weber not ban such terms as "epoch," "phase," and "stage" from the cultural sciences due to their evolutionary connotations? Did he not time and again warn against using such terms because they mislead one "to treat them as real beings in the manner of the organism with which biology is concerned, or as a Hegelian 'idea,' which lets its individual components emanate out of itself?"[73] Indeed, there can be no doubt that Weber vehemently attacked such concepts of evolution. They were based on a theory of concept formation that did away with the *hiatus irrationalis* between the concept and reality and identified development with progress (*Wertsteigerung*).[74] In his view, there is neither a lawful succession of universally repeated stages nor an inherent unity to any one stage such that its historical manifestations can be derived from its general character. Instead, the individual constellation of factors has to be addressed. Each individual constellation is caused by other individual constellations. Employing constructs like epochs, phases, and stages is therefore dangerous indeed. These constructs are acceptable, however, as long as they are used as heuristic devices and as conceptual means of representation, but not as means of drawing conclusions, whether by way of deduction or analogy. In fact, in the former regard, they are even unavoidable. For this reason, Weber formulates his stage concept in the following manner: "If we construct a 'cultural stage,' this mental construct solely means, in terms of the judgments it implies, that the individual phenomena that we summarize conceptually by means of it are 'adequate' to one another, possessing—one could say—a certain degree of intrinsic 'affinity,' with one another. It never entails, however, that they follow from one another according to any kind of lawfulness."[75] This expresses a methodological understanding of the stage concept suggested by Heinrich Rickert. Developmental stages result from a value-related combination of external historical connections and their internal structuring, whereby the "telos" is provided by the value chosen and conditioned by it (Rickert terms this "conditional-teleological").[76]

In this limited sense, Weber accepts the construction of developmental phases, stages, or epochs. Like Rickert, he holds them to be indispensable for structuring a historical nexus formed on the basis of a value relation. It is no coincidence that the division of topics planned by Weber for the "Handbook of Political Economy" (later named the "Outline of Social Economics") started with an article on "Epochs and Stages of the Economy" ("Epochen und Stufen der Wirtschaft"), which was then changed into "Economic Stages of Development" ("Volkswirtschaftliche Entwicklungsstufen"). In fact, the first volume of this multiauthor effort, distributed in 1914, began with Karl Bücher's classification of European economic development into the stages of the closed household economy (including the *oikos* and corvée labor [*Fronhof*], the urban economy, and the national economy [including the closed state economy (*Staatswirtschaft*) and the more or less open capitalist economy]).[77] As we know from his correspondence, Weber considered Bücher's exposition completely inadequate, and this estimation played some role in motivating him to revise his own contribution to the "Outline," which has been posthumously handed down to us as the first version of *Economy and Society*.[78] Nevertheless, he certainly did not consider this article inadequate merely because Bücher employed developmental stages, but because of the very schematic way in which they are employed and more generally, because of the extremely crude and undifferentiated depiction he offered of the different communal and associational forms, lumped together as "economic support groups" (*Versorgungsgemeinschaften*).[79]

The concept of phase, epoch, or stage thus serves Weber as a mode of representation with which to internally subdivide Mediterranean-Occidental development. It produced subunits of historical phenomena possessing a certain degree of inner relatedness, with modern Western rationalism providing the (heuristic) telos for their construction. It was in this sense that he spoke, as early as in the studies on Protestantism, of the capitalism of the heroic age in contrast to that of the iron age. In the "Anticritiques" we find the distinction between ancient, medieval, early modern, and modern capitalism; in the *General Economic History*, probably following Sombart's suggestion, we find the distinction between the precapitalist and capitalist age, the latter being subdivided yet again into an early and advanced stage.

A classification of a different kind was offered by Ernst Troeltsch in his "universal history of the ethics of Western Christianity"[80] for religious development. For him, the early church, medieval Christianity, and Protestantism formed, in relation to one another, relatively closed developmental realms. Nevertheless, they all made up part of a larger continuity in which the "essence" of Christianity was articulated in different, mutually related formations. Important in all of this, however, is the fact that neither in the internal subdivision of Western economic development nor in that of Western religious development are the stages—so conceived—relativized as being preliminary to some final condition or negatively evaluated. Instead, they remain stages in their own right and with their own internal logic. In his interpretation of medieval Catholicism, Ernst Troeltsch found a very fitting way to put this: "Medieval religion and its social teachings are not a distortion of the 'essence of Christianity,' nor are they a developmental phase of the Christian idea serving other purposes. Instead, they represent an articulation of religious consciousness in keeping with the general constellation, possessing its own assets and truths, and its own errors and horrors."[81]

Thus, the internal classification leads to subunits with, as it were, both substantive and temporal references. Substantively, it refers to structural principles that have internal and external sides, motivational and institutional components.[82] Temporally, they refer to a historical span of time in which a certain structural principle is predominant. In this sense, for example, Werner Sombart distinguishes the precapitalist from the capitalist economic epoch. In the precapitalist epoch, the principle of primary want satisfaction or self-sufficiency (*Eigenwirtschaft*), with empiricist technology and traditionalist management, predominates. In the capitalist epoch, the principle of market production (or of a monetary exchange), with scientific technology and rationalist management, prevails. Further differentiations arise from the facts that economic principles can take on a variety of forms, for example, the principle of primary want satisfaction the form of a peasant village or a manor, and that transitional ages can be conceived in which several principles compete. Thus, Sombart views the time of rebirth of the exchange economy in Western cities as such a transitional period. Nevertheless, initially, at least in the urban crafts, the aspect of customary sustenance, the provision of inhabitants in accordance with their status, remains intact. It is only gradually, on the basis of particular circumstances, that the market principle penetrates traditional relationships and begins to replace them. Thus, the age of early capitalism is reached, in which the principle of relatively self-sufficient want satisfaction is seriously challenged by the market principle.[83]

The *General Economic History* shows that Weber thought along similar lines. An economic epoch can then be termed typically capitalist only "if the satisfaction of needs is predominantly capitalistic in such a way that if this type of organization is imagined away, the want satisfaction would have to collapse."[84] This is the underlying meaning of his view that although politically organized capitalism has existed in all previous history and the first moves in the direction of market-oriented capitalist enterprise occurred relatively early, there is but one capitalist epoch, the modern age. Its historical preconditions arose, however, in a number of different precapitalist economic epochs, including not only the early capitalist age but also antiquity and the Middle Ages.

Yet, the economy is only one of several societal spheres. As much as a "universal history of culture" such as Weber's *Collected Essays in the Sociology of Religion* must pay special attention to its spirit and form in its developmental history, equally must it attend to the "elective affinities" between this developmental history and that of the other spheres, especially of religion and politics. For this reason, the division into stages or epochs involves more than simply economic principles; it involves configurations of order that shape an entire civilization. A series of such epochs and their linkages by means of historical legacies must provide the basis for explaining modern culture, especially modern economic culture. Cultural science, in Weber's understanding, thus sees itself confronted by four tasks, which are mutually independent but at the same time interrelated: (1) developing typologies (*Kasuistiken*) of clear (historical) concepts and establishing general rules of occurrence is the task of theoretical cultural science; (2) identifying (individual) constellations, and (3) making causal attributions, as well as (4) estimating developmental tendencies connected to contemporary constellations is the task of historical cultural science. Weber described these four tasks in the essay "Objectivity":

The determination of those (hypothetical) "laws" and "factors" would in any case be only the first of the many operations that would lead us to the desired knowledge. The analysis of the historically given individual configuration of those "factors" and their significant concrete interaction, conditioned by their historical context, and especially the rendering intelligible of the basis and kind of this significance would be the next task to be achieved. This task must be achieved, it is true, by the utilization of the preliminary analysis, but it is nonetheless an entirely new and distinct task. The tracing as far into the past as possible of the individual features of these historically evolved configurations which remain significant for the present, and their historical explanation by antecedent and equally individual configurations would be the third task. Finally, the prediction of possible future constellations would be a conceivable fourth task.[85]

The division into epochs is removed from the history of events but still related to it. At least Weber's scattered remarks seem to justify such an interpretation. In a comparison between the Chinese and the Western political and economic orders, Weber refers to those revolutions decisive for the political and economic destiny of the West, "the Italian revolution of the twelfth and the thirteenth centuries, the Netherlands' revolution of the sixteenth century, the English revolution of the seventeenth century, and the American and French revolutions of the eighteenth century."[86] A passage from the second version of *Economy and Society* practically reads like an explanation of this first quote:

The major forerunners of the modern, specifically Western form of capitalism are to be found in the [medieval] urban communes with their particular type of relatively rational administration. Its primary development took place from the sixteenth to the eighteen centuries in Holland and England, whose status [*ständische*] order was distinguished by the unusual power of the bourgeois strata and the preponderance of their economic interests. The fiscal and utilitarian imitations, which on the Continent were introduced into the purely patrimonial states or states with feudal legacies, have in common with the Stuart system of monopolistic industry the fact that they do not stand in the main line of continuity with the later autonomous capitalistic development.[87]

Political and economic destiny is, however, joined by religious destiny; it is linked with the former in a variety of ways but cannot be deduced from it. Its decisive revolutions include not only the Reformation and its primarily seventeenth-century consequences, but also the radical changes in the eleventh and twelfth centuries connected to the separation of the Western church from the Eastern church, the Gregorian reforms, and the Investiture Struggle.[88] From the junction of the political and economic with religious "destinies" three great transformations result, at least for the developmental history of Western Europe. The transformation from the eleventh to the thirteenth century produced some external historical preconditions for modern capitalism. The transformation from the sixteenth to the eighteenth century gave rise to internal historical preconditions for modern capitalism. The "new spirit" and the already largely complete form entered into a genuine elective affinity such that a development unobstructed by any spiritual restraints could take place. Here, spirit and form are not merely not at odds; they augment each other. The transformation in the nineteenth and twentieth centuries established victorious capitalism, with its rational organization of formally free labor, on a mechanical basis once and for all; it "emancipates" itself from all religious, indeed, from all ethical foundations.

In other words, from a primarily economic perspective we observe first "the late medieval, still highly unstable processes of capitalist development,"[89] then, the early capitalist development, especially its spiritual side,[90] which brings forth the man of vocation, who, in contrast to the medieval Catholic and the Lutheran, needs make no compromises "in order to feel at one with his activity."[91] Finally, we encounter advanced capitalism, which achieves hegemony once and for all both over all traditionalist economic mentalities and over all economic systems oriented around Sombart's principle of relative self-sufficiency. In Weber's eyes the capitalist system would reach its ecological limits only in the very distant future. As Werner Sombart reports: "When I once spoke with Max Weber about the future and we raised the question when the witch's sabbath that humanity in the capitalist countries had been in since the beginning of the nineteenth century would end, he answered, 'When the last ton of ore will have been smelted with the last ton of coal.'"[92]

Two points now emerge clearly. First, it would be wrong to assume that Weber connected the decisive transformation that ultimately led to modern capitalism (and to modern rationalism) solely with the Reformation and its consequences. The latter is important, but it alone did not produce all of the important historical preconditions. Second, Weber certainly would not have judged the first transformation as the crucial turning point in Western European development, as recent investigations tend to do.[93] Nevertheless, as the opening passage of *Ancient Judaism* shows, he treated the cultural significance of "the Roman Catholic Church resting on the Roman concept of office" and "the medieval order of estates" as equal to that of ascetic Protestantism for the development of Western Europe, even though, for the economic development, he deemed the medieval urban expansion even more significant than the "papal revolution."[94] Nonetheless, regardless of how one places the accents, Weber considered the High Middle Ages a phase of important, largely institutional transformations for Western Europe. On a smaller scale, this is already demonstrated by his dissertation.

When Randall Collins conjectures that had Weber written his planned study of medieval (*sic*) Christianity, he would then have realized that the High Middle Ages were the most important of all institutional turning points on the path to capitalism—"his commitment to the vestiges of his Protestantism argument may have kept him from recognizing this earlier"[95]—one can only wonder about the knowledge of Weber's work possessed by an author who sought to write *Weberian Sociological Theory*. Weber neither overlooked the historical significance of the High Middle Ages for the singular development of the West in general and for Western capitalism in particular, nor does a contradiction exist between the thesis of a largely institutional transformation in the Middle Ages and a largely motivational transformation in the post-Reformation period.

Yet a third point is important in this context. Marx not only identifies the history of the West with that of humanity, but also, owing to his concept of the feudal mode of production, fails to recognize the historical significance of both the medieval and the post-Reformation transformations. In contrast, Weber's approach is safeguarded against this kind of normative Eurocentrism[96] and against a periodization of the history of the West according to which the "great transformation" is largely identical with the great political revolutions of modern times, chiefly with the French Revolution.[97] Admittedly, Weber's subdivision into epochs, his periodization, remains vague. And it also appears to receive a different accent for every different subdevelopment. Moreover, he often operates with the triad of antiquity, Middle Ages, and modernity. Nevertheless, there are immanent reasons why his approach is open to revision in this regard, especially since he evidently emphasizes the decisive points for the pre-Reformation phase of development. Even his critics admit this. In his basic study of the genesis of the distinctive legal tradition of the West, Harold J. Berman writes (even though his closing remarks blur the differences between Marx and Weber too much) that Weber

confirms many of the root facts that form the foundation of the present study: that the Investiture Struggle of the late eleventh and early twelfth centuries laid the foundations for the separation of church and state, that the new canon law of the twelfth century was the first modern Western legal system, that the reciprocity of rights and duties of lord and vassal distinguished Western feudalism from that of other societies, that the Western city of the twelfth century and thereafter was unique in conferring constitutional rights upon its citizens. Yet Weber is prevented from drawing the right conclusions from these facts by his historiography, which postulates a sharp break in the sixteenth century between the Middle Ages and Modern Times, and between feudalism and capitalism. For Weber, as for Marx, Western law is bourgeois law, capitalist law, or in Weber's peculiar terminology, bureaucratic law, formally rational law.[98]

The study of Western Christianity, starting from the studies of ancient Judaism and ancient Christianity,[99] undoubtedly would have devoted great attention to the formation of the Roman church—in Weber's view the first rational bureaucracy in world history—and its relationship not only to the movements of orthodox religious virtuosi, but also to the feudal, *ständisch*, and urban political powers. His interpretation is adumbrated in the first version of *Economy and Society*, especially in the sociologies of law and domination.[100] In other words, this study would certainly have analyzed the first transformation before moving on to the second one, and thus to that transformation that is primarily described in the studies of Protestantism. As mentioned earlier, this study would have also removed the latter ones from their isolation and developed the other side of the causal chain. In this sense, there really is, as Randall Collins correctly suspects, "the Weberian revolution of the High Middle Ages."[101]

The Object of Explanation: Market-Oriented
Capitalist Enterprise with Free Labor

Before this revolution of the High Middle Ages can be characterized, the distinctive features of modern Western capitalism have to be clarified. In other words, what are its defining qualities that ultimately have to be explained? The ideal-typical class concept of capitalism—economic action based on the expectation of profit through the exploitation of exchange opportunities, or, economic action that seeks utilization of capital for ever-renewed profit—does not suffice here. Instead, one has to specify those of its qualities that do "not exist in this way in other epochs of the formation or are specifically different in degree."[102] Although Weber repeatedly emphasizes that the definition of such complex formations as modern capitalism can never be made at the outset of an investigation, but is only "possible as the result of a synthesis undertaken step by step,"[103] Karl Marx's proposition that research and its subsequent synthesis are always two distinct processes holds for Weber as well.[104] In fact, Weber too prefaces at least the *Collected Essays in the Sociology of Religion* with the results of the synthesis he has achieved step by step, conclusions known as the "Author's Introduction."[105]

In my view, the definition of specifically modern Western capitalism is made up of three complexes of qualities, which Weber does not always keep separate. The first complex is related to the modern capitalist enterprise, the second to the modern capitalist economic order, and the third to the modern capitalist spirit. Modern capitalism is first characterized by the pursuit of profitability undertaken by profit-seeking enterprises (*Erwerbsbetriebe*), that is, by units continuously oriented toward profit, in contrast to households or budgetary units oriented toward their own want satisfaction. Furthermore, these units combine the three factors of production: labor, the material means of production, and management in an establishment, such as a workshop or an office. Strictly speaking, the concept of the profit-seeking enterprise includes only the case in which the economic firm and the technical establishment are identical.[106]

The modern profit-seeking enterprise can be more precisely described by means of three features: the existence of formally free labor and its combination with machines and apparatus ("fixed capital"), which leads to the technically defined specialization and

interlinking of labor processes; the internal and external autonomization of the profit-seeking enterprise vis-à-vis the household,
which is seen in its spatial separation (between living quarters and
the workshop or office), in its legal separation (between private
wealth and the capital of the firm or establishment), and in separate accounting (between the administration of wealth on the basis of [monetary] householding and capital accounting on the basis
of double-entry bookkeeping [*doppelte Buchführung*]); and the
disconnection of the fate of the capital of an enterprise from that
of the wealth of an individual owner, which is reflected in the
separation between the management and the ownership of the material means of production (of "fixed capital").[107] The modern capitalist manufacturing enterprise (*Gewerbebetrieb*) is typically a
factory business in the legal form of a joint-stock company, and
the modern capitalist commercial enterprise, an office business in
the legal form of an unlimited partnership. As such, they belong
in the category of "firm[s] conducted on the basis of capital
accounting."[108]

Weber defines the modern capitalist firm, analogously to the
modern state, on the basis of the means specific to it. Whereas the
modern state is defined in terms of its monopoly of legitimate
physical force, the modern capitalist firm is defined in terms of
capital accounting. The degree of formal rationality of modern
capitalist profit-seeking enterprises is ultimately tied to the degree of rationality of its capital accounting. The latter is, however,
not merely dependent upon the aforementioned features, but also
upon those connected to the capitalist economic order as a market
economy because "a maximum of formal rationality of capital accounting in production enterprises"[109] can be obtained only if the
three aforementioned features are joined by three further ones: the
"commercialization of ownership shares in enterprises through
the various forms of securities" that promotes the separation of
the household from the profit-seeking enterprise and of wealth
from capital, and above all, that sets "the capital at the disposal of
the enterprise" free from "the private wealth of the owners" and
its destiny;[110] a monetary system monopolized and secured by the
state; and the most far-reaching freedom and openness of markets
possible (markets for commodities, labor, capital, money, etc.), enabling the "specialization of autocephalous and autonomous units
in a market economy [to arise], which are oriented only to their
own self-interest, formally only to the regulations of a formal-

order-enforcing organization." The "pure *Rechtsstaat*," the lais-sez-fair state, which admittedly represents a conceptually limiting case (*Grenzfall*), is an example of such a formal order. In reality, the modern constitutional state, like all political associations, is an organization that regulates the economy, and the only question is how much it limits itself to formal regulation.[111]

Where unfree labor is predominant or the material means of production are mere tools, where the divisions between wealth and capital, income and profit, household and enterprise remain unstable, and where the fate of the enterprise's capital remains intimately connected to that of the wealth of individuals, the organization of labor characteristic of specifically modern Western capitalism is lacking in one way or another. Where, as was in part the case in imperial Germany, the stock market is insufficiently organized and its brokers are not sufficiently professionalized,[112] where the monopolization of the monetary system by the state is lacking, and above all where political powers exercise substantive economic regulation, the "satisfaction of wants that results from action purely oriented to advantages in exchange on the basis of self-interest" is lacking in one way or the other.[113] As long as want satisfaction through markets does not yet prevail, individual cases of modern capitalist profit-seeking enterprises or of a capitalist organization of labor may occur, but they do not determine economic life as a whole. They can cease to exist "without introducing any overwhelming change."[114]

In the sense of this combination of micro- and macroeconomic features, Weber spoke of "capitalism based on enterprises with rational organization of (formally) free labor" in his "Author's Introduction." He added the adjective "bourgeois" to this summarizing definition, however.[115] This refers to a social stratum, a "social carrier," as well as a "spirit," a specific economic mentality. In terms of the latter, bourgeois means that neither the seigneurial mentality of provision according to status, the peasant or artisan mentality of sustenance, nor the speculative mentality of adventure capitalists is predominant, but rather that there has come about a rational moderation of the pursuit of profit that lets itself be governed by the principle of calculability based on capital accounting and market competition. It is the spirit of proving oneself in one's vocation that is satisfied by the (formally) peaceful utilization of capital solely for the sake of capital utilization and for no other purpose.[116]

Thus, Weber distinguishes economies based on the household

from those based on acquisition, and within the latter, peaceful from violent acquisition. The first distinction is based upon the dichotomies of household versus profit-seeking enterprise, want satisfaction versus profitability, and wealth versus capital. The most important dichotomy connected to the second distinction is whether political or market opportunities are exploited. Only the latter leads in the direction of formal, rational capital accounting. Moreover, only by progressing in this direction can one reach the bourgeois enterprise, whether it is understood primarily in terms of manufacture, of commerce, of banking, or of a stock exchange. Economic activity within the frameworks of the household or of politics has always existed both in form and spirit; the same does not hold for economic activity by means of the capitalist organization of labor in relatively free and open markets. This kind of economic activity is instead specifically Western and, in its formal rationality, specifically modern. For this reason, the historic claim made in the second version of *Economy and Society* reads:

It is only in the West that we find rational capitalist enterprises with fixed capital, free labor, the rational specialization and interlinking of labor processes, and the purely market-determined supply functions based on such enterprises. In other words, only here do we find the capitalist form of the organization of labor, which, formally speaking, is purely voluntary, as the typical and predominant form of satisfying the needs of the broad masses, with expropriation of the workers from the means of production and appropriation of the firms by the owners of securities. It is only here that we find public credit in the form of issues of government securities, the "going public" of business enterprises, the floating of security issues and financing carried on as the specialized function of rational business enterprises, trade in commodities and securities on organized exchanges, money and capital markets, and monopolistic organizations as a form of the rational organization of production and not only of trade.[117]

And, one can add, only here can be found the concomitant spirit of economic activity as a vocation.

To sum up, the specificity of modern Western capitalism consists of its being bourgeois capitalism based on the enterprise, with its rational organization of formally free labor. For this reason, it is only here that the opposition between big industrialist and wage laborer exists, as well as the national class division between bourgeoisie and proletariat. In contrast, the ancient world is characterized by the local and interlocal opposition between creditors and debtors, and the medieval world by that between putters-out and those whom they employ.[118] As with Marx, for Weber modern capitalism first of all rests upon the separation of what was originally "organically" connected: of the worker from the means, materials, and place of labor; of the business from the household; of the business capital from personal wealth; and of the economy from the state. Nevertheless, Weber's primary concern is not, like Marx's, the expropriation of the worker from the conditions of his self-realization, but rather the autonomization of business establishments. And, in contrast to Marx, he is not satisfied with the analysis of only the objective side of the process. One must also devote a truly independent chapter to the subjective side, to the conception of the business as a "mystical entity," as a "cause" transcending individuals. This is the reason why even the *General Economic History* ends with a chapter sketching "The Evolution of the Capitalist Spirit." That the latter cannot be understood merely as the function of objective economic conditions is emphasized both in the "Conceptual Introduction" to this lecture series[119] and in the "Author's Introduction" to the *Collected Essays in the Sociology of Religion*, and thus in two of his last writings. Especially the latter of these two texts contains a radical rejection of any kind of one-sidedly economic, and, one could also say, of any kind of one-sidedly institutional explanatory model of modern Western capitalism. If one seeks to explain the origins of modern economic rationalism, one undoubtedly must recognize "the fundamental importance of the economic factor, above all take account of the economic conditions." But, Weber continues, "at the same time the opposite causation must not be left out of consideration." It is oriented toward "the ability and disposition of men to adopt certain types of practical rational conduct"—conduct that is linked to faith in certain ethically founded conceptions of duty.[120]

The First Transformation:
Three Revolutions Intertwined

The Papal Revolution

The question must now be taken up, What did the first transformation contribute to the rise of the capitalist organization of formally free labor, to the modern market economy, and to the bourgeois mode of conduct as defined? Which historical preconditions did it give rise to? In order to shed light on this, one must provide a short explanation of the shifts Weber saw occurring subsequent to this transformation. To put it simply, Weber refers to the economic and political as well as the religious legacy of late antiquity as it made its way down from Diocletian and Constantine to Charlemagne.

The young Weber had already touched on this theme. In his 1896 lecture, in which he addressed an educated public on the decline of ancient culture (including some claims he was later to revise in "Agrarian Sociology"), he presented Charlemagne as the belated executor of Diocletian's will. In Weber's view at that time, the history of Western Europe began where that of late antiquity ended—in a ruralized inland culture. The maritime and urban culture of Mediterranean antiquity had perished in its revision to a subsistence economy and a concomitant ruralization.[121] This process stripped all of its leading institutions—the standing army, the salaried officialdom, the interlocal exchange of commodities or the city—of their economic basis. They were replaced by a rural manorial system, which in turn provided the beginnings for the economic and political development of Western Europe. In the Carolingian age, the political unity of the West was reawakened on the basis of a strict economy in kind:

The manors are the centers of civilization, and they also support the monasteries. Manorial lords run the political system, and the greatest manorial lord is the king himself, a rural illiterate in his way of life. The king has his castles in the country, and he has no capital; he is a monarch who travels . . . even more than monarchs travel today. He travels so much because he goes from castle to castle to consume what has been stored up there for him.[122]

Unlike the situation in many Oriental manorial systems, the overlords did not stand directly opposite a mass of subjects differentiated according to sibs and occupations. Instead, he "stands as one landlord [*Grundherr*] above other landlords, who as local honoratiores wield an autonomous authority within their respective local domains."[123] A patrimonial state of this kind, which in spite of its external unity was internally decentralized, and which was lacking the concept of the city in its administrative-legal sense, was not capable of supporting anything like the differentiated and refined urban culture of antiquity. Necessary preconditions of the latter were the development of a monetary economy and above all of a market economy. Therefore, the young Weber viewed the urbanization and state formation of this rural inland culture as the decisive processes for Western development. This too is attested to by his lecture, which closes with the following words:

It was only when the medieval city developed out of free division of labor and commercial exchange, when the transition to a national economy made possible the development of burgher freedoms, and when the bonds imposed by outer and inner feudal authorities were cast off that—like Antaeus—the classical giant regained new power, and the cultural heritage of antiquity revived in the light of modern bourgeois culture.[124]

Admittedly, the Weber of 1896 explored economic and social history largely without reference to the history of religion. Nonetheless, he did remark in his lecture that in the process of decline a tremendous process of recovery and revitalization also occurred in which Christianity played an important role. Family organization and private property were returned to the masses of the unfree, and Christianity invested this return of the "speaking inventory" into the circle of humanity "with firm moral guarantees."[126] In "Agrarian Sociology," Weber also largely left out religious history, which he had in the meantime discovered.[125] Here he merely objects to the notion that Christianity arose from motives of social reform or even of social revolution and was originally a proletarian movement.[127] Only with the two major projects does Weber take the religious aspect that had guided the studies of Protestantism systematically into account. It is true, however, that one finds only allusions to the period from the Constantinian turn until the Gregorian reforms.[128]

These allusions are mostly to the history of the church, a topic where Weber largely shared Troeltsch's contentions. To fill in the gaps we can, therefore, partly rely on Troeltsch. Following him, we see that a church that was regionalized in comparison to that of late antiquity was in keeping with the early medieval patrimonial state, externally "unified" through gradual expansion and internally decentralized. Troeltsch viewed the "splitting up of the imperial church to Germanic-Roman national churches [Landeskirchen]" in the West[129] and their subsequent new relationship to the world, as one of the decisive preconditions for a development at the end of which a new universalist imperial church, distinct from both the old Roman and from the Eastern church, could emerge.[130] The church that was universalized and politicized by the empire of late antiquity in order to support the unity of the realm had accommodated itself to the empire but was not intrinsically connected to it.[131] Only in the period of national churches, which seemingly signified a "complete dissolution of the imperial church and an apparently final abolition of the canon law of the early unified church,"[132] did a genuine *interpenetration* of the spiritual and the secular take place. This certainly initially occurred under secular authority.

A spiritual-worldly organization resulted that, in Weber's view, was "predominantly caesaropapist."[132] Whereas Troeltsch focused largely upon the inner Christianization of the West, Weber placed the external Christianization at the center of his analysis. The closer the alliance between the highest patrimonial lord and the church, the more the power of local forces tended to remain in check. For Troeltsch as for Weber, this (inner and outer) alliance bore fruit in the Frankish, and, above all, the German national church. Weber remarks,

> In Germany, in particular, the king attempted, at first with the greatest success, to establish a countervailing power to the local and regional powers; in the bishops he created a clerical estate of political honoratiores to compete with the corresponding secular stratum. Because bishoprics were not hereditary and the bishops not locally recruited and interested, they appeared solidary with the king by virtue of their universalistic interests. Furthermore, the seigneurial and political powers granted to them by the king remained even legally in his hands.[134]

Through this inner and outer interpenetration of the secular and the spiritual, the old parallelism of universal church and Roman Empire could be replaced by a new unitarianism of the (Germanic and Roman) national church and patrimonial domination. For Weber, this finds expression precisely in that caesaropapist linkage of political and hierocratic domination that the Carolingians achieved in the Frankish realm and that, after the divisions in the empire, was maintained in the German region under the Ottonians and early Salians.[135] This linkage, indeed this melding of church and "state," had far-reaching consequences. As Harold J. Berman observed: "Contrary to modern ideas of the separateness of the church and the state, the church in the year 1000 was not conceived as a visible, corporate, legal structure standing opposite the political authority. Instead, the church, the *ecclesia*, was conceived as the Christian people, *populus christianus*, which was governed by both secular and priestly rulers (*regnum* and *sacerdotium*)."[136]

With the revitalization of the imperial idea through the establishment of the Holy Roman Empire (later called the Holy Roman Empire of the German nation), however, the idea of a universal church also had to regain attractiveness.[137] Decisive for our context is the fact that national churchdom had set the stage for a relatively unified Christian culture (*Einheitskultur*), which, in comparison to the early church and to the development of the Eastern church, provided a historically new precondition for a positive relationship between hierocratic and political domination.

According to Troeltsch, the development toward an outer and inner unified Christian culture culminated in the reform of Gregory VII. In the time separating Gregory from Augustine, not only was a unified church of priests consolidated (in Weber's terms, an institution of grace based on the charisma of office) but also "a new relationship to the state" was established, "where the state appropriates the spiritual norms and goals of life, internally joining its own structure with that of the church, and in this way submitting, directly or indirectly, the general life of society to the norms of the church."[138] This was mostly due to the success of the Gregorian movement. The Gregorian reforms must be regarded, therefore, as a major event in the history of the West.

For Weber, the Gregorian movement was an example of a reform movement of a restored church, which, as a rule, attempts to eliminate the autonomous charisma of political domination and to transform caesaropapism into theocracy. He considered the struggle between hierocratic and political domination as a conflict over the distribution of power. At least in Italy, an aristocratic stratum of religious intellectuals "joined forces with an emerging bourgeoisie against the feudal powers."[139] As is well known, the struggle ended with a compromise, whereby the coalition between hierocratic and political domination of the Carolingian age and of the first phase of the Holy Roman Empire was replaced by a separation of powers. It bound both sides to specific inner and outer limits to legitimacy, while simultaneously leaving their autonomous sources of legitimacy intact. This did not exclude the possibility that occasionally the old alliance could revitalize itself under changed conditions.[140] Nevertheless, from the perspective of Weberian sociology, the Investiture Struggle resulted in an institutional invention with lasting effects, for it set the stage for a situation in which neither caesaropapism nor theocracy could ultimately prevail but only a tension-filled dualism between political and hierocratic domination. This was one reason why the culture of the Western Middle Ages, marked by what Harold J.

Berman termed the "papal revolution," came to fill a unique position in comparative terms. As Weber summarized it:

At least from a sociological viewpoint, the Occidental Middle Ages were much less of a unified culture [*Einheitskultur*] than the Egyptian, Tibetan, and Jewish cultures after the hierocracy's victory, or than China since the triumph of Confucianism, Japan—if we disregard Buddhism—since the victory of feudalism, Russia since the rise of caesaropapism and state bureaucracy, and Islam since the definite establishment of the caliphate and the prebendalization of domination; finally, even Hellenic and Roman culture were more unified than medieval Europe. This generalization appears to be largely correct even though all these cultures were unified in a different sense.[141]

This conclusion seems to contradict Troeltsch's thesis of the Middle Ages as a relatively unified culture. On a closer inspection, however, this is not the case. Of course, Weber sought to modify Troeltsch's analysis in a specifically sociological direction, but he accepted Troeltsch's interpretation of the repercussions of the Gregorian reforms. Strictly speaking, he depicted the relatively unified Christian culture of which Troeltsch spoke as a relatively unified *ecclesiastical* culture. It was based on the ideas that the secular had to be relativized in terms of the spiritual and the non-religious in terms of the religious in such a way that all spheres of life could be Christianized without losing their relative autonomy. This called for a particular type of hierarchy, with the institution of sacramental grace as its point of reference. Through the institution of sacramental grace everyone could in principle participate in the "union" with the divine, regardless of status or occupation. To obtain access to salvation, it ultimately sufficed to be obedient to an institution by virtue of the sacrament of penance. In Troeltsch's view, the primary result of the Gregorian reforms was the realization of the unity of Christian-ecclesiastical culture in this sense. It provided leeway for autonomous developments outside the church. The Gregorian and post-Gregorian world view gained support from dogmatic developments in the twelfth and thirteenth centuries, however. Three new dogmas resulted, with the first two remaining implicit and the third receiving official formulation. They expanded upon the prior foundations of dogma in "church, canon, and tradition and . . . the christological trinity." These three new dogmas were "(1) the dogma of the universal episcopacy of the Pope, (2) the dogma of the superordination of the spiritual power over the worldly power, and (3) the dogma of the administration of grace through the seven sacraments."[142]

Weber too viewed the Gregorian reforms as the decisive step in the full development of the Western church as an institution of sacramental grace.[143] Its combination of institutional and sacramental grace, its organization of confessionals and penances that "combined the techniques of Roman law with the Teutonic conception of fiscal expiation (*Wergeld*)" achieved "the Christianization of Western Europe with unparalleled force."[144] But this ecclesiastic articulation also implied that "the ultimate religious value is pure obedience to the institution, which is regarded as inherently meritorious, and not concrete, substantive ethical obligation, nor even the qualification of superior moral capacity (*Virtuosenqualifikation*) achieved through one's own methodological ethical actions."[145] This left room for the autonomous development of knightly-manorial, bourgeois-urban, and peasant-rural cultures.[146] Therefore, there are "limits of effectiveness" to Troeltsch's relatively unified culture of Christianity. Two are especially important for Weber: first, this culture does not ultimately force the individual to conduct his life in a rationally methodical way,[147] and second, it relativizes the "tension between religious ethics and the nonethical or unethical requirements of life in the political and economic structures of power within the world."[148] Thus, paradoxically, this culture did not enforce uniformity in legitimation and organization, as it might appear, but rather made possible, under the canopy of a Christian symbolic universe, a certain pluralism.[149]

This paradox holds not only for the medieval configuration as a whole, but also for its religious sphere. This is seen in the manner in which the endemic unity-threatening conflict in the early church—between a "sect-like" monasticism based on personal charisma and a "church-like" priesthood based on the charisma of the office—was ultimately regulated by the medieval church,[150] for the church reform movement under Gregory VII linked itself to the monastic reform movement that arose in Cluny.[151] Here, too, Troeltsch's unity thesis, put in sociological terms, goes to the core of Weber's concerns. It shows that, in the framework of a relatively unified ecclesiastical culture, asceticism and monasticism no longer are ends in themselves but are means serving general aims of the church.[152] Here, too, the idea of a particular type of hierarchy applies. As in the case of church and "state," Troeltsch points to a decisive shift from late antiquity to the Middle Ages. Weber assessed this reform in the same way. It is his thesis that the tension between monasticism and hierocracy, which is certainly not limited to Western Christianity, found a specific "solution" "by integrating the monks into a bureaucratic organization; subject to a specific discipline and removed from everyday life by the vows of poverty and chastity, they became the troops of the monocratic head of the church."[153]

By linking hierocratic and monastic reform to the unified culture of the church, the "surplus achievement" arising from adherence to the *consilia evangelica* can become a creative instead of a destructive source for the church. It can, usually by means of the establishment of new monastic orders, work against the routinization, especially against the feudalization, of the church. Naturally, after a charismatic period, the new orders are also subject to these processes. But before this occurs, they increase the miraculous powers of the church by adding to the "repository of blessings" that the church has at its disposal "for the benefit of those deficient in charismatic gifts."[154]

What Troeltsch termed the "ecclesiastic transformation of monasticism" was for Weber the process of "making the monk fit for work on behalf of the hierocratic authority—the foreign and home mission and the struggle against competing authorities."[155] This process of integration, which found its high point in the policy of Innocent III, can be sociologically described as a process of inclusion by which the monks were to become "the elite troops of religious virtuosi within the community of the faithful."[156] Integration by virtue of inclusion has to be distinguished from integration by virtue of assimilation. The former favors internal pluralization, the latter does not.[157] The recognition of special moral codes and special organizations within the church naturally does not imply the irrevocable disappearance of the tension between office charisma and personal charisma. On the contrary, integration by virtue of inclusion increases the potential for internal tensions. This integration adds to the religious stratification between the virtuosi and the masses (or the laity), found in all major religions, and the stratification between different religious virtuosi (for example, between higher and lower clergy, between monks and priests, between high and low monks, between monastic orders and tertiary orders, between male and female orders). Moreover, it is also probable that this religious stratification will become linked to social and economic stratification (as the aristocratic predominance in church and monastery shows).

Thus, the internal pluralization concomitant with the process of inclusion fails to threaten the unity of culture only as long as the differentiated units actually remain a part of the hierocratic regimentation of life. This in turn has an effect upon the shaping of the membership role. It becomes formalized. This formalization is seen in the codification and legalization of role expectations and in the concurrent sanctions.[158] Precisely this internal pluralization appears to have occurred in the course of Gregorian reforms. Evidence of this is provided by the fact that "excommunication against those who were persistently disobedient and unbelieving" was in fact relatively effectively carried out.[159] Gregory's great weapons were, as Troeltsch put it, "exclusion from the sacraments and excommunication, those of his successors the interdict and the declaration of a crusade."[160] Exclusion from the church, however, usually also led to social and economic boycott, for which it provided the legitimation.[161]

Here another reflection of Weber's applies. In a church rich in dogma, as the Christian church is in comparison to other hierocracies,[162] the personal acceptance of dogmas, the *fides explicita*, can certainly become a membership criterion, especially for religious virtuosi who possess or should possess a corresponding "theological intellectualism."[163] This can also enhance internal tensions, however. Christianity as a religion of faith is marked from the outset by an anti-intellectual quality. One way out is to reduce *fides explicita* into *fides implicita*, to leave it, at least for the laity, at the declaration of trust in the church.[164] But, as a consequence of this, a genuine religiosity of faith stands, in its decisive convictional quality, opposed to theological intellectualism. For the pious, one's own intellectual strength is always inadequate; conviction transcends intellectuality.[165] The codification and legalization accompanying the formalization of membership could thus appear, particularly to the genuinely faithful, as a mere externality (*Veräußerlichung*). The individualism of faith and conviction inhabiting Christianity from the beginning could therefore be brought under control only with difficulty by means of an inwardly pluralistic, outwardly unified church culture.

If one follows Herbert Grundmann's depiction of religious movements, which includes the women's movements, in the twelfth and thirteenth centuries, the inclusion strategy asserted here forces all medieval religious movements to make the decision either to assimilate themselves to the ecclesiastic forms of the *vita religiosa*, that is, to become a monastic order, or to free themselves from the ecclesiastic organization and thus separate themselves from the church in general, that is, to become a sect, a heresy.[166] This is the reverse side of the relatively unified church culture, with its tendency toward codification and legalization, that certainly offered special paths to salvation for Christians in accordance with their "religious sensibility," insofar as this did not violate the basic maxim of *"extra ecclesiam nulla salus."* In contrast, however, non-Christians were subject to extreme pressures to assimilate, or, as in the case of the Jews, subject to extreme pressure to segregate, and above all, "false Christians" were threatened by persecution and extermination. The most important ideals of the Christian religious movements, poverty and the apostolic life, represented a permanent challenge to the hierocracy. As with itinerant preachers of early Christianity, there was an anti-institutional atmosphere surrounding medieval ones. They did not easily recognize "the *ordo* of the hierarchical church."[167] Thus, where religious movements escaped inclusion, they worked against the unified church culture. Their very existence threatened a legitimation claim based on the charisma of the office. These heretical movements also prepared the soil for an innerworldly asceticism directed against the sacramentalism of the church, then brought to maturity by ascetic Protestantism. Weber would have paid special attention to these movements had he finished his project.[168]

In addition, however, one must not forget another, much more important aspect of the religious development of the Middle Ages: the movement of rationalization that in Weber's view arose on the basis of the relatively unified medieval church culture. The first rational advances were achieved by monks in the service of the hierocratic regimentation of life. These advances took place not only in science and music, but also in the economy.[169] For Weber, the monastic communities of the West were the "first rationally administered manors and later the first rational work communities in agriculture and the crafts," and the Western monk, the first man of vocation.[170] Because medieval monasticism ultimately did not persist in radically resisting the church but was instead included in the latter, it was capable of achieving the "economically improbable."[171] This was true because the monk proved himself by means of special achievements, and thus was able, at least in part, to link his own life with the ethically so effective notion of achieving *certitudo salutis* on the basis of one's own efforts.[172] This economic capability was also due to the fact that in Western monasticism labor as an ascetic instrument was "developed and put into practice far more consistently and universally" than elsewhere.[173]

Both the idea of proving oneself and the asceticism of labor, connected with Christianity from the outset, were allowed to move into the forefront and to become effective forces. Only because the special ethics and organization of the monastery were recognized as integral parts of church life was it possible for an "ethically systematized method of conducting life" to develop in subareas of the church despite the prevalence of institutional sacramentalism.[174] No matter how much this institutional sacramentalism, centered around the confessional, had an undeniably disciplining power upon the believer's conduct, it ultimately relieved rather than intensified psychic pressure and was thus not a force serving to unify one's life from within. In typological terms, the "free" monk as mendicant and itinerant represents in practice the prototype of an antieconomic and antirational seeker of salvation who is totally self-sufficient and struggles solely for his salvation. In contrast, the "church-integrated" monk uses his special ethic to rationalize his conduct in accordance with the structures of the establishment of which he is a part. This form of conduct, not least of all because of its asceticism of labor, has a positive effect upon economic activity: "The very fact that the monks were a community of ascetics accounts for the astonishing achievements that transcend those attainable through routine economic activities."[175] The medieval church remained "in movement" not least of all because of such rational achievements of its monks. In this sense, it existed in tension not only with political domination and heretical religious movements, but with its own monastic orders as well.

However, the hierocracy also provided rational achievements of its own. Because it destroyed the national church system, integrated monasticism, codified and legalized the membership role, and artfully elaborated on sacramentalism, the hierocracy was forced onto rational paths, especially in questions of organization. As I mentioned earlier, Weber considered the medieval Western church the first rational bureaucracy in world history. As such, it developed into a corporation in the specific sense of the word. A harbinger of this legal construct was already found in the canon law of late antiquity. It took on that shape, decisive for later Western development, however, in the Gregorian reforms:

After the declaration of war on the private ownership of churches [*Eigenkirchenrecht*] in the Investiture Struggle, canon law elaborated a coherent ecclesiastical corporation law, which, due to the ecclesiastic peculiarity in authority and organization, had to differ from the corporation law of both voluntary associations and status organizations. But this very ecclesiastical corporation law, in turn, markedly influenced the development of the secular corporation concept of the Middle Ages.[176]

The Feudal Revolution

Thus, in the perspective of universal history medieval Western monasticism, because of its asceticism of labor, and the medieval Western church, because of its corporate character, possess a special quality. These qualities combined propelled the monastic charisma of the person and the priestly charisma of office onto rational paths of development. In addition, with the dissolution of the Carolingian empire political domination also changed. Out of a manorial system that was based largely upon a natural economy, a fief-based feudalism emerged.[177] Although this development ultimately weakened central political authority as an organization vis-à-vis local political authority and the centralized church, feudalism did strengthen the basis of its legitimacy in its own right. The feudal relationship is not only "a marginalized case of patrimonialism that tends toward stereotyped and fixed relationships between lord and vassal," but also the result of the routinization of a charismatic relationship. Indeed, it is only from this viewpoint that "certain specific features of feudal allegiance find their proper systematical location."[178]

Only this twofold character of Western feudalism, the specific way in which it combines traditional and charismatic elements of legitimacy, makes possible Western knighthood, with its unified mode of conduct based on honor. In this way, however, the religious forms of charisma are confronted by a genuinely political form of charisma. Similar to "ecclesiastic" monastic charisma that maintained a strongly personal element without divesting itself of its institutional bonds, this political form of charisma also had an intermediary character. It legitimated a political association that "is different both from patrimonialism and from genuine or hereditary charisma."[179]

Feudally transformed manorial patrimonialism is, however, not only characterized by regulating the extrapatrimonial relationships through a "very demanding code of duties and honor" derived from military rather than religious sources; even in its fullest development the feudal relationship compels the merging of the "seemingly most contradictory elements . . . on the one hand, strictly personal fealty, on the other, contractual stipulation of rights and duties, their depersonalization by virtue of the rent nexus, and finally hereditary control of the possession."[180] Like the internally pluralistic hierocracy, the feudal association was also capable of an extraordinary internal differentiation. Like the former, it thus represented a formation permeated by tensions. Moreover, the feudal association required not merely freemen who took on military and, within limits, administrative service; it also required a certain measure of "the rule of law."

In the earlier version of *Economy and Society*, Weber talked of "free feudalism" and classified Western feudalism as the "most consequential" case of it.[181] Interestingly enough, in the newer version he did not reiterate this conceptual usage and the typology connected to it. The reason might be that a "vassal in the specific meaning of the word had to be a free man, not subordinate to the patrimonial power of a lord."[182] Thus, one can sensibly speak of this kind of feudalism only where this precondition is satisfied. In addition, however, it is also based on status contracts. Although the two parties have unequal rights, reciprocal obligations of loyalty form its basis.[183] To the extent that this right of freely entering a contract was curtailed, whether by considering the grant hereditary, or even by considering it as "part of the maintenance fund for the members of the knightly estate" and thus by compelling the lord to fill every vacancy,[184] the "system" lost its originally personalist quality but gained a special contractual one. As Weber put it in the older version of *Economy and Society*:

This very permeation of the whole system with the guarantee of the fief-holder's position through a bilateral contract was very important for the development of feudalism; this guarantee transcended the mere granting of privileges by the lord and, in contrast to the appropriation of benefices, it was not just a purely economic matter. It turned feudalism into an approximation of the *Rechtsstaat*, at least in comparison to pure patrimonialism, with its juxtaposition of traditional prescription and appropriated rights, on the one hand, and arbitrariness and discretion on the other. Feudalism is a "separation of powers," but unlike Montesquieu's scheme, which constitutes a qualitative division of labor, it is simply a quantitative division of authority. The idea of the social contract as the basis of the distribution of political power, an idea which led to constitutionalism, is anticipated in a primitive fashion.[185]

Thus, the "feudal revolution" of the eleventh and twelfth centuries resulted in a further pluralization of medieval culture. The church bureaucracy, primarily legitimated in terms of the charisma of office, was confronted by a contrary principle of organization and legitimation. It is true that religious life penetrated political life and vice versa, for example, in the feudalization of the church or in the "bureaucratization" of politics by means of the integration of the clergy into feudally organized administrative staffs. It is also true that there was an intrinsic link between the monastic and knightly modes of conduct—witness the various orders of knights. Nevertheless, these different principles retained their significance in developmental history, for, as a rule, "warrior nobles, and indeed feudal powers generally, have not readily become the carriers of a rational religious ethic."[186] In general, the honor-oriented feudal ethic and the salvation-oriented religious ethic tend to contradict one another,[187] and a feudal association, with its "systematically decentralized domination," is practically the exact opposite of a rational bureaucracy.[188] Above all, however, with the realization of the feudal principle, a constant struggle between the central authority and the centrifugal local authorities had to result. This was especially true where the "grant" included judicial and military powers. The feudal overlord was constantly in danger of being disempowered by the fief-holders. Although he could take "system-conforming" countermeasures,[189] these usually remained largely ineffective as long as he refrained from establishing his own patrimonially or nonpatrimonially recruited administrative staff. The more legal corporations, which gradually became more *ständisch*, formed out of the union of fief-holders, and the more feudal polity, which after all was no state, became a proper *Ständestaat*, the more bitter the struggle became. According to Weber, the *Ständestaat* "owed its existence" to Western feudalism: "'*rex et regnum*' (*Ständestaat*) in the Western sense was known only in the West."[190]

There are thus primarily three conflicts that arose with the papal and feudal revolutions and ultimately fractured the medieval culture: the conflict between heretic and monastic personal charisma and the charisma of priestly office; that between feudal and *ständisch* contractualism; and that between a bureaucratic church and an initially nonbureaucratic, indeed, antibureaucratic political association. In Weber's view—as the first epigraph of this essay attests—the Western medieval configuration was forced to resolve these very conflicts. The resulting arrangements, primarily institutional inventions, became contributing factors to the singular development of the West.[191]

Admittedly, this rough sketch would remain much too incomplete if one were not to take into account a third "revolution," that of the city,[192] which, together with the papal and feudal revolutions, created further important historical preconditions for the

singular development of the West.[193] The papal revolution gave a
crucial impetus to the monastic world of vocation and showed the
way to "legislation by rational enactment."[194] Furthermore, it
gave the Western world a relatively formal-rational sacred law in
the form of canon law and a relatively rational bureaucratic institution in the form of the church. The feudal revolution created
Western knighthood, with its innerworldly unified mode of conduct and the idea of the contractual character of political power.
In contrast, the "urban revolution" contributed to the development of the secular concept of the corporation and to the "birth"
of a particular urban citizenry. Only because central authority
could later join up with this bourgeoisie did its struggle with the
"successors" of the feudal administrative staffs, the ständisch corporations, ultimately end in victory, for in order to expropriate the
latter, a peculiar constellation of forces was required. As Weber
notes: This constellation "was influenced by the rise of the bourgeoisie in the towns, which had an organization peculiar to Europe. It was in addition aided by the competition for power by
means of rational—that is, bureaucratic—administration among
the different states. This led, from fiscal motives, to a crucially
important alliance with capitalist interests."[195] The rise of the
burghers, with an urban organization and legitimation peculiar to
Europe, however, dates back to the twelfth and thirteenth centuries. Therefore, this development must now be analyzed.

The Urban Revolution

The city, of course, is not specific to the Middle Ages. As
Weber's analysis of the demise of antiquity shows, he perceived a
genuinely urban culture over wide stretches of Mediterranean history. Nevertheless, as important as urban development in antiquity was for the concepts of the citizen (Bürger), of the community
as a corporate body, and of democracy, "neither modern capitalism
nor the state as we know it developed on the basis of the ancient
city."[196] Both belong to the history of the urbanization of medieval
rural culture, so to speak. In fact, Weber attributed a "special developmental position"[197] vis-à-vis both Asian and Mediterranean
cities to the Western medieval city as it gradually arose in the
wake of the dissolution of the Carolingian empire. He also ascribed a special role to the city of the modern patrimonial states
that succeeded the Ständestaat. By then, the city had again "de-
generated" into an administrative district of a larger unit.

But because of its history in the High Middle Ages, the city retained at least some corporative powers and a limited right to self-government. This was due to the fact that the medieval urban development led to a "revolutionary . . . innovation":[198] to the autonomous and autocephalous corporation of burghers based on fraternization. This corporation included the rights to impose statutes (*Satzungsrecht*), to appoint officials, to levy taxes, to regulate markets, to employ a commercial and industrial police, and to launch an economic policy of its own, combined with efforts to bring the noncitizen strata into at least economic dependency.[199] Some of these features dated back to antiquity. But they reached their full development only when a new principle of organization and legitimation replaced traditional secular or spiritual authorities.

Of course, the Mediterranean-Occidental city of antiquity already possessed the quality of an "institutionalized association, endowed with special characteristic organs, of people who, as 'burghers,' are subject to a special law exclusively applicable to them and who thus form a legally autonomous status group."[200] In this sense, there is continuity between antiquity and the Middle Ages. However, the autonomy and autocephaly of the ancient city were linked, in terms of external relations, to a greater extent to "transformations based purely on military factors,"[201] and, in terms of their internal relations, to the remnants "of religious exclusiveness of the sibs toward each other and toward the outside."[202] These remnants ultimately prevented the ancient city from radically opposing the principle of the sib with the secular concept of the corporation, and from interpreting this latter in a purely "bourgeois" manner, that is, in radical opposition in every form of rule by sib (*Geschlechterherrschaft*). The fact that these developments occurred in the Middle Ages to a marked degree, even though not everywhere, can be traced back to two circumstances: the structure of the medieval political associations and Christianity.

Before we explore this relationship that is so essential to Weber's view of Occidental Christianity more closely, two points should first be made clear: the thesis of the challenge to seigneurial authority, which can also be called the usurpation thesis, is not a thesis explaining the genesis of the medieval city;[203] and the medieval city creates neither modern capitalism nor the modern state. The bourgeois producer cities (*Gewerbestädte*) of continental northern Europe,[204] which in connection with his explanatory model interested Weber the most,[205] did not usually arise for political, let alone for military reasons. Their genesis instead can be traced to economic motives and to the "concessions from the political and seigneurial powerholders integrated into the feudal military and office structure." They certainly also initially remained oriented toward the economic interests of their concessionists, who resided largely outside the city.[206] Correspondingly, their growing autonomy and autocephaly owed less to a politically motivated desire to usurp power than it did to a specific power constellation: the lack, on the part of feudal lords, of a "trained apparatus of officials" that could have effectively controlled the cities, and "competition of nonurban powerholders among themselves, in particular the conflict of the central power with the great vassals and with the hierocratic power of the church."[207] Of course, there were also usurpations of power, to which the history of some Italian cities and especially the history of the city of Cologne testify.[208] But it was not these few revolutionary changes that Weber considered decisive.

Crucial instead was the step-by-step move toward a "new" principle of organization and legitimation, that of urban democracy, particularly by the primarily economically oriented cities and their commercially and industrially active members—a move facilitated by the structural weakness of the nonurban powers. This sometimes led to the voluntary granting of expanded urban privileges on the part of the cities' feudal concessionists.[209] Above all, however, the autonomy of the cities remained a "historical interlude."[210] Therefore, the medieval city—or more precisely, the bourgeois producer and inland city—was also "in no way the only significant antecedent developmental stage and certainly not itself the carrier" of modern capitalism and the modern state. Nevertheless, it was "a crucial factor in their rise."[211]

What made the medieval city into such a crucial factor, and what role did Christianity play in this? With regard to the first question, Weber cited geographical, military, and cultural circumstances.[212] The first two have already been referred to. For most of the feudal lords, who resided in their castles and not in the cities, the establishment of new cities was an economic, not a "military measure."[213] The cities established for economic reasons usually remained, even in the case of gradual usurpation, primarily economically oriented. But they could exploit the room to maneuver granted to them as a result of the seignorial rivalries, and they used it often to promote self-government. Moreover, this strategy had antifeudal consequences, especially the tendency to dissolve *stän-*

disch connection between town and country. As Weber repeatedly underscored, the knightly and bourgeois modes of conduct, when brought to their logical conclusions, are indeed incompatible. The burgher, with his orientation toward "function," and the knight, with his senses of "being," are the social bearers of different world-views and attendant modes of conduct. The fact that they stand in the sharpest contrast is perhaps nowhere more clearly seen than in their stances toward earning a living. Where the bourgeois mode of conduct came into its own, it displayed a much greater elective affinity with that of the monastic and church official than with that of the knight. It lacked "the features of playfulness and elective affinity to art, of heroic asceticism and hero worship, of heroic honor and heroic hostility to the utilitarianism of business and office—features that feudalism inculcates and preserves."[214]

This development of the city as a corporate body was nurtured by religious sources. Here Christianity enters in. Because of the events of Antioch and the subsequent dispute between Peter and Paul that ended in the latter's "victory" and the devaluation of all ritual barriers of birth for the Christian community,[215] Christianity had in principle devalued all criteria hindering fraternization among the faithful. Thus, the city as a corporate body could take a bourgeois turn.[216] Weber stressed the important role played by the Christian community, even though it was "only one of the many symptoms pointing to this quality of the Christian religion that, in dissolving clan ties, importantly shaped the medieval city."[217]

This role must not be misunderstood as implying that the medieval city was a mere appendage to the church's principle of organization and legitimation. The city remained instead a secular association, even if membership in it was premised upon "full membership in the parish community."[218] Here, too, one can again make recourse to the thesis of the relatively unified Christian culture, for here we see the religious barrier to inclusion that still existed even for the bourgeois producer city. Whoever lacked full membership in the church community and did not or could not participate in the Eucharist was unable to attain the personal legal status of a full citizen. This qualification did not prevent the granting of citizenship to strangers moving to the city, such as traders from other nationalities or places, but it did prevent the granting of citizenship to members of non-Christian communities of faith. Naturally, this primarily involved the Jews, who, even though they were summoned to the cities for economic reasons, remained in a special position, which Weber compared to that of Asiatic guest peoples.[219] In spite of a division of labor connecting them to the urban economy, they remained outside of the burgher association. This was also true for other "guest peoples" who were usually called into the country as traders through princely concessions.[220] In the case of the Jews, this refusal of inclusion had a special quality: it was, according to Weber's thesis, not only forced upon them, but they in part also sought it out. Because of their dietary codes, the pious medieval Jews could offer Christians hospitality but were not allowed to accept any reciprocal offers. Moreover, marriage with Christians was excluded.[221] Thus, the medieval commercial city, too, remained a religious association, which could be joined only by the individual as a Christian. Among the Christian burghers, however, clan (*gens*) and sib membership were not allowed to prevent fraternization. In this way, clan and sib associations were removed as primary elements in the constitution of burgher communities.

Of course, this did not mean that these communities were not organized into subassociations or were not acquainted with class and status-group stratification. On the contrary, in terms of both status groups and economic opportunities, the world of the burghers remained stratified. In his sociology of religion, in particular, Weber repeatedly emphasized that the bourgeois state displayed an unusual amount of heterogeneity. For this reason, the thesis of the class-conditioned nature of religion, which within limits is certainly fruitful, is very difficult to apply to them. The medieval commercial city was not a homogeneous formation, either. Like the church, the internal pluralism of the city can be understood as the result of inclusions, either granted or struggled for. The "free" subassociations corresponded to the city as a "free" association. They served an array of purposes, religious or social (*confraternitates*),[222] occupational (guilds of artisans or merchants), or political ("parties"). There were constantly conflicts between them. As were the ecclesiastic and feudal spheres, the autonomous urban association was also marked by internal pluralism and the unique dynamics accompanying such a constellation.

Thus, though the "full citizens" confronted each other as formal equals, they were usually also materially unequal. Indeed, even formal equality, for example, the participation in urban government, was hardly always democratically organized. In particular, the growing domination of the guilds, which increasingly became the real constituencies of the urban commune, led to a strict subdivision along status-group lines within the city that were connected to the monopolization of economic opportunities. Like the polis of antiquity before it, the medieval urban community provides no support for a romantic vision of democracy. However, the guild structure as a system of inequality based upon occupational status groups had two far-reaching consequences: it ignored status differences outside the city, and it replaced the personal association of lineage and sib with the "impersonal" occupational association. Even though the upper guilds in particular tended to turn "into plutocratic corporations of rentiers," the guild structure as a whole led to "an increase in the power of a specifically urban stratum either directly participating in commerce and industry or indirectly interested in it: the bourgeoisie in the modern sense."[223] Moreover, the guild structure resulted in the medieval city's becoming "a structure oriented immeasurably more than any city of antiquity—at least during the epoch of the independent polis— toward acquisition through economic activity."[224] To the extent that the increasingly closed guild system came under pressure from the putting-out system to open itself, the increase in rationality yielded by the interlude of medieval urban autonomy could be harnessed for market-oriented action.[225]

The claim of some cities to autonomy and autocephaly thus formed, within the medieval configuration, a further source of tension fraught with developmental significance. A new principle of organization and legitimation came into play that did not match that of feudalism, the charisma of office of the church, or the personal charisma of monasticism, namely, the corporate organization of secular associations and its democratic legitimation. Of course, the church also possessed a corporate character, but not in the context of an oathbound political union. Feudalism also rested upon political contracts of fraternity, but not between members of a corporate body. Thus, the autonomous and autocephalous medieval city gave rise to the idea of a democratically legitimated corporate body, in opposition to hierocratic and feudal associations. In an address in Vienna in October 1917 on the problems of a sociology of the state, Weber incorporated this principle into his typology.[226] However, for the explanatory model discussed here it is crucial that the autonomous and autocephalous medieval city helped bring about the birth of a bourgeoisie oriented toward larger markets.

It is true that in many of the medieval cities autonomy and autocephaly was either not fully realized or lasted only a short period

of time. But this was sufficient to give rise to important preconditions for the specific development of the West. Aside from new
forms of production, such as free domestic industry, and new
forms of commerce, such as the unlimited partnership, the medieval cities had contributed to the establishment of legal institutions—such as the annuity bond, the stock certificate, the bill of
exchange, the mortgage secured by real estate, and the deed of
trust[227]—that proved important for modern capitalism. One
should also mention the accounting system, developed primarily
by the medieval Italian cities, which made the West, according to
Weber, the "site of monetary accounting" par excellence.[228] But
above all, it is the concept of the secular political corporation (politische Anstalt) that makes the difference. Whereas the role of religious membership was partly formalized through the Gregorian
and post-Gregorian church, the role of political membership was
partly formalized through the medieval city. If one adds the contractual element, stemming from feudalism and later "objectified" through the Ständestaat, one has the main ingredients that
Weber regarded as crucial for the Western trajectory to modern
capitalism.

However, if the bourgeoisie wanted to maintain its primarily
economic orientation, it required an institutional framework transcending the city and its hinterland. It needed, as it were, a state
economic policy instead of a mere urban economic policy. This
state policy was initially provided by mercantilism, even though
the form it took was unfavorable to an economically oriented capitalism.[229] The bourgeoisie also needed expanded markets and mass
purchasing power. Both were first provided by the absolute states,
which replaced the Ständestaat and preceded the modern Rechtsstaat. They did this by means of war and luxury, and later, by
means of democratizing luxury and by reducing the degree of exploitation that had existed before.[230] In sum, it was first within
this institutional framework that an urban bourgeoisie could become a national bourgeoisie.

This shift presupposed not only modern business enterprises in
the shape of domestic industries, manufactures, and factories, but
also the transition to a mode of want satisfaction that relied primarily on the market economy. Moreover, it also required a specific economic ethos. Although the medieval producer city as a
Christian city had already provided an antimagical and above all
antifeudal direction, the idea of economic activity as an area of
proving one's religious calling still remained largely alien to it.

This necessitated a second transformation—a transformation less from without than from within. According to Weber, this transformation was an achievement of the post-Reformation period, which also marked the final dissolution of the relatively unified culture of the church. As Weber put it in the *General Economic History*, "In the last resort the factors that produced capitalism are the rational continuous enterprise, rational accounting, rational technology, and rational law, but again not these alone; they had to be supplemented by the rational spirit, the rationalization of conduct, and the rational economic ethos."[231]

The Second Transformation: The Religious Foundation of Bourgeois Conduct

Weber never intended to dispense with "ideal factors"—more precisely, with "the psychology of acquisition" (*Erwerbs-Psychologie*)[232]—in offering an explanation of the genesis of modern capitalism or in his planned study of Western Christianity. This assertion results not only from the theoretical and methodological considerations given above, but also from substantive considerations: No later than the time of the first version of the *Protestant Ethic*, he realized that there was a connection between the genesis of "that powerful economic world, bound to the technical and economic conditions of mechanical production"[233] and the genesis of an ethical concept of duty, of a specific vocational ethos.[234] In order to understand this side of the problem, he called for "psychological" analyses[235] that left behind the notion of psychology that was prevalent in economics. Particularly in the second phase of his work, when he lays the methodological and substantive basis for an "interpretive psychology,"[236] both of these aspects play an important role in Weber's analysis. In the dispute with Felix Rachfahl, for example, Weber was not content merely to reiterate the argument that the form and spirit of capitalism "may very well occur separately."[237] Instead, he went on to emphasize that the analysis of the spirit independently of the form remained his main concern:

Let me be permitted to ask anyone not interested in this "psychology" but only in external forms of economic systems to leave my efforts unread, but just as much to leave it to my discretion whether I want to interest myself in this psychic side of modern economic development, which in Puritanism achieved a peculiar balance with regard to the great inner tensions and conflicts between "vocation," "life" (as we like to say today), and "ethics," a balance that never before and never again existed in this manner.[238]

The fact that this psychology was not to be based on assumptions either of classical or neoclassical economics or of the older or younger historical school can already be inferred from the choice of concepts Weber employed: instead of acquisitive and social drives, he chose material and ideal interests, interests from without and interests from within; instead of an axiomatic or empirical social psychology as the basis of the cultural sciences, he attempted "to analyze the specific effects of a definite motive, a motive analyzed on its own terms and in view of its own inherent consequences to the greatest degree possible."[239] Therefore, attention has to be paid to the ideal foundations that help to shape and maintain such a motive, for motives, in contrast to drives, are symbolically structured psychic components that vary according to the symbolic universe of which they are a part.

Thus, according to its own premises, Weber's "psychology" could not be a psychology of an acquisitive drive, but rather a "psychology" pointing to the mutual adaptation of ideas and interests. It involved the cultural modification of that psychic component that in the outmoded psychology of economics had been termed the "acquisitive drive."[240] This modification, which he conceives of as a rational moderation in this case, cannot be understood as the result of skillful and prudent adjustment to capitalist institutions. The "spirit," which moved the "new-style" entrepreneurs *and* workers, required—this was and remained Weber's conviction—an investigation "from within" the subject. Indeed, the question was, How could one want to be a self-restrained specialist in one's calling if one did not have to be? Thus, action was involved here that one carries out for its own sake and not, at least not primarily, on the basis of outside compulsion and as a means to an end.[241] This required the commitment to an ethically conceived duty. According to Weber, under traditional conditions religious forces had the most lasting influence on such conceptions. Here, the psychological lever was provided by the desire for salvation and the religious interpretation of from what, for what, and above all how one could be saved.

Christianity, in contrast to the other salvation religions, ultimately strove for salvation "from radical evil and the servitude of sin" and hoped for "the eternal and free benevolence in the lap of a fatherly God."[242] Salvation, moreover, was tied to the idea of proof. It was not to be effected in terms of the conception of reciprocity underlying almost all religious ethics, whereby one could ultimately earn one's salvation. Christianity instead required an individual actively to fulfill God's commandments for their own sake in this life. Part of this life consisted of one's economic action; for this reason, the question facing all salvation religions was, To what extent is economic action relevant to salvation? All religions, by the end of their charismatic phase, naturally have to accept the fact of economic life and take a position on it. Thus, the question is further, To what degree do they vitiate traditional economic mentality?

Weber states that the medieval church, like the feudal nobility and the urban artisans, supported the spirit of economic traditionalism, with its economic ethic, as almost all hierocracies do. Admittedly, in accordance with its internal pluralism, there was no unity in the church's positions toward religiously pleasing economic action; the more it allied itself politically with the financial powers, especially those of Italian cities, the more it grew ready to treat the pursuit of profit "for its own sake" as nonmoral, rather than immoral. In this way it could be accommodating without losing face.[243] Yet nothing changed the fact that economic activity neither for the sake of "acquisition as the ultimate purpose of life" nor "for the satisfaction of material needs"[244] could have any positive significance for salvation. The maxim incorporated into canon law (*Corpus Iuris Canonici*), "*Deo placere vix potest*,"[245] was for Weber an expression of this basic state of affairs. Although one can make a profit without endangering one's salvation, this activity is no basis at all for hopes of redemption. An intrinsic connection between one's economic and salvational fate did not exist for the medieval church. It

does not condemn the acquisitive drive (a concept, by the way, which is wholly imprecise and better not used at all); instead, the church condones it, as it does all worldly things, in those who do not have the charisma necessary for adhering to the *consilia evangelica*. However, the church cannot bridge the gap between its highest ethical ideals and a rational, methodical orientation toward the capitalist enterprise that treats profit as the ultimate goal of a vocation and—this is the main point—regards it as a measure of personal virtue.[246]

Even though Weber viewed the doctrine on usury and the just price, for example, as rather ineffective, he nevertheless viewed the economic ethic of the pre-Reformation church as the ideal base for the "traditionalist and 'minimum subsistence' measures" of precapitalist forces.[247] If the religious ethic is supposed to contribute to breaking with the "spirit" of economic traditionalism, his argument goes, the mere religious toleration of acquisition for acquisition's sake must to be replaced by proving oneself in religious terms through acquisition for acquisition's sake. Only in this way could the deep inner conflict and tension between conscience and action be overcome without false compromises, conflicts in which "earnest Catholic believers" of the pre-Reformation period ultimately remained entangled through their capitalist activities.[248]

Thus, the consideration of motivational constellations reveals the same tensions and peculiar balancing of these tensions that we observed in the context of institutional constellations. Only when both kinds of constellation are taken into account can one understand how the completely "unnatural," indeed, absurd "conception of money-making as an end in itself to which people were bound as a calling" can arise.[249] The fact that Weber did not consider the thesis of the external accommodation to capitalist institutions to be convincing, at least not for explaining the genesis of modern capitalism, has already been emphasized.[250] However, he was also not satisfied with the thesis of the internal accommodation to capitalism insofar as it was connected with utilitarian or pragmatic premises.[251] A revolution in mentality—a revolution from within—was required, and it was not probable without religious-ethical premises. Hence, that revolution had to be explained in terms of a tension between these premises and the interest in salvation and its ultimate resolution.[252]

Unlike Marx, then, Weber was from the outset interested not in primitive accumulation, but in the bourgeois mode of conduct: "[W]hat was central here was not the mere accumulation of capital, but the ascetic rationalization of the whole of life in one's calling."[253] Where the "spirit" of modern capitalism appears, it "provides itself with capital for its activity, and not vice versa."[254] Long before bourgeois conduct emerges, money exists for investment in the form of commercial or venture capital. The question is not whether great monetary wealth is accumulated, but rather under which institutional, and above all, motivational conditions existing wealth flows into productive channels. Even the compulsion to save connected to ascetic rationalization in no way interested Weber primarily in economic terms; after all, extensive restriction of consumption could endanger capitalist development by depressing demand. The studies on Protestantism are not analyses of the ideational roots of primitive accumulation. The compulsion to save is much more an expression of a stance taken against the enjoyment of instinctual life in all social spheres, and at the same time, against a seignorial mode of conduct. In religious terms, it is directed against the idolatry of the flesh, or put profanely, against egotism, which is opposed by unconditional sacrifice and service for an impersonal cause. To be able to interpret profit-oriented activity in this sense, an ethic is required as a vehicle for establishing the unbroken unity between the certainty of religious salvation and the innerworldly asceticism of calling. This ethic was ultimately made possible only by ascetic Protestantism, not by Catholicism, Lutheranism, or Judaism, or by any philosophical teachings, either.

Until his death Weber held fast to this thesis on the "psychic side of modern economic development," first developed in his studies of Protestantism and then placed in a broader comparative perspective in the chapter on the sociology of religion in the first version of *Economy and Society*.[255] This persistence is evident from the countercritique of the arguments of Lujo Brentano and Werner Sombart that he inserted into the second version of the *Protestant Ethic*. Whereas Brentano interpreted the "spirit" of modern capitalism as the result of a removal of the moral controls in the pursuit of money, Sombart viewed it, following Weber, at least for the early capitalist phase, as the result of a moral tempering of acquisitive pursuits; however, he negated Weber's claim of a special role for ascetic Protestantism. In analyzing critique and countercritique, we can discover Weber's "last word" on his Protestant Ethic thesis.

For Brentano, capitalist spirit means the unrestricted pursuit of money, a form of conduct that no religious ethic has ever condoned. Correspondingly, he held the Puritan ethic to be the "traditionalist economic ethic of the petty bourgeoisie."[256] He accused Weber of having falsely interpreted the Christian emancipation from economic traditionalism and having neglected the truly decisive pagan emancipation. Substantively, according to Brentano, capitalist development depends primarily on commerce, money-lending, and war;[257] ideationally, however, it arises from empirical philosophy, and he cites Machiavelli as its representative.[258]

In contrast, Sombart, after renewed reflections on the intellectual history of modern economic man, initially came to the con-

clusion that Puritanism equals Judaism in morally tempering acquisitive pursuits.[259] A short time later, however, he expanded this
conclusion about the connection between religious and capitalist
ethics to include Catholicism—in particular to Thomism and the
ethics of Anthony of Florence and Bernhard of Siena—and to
philosophical utilitarianism, which he traced from the family
books of Leon Battista Alberti to Benjamin Franklin.[260] Sombart
argues that Alberti's doctrine of virtues anticipated that of Franklin and that the most important teachings of Thomism, like those
of Judaism, agreed with the teachings of Puritanism.[261] Everywhere one finds bourgeois virtues recommended: industry, utility,
frugality, and honesty were the focus of attention. The active life
instead of the life of idleness, occupying oneself with useful things
instead of with play, moderation instead of excess, frugality instead of luxury, honesty instead of cheating—these were the values inculcated by both Alberti and Franklin, as well as by Jewish,
Scholastic, and Puritan authors. The only thing that Puritanism
added to Thomism was the repression of the aesthetic desire for
splendor, for the *magnificentia*: "Perhaps the greatest service that
the Puritan and Quaker ethics performed for capitalism, insofar as
the latter was marked by bourgeois spirit, was the development of
frugality [*parsimonia*] into stinginess [*parvificentia*]."[262]

Just this short characterization of the two counterpositions
should make it clear that, for Weber, Sombart rather than Brentano
posed the greater challenge.[263] In Brentano, the revolution in religious mentality was, so to speak, excluded by definition as a possible historical precondition for the genesis of modern capitalism.
If the spirit of modern capitalism is equated, as in Brentano's writings, with the unrestrained pursuit of money, then not only "all
conceptual precision is lost,"[264] but all understanding for the bourgeois mode of conduct (*bürgerliche Lebensführung*) as a major
condition of modern culture, for "at all periods of history, wherever it was possible, there has been ruthless acquisition, bound to
no ethical norms whatever."[265]

In contrast, not only did Sombart recognize the significance of
moral forces for the rise of modern economic man, but he also distinguished entrepreneurial from bourgeois spirit. Pirates, feudal
lords, bureaucrats, speculators, great merchants, and artisans
seeking to improve their station, for example, can be imbued with
entrepreneurial spirit; it is the spirit of all economic supermen
who possess the will and the ability to be economically successful
by means of farsighted, well-planned, and coordinated action that

is venturesome but calculated. Entrepreneurial spirit is one thing, however, bourgeois spirit is something else. Only if the former is penetrated by the latter does a rationalization of economic management set in, according to Sombart. Thus, the spirit of capitalism arises out of a combination of the soul of the entrepreneur and the soul of the bourgeois. Moral forces, however, are among those forces that shape the soul of the bourgeois. Hence, for Sombart, too, capitalist spirit means the restraint of the pursuit of acquisition by binding it to an ethic in the framework of a rationalizing and methodical conception of life. He expressly remarks, however, that this means of restraint holds only for the spirit of early capitalism and not for that of advanced capitalism.[266]

Consequently, Sombart joined with Weber against Brentano in holding that the spirit of modern capitalism contains elements of bourgeois spirit and rests upon an ethical basis. Not the pursuit of utility and happiness, but the pursuit of "duties" has to be the decisive psychological lever for revolutionizing traditional economic mentality in its seignorial (feudal, patrimonial, patrician), artisanal, or peasant forms. Sombart also agreed with Weber that there is a distinction to be made between the early-capitalist and the advanced-capitalist spirit. Differences emerge in their respective analyses of the psychological level and how this distinction is to be interpreted. These points are interrelated. Because Weber ultimately considers Sombart's intellectual history of modern economic man to be wrong, he also has a different assessment of the transformation of the bourgeois mode of conduct in the transition to advanced capitalism, which represents the third transformation.

What is wrong with Sombart's intellectual history of modern economic man? Even though Weber does not comprehensively criticize it anywhere in his work, objections concerning method, theory, and substance can nevertheless be discerned.

The objection to method can be dealt with quickly. Although Weber himself never explicitly formulated it, it is implicit in his very approach. In his intellectual history of modern economic man, Sombart investigates primarily doctrines. It is only marginally, if at all, that he takes up their pragmatic psychological effects.[267] This, however, was precisely the focus of Weber's "psychology." Weber emphasized time and again that one cannot confine oneself to the analysis of doctrines but must take into account their pragmatic psychological effects.

The theoretical objection to Sombart's work is of greater importance. It concerns the relation between prudential doctrines (*Klugheitslehre*) and ethics. Weber diagnoses a fundamental difference between them, which Sombart totally ignores. One example is the manner in which Sombart describes the relationship of the "aristocratic" Renaissance man of letters, Alberti, to the "bourgeois" American, Franklin. According to Weber, Sombart misses the decisive points. It is not only that Alberti's instructions, in contrast to those of Franklin, tend to be oriented more toward the household and the investment of wealth than toward market operation and capital utilization; it is not merely that the audience he addresses tends to be made up of aristocratic, humanistically educated patricians rather than of petit bourgeois masses. When Alberti speaks of economic rationalism at all, religious pathos is entirely missing. Instead, it is "as if Cato's homely wisdom were taken from the field of the ancient slave-holding household and applied to that of free labor in domestic industry and the metayer system."[268] This form of wisdom, however, cannot have much of a psychological impact. It is one of the crucial premises of Weber's approach that

a religiously based ethic places very definite psychological sanctions (of a noneconomic character) on the conduct it calls forth, sanctions that remain highly effective as long as religious faith stays intact, and these sanctions are precisely what a mere doctrine on the art of living such as that of Alberti does not have at its disposal.[269]

"Psychological" here means that by means of norm-conforming action emotional states are produced (e.g., the feeling of being an instrument or a vessel of God) that can be enjoyed in the "here and now," regardless of whether the promises of redemption are directed toward a world beyond or a future thisworldly state.[270] Moreover, these emotional states are completely independent of economic or other achievements in the world. Admittedly, even in Franklin one finds utilitarian undertones. This is something that Weber had already emphasized in the first version of the *Protestant Ethic*. There is still a difference, however, if a position is in its very conception nothing more than a doctrine of prudence, or if it represents an already partly secularized religious ethic. According to Weber, the former applies to Alberti and related writers, the latter to Franklin.

Thus, in contrast to Alberti, Franklin offers ethically tinged maxims for living; they are moral rules (and not technical ones), with the concomitant sanctions. Sombart fails to see this. Instead, he attributes to a doctrine of prudence something only a (religious) ethic can achieve: the ability to be a life-transforming power from within.[271] This of course does not imply that every (religious) ethic achieves this, and even if one does, there is no implication that because of this achievement it automatically revolutionizes a traditionalistic economic mentality. This implication would presuppose a singular religious ethic and a singular religious practice through which this ethic is interpreted, for the practice represents, so to speak, the medium in which the religious foundations and the church structures, as well as the material and ideal interests of the believers meet.[272] Now, Sombart did not only treat doctrines of prudence and ethics along the same lines; he did the same with the Jewish, Catholic, and Puritan/Quaker ethics, without clarifying whether their superficially similar prescriptions were also connected to similar practices.

This brings us to the substantive objections, which are without a doubt the most serious ones. Weber took up Sombart's challenge not least because it offered him the opportunity to underscore once again the unique position of ascetic Protestantism in the analysis of the motivational side of modern economic development. Let me reiterate: his attempt to divest the studies of Protestantism of their isolated character and to locate them within overall cultural development did not result in relativizing the thesis. Ascetic Protestantism retained its uniqueness vis-à-vis all important Asian religions, and vis-à-vis medieval and modern Judaism, pre-Reformation Catholicism, and Lutheranism. That Sombart's analysis not only obscured all distinctions between the psychological effects of doctrines of prudence and those of ethics, but also, more importantly, led to the elimination of the unique position of ascetic Protestantism, turned his intellectual history of modern economic man for Weber into a "book full of [unfounded] theses [*Thesenbuch*] in the worst sense of the expression."[273] Weber's "counterthesis" was that neither medieval or modern Judaism nor pre-Reformation Catholicism had brought forth the bourgeois mode of conduct, the practice of proving oneself in one's calling. It must be attributed to ascetic Protestantism and to nothing else. (Both agreed that Lutheranism did not qualify as a source of the bourgeois mode.)

As early as 1913–14, in the religion chapter of the older version of *Economy and Society*, and even before the study of ancient Judaism took monographic form, Weber marked out his position in regard to Sombart's claim that Judaism is Puritanism: "Neither that which is new in the modern economic system nor that which is distinctive of the modern economic mentality is specifically Jewish in origin."[274] In 1919–20, after he had devoted a historical investigation to ancient Israel and ancient Judaism, he reiterated this conclusion regarding the motivational side of economic development: "Judaism was on the side of political or speculative 'adventurist capitalism': its ethos was, in a word, that of pariah capitalism. Puritanism, by contrast, was the vehicle for the ethos of the rational bourgeois enterprise and the rational organization of labor. It took from the Jewish ethos only what fitted into this framework."[275]

The historical investigation of ancient Judaism had demonstrated that the Jewish order of life, with its concept of God and its "highly rational religious ethic of innerworldly action, free of magic and all forms of irrational pursuit of salvation,"[276] constituted an important historical precondition for ascetic Protestantism. Nevertheless, neither the medieval nor the modern religious practice of Judaism led to the spirit of proving oneself in one's vocation. It did not lead to this pride in a bourgeois business morality whose followers "refused to have anything to do with the 'courtiers and project-makers' of the large-scale capitalist type, whom they looked on as an ethically suspect class."[277] In marked contrast, despite ritual barriers, these representatives of a "nonbourgeois" capitalism were among the most important business partners of a wealthy Jewry that was specialized in commerce and especially banking, as well as in the financing of the state.[278] Of course, medieval and modern Jewry did not consist only of wealthy strata. It also included petit bourgeois and quasi-proletarian sections, artisanal strata, and, in more recent times, a "massive ghetto proletariat."[279] But in spite of the enormous range of its economic activity and social situation, and despite a religious ethic free of magic and oriented to innerworldly action, "the organization of industrial labor in domestic industry and in the factory system . . . was strikingly—though not completely—missing."[280] What was completely missing, however, was that rational moderation of the so-called acquisitive drive that was intrinsic to ascetic Protestantism.

What were the causes of this absence? The most important have already been mentioned. They are connected to the Jews' status as a guest people. It is Weber's thesis throughout that this status produces a legally and factually precarious situation, and it is a condition that does not lead to the overcoming of the dualism of in-group and out-group morality so characteristic of all traditional economic behavior: that which is prohibited to fellow believers is permitted to strangers to the faith. This does not mean that in relations to outsiders the principle of formal legality is missing, as Sombart believes. It does mean, however, that the economic mentality does not overcome traditionalism here, for in in-group relations, the standpoint of subsistence is predominant, and in out-group relations, the standpoint of a "completely impersonal management of business"[281] tied to the norms of formal legality and fairness, which moves, so to speak, in a sphere indifferent to religious salvation is predominant. Where external circumstances permit it, this type of business management tends to orient itself toward the economic exploitation of power- and market-based opportunities. But a stimulus toward a bourgeois mode of conduct does not arise. Let us be clear about it: neither the supposedly conventional adherence of Jews to the law nor the rights of aliens in Jewish law hinder a development of Jewish mentality in this bourgeois direction; what is missing is the idea of religious proof through economic conduct.[282] As Julius Guttmann confirms, this is something not found in Jewish ethics.[283] The religious self-evaluation of the pious Jew remains completely independent of his economic success. Only in ascetic Protestantism were the two connected in a positive way.

Weber had already emphasized in the first version of the *Protestant Ethic* that pre-Reformation Catholicism and Lutheranism also lacked this connection. Just as Sombart's equation of Judaism and Protestantism was incorrect in a crucial respect, so too was the equation of Thomism or quattrocento mendicant theology with Puritanism. The causes for the lack of connection are different from those in Judaism, but the result is similar: the stimuli arising from a radicalized idea of proving oneself, which lead—owing to the concomitant psychological lever—to a pervasive moralization of all of life, are not in place.

Without question, Weber would have elaborated on his interpretation of pre-Reformation Catholicism in his study on Western Christianity. He would also have discussed some affirmative relationships between the Catholic economic ethic and modern capitalism. Moreover, he would have further extended his analysis of the continuity between otherworldly monastic asceticism and innerworldly vocational asceticism that he had already established in the first version of his *Protestant Ethic*.[284] He also intended to treat post-Reformation Catholicism in greater detail. Nevertheless, his main thesis on pre-Reformation Catholicism was set. Outside of the heterodox pre-Reformation movements and isolated tendencies of pre-Reformation monasticism, as Weber explicitly emphasized once more in the second version of the *Protestant Ethic*, "the characteristic Protestant conception of the proof of one's own salvation, the *certitudo salutis* in a calling," was lacking, "and thus the psychological sanctions that this form of religiosity placed upon '*industria*'" were also lacking.[285] The cause for this lack was not that Catholicism had not developed ideas in this direction; rather, it was that Catholicism remained an institution of sacramental grace. Let me quote what I view as a central passage, added by Weber to the second version of the *Protestant Ethic*:

> Of course, the Catholic ethic was an ethic of conviction. But the concrete *intentio* of the single act determined its value. And the single good or bad action was credited to the doer, determining his temporal and eternal fate. Quite realistically, the Church recognized that man was not an absolutely clearly defined unity to be judged one way or the other, but that his moral life was normally subject to conflicting motives and his action contradictory. Of course, it required as an ideal a fundamental change of life. But it weakened this requirement (for the average) person by one of its most important means of power and education, the sacrament of absolution, the function of which was connected with the deepest roots of Catholic religiosity.[286]

Thus, the unique position or role of ascetic Protestantism, and of Calvinism in particular, vis-à-vis Judaism and Catholicism, which Sombart contests, results from the radicalization of the conception of the proof of one's own salvation. This radicalization has both an ideal and an institutional side. The ideal side is connected to the combination of the ideas of proof and predestination, which in turn is joined to a specific conception of God, namely, the "absolute, sovereign character of God's will," whose grace is "completely unearned."[287] Institutional radicalization refers to the role of sacramental grace, whose claim to possess redemptive charisma is rejected; it now exists stripped of all magical force. Ideal radicalization destroys the ethical conception of reciprocity; institutional radicalization abnegates the possibility of periodic exoneration or moral transgressions. Now ethical commandments have to be fulfilled exclusively for the sake of God's glory, or in secular terms, out of respect for the law.

In this context, individual good works no longer suffice, but only the conducting of one's life in a systematic, unified, and methodical way in the service of God, or in secular terms, in the service of a cause, to which one has to be unconditionally committed. Only where such "faith" exists is the individual capable of gaining detachment from his world and from himself. Only then does he become an "inner-directed personality" in the strict sense of the term. When this conception of life takes hold of laymen involved in everyday economic life, it is probable that the economic realm will be interpreted as a sphere where one can prove oneself in an ethically relevant way. This is especially the case if these laymen do not belong to positively privileged strata and are rising economically. Even in the first version of the *Protestant Ethic*, in which Weber deliberately excluded any analysis of the class-conditioned character of religion, he had already pointed out that it was not the upper bourgeois classes but the "rising middle and lower-middle bourgeois classes" that became the "typical vehicle of the capitalist ethic and the Calvinist church." By fusing material and ideal interests, they initiated a revolution from within the individual. At the end of this revolutionary process we find a specifically bourgeois mode of conduct. Proving oneself in one's vocation can then take on a purely secular meaning.

Weber's Protestant ethic thesis has frequently been reconstructed and even more frequently been criticized in historical terms.[288] I will not take that up here. What I view as the crucial aspect in this context, however, was not always recognized in this literature, the fact that Weber's primary concern involved providing evidence of extreme psychic tension and its peculiar compensation. Ascetic Protestantism intensifies the psychic tension characteristic of all salvation religions between the "world" and the "hinterworld" understood as "the world above," and between promise and fulfillment, until the very idea of reciprocity—the conception of compensation for thought and action pleasing to God—itself ultimately becomes obsolete. Ascetic Protestantism does this for both the cognitive and the ethical realms. The "hinterworld" as the world above, personified in a radically transcendent being, the hidden God, is completely beyond human understanding, and no human action is capable of moving this God, whose decrees are not only unchangeable, but can also never lose their validity.[289] The believer is placed under this extreme inner tension, and initially, moreover, without any hope of lessening this tension. The salvation of church sacraments, indeed all inner means "of periodically discharging the emotional consciousness of sin," was lost.[290] Moreover, church structure in the form of the sect church or the pure sect, with its tendency to increase social control and to compel each member "to socially prove himself in the circle of his peers,"[291] intensified the already extreme pressure from within by pressure from without. All that remains, under such social and psychic conditions, is the continuous proving of oneself by means of innerworldly asceticism in the form of the asceticism of labor; for all other courses are excluded by the "radical exclusion of magic from the world."[292] Man must make himself completely into an instrument at the service of his God. In this way he learns what it means to do something for its own sake. The atmosphere in which this occurs is one of "pathos-filled inhumanity,"[293] of inner loneliness and a "disillusioned and pessimistically inclined individualism."[294] Those who live in such inner tension without being destroyed by it must respond to it by psychically rationalizing the way they conduct their lives.

Of course, even a person who tends to be heroic is not capable of withstanding this inner tension without some form of psychic compensation (*Ausgleich*). This is the context of Weber's famous construct according to which the unique compensation that ascetic Protestants discover consists in the interpretation of economic success as a sign of election. In this way, however, one's worldly vocation gains salvational significance, but—and this is the crucial point—without in any way reducing the psychic pressure continuously to prove oneself, much less identifying the meaning of life with vocational success. Even as its religious roots begin to die, as this religious mode of conduct is "secularized," this psychic constellation initially remains intact. Not just the Puritan, but the already largely secularized Benjamin Franklin wished to be a man of vocation without having to be one; the ethos of vocation as a cause is involved here.[295] The idea of the duty of one's calling is at the heart of the bourgeois mode of conduct. In psychic terms, it is for this reason just as far removed from the seignorial, artisanal, and peasant modes of conduct as from a world of "Faustian omnicompetence."[296]

In this sense, innerworldly asceticism is a central bourgeois virtue. It is the source of that rational moderation of the so-called acquisitive drive that Weber places at the center of his analysis. Judaism promotes rational innerworldly action but not asceticism, whereas Western monasticism provides support for asceticism but not for rational innerworldly action. Ascetic Protestantism first brought together these two historical "legacies." It also found a social group as a vehicle for this synthesis that owes its genesis primarily to the development of the medieval city. This development was joined by the development of capitalist institutions discussed earlier, whose origins stretch in part as far back as antiquity. They all represent important historical premises that enabled the second transformation to inaugurate a "development [that is] psychologically also of unbroken consistency."[297] The maxim *Deo placere vix potest*, with which capitalist acquisitive pursuits had been previously restrained, is now done away with; the capitalist pursuit of acquisition, and more generally, vocational labor is no longer deemed to be religiously immoral or even of a morally indifferent character; it is now held to be morally relevant. This transformation from within cannot be interpreted merely as a product of accommodation to the capitalist form of economy. Form and spirit possess their own histories. Their lines of development have to intersect in order for each to be able to separate itself from its previous "partner"—form from politics and spirit from religion—and establish new ties.

This new fusion occurs, for Weber, in the sixteenth and seventeenth centuries, making them the "heroic age of capitalism,"[298] that epoch in which an inwardly strengthened capitalism is joined by powerful external allies in the form of patrimonial states with a relatively modern bureaucracy. It is at the same time that age in which the mode of want satisfaction is still not predominantly capitalistic, in which household principle and market principle vigorously compete. The struggle is decided in favor of the market principle only in the nineteenth century, thus beginning the "iron age of capitalism."[299] This marks the third transformation, in the course of which the constellation of factors once again undergoes a fundamental change vis-à-vis the two preceding transformations. Let us raise, then, as a final question, What are the main changes to be found here?

The Third Transformation: The New House of Bondage

In order to characterize this third transformation, it is helpful to take a last look at Sombart. As I mentioned before, he distinguishes between early and advanced capitalism and between the bourgeois of the old and the new style. Whereas for the old-style bourgeoisie, man remains the measure of all things (*omnium rerum mensura homo*), for the new-style bourgeoisie this is not the case: here, it is not man but acquisition, or rather business, that is at center stage. The bourgeois virtues according to which the old-style bourgeoisie lived have now "become objective components of the business mechanism."[300] Objectification is the word that best sums up this process. By means of this contrast, Sombart comes to the thesis that "In the age of early capitalism, capitalism is made by the entrepreneur; in that of advanced capitalism, the entrepreneur is made by capitalism."[301]

At first glance, it appears that Weber argues similarly. He also states that capitalism, when victorious and founded on a mechanical basis, objectifies all economic and, indeed, social relationships and no longer requires a bourgeois mode of conduct. Capitalism now actually produces those human beings it needs to function, and this holds for both laborers and entrepreneurs. Whereas the Puritan and his secular successors in the mold of Benjamin Franklin still desired to be men of vocation, "we are compelled to be."[302] In this way, the vocation is in danger of losing the inner support it gained in early capitalism; and that danger increases the more consistently that victorious capitalism, on the basis of its unparalleled success, constructs its new house of bondage. This bondage is, in contrast to the old, one of golden chains.[303] Its defining marks are mechanized petrifaction and a frantic effort to take oneself seriously, combined with vanity, that "deadly enemy of all devotion to a cause and of all detachment, including above all, detachment towards oneself."[304] As was the case with otherworldly monastic asceticism, it appears that here, too, innerworldly vocational asceticism falls prey to its own successes. However, whereas the former continuously provoked reformations, the latter is threatened by mechanized petrifaction.[305]

Nevertheless, the similarity here between Sombart and Weber is only superficial. For Weber, objectification is a basic motif located at the heart of a religiously or a secularly interpreted bourgeois mode of conduct. It is not the product of a development of the capitalist form but rather the result of the original psychic constellation—that one must subordinate oneself to a cause. It is the Puritan entrepreneur, Sombart's old-style bourgeois, whom Weber characterizes as the embodiment of objectification: "The thought that man has an obligation towards the possessions entrusted to him, to which he subordinates himself either as obedient steward or actually as a 'machine for acquisition,' lays its chilly hand on life."[306] This feeling remains part and parcel of the bourgeois mode of conduct as long as it maintains its value orientation.

That this feeling could be lost, that even what seem from the outside to be the greatest of successes remain burdened by "the curse of futility to which all finite creatures are subject"[307] is what troubles Weber in regard to the third transformation. It is an apprehensiveness that prompts him to pose the question of the meaningfulness of a life under the conditions of a victorious capitalism. It also motivates him to ascertain what the remaining possibilities are for bourgeois conduct inside and outside of the process of the exploitation of capital. What is the meaning of vocation in a world of technically trained specialists? Where and how can the vocational ethos still be realized under the conditions of victorious capitalism? What can be done in this sense to maintain vocation as a cultural force? If one allows free rein to the advanced-capitalist developmental tendencies, there would ultimately be only those "last of men" in a godless and prophetless age that are spoken of in Weber in the end of *Protestant Ethic* and in Nietzsche at the beginning of his *Zarathustra*.[308] Weberian answers to these troublesome questions can be found in Chapter 1 of this book.

Let us conclude with an observation regarding Weber's explanatory model employed in his analysis of the rise of the West. In keeping with the requirement he raised in the "Author's Introduction," I have taken into account institutional conditions in favor of modern capitalism. I have also paid attention to the "causal relations running in the opposite direction," meaning the causal role played by the capability and disposition of human beings to take up a bourgeois mode of conduct. In contrast, for example, to Randall Collins's reconstruction, I have not offered a closed causal chain of factors, nor, as he does, distinguished between ultimate, background, and mediating conditions (conditions for which it remains unclear whether they are to be understood logically or temporally).[309] Weber was acquainted with neither a closed causal model nor a classification of conditions in this sense. He was acquainted only with constellations of factors classified according to epochs and with inner and outer historical preconditions, which are important or unimportant according to whether they can be connected in an adequate or only a coincidental fashion to consequences on the institutional or psychic level. Above all, however, Weber was acquainted with historical legacies. Certain factors arise and continue to exist "inconspicuously" until, on the basis

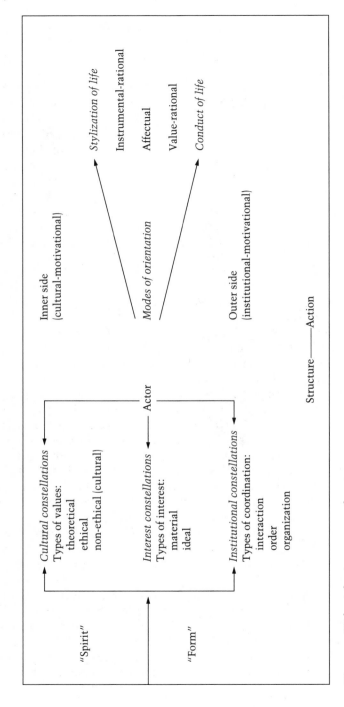

Figure 5. Weber's basic conceptual apparatus.

of historical coincidences, they get "caught up" in a constellation of factors in which they suddenly take on (causal) cultural significance for modern capitalism, even though they were not "invented" for this purpose. The medieval development of the city is one example. The historical intermezzo of urban autonomy creates institutions and bourgeois strata whose cultural importance for capitalism develops only very much later, in the sixteenth and seventeenth centuries, as the bourgeois mode of conduct arises from completely different historical sources. In this sense, Weber's explanatory model consists of the characterization of a sequence of individual constellations of inner and outer factors classified according to epochs. Of course, it is controversial whether the causal attributions claimed, especially in the light of new research, still retain their validity. Nonetheless, the explanatory model remains exemplary for historical sociology (see Figure 5).

Epilogue
Action, Order, and Culture

The depiction of Max Weber's political-philosophical and histori-cal-sociological profile invites an afterthought. What does it mean to pursue a line of reasoning that Weber himself eventually labeled interpretive sociology?

After Weber had partly recovered from his breakdown and re-sumed writing in the spring of 1902, he addressed methodological issues. This is no accident. The personal crisis had made him even more sensitive to the scientific crisis in economics than he had been before the breakdown. The general presuppositions guiding everyday scientific work in his field appeared to him misunder-stood or misconstrued. Weber tried to come to terms with the logi-cal problems of historical method as understood by the Historical School in German economics. He laid open the weakness of this ap-proach through a critique of Wilhelm Roscher's historical method. Neither positivism nor intuitionism served him as models; in-stead, he proceeded from the logical distinction between a theo-retical and a historical approach. Unlike many contemporaries, he regarded the Historical and the Theoretical Schools in German economics not as two different kinds of economics ("*zwei Natio-nalökonomien*," as he put it in the essay on objectivity), but as two sides of one coin.

To clarify this logical distinction, Weber relied on Heinrich Rickert's juxtaposition of generalizing and individualizing con-cept formation. The difference, he contended, must be grounded logically rather than ontologically. The quality of the object does not matter, but the mode of abstraction does. Regardless of its quality, we can always turn an object into either an exemplar of a class or an "historical individual." Nevertheless, Weber did not disregard the quality of the object altogether. From the outset he stressed that human utterances and actions are accessible through interpretation, from within. This accessibility gives them a special status vis-à-vis objects to which we cannot ascribe modes of orientation. Where such access is handled in a methodically controlled manner, a subgroup of sciences is established that does not fit the common distinction between natural sciences and sciences of the mind. This subgroup can be called sciences of action (*Handlungswissenschaften*). Economics belongs to it. Insofar as economics pursues a theoretical perspective, it contributes to action theory.

From early on, therefore, methodological problems are intertwined with problems of a theory of action in Weber. Both are developed side by side and step-by-step. It is true that first, methodological issues come to the fore. But the linkage is never severed. Action theory requires a theory of interpretation and vice versa. Weber's mature position, as laid down in the first chapter of *Economy and Society* ("The Basic Sociological Terms") corroborates this view.

In action theory Weber starts with the economic paradigm of an actor engaged in the rational pursuit of self-interest. Here, the course of action can be construed as the actor's adaptation to a situation in order to optimize his success. Interpretation remains pragmatic, based on the reconstruction of the logic of a situation. The point of view of the participant and the point of view of the observer coincide. This does not wipe out the logical distinction between the two perspectives, but it indicates that interpretation as an analysis from within becomes almost indistinguishable from observation as an analysis from without.

After 1902 Weber corrects this economic paradigm methodologically as well as theoretically. Methodologically, he discovers psychological interpretation without subscribing to Dilthey's views. An important intermediate step toward this discovery is his study on the psychophysics of industrial labor. In the course of this study Weber familiarizes himself with the psychology of his time and its potential to analyze subconscious and preconscious processes. This includes experimental psychology and psychopathology, especially the work of Emil Kraepelin and his disciples. This school proves to be especially strong in analyzing reactive behavior by way of observational explanation. It forces interpretive sociology to acknowledge an important line of demarcation: Every course of action is codetermined by processes beyond the actor's meaningful orientation. Here, interpretation does not apply.

This is not the whole story. There are also cases where the actor is meaningfully oriented, but where this orientation is hidden either from himself or from the observer. What Weber later terms "affectual orientation" is a case in point. This opens up a whole range of possibilities beyond observational explanation or pragmatic interpretation. It is the realm of psychological interpretation, which requires a true analysis from within. This does not turn interpretive sociology into a subjectifying discipline, however. Psychological interpretation serves causal attribution, for interpretation facilitates the explanation of a course of action; it is not opposed to it.

This methodological correction of the economic paradigm is associated with important theoretical alterations. As affectual-oriented action shows, action theory cannot rest its case on success-oriented action alone. This holds true even if we neglect nonrational orientations and concentrate only on rational orientations, for success-orientation is joined by value orientation that is also capable of being rationalized. It is not simply a variant of success-orientation. As early as the *Protestant Ethic* of 1904–5, Weber tried to convey this message to his fellow economists. With the Stammler essay of 1907 he definitely prepared the ground to demolish the economic paradigm in the theory of action. Success-oriented and value-oriented action cannot be reduced to each other. They are on equal footing.

Action always implies relationships to objects. They are part of the situation and can be physical, social, or cultural. The actor is conditioned by objects and oriented toward objects. He is constrained and free to choose. To strike a balance, he has to define a situation. In doing so, he is always confronted with the problem of single or double contingency.

In "Basic Sociological Terms" Weber summarizes his methodological and theoretical findings. He distinguishes between observational and interpretive explanation, and, within the latter, between a psychological and a pragmatic mode. There are also hints of a third type of interpretation, the reconstruction of meaning patterns and systems of rules. This third type of interpretation, although sufficiently developed in other parts of the work, is not given its proper due here, as Alexander von Schelting rightly observed a long time ago. Weber also distinguishes between four modes of orientation: traditional, affectual, instrumental-rational, and value-rational. These distinctions can be arranged in a sequence according to the following dichotomies: routinized versus nonroutinized, spontaneous versus rule-bound, bound by technical rules versus bound by normative rules. Every meaningful orientation can be routinized (traditional or habitual). In this case it becomes almost indistinguishable from reactive behavior. Spontaneous orientation (affectual or emotional) is also almost indistinguishable from reactive behavior. But contrary to routinized orientation, it is capable of being sublimated and therefore has a developmental potential of its own. If sublimation goes far enough, spontaneous orientation can turn into rule-bound orientation. This is open to rationalization. Its direction is determined by the type of rule (see Figure 6).

In "Basic Sociological Terms" Weber builds upon these modes of orientation. No action theory that deserves its name can forgo this analysis. Interpretive sociology would not be sociology, however, if it confined its distinctions to this level of analysis. Modes of orientation must be coordinated, especially in situations of double contingency. Many interpreters of Weber's work have been puzzled by the fact that he seems to supply two typologies of action, the first in section 2, the second in section 4 of "Basic Sociological Terms." This puzzle can be resolved by introducing the crucial distinction between modes of orientation and modes of coordination. These are two independent and yet interdependent dimensions of sociological analysis. The transition from orientation to coordination is accomplished in section 3 under the label "social relationships." Order and organization are then introduced as concepts that presuppose the concept of social relationship. An order requires rules ("a social relationship will be called an 'order' only if action is approximately or on the average oriented to certain determinate 'maxims' or rules"); an organization requires carriers of sanctions. The architecture of the "Basic Sociological Terms" reflects this conceptual strategy (see Figure 7).

Although section 4 deals with modes of coordination, it resembles section 2 in its internal structure. This is not accidental, inasmuch as Weber applies similar dichotomies. Coordination can be routinized or nonroutinized. If nonroutinized, it can be spontaneous or rule-bound. If rule-bound, the mode of coordination depends on the type of rule applied. The only difference is that the case of spontaneous coordination is not developed. The emphasis is on coordination by virtue of interests and by virtue of legitimacy, as in the sociology of domination in general (see Figure 8).

Observational explanation	Interpretive explanation	Reconstruction
Reactive behavior	Action or social action	Culture
	Traditional or habitual Affectual or emotional Instrumental-rational Value-rational	System of rules
Reactive imitation and behavior conditioned by crowds	Means-end	Symbol/sign-symbolized/signified
Stimulus-response "Mechanical" causality	Motivational "causality"	Noncausal relations

Figure 6. Weber's typology of action orientation.

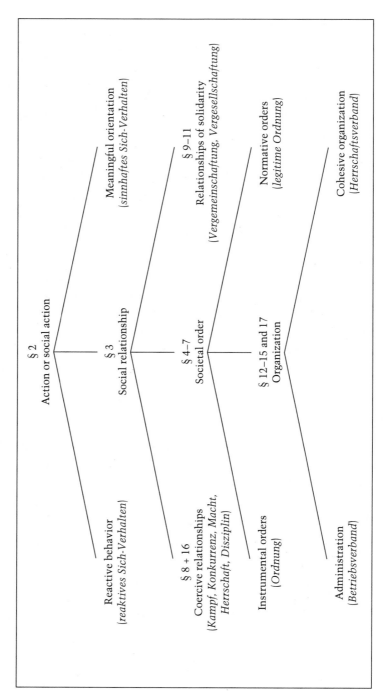

Figure 7. Weber's architecture of the basic sociological terms.

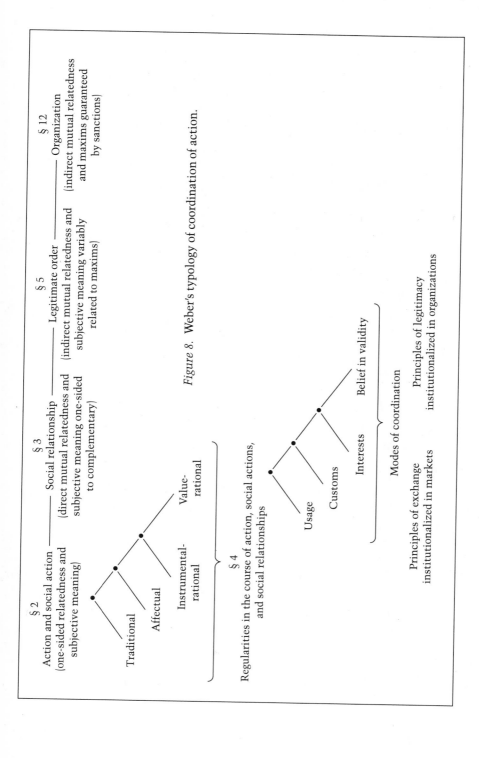

Figure 8. Weber's typology of coordination of action.

This is not the place to pursue Weber's conceptual strategy further or to fill the gaps in his conceptual apparatus.[1] Suffice it to say that the distinction between modes of orientation and modes of coordination is not enough. Interpretive sociology always requires an analysis that includes culture. We will never be able to understand orientation or coordination without the interpretive reconstruction of patterns of meaning and systems of rules. This holds true although culture is usually institutionalized in organizations, orders, and social relations and internalized by actors. It holds true, although only through actors' conduct are modes of coordination and cultures reproduced. Interpretive sociology requires an analysis of the interplay between action, order, and culture. It calls for a three-level analysis. This is the most important reason that Weber rejected not only a merely materialist or idealist construction of history but also a merely institutionalist or mentalist one.

Reference Matter

Notes

« *Introduction* »

1. Cf. Arendt and Jaspers 1985: 603.
2. Jaspers 1988: 32, 94–98.
3. Cf. Arendt and Jaspers 1985: 671–72, 695–96.
4. Cf. Roth and Schluchter 1979.
5. Cf. Schluchter 1981.
6. Cf. Schluchter 1989.
7. Notable exceptions are, for instance, Poggi 1983 and Lehmann and Roth 1993.

« *Chapter 1* »

1. Both speeches have been edited for publication as part of the *Max-Weber-Gesamtausgabe*, several volumes of which have already appeared. The present essay was originally published in German, in abridged form, as an introduction to the volume in which the two essays were reprinted. Cf. Weber 1992.

2. Cf. Jaspers 1988: 81.

3. Jaspers 1988: 50. In German one can distinguish "national," akin to the English "patriotic," from nationalistic. Weber himself always tried to make this distinction. "National" is not to be identified with the state. Of course, nation and state, as the inner and outer sides of one complex, have to be placed in relation to one another. Nevertheless, one represents the "spirit" and the other, the "form." On the problematic aspects of Weber's political thinking in this respect, see Mommsen 1974. Jaspers held Weber to be "the greatest German of our age." He had already characterized him in this way in 1920 and 1932. In 1958, regarding Weber the politician, he added: "His point of departure was a powerful German Em-

pire—whose defeat in the First World War he experienced just before his death, while hoping for its restoration. Today, all politics are based on new historical premises that lay outside of those that Weber practically considered. Max Weber reminds us of a past irrevocably lost in which he followed paths that were rejected by Germany. His basic political convictions, however, are everlasting" (Jaspers 1988: 50).

4. E.g., Maurenbrecher 1917: 104. Above all, in the two 1917 Lauenstein conferences on culture, Weber came to terms critically with Maurenbrecher and his views.

5. The struggle of the nations is, of course, supposed to employ peaceful means, and consist of competition within the framework of the League of Nations. However, whether one could be a national pacifist in this sense depends, as desirable as this may be, not on the Germans alone. On this, cf. Weber 1988: 109.

6. The dangers of this type of politics, expressed above all in its pursuit of peace through victory (*Siegfrieden*) and the annexation desires connected to it, are already described in Weber's speech of October 27, 1916, in Munich, on Germany's place among the European world powers. Cf. Weber 1984: 153–94, esp. 164–69.

7. On this hope, see Weber's speech on Germany's restoration (*Wiederaufrichtung*) from January 2, 1919, before a largely student audience in Heidelberg, about which several newspaper reports exist. See Weber 1988: 415–28, esp. 419–20.

8. Cf. such formulations as in "Deutschlands künftige Staatsform," Weber 1988, 106–7, where one finds statements such as the following: much more important than specific technical solutions to the problem of governing is the question "whether the bourgeoisie will produce in its masses a new *political spirit*, self-confident and ready to accept responsibility. Up until now, for a period of decades, the spirit of 'security' has predominated: sheltered in the protection of authorities, fearing all boldness or innovation, in short—the cowardly *will to impotence*." Before the turn of the century, Weber had already polemicized in similar form against the smug bourgeoisie, for example, in his Freiburg inaugural address.

9. Cf. also in this context the appeal of January 30, 1919, of the *Deutsche Demokratische Partei* (DDP) to democratic youth, which Max Weber also signed. Reprinted in Weber 1988: 513–17.

10. According to Jaspers 1988: 81.

11. According to a newspaper report, Weber anticipated a period of darkness and chill for Germany in the speech on Germany's restoration. Cf. Weber 1988: 419. This period also appears in modified form in "Politics as a Vocation." Cf. Weber 1978c: 128 (Weber 1971: 559).

12. On the dating of the addresses, cf. the excursus at the end of this chapter.

13. Even though it is not known exactly when Weber resumed working on these manuscripts, one can conclude from the title of the lecture

course he gave in Vienna in the summer semester of 1918 that he fell back on his still unpublished contribution to the *Grundriß der Sozialökonomik* (hereafter referred to as the *Outline*), a collective enterprise which Weber had conceived of and coordinated since 1909 and to which he wanted to contribute his major study "The Economy and the Societal Orders and Powers." According to the university course catalogue, the lecture course was entitled "Economy and Society (Positive Critique of the Materialist Concept of History)." According to Marianne Weber, Weber presented the results of his research in the sociologies of religion and domination (state) and thus, probably, two of the core elements of the old version of "The Economy and the Societal Orders and Powers," as intended for the handbook. Cf. Marianne Weber 1926: 617; and as supplementation, Heuss 1963: 225. Weber had already presented the basic components of his sociology of domination on October 25, 1917, in Vienna. There was a newspaper report on it in the *Neue Freie Presse*, No. 19102, October 26, 1917, p. 10.

14. In 1917, Weber began to write extended political articles—in sequel form—for the *Frankfurter Zeitung* on technical questions of government in the reorganization of Germany. In November 1918 he even temporarily became a kind of freelancer in its editorial office; and starting in December 1918 he actively supported the DDP's election campaign. The most important results of his political journalism were probably the two sequels of articles also published as pamphlets: "Wahlrecht und Demokratie in Deutschland" (Suffrage and democracy in Germany) and "Parlament und Regierung im neugeordneten Deutschland" (Parliament and government in a reconstructed Germany). Cf. Weber 1984: 344–96; Weber 1984: 421–596.

15. On this departure, cf. Weber 1984: 23–24. Weber applied for his discharge due to the imminent disbanding of the reserve hospital commission and the accompanying reorganization of relations of command. From October 1, 1915, on he was back in civilian dress, although he continued to go to his office regularly for a while in order to train his successor. Cf. Marianne Weber to Helene Weber, October 1, 1915 (private collection of Max Weber-Schäfer): "Yes, and Max is walking about today for the first time again in civilian dress, even though he's in the office the whole day, for his successor is not up to the task at all, and I don't know how it will work out. I am also sad and displeased that Max has to leave this work before the end of the war, work with which he has become one and to which he had dedicated himself with a moving sense of duty despite its 'mindlessness.'"

16. The plan and the implementation of the lecture series admittedly diverged from one another, as I shall show. See also the "Editorische Berichte" (Editorial reports) in Weber 1992.

17. On the development of Weber's work, cf. Schluchter 1989, part 4.

18. The sole public scholarly address from the time of his breakdown in health until the beginning of 1917 was Weber's speech at the congress

in St. Louis in 1904, published in 1906 as "The Relations of the Rural Community to Other Branches of Social Science." The first public (political) speech he held at all following his breakdown in health was on August 1, 1916, in Nuremberg, addressed to the party-unaffiliated lobby German National Committee for a Negotiated Peace (Deutscher National-Ausschuß für einen ehrenvollen Frieden), of which only newspaper accounts remain (Weber 1984: 648–89). Immediately after his trip to America, Weber gave a report of his impressions of the "New World" in a public meeting of the local chapter of the National Social Association (Nationalsozialen Verein) in Heidelberg, on which Johannes Leo reported. Cf. Leo 1963: 17–18. The remaining scholarly or political addresses, and all other remarks by Weber in the period between 1898–99 and the middle of 1916 were made either in settings largely closed to the public before a select audience, such as the lecture on the value-judgment debate in January 1914, or as part of discussion, and thus were largely ad hoc and spontaneous in nature. Only in 1917 did Weber once again launch into political and scholarly lecturing activities on a larger scale. The first public university lecture that he held after his illness did not take place until as late as the summer semester of 1918 at the University of Vienna.

19. On May 14, 1914, for example, Marianne Weber wrote to Helene Weber (private collection of Max Weber-Schäfer): "I hope Max finishes his large handbook article in the fall. Then it would probably be my deepest and ever-present desire for him to decide once again—at least in the form of occasional *lectures*—to address the youth. Will that happen, however? The psychological inhibitions that keep him from doing that must still have great power over him. However, at some time the spell must be broken!"

20. On November 6, 1914, Marianne Weber wrote to Helene Weber (private collection of Max Weber-Schäfer): "Indeed, Sundays, though our youth are almost completely gone, are always full. Now we sit crowdedly in Max's room. . . . Indeed, when will the time come when Max sits at his desk again? At the moment, he does not even have his inkwell there."

21. Cf. above all the essays "Zur Frage des Friedenschließens" (On the question of making peace) and "Bismarcks Außenpolitik und die Gegenwart" (Bismarck's foreign policy and the present) in Weber 1984: 49–92, which had already been written in 1915. Weber oriented himself in his foreign-policy analyses on military security, economic interest, and national cultural identity. In his view, every nation has to create a viable balance between these three rational principles of foreign policy, and that holds for Germany also. On this point, cf. Weber 1984: 189. From the very beginning, Weber came out for a peace of mutual understanding (*Verständigungsfrieden*), against the annexation of Belgium in the West, and for a Polish nation state as a buffer against Russia in the East.

22. On this, cf. Weber 1984: 134–52, 645–47.

23. Cf. for example, Max Weber to Marianne Weber, May 16, 1916 (private collection of Max Weber-Schäfer): "*Once* I start working on Chinese

and Indian matters, I feel very well and able to work; I long to do such work."

24. On this aspect of the development of Weber's work, cf. Schluchter 1989, chapter 13.

25. Marianne Weber to Helene Weber, October 12, 1916 (private collection of Max Weber-Schäfer). The passage in the letter containing the quote reads: "Max has just immersed himself in the Old Testament, analyzing the Prophets, Psalms, and the Book of Job—and he sometimes reads to me some of his newest writings in the evening—that does good after all the day's distractions."

26. On the role of pre-exilic prophets, see Schluchter 1989, chapter 5. On the change from historical treatment to a treatment of contemporary relevance, or more precisely of personal and contemporary relevance, see Marianne Weber 1926: 604–5. In her estimation, in 1916, the pre-exilic prophets of doom now appeared to Weber "as the first 'political demagogues' historically attested to"; his analysis of Jeremiah, like that of the Puritans, especially let "strong inner involvement show through." In a speech from December 1, 1918, Weber formulated his need for independence in political questions, according to a newspaper account, in the following way: he would not join the Social Democratic Party, even though he was almost indistinguishable in his stance from many members of that party "because he could do without *independence in the expression of his opinion* vis-à-vis the demos even less so than vis-à-vis the forces of authority." Weber 1988: 379.

27. On this perspective, cf. the felicitous remark by Karl Jaspers on the relationship of consciousness of past and present in Weber in Jaspers 1988, 83.

28. After his first hours of lecture in Vienna, he wrote on May 7, 1918 to Marianne Weber (private collection of Max Weber-Schäfer): "No—I was born for the *quill* and for the *public platform*, not for the lectern."

29. On this speech, cf. the "Editorial Report" and the newspaper accounts of the speech reprinted in Weber 1984, 649–55.

30. "Deutschlands weltpolitische Lage" (Germany's political situation), Weber 1984: 153–203; held before the Progressive People's Association (Fortschrittlicher Volksverein).

31. This expression is found in Marianne Weber. In a letter to Helene Weber from August 7, 1916 (private collection of Max Weber-Schäfer), one reads, "The address recently in Nuremberg was apparently a brilliant success for him. But the audience did not know him, and he was not allowed to take a poke at the Pan-Germans, and that made him angry. The first *public* and political address for 17–18 years. Whether the lion has now got a taste of blood!? He complained terribly about the necessity of being cautious and conciliatory! He really is the *combative* hero."

32. Admittedly, Weber also did not want to hear of ceding Alsace-Lorraine. Its treatment as a state of the empire (*Reichsland*) with special status, he considered, however, a mistake. Cf. his debate with the group

around Ernst Toller in 1917 in Heidelberg; see the account by Käthe Leichter (Leichter 1963, esp. 140).

33. Weber 1984: 192.

34. Aside from the major constitutional writings, chiefly from 1917, such as "Suffrage and Democracy in Germany" (see Chapter 1, n. 14) and the first version of "Parliament and Government"; cf. Weber 1978b), cf., e.g., his 1919 speech on Germany's restoration, Weber 1988: 415 (see Chapter 1, n. 7).

35. This flight was one of the reasons why Weber did not immediately join the Deutsche Demokratische Partei (DDP), which had grown out of the Deutsche Volkspartei (DVP), but only did so after a short delay. He had defended the monarchy as an institution in the framework of an authentic parliamentarianism until events no longer made this defense possible. He did not want to present himself as a republican from one day to the next. In spite of this prudence, he quickly joined the DDP, signing its electoral program and campaigning for it in December 1918 and January 1919. The election appeal can be found in Weber 1988: 501–4.

36. On this formulation, see "Science as a Vocation" (Weber 1973: 612).

37. Weber 1984: 192.

38. This was the major motivation behind Weber's ever increasing invective against Kurt Eisner, which also left its mark on the speech "Politics as a Vocation." Indeed, this address took place after Eisner had taken on the position of governor of Bavaria on November 7–8, 1918, and before he was murdered, on February 21, 1919, by Count Arco-Valley. According to newspaper accounts, especially in his election campaign speech from January 14, 1919, in Fürth, Weber condemned "in the sharpest possible terms . . . the special treatment given by the Bavarian government to the question of war guilt," and emphasized that Eisner's publications had "caused immeasurable damage." Eisner had published on November 23, 1918, without the approval of Berlin, passages from reports that the Bavarian embassy in Berlin had made to the Bavarian government in July and August of 1914. Cf. Weber 1988: 453–54. In a letter to Else Jaffé from this period, probably from February 10, 1919 (private collection of Eduard Baumgarten), Weber characterized Eisner as a "demagogue without any political conscience." On Weber's fundamental position on this question, which—in spite of his rage about "the doings of the current dilettantish regime" and about literati such as Eisner, Mühsam, Landauer, and Toller—also reflects his principled standpoint on the relationship between politics and ethics, see his article, "Zum Thema der 'Kriegschuld,'" (On war guilt) of January 17, 1919, in Weber 1988: 177–90.

39. Weber 1949: 18 (Weber 1978c: 84); Weber 1973: 508–9.

40. Cf. Weber 1978c: 223, 225; Weber 1971: 558, 560. In the second of these passages (Weber 1978c: 225), Weber distinguishes three reactions: "Embitterment or philistinism, simple apathetic acceptance of the world

and of one's profession, or third, and far from least common, mystical escapism in those who are gifted in that direction or—as is frequently and regrettably the case—who force themselves into it to follow the fashion." The first two, however, are variants of adjustment to the world.

41. A report on this address is found in *Das jüdische Echo. Bayerische Blätter für jüdische Angelegenheiten* 4 (January 26, 1917), 40–41. It was a weekly newspaper appearing every Friday. Weber's public address took place on "Wednesday evening in front of a large public" (40).

42. Of interest is the conclusion of the newspaper account (see n. 41), it reads: "An unexpectedly large—mostly Jewish—audience followed the very captivating address. It did not always display a strict structuring of the material (in part because Prof. Weber had only reckoned with a non-academic public, and thus occasionally spent more time than intended on details that were necessary for overall understanding), but it provided a host of interesting details. The majority of the audience left with the impression that they had heard things here that most had never previously heard about" (ibid., 41).

43. Cf. the account in the *Neue Freie Presse*, No. 19102, October 26, 1917, p. 10. On the question of a three- or four-part typology of domination, cf. Schluchter 1989, chapters 6.6 and 11. Weber was in Vienna for negotiations on the possible terms of his appointment to the University of Vienna, where the law faculty had recommended Weber alone (*unico loco*) as the successor to the deceased Eugen von Philippovich.

44. Held at the Fortschrittlicher Verein. Cf. Weber 1984: 712.

45. It is not certain whether Weber actually held this address; it is mentioned in correspondence several times. Despite the most intensive research, neither an announcement nor a report of the speech has yet to be found. The date is also uncertain. In the letters of Max Weber, talk is of September 18; in a letter from Marianne Weber to Helene Weber, however, September 14 is mentioned. On September 13, Marianne Weber wrote (private collection of Max Weber-Schäfer): "Tomorrow Max is delivering an address in an adult education course in Heppenheim on 'State and Constitution.' We (Tobelchen [her companion] and I) are going along, and it will be the first time that I have heard him publicly speak since St. Louis, and thus in thirteen years."

46. Weber emphasized at the beginning of his political address of November 5, 1917, that he was speaking as a politician, not as a scholar, just as he emphasized in "Politics as a Vocation," more than one year later, that he was speaking as a scholar and not as a politician.

47. Weber claimed that Germany had to enter the circle of the world's master peoples (*Herrenvölker*), and thus used a term that has in the meantime lost its innocence. According to newspaper accounts, however, the term simply applied for him to peoples "who had gained control over their own government and are more than just the objects of legislation." Cf. Weber 1984: 713, 727.

48. The event ended with the acceptance of a resolution, the contents of which well reflect Weber's position on problems of domestic and foreign policy. It is reprinted in Weber 1984: 722.

49. Marianne Weber also mentions talks in the summer of 1917 on Indian castes, Jewish prophets, and the sociological foundations of music. Cf. Marianne Weber 1926: 607. These talks were probably readings in private circles.

50. Cf. Marianne Weber to Helene Weber, November 1, 1917 (private collection of Max Weber-Schäfer): "Max came home from Vienna in a very cheery mood yesterday evening after being gone for ten days. They had paid court to him intensively there, had accepted all his conditions, and want him to hold a [weekly] two-hour trial lecture course to test whether his energies are sufficient for a professor's chair, etc. I do not think he will ultimately decide for Vienna, but this summer semester that lasts only three months and imposes on him only a very modest teaching obligation, and in addition is a welcome opportunity to gain political insights and to have all kinds of engaging new people around him, is very tempting to him, and I guess I can't begrudge him that."

51. Cf., for example, Max Weber to Mina Tobler, August 28, 1917 (private collection of Eduard Baumgarten), in which one reads this about the political situation: "I now view the future with optimism even with all the apprehensions remaining. If we are reasonable and do not believe that we can rule the world, we will surely come through it all with honor, militarily and otherwise. But it would be good, if it were to end."

52. Cf. n. 20 above.

53. On the history of this house in Heidelberg, see Lepsius 1989.

54. On this, cf. Weber's own distinction between teacher and leader in "Science as a Vocation," Weber 1973: 605. See also the statements of participants cited in the "Editorial Reports" in Weber 1992.

55. Löwith misdated the address and claimed that it was "published verbatim as it was spoken." Cf. Löwith 1986: 16. Because Löwith writes that the war first ended for him in December 1917, one has first to assume that he could not have heard the address on November 7, 1917, and that it took place later (or even twice). This assumption would be unfounded. An examination of the registration lists at the University of Munich shows that Löwith was already registered in the winter semester of 1917–18; thus, his recollection could very well (and also must) refer to November 7. That Weber's address was not printed verbatim as spoken can be gathered from its publication history. On this, cf. the "Editorial Report" in Weber 1992.

56. Löwith 1986: 16–17.

57. Löwith 1986: 17.

58. Max Weber to Else Jaffé, January 22, 1919 (private collection of Eduard Baumgarten).

59. On this, cf. the "Editorial Report" on "Politik als Beruf," Weber 1992.

60. Cf. the account of the *Heidelberger Neuesten Nachrichten* on Weber's election speech of January 2, 1919, in Heidelberg, on Germany's restoration, Weber 1988: 419.

61. Cf. Weber 1984: 99–125.

62. On this bitterness, cf., for example, Weber 1988: 432, 453–54, as well as the statements dictated in pure rage about Liebknecht and Rosa Luxemburg prior to their murder (Weber 1988: 441).

63. Cf. "Politics as a Vocation," Weber 1971: 548.

64. Heuss 1963: 225.

65. Max Weber to Marianne Weber, May 7, 1918 (private collection of Max Weber-Schäfer).

66. Max Weber to Marianne Weber, June 20, 1918 (date unverified; private collection of Max Weber-Schäfer).

67. Max Weber to Mina Tobler, May 7, 1918 (private collection of Max Weber-Schäfer).

68. Cf. Lepsius 1977. Indeed, Weber had regularly delivered speeches in Munich since his "return to the public realm": before the Progressive People's Association (Fortschrittlicher Volksverein), before the Social Science Association (Sozialwissenschaftliche Gesellschaft), and before the Munich Free Students Association (Freie Studentenschaft). Moreover, the *Münchener Neuesten Nachrichten* had turned into a forum for his political articles, second only to the *Frankfurter Zeitung*. He also had personal relationships (Else Jaffé) in the city.

69. Max Weber to Else Jaffé, January 20, 1919 (private collection of Eduard Baumgarten).

70. Guenther Roth considers four of Weber's political hopes unrealized: "to influence significantly the drafting of the new constitution, to get himself elected to the Weimar national assembly, to help organize an international campaign against the imputation of Germany's war guilt, and to be taken seriously as an adviser at the Paris Peace Conference." Cf. Roth 1989: 138. Starting from this supposed failure, Roth then comes to the question: "How do we get from Weber the frustrated politician to Weber the driven scholar?" The answer: "Weber's return to single-minded scholarship was not only an act of renunciation in an obvious sense, but in some way also a continuation of his political war with other means" (Roth 1989: 145). This continuation is shown by the "new objectivity" that marks the style and form of his subsequent scholarly work, oral and written. It can be seen, for example, in the "Basic Sociological Terms" ("Soziologische Grundbegriffe") and the new version of *Economy and Society* in general. One can raise the following objections to these arguments: First, even before leaving the military hospital administration Weber was already "the driven scholar." Second, the supposedly new objectivity is the same old one that Weber demanded and practiced, for example, in the essay on value freedom as well as in "Science as a Vocation" and long before, and that is intimately connected to his concept of personality. Third, the form of the second version of *Economy and Society* is the

result of an increasing division of labor between the handbook contribution and the writings on the economic ethics of the world religions. On this form, cf. Schluchter 1989, chapter 12. Thus, none of these points are related to Weber's retreat from politics in any basic way.

71. Of the three qualities that a politician, according to Weber, is supposed to possess—namely, passion, a sense of responsibility, and a sense of proportion (or perspective)—Weber sometimes lacked the last of these in the positions he took in everyday politics. This lack can be seen in his election speeches of December 1918 and January 1919. In the heated political atmosphere of the election campaign, he, too, occasionally made statements he would never have committed to paper.

72. Perhaps Karl Jaspers saw this clearer than anyone else. Cf. Jaspers 1988: 67–68.

73. In point of fact, only his temporary commitment to the DDP can even be interpreted to qualify as political actions.

74. Cf. Weber 1958a: 77; Weber 1971: 505.

75. Cf. Weber 1958a: 79; Weber 1971: 508.

76. Cf. Birnbaum 1963: 21.

77. For evidence to this effect see Schluchter 1989, chapter 12.

78. This conflict was also present during the period in Munich in which, as in Vienna, Weber enjoyed great success with his lectures. He lectured before several hundred students, customarily in the Auditorium Maximum. Nevertheless, the lectures gave him small pleasure: "The lecture course is an obligation—*not* pleasant, it does not suit me at all. Writing style and speaking style are different, something so many people are strangely enough capable of forgetting or repressing. A 'lecture,' however, is writing-speaking style, for the d[amned] lads are indeed *supposed* to take notes, and I myself know for how little that is good" (Weber to Mina Tobler, January 3, 1920 [private collection of Eduard Baumgarten]). And even earlier: "What is so 'demanding' about lectures—I see it now—is that my speaking and writing style are totally different. I can only speak without inhibition when I speak extemporaneously (on the basis of notes). In my course, however, I have to provide 'responsible' formulations, and that is ridiculously demanding, at least for me, for I then speak in writing style, i.e., inhibited, agonized, practically physically maltreating my brain" (Weber to Mina Tobler, July 27, 1919 [private collection of Eduard Baumgarten]).

79. This simplification also had a personal side to it. The constellation of Max Weber, Marianne Weber, Mina Tobler, Else Jaffé, and Alfred Weber had changed. A complete picture can emerge only by taking that change into consideration, something that cannot be done here.

80. Cf. Marianne Weber to Helene Weber, February 13, 1919 (private collection of Max Weber-Schäfer): "Such a great offer is here from *Bonn*—only a two-hour teaching obligation, everything one wants, and 20,000 MK guaranteed income!!—that it is really exciting. Now it is only a question as to whether Munich will agree to allow Max to lecture on sociology

and the theory of the state instead of on economics [*Nationalökonomie*], and to a limited teaching obligation (four hours). Then we will naturally go to Munich, even though the *salary* offered there is only very modest."

81. Cf. Max Weber to Marianne Weber, June 16, 1919 (private collection of Max Weber-Schäfer): "I just sent my course announcement to the administration, start on *Tuesday* (5–6 P.M.) ('Die allgemeinsten Kategorien der Gesellschaftswissenschaft')." For the winter semester of 1919–20, he first announced two hours on "Economic History" ("Wirtschaftsgeschichte") and two hours on "States, Classes, and Status Groups" ("Staaten, Klassen, Stände") but then cancelled the latter for the sake of the former, which ultimately became the four-hour "Outline of Universal Social and Economic History" ("Abriß der universalen Sozial- und Wirtschaftsgeschichte"). In the summer semester of 1920 he lectured on the "General Theory of State and Politics (Sociology of State)" ("Allgemeine Staatstheorie und Politik [Staatssoziologie]") (four hours) and on "Socialism" ("Sozialismus") (two hours). With the exception of "Economic History," these are all topics that are directly connected to the handbook article. It is known that Weber offered "Economic History" only in response to the urgings of his students. He wrote to Mina Tobler in January 1920 on this reluctance to deliver the lecture (private collection of Eduard Baumgarten): "*This* material bores me, given the unworthy haste with which it is presented."

82. See Schluchter 1989: 425, 443.

83. Weber thoroughly read the manuscripts on aesthetics that Lukács wrote from 1912 to 1918 in pursuit of the postdoctoral lecturing qualification in philosophy at the University of Heidelberg. His reading is also reflected in "Science as a Vocation," cf. Weber 1973: 610. Of course, Mina Tobler also represented an important dialogue partner on questions of music.

84. Weber wrote on November 8, 1919, to his publisher, Paul Siebeck, that he wanted to give his contribution to the handbook a "didactic form . . . that I consider appropriate in order to finally treat 'sociology' in a strictly objective and scholarly manner instead of as the dilettante achievements of ingenious philosophers." This statement should not lead one to conclude that he planned to write a dry and abstract book. Weber expressly rejected this possibility.

85. As written in "Politics as a Vocation," Weber 1958a: 128; Weber 1971: 560.

86. Cf. Weber 1988: 419.

87. Cf. Marianne Weber 1926: 647–48. The transcription of the original is corrected in Mommsen 1974: 347.

88. Cf. Schluchter 1989, chapter 9, esp. 313.

89. Cf. Weber 1988: 191–95. The date of Weber's resignation is uncertain. Cf. ibid., 191.

90. The address took place in front of the Political Association of German Students (Politischer Bund deutscher Studenten [Bund deutsch-

nationaler Studenten]) in Munich. In a public announcement, it was stated: "Only students will be admitted." In addition, Weber announced publicly at this event that in taking over the professorship of Lujo Brentano he would be leaving politics. On March 14, 1919, the *Münchener Zeitung* carried the following item: "In a student meeting [reported about elsewhere in the newspaper], the democratic politician, Prof. Max Weber (Heidelberg) declared that at the moment when he intends to join the teaching staff of the University of Munich, he will *take leave of politics.* It is too difficult both to pursue politics and to convey the useful facts and knowledge of science. Apparently Weber is of the view that, as the successor to Brentano, the Munich professorship entails a greater range of tasks of teaching and scholarship than those in Heidelberg, since it is known that he was zealously politically active there." Cf. Weber 1988: 483. Clearly the newspaper was not aware that since his illness, Weber had not held any courses in Heidelberg.

91. Weber 1988: 482–84.

92. Cf. the account of the first Lauenstein conference from May 29 to May 31, 1917, where one passage reads: "Prof. Weber came out against the youth movement, which he clearly saw only in terms of the Wyneken movement; he did this with such sarcasm that he lost a great deal of the initial sympathies of his audience." Cf. Weber 1984: 703. Weber's rejection of Wyneken is also expressed in another document that is connected directly to "Science as a Vocation" and "Politics as a Vocation." In a letter from Frithjof Noack to Marianne Weber of October 26, 1924 (private collection of Max Weber-Schäfer), in which Noack reports on his research on the genesis of the two speeches, one reads: "Weber was above all happy that the speech on education was not held by Wyneken, whom he disdained intensely as a 'demagogue of youth, etc.'" This disapproval becomes all the more poignant given the fact that Weber's brother Alfred was a declared follower of Wyneken. On the latter's effects on others, see also the correspondence between Wyneken and Walter Benjamin, who after initial support, completely broke with him. See Götz von Ohlenhusen 1981. Further, see Benjamin 1977, esp. vol. 2, bk. 1, 60–66 (on the relationship between the Freistudentenschaft and the Freischar), and vol. 2, bk. 3, 824–88. The letter in which Benjamin breaks with Wyneken is found in vol. 2, bk. 3, 885–87.

93. On this last point, see once again the newspaper account (Chapter 1, n. 89) in Weber 1988: 484.

94. Cf. Schulze and Ssymank 1932: 381.

95. The expression *Finke* (finch) was originally a term of ridicule, similar to the expression *Wilde* (savages) and used in the same way.

96. Schulze and Ssymank 1932: 420. Cf. also the leaflet *Der freistudentische Ideenkreis. Programmatische Erklärung* (The ideas of the Free Student Movement) (hereafter Behrend 1907). The Free Students came out against the "drunken student in fraternity colors" as the prototype of students and against the "predominance of the principle of student soci-

eties, morning and early evening drinking, class divisions, and the limited interest in education" in student life. Cf. Behrend 1907: 18. Instead of this, they advocated self-education in the framework of an academic cultural community for which the idea of the unity of the scholarly disciplines, the unity of research and teaching, and the unity of those teaching and those taught remained definitive.

97. On the principle of tolerance and neutrality, see Behrend 1907: 29. The principle of neutrality, incidentally, in no way excluded the idea of a political education. Quite to the contrary, it was one of the distinctive characteristics of the Free Students that they emphasized the importance of political education, and thus, in those university departments (*Abteilungen*) in which they practiced their educational work, they gave special regard to the social sciences. Cf. Behrend 1907: 33.

98. Immanuel Birnbaum, who after studying in Freiburg and Königsberg came to Munich in the summer semester of 1913 and quickly rose to the top ranks of the Munich Free Students Association, writes in his memoirs: "However, the student movement in Munich also attracted me strongly. It had given the basic idea of the Free Students Association a new programmatic turn: it no longer raised claim to all nonincorporated students as free students; instead, it declared its organization to be an academic party that sought to defend equal rights, elected student representatives, and advocated expanded student self-education." Birnbaum 1974: 45.

99. Cf. Behrend 1907: 5–6.

100. Between 1872 and 1919–20, the number of university students rose from circa 16,000 to circa 118,000. On this increase, see Schulze and Ssymank 1932: 428, 465.

101. Cf. their leaflet "German Free Academic Youth, 1913, on the celebration at the Hohen Meißner" ("Freideutsche Jugend. Zur Jahrhundertfeier auf den Hohen Meißner 1913"). The following associations are listed there: Deutsche Akademische Freischar (Free Academic Youth), Deutscher Bund abstinenter Studenten (German Association of Abstinent Students), Deutscher Vortruppbund (German Advance Guard Association), Bund deutscher Wanderer (Association of German Ramblers), Jungwandervogel (Young Hiking Enthusiasts), Österreichischer Wandervogel (Austrian Young Hiking Enthusiasts), Germania-Bund abstinenter Schüler (Germania Association of Abstinent School Students), Freie Schulgemeinde Wickersdorf (Free School Community of Wickersdorf), Bund für Freie Schulgemeinden (Association for Free School Communities), Landschulheim am Solling (Outdoor School on Solling Mountain), Akademische Vereinigungen Marburg und Jena (Academic Associations of Marburg and Jena), Dürerbund (Dürer Association), Comeniusgesellschaft (Comenius Society), Bodenreform (Land Reform), Völkerverständigung (International Understanding), Frauenbewegung (Women's Movement), Abstinenzbewegung (Abstinence Movement), and Rassenhygiene (Racial Hygiene).

102. See Schwab 1914. The group around Wyneken—the Free School Community of Wickersdorf—quickly withdrew (or rather, were forced out).

103. See Schulze and Ssymank 1932: 459–60. According to the authors, the movement really stayed alive at only five universities after the outbreak of war.

104. On Foerster's position, cf., for example, his book *Politische Ethik und Politische Pädagogik* (On political ethics and pedagogics), Foerster 1918, esp. 327–48 ("Cæsar and Christ"). In this chapter, Foerster comes to terms with above all Otto Baumgarten, Max Weber's cousin.

105. Cf. Birnbaum 1974: 59.

106. On this see Schulze and Ssymank 1932: 459–60. Cf. also the declaration of Heidelberg students, signed by, among others, Ernst Toller and Elisabeth Harnisch (*Die Tat. Monatsschrift für die Zukunft deutscher Kultur*, 9 [Sept. 1917–18], p. 820).

107. Weber 1949: 6; Weber 1973: 494.

108. Weber 1949: 4; Weber 1973: 492. Weber gave the following judgment of Foerster in "Politics as a Vocation": "My colleague, Mr. F. W. Foerster, whom personally I highly esteem for the undoubted honorableness of his convictions, but whom I reject unreservedly as a politician." Cf. Weber 1958a: 122; Weber 1971: 553.

109. Immanuel Birnbaum to Max Weber, November 26, 1917 (private collection of Max Weber-Schäfer). Cf. also the "Editorial Preface" on "Science as a Vocation" in Weber 1992. The German names of the groups in common opposition to Weber were: the "'Bildungs'-Freunde" and the "Schwärmer für den 'wissenschaftlichen Verstandesgebrauch.'"

110. This is especially true for Husserl's critique of the reduction of epistemology (the theory of knowledge) to cognitive psychology (the psychology of knowledge). In order to avert such reductionism, Weber based his arguments on, among other things, Husserl's *Logical Investigations* (*Logische Untersuchungen*). Naturally, this basis is not sufficient for inferring any sympathy on Weber's part for the phenomenological method. Southwestern German neo-Kantianism also battled against the reduction of epistemology to cognitive psychology.

111. Both Husserl and Weber discuss such naturalistic self-deceptions, in part, in terms of the same authors, for example, Wilhelm Ostwald. Cf. Husserl 1911, esp. 295; and Max Weber, "'Energetische' Kulturtheorien" ("Energetic" theories of culture), in Weber 1973: 400–26.

112. For a comprehensive discussion, see Chapter 2. Helmuth Plessner gave the following evaluation of Weber's relation to Husserl: "Weber respected Husserl's seriousness, but he found his cause to be loathsome." Cf. Plessner 1963: 33.

113. Weber 1949: 2; Weber 1973: 490.

114. Weber 1949: 3; Weber 1973: 491.

115. Weber says this in reference to the last forty years of development in economics. Cf. Weber 1949: 3; Weber 1973: 492.

116. Weber 1949: 3; Weber 1973: 491.

117. Weber 1949: 3; Weber 1973: 491.

118. In typological terms, Weber actually distinguishes three different kinds of education: charismatic education on the basis of non-everyday ("extraordinary") knowledge, by means of which a natural gift already present within a human being is led to manifest itself; cultural education on the basis of formative knowledge, by means of which the character of the human being is cultivated; and specialized training on the basis of specialized knowledge, by means of which a human being is trained to be able to perform useful functions. Cf. Weber 1989: 302ff.

119. Weber 1921, I: 204; Weber 1958b: 182; and *Zarathustra* in Nietzsche 1960, vol. 1.

120. Cf. Weber 1949: 3; Weber 1973: 491.

121. Weber 1921, 1: 203; Weber 1958b: 181. It is known that Weber viewed the later works of Goethe, notably *Faust II* and the *Wanderjahre*, as taking leave of this ideal. This estimation also played a role in his critique of neo-idealistic efforts, especially as it developed in the circle around the publisher Eugen Diederichs, and it played a central role at the Lauenstein conferences (Weber's brother Alfred also sympathized with these circles, which also included parts of the Free German movement). On the efforts of Eugen Diederichs in general, see Hübinger 1987: 92–114; and further, Diederichs n.d., esp. 270–308. On organics, harmony, and humanity as guiding concepts of German classicism, see also Lukács 1953: 57–75. For Weber, Gundolf's book was important; cf. Gundolf 1916.

122. Weber 1978c: 73; Weber 1973: 493.

123. Kant termed this the distinction between the private and public use of reason. Cf. Kant 1977, A: 487, 488 (*Beantwortung der Frage: Was ist Aufklärung?*).

124. Weber 1978c: 72; Weber 1973: 493. Weber speaks of the "unassailability of the academic chair" (Weber 1949: 5; Weber 1973: 493). This is meant in an institutional sense. It naturally does not mean that those studying are not allowed to criticize a presented doctrine. Weber also recognized that doubt and critique are the elixir of life. With Fichte, he declares: "For the most radical doubt is the father of knowledge." Cf. Weber 1978c: 75; Weber 1973: 496; and Fichte 1962 (*Sittenlehre. Drittes Hauptstück* section 15).

125. Weber 1978c: 72; Weber 1973: 493.

126. A good example of this effect is in the account by Julie Meyer-Frank, who started studying in Munich in the winter semester of 1917–18, and who also witnessed Weber, aside from in his two public addresses, in his Munich lecture courses and seminars. She wrote: "In contrast, Max Weber lectured with precise emphasis, like a conductor accompanying the rhythm of his speech with his hand, a hand oddly delicate for this large-headed, tall man. I attended his major lecture courses on the 'Sociological Categories' and 'Social and Economic History' and took part in his seminars. I know that the sociological categories, worked into his book

Economy and Society (Wirtschaft und Gesellschaft), today causes students great difficulties, and that they have a hard time getting through its abstract formulations. Then, however, we followed tensely, even with anxious excitement, the short sentences that like the whiplashes of an inexorable logic gave definitions, abstract exegesis, and vivid examples, each full of meaning, and taken as a whole, providing new knowledge. I have never copied out lecture notes so carefully as these and never before or since been so conscious of having learned." Cf. Meyer-Frank 1982: 216. She was also a member of the Munich Free Students Association. A different recollection is presented by Helmuth Plessner, who also attended the lecture course on the sociological categories: "Attendance quickly dropped, which was fine with him. Presentation was not his forte, neither in lecture nor in book form. Prophecy from the lectern of all places he despised. An overcrowded lecture course—or was it one of the then-frequent student meetings?—he began with the quote from George: 'Just their numbers is a crime.' He discarded all his rhetorical skills when he taught. In the 'Category' course, he provided a true picture of this-worldly asceticism, as far as I remember, pure definitions and explanations, providing only the quintessence, the crème de la crème (*Trockenbeerauslese, Kellerabzug*)." Cf. Plessner 1963: 34.

127. Cf. Mahrholz 1919: 230. Mahrholz was, incidentally, chairman of the function at which Weber gave his "Politics as a Vocation." He already knew Weber from the first Lauenstein conference. On the occasion of this conference, incidentally, Edgar Jaffé had written something similar, without doubt in reference to Max Weber: "The sermon of resigned labor and modest honesty appeared like the sun bathing this grave [of the spirit] in gold with its last rays, a sun that had lost its ability to warm." Cf. Jaffé 1917: 995.

128. His reaction to Weber has already been cited. Cf. the passages noted at Chapter 1, notes 56 and 57.

129. Several names are found in the transcript of the talk between Birnbaum and Horst J. Helle, March 3, 1982 (Birnbaum 1982: 4); others are found in König and Winckelmann 1963.

130. Cf. Birnbaum 1974: 60–61.

131. Birnbaum writes that he has participated in Freiburg in the Akademischer Freibund (Free League of Students), "an informal student association with leftist-liberal political tendencies" (Birnbaum 1974: 38). In his talk with Helle, he even stated that Weber had sent him to the SPD (Social Democratic Party), and not only him, but his friend Mahrholz and others! Birnbaum 1982: 10–11.

132. Cf. Birnbaum 1974: 75.

133. On the details, cf. the "Editorial Reports" in Weber 1992.

134. Schwab 1917: 104.

135. Schwab also speaks in this context of "West European–American humanity." Cf. Schwab 1917: 105.

136. In addition to the Free Students, Schwab named the George cir-

cle, the Wandervogel (Hiking Enthusiasts), Sprechsaal and Anfang (Beginning), the Free Academic Youth, the Abstinent Students, Lietz, Wyneken, and the "whole Wickersdorfer circle." Cf. Schwab 1917: 105.

137. Schwab 1917: 104. Further, see the Editorial Report on "Science as a Vocation" in Weber 1992.

138. See Editorial Reports, Weber 1992.

139. That Weber takes up the Greek world in "Science as a Vocation" is possibly owing to Schwab and his backward-looking utopia, and not, as is sometimes claimed, to Georg Lukács, who, in his "Theory of the Novel" ("Theorie des Romans") characterized the bourgeois era as the era of complete wickedness (in reference to Fichte) and—like Schwab—contrasted this era to the age of the Greeks. Cf. Lukács 1916, esp. part 1, "Closed Cultures" ("Geschlossene Kulturen").

140. Weber 1958a: 135; Weber 1973: 588–89.

141. Weber 1978c: 73; Weber 1973: 494.

142. On this concept, cf., e.g., Weber 1984: 606; on its interpretation, see Schluchter 1989, chap. 10.

143. Weber 1984: 606–7.

144. For a comprehensive analysis of the demarcation of these three roles from one another and their normative and institutional contexts, see Schluchter 1984: 65–116.

145. Weber 1978c: 222; Weber 1971: 557 (cf. also Weber 1958a: 125–26).

146. Weber 1978c: 223; Weber 1971: 558 (cf. also Weber 1958a: 126–27).

147. Weber 1958a: 127; Weber 1971: 559.

148. Weber 1978c: 214; Weber 1971: 547.

149. On this, cf. the telling formulation in Weber 1949: 23–24; Weber 1973: 514.

150. Weber 1958a: 127; Weber 1971: 559.

151. On this, see the Editorial Report on "Politics as a Vocation" in Weber 1992.

152. Weber 1978c: 219; Weber 1971: 553.

153. Weber 1978c: 214; Weber 1971: 547.

154. Just a few months before delivering "Politics as a Vocation," Weber had given a critical accounting of the delusionary and realistic trends within socialism in his Vienna speech of June 13, 1918, on "Socialism" ("Der Sozialismus") which shortly thereafter appeared as a booklet. In it, he took up the general strike and terrorism as means of revolution and the "*romanticism* of revolutionary hope" connected to them that was so "spellbinding for these intellectuals." Cf. Weber 1984: 628. In his Munich speech from November 4, 1918, on "Germany's Political Reorganization" ("Deutschlands künftige Staatsform"), he took on a "minority" of leftist intellectuals "strongly moved by revolutionary chiliasm," including the anarchist Erich Mühsam and the Bolshevist Max Lewien. Cf. Weber 1988: 359–69. In his speech from January 28, 1919, on "Politics as

a Vocation," Weber presumably found in his audience—aside from Free Students, Free Germans, and "a group of younger students with poetically revolutionary attitudes (Trummler, Roth),"—Ernst Toller, who was a member of Eisner's government at that time. Weber's relationship to Erich Trummler and Ernst Toller went back to the Lauenstein conferences. On the makeup of the audience addressed by "Politics as a Vocation," cf. Frithjof Noack to Marianne Weber, October 26, 1924 (Max-Weber-Archiv, Munich). Knud Ahlborn could have been one of the Free Germans present. He was a member of the Free Academic Youth, was close to the proletarian youth movement, and had also taken part in the Lauenstein conferences.

155. Weber 1978c: 214; Weber 1971: 547.

156. Weber 1978c: 214; Weber 1971: 547.

157. Weber 1978c: 73; Weber 1973: 493.

158. Weber 1978c: 73; Weber 1973: 493.

159. As written at the end of the study of ascetic Protestantism (Weber 1958b). Cf. Weber 1978c: 170; Weber 1921, 1:203.

160. Cf. Frithjof Noack to Marianne Weber, October 26, 1924 (Max-Weber-Archiv, Munich). Cf. also Weber's testimony as witness in the legal proceedings against Ernst Toller and Otto Neurath, Weber 1988: 485–95. Julie Meyer-Frank reports that just after the end of the address "Politics as a Vocation," those present had to leave the auditorium because followers of Eisner wanted to break up the meeting. Shortly before the address, Weber had called Eisner the "buffoon of the bloody carnival." On this, see Meyer-Frank 1982: 213–14.

161. Weber 1949: 192; Weber 1973: 132.

162. Cf. Weber 1958a: 137; Weber 1973: 591, where Weber states that "even with a personality of Goethe's rank, it has been detrimental to take the liberty of trying to make his 'life' into a work of art."

163. Weber 1949: 192; Weber 1973: 132.

164. Gundolf 1916: 4.

165. This distinguished him not only from the followers of Stefan George, but also from those of Nietzsche.

166. One need only think of the concluding passages of "Politics as a Vocation," with its quote from Shakespeare's Sonnet 102; Weber 1978c: 224; Weber 1971: 559.

167. On publication history, cf. the Editorial Reports in Weber 1992.

168. Curtius 1919.

169. Kahler 1920. This book was published by the same publisher (Georg Bondi-Verlag) as that of the Stefan George circle.

170. Salz 1921.

171. Troeltsch 1981b.

172. Scheler 1922.

173. It is sometimes conjectured that Walter Benjamin took up "Politics as a Vocation" in his "Zur Kritik der Gewalt" ([Critique of force] Benjamin 1921). There is however, neither philological nor substantive evi-

dence for this claim. Although ultimately published in the *Archiv für Sozialwissenschaft und Sozialpolitik*, the piece was apparently originally to be published in *Die weissen Blätter*.

174. A certain shift recently resulted from the part played by the distinction between the ethics of conviction and responsibility in the controversy surrounding the German peace movement.

175. Weber 1958a: 152; Weber 1993: 609.

176. Curtius 1919: 202.

177. Curtius 1919: 203.

178. Cf. Kahler 1920: 8.

179. Kahler 1920: 15.

180. Cf. Kahler 1920: 27ff.

181. The following passage makes this especially clear: "The development of the world is taking place in Germany today. Germany has been pushed to the absolute limits of deprivation, because it is to give birth to the great transformation. Germany is the scene of the breakdown of the old because it is to be the scene of the triumph of the new. Nowhere else have we experienced the conceptual decomposition of the organic form to such an extent. Nowhere has this terrible type of functional man, of the man of performance, of man as [mere] part, developed in such exemplary purity as in Germany: this totally inhuman creature, all of whose communal ties of blood and soul have been severed, whose whole life revolves around the rationally material species of activities he has learned, indeed, who appears to be nothing more than this activity that has been taken out of, abstracted from, and stabilized outside of all living context" (Kahler 1920: 35).

182. Kahler claims that Weberian rationalism forms the lowest stratum of knowledge, the stratum of mere facts. This stratum is subordinate to knowledge of "higher, more comprehensive, *viable becoming and advancing*," as it is expressed in Bergson's intuitionism. Both strata of knowledge, however, have to be reintegrated with the highest and ultimate form of knowledge, that arises from the penetration of the "highest, most comprehensive, complete basis of *eternal being*" possible only on the basis of contemplation (*Schauen*), and thus as a result of a Platonizing contemplation of essences (cf. Kahler 1920: 46).

183. Kahler 1920: 65.

184. Kahler says that this form of knowledge that is the product of the spirit and not of the intellect has to be distinguished from the form of faith and that of art insofar as "it is unable to take on either mythical personal or symbolic shape" (Kahler 1920: 65).

185. Kahler 1920: 39.

186. The parallels to contemporary debate on modernity and postmodernity are evident.

187. Cf. the analyses in Troeltsch 1981b: 654 and, in greater detail, in Troeltsch 1922, esp. chapters 1 and 3, part 6.

188. In Arthur Salz's words in his critique. Cf. Salz 1921: 11.

189. One is tempted to interpret a passage from the "Vorbemerkung" (Author's introduction) to the *Gesammelte Aufsätze zur Religionssoziologie* (Collected essays in the sociology of religion) as a direct reaction to Erich von Kahler's pamphlet: "Fashion and the zeal of the *literati* would have us think that the specialist can today be done without, or degraded to a position subordinate to that of the seer. Almost all sciences owe something to dilettantes, often very valuable viewpoints. But dilettantism as a guiding principle would be the end of science. He who yearns for a vision should go to the cinema, though it will be copiously offered to him today in literary form for the present field of investigation as well" (Weber 1958b: 29; Weber 1921, 1:14). What we do not know, however, is whether Weber was able to read Kahler's essay. Even though the latter was apparently finished by November 1919, it was only published shortly after Weber's death (cf. Kahler 1920: 5). It is conceivable that Weber knew of Kahler's attack, especially because Salz was both a friend of Kahler's and in close contact with Weber in Munich. Salz could have at least informed Weber of the manuscript, and perhaps he even provided it to Weber.

190. Salz 1921: 73ff., esp. 77. On the relationship of classical German philosophy and the French Revolution generally, see Henrich 1990: 73ff.

191. Salz 1921: 29.

192. This preference does not, of course, imply that he completely identified with Weber's position. He, too, appears to have dreamed of the return of a charismatic age, in which, as in the Renaissance, science also develops visionary and poetic powers and the scientists also can be permeated by a Faustian and ecstatic sense of life. He, too, appears to have ultimately sought the reconnection of modern science with life that goes beyond Weber's "minimalist program for the scholar from vocation." However, he opposed a theocratic philosophy of restoration that signified a return to the Middle Ages or the wisdom of the East and opposed above all the dictatorship of the few concomitant with such a restoration. Cf. Salz 1921: 11, 13, 61ff, 91. Nonetheless, in spite of his orientation to the West, Salz still holds fast to Germany's special mission. Salz 1921: 81ff.

193. Troeltsch 1981b: 675.

194. Troeltsch 1981b: 673.

195. Troeltsch had above all the works of Friedrich Gundolf in mind, but also Count Keyserling's School of Wisdom and the anthroposophy of Rudolf Steiner. The background here is supplied by developments in intellectual history associated with the names of Schopenhauer, Nietzsche, Bergson, Dilthey, Simmel, and Husserl. Kahler also considered Gundolf's book on Goethe as an example of the new science!

196. Troeltsch 1981b: 673.

197. Cf. Curtius 1919: 202.

198. Scheler 1922: 20.

199. Cf. Scheler 1922: 19.

200. Scheler 1922: 25.

201. Cf. Rickert 1926: 234.

202. Rickert 1929: xxv.

203. Rickert 1926: 235.

204. Not everyone did. Curtius, for example, accused Weber of having taken his concept of science "from the mechanical natural sciences" and having oriented it around "the contemporary ideal of meticulousness." Cf. Curtius 1919: 201.

205. A balanced assessment of the different worldviews (Weltanschauungen) that played a part, not least of all in conjunction with "Science as a Vocation," is reached by Eduard Spranger. He distinguishes presuppositions that are immanent in science from those that are transcendent to it. Weber's position on the status of the latter he considers representative of the view of the older generation. He discusses, in addition to Scheler's stance, the counterpositions of Erich Rothacker and Theodor Litt; he also draws the broad contours of his own position, which focuses on self-critique and reaching understanding on the basis of reasons. In this way, he comes very close to Weber's position. Cf. Spranger 1929.

206. That Weber did not advocate a simplistic relativism was first emphasized by Dieter Henrich in his dissertation. Cf. Henrich 1952, part 2. For my part, I have sought to develop Weber's value theory from the perspective of a regulative universalism. Cf. Chapter 2.

207. Jaspers 1988: 46.

« *Chapter 2* »

1. See Roth 1987a: 207–8. On the intended audience of the speech, see Roth and Schluchter 1979: 113–16.

2. See Weber 1971: 539; Weber 1958a: 120. On distinguishing the ethic of responsibility from mere Realpolitik, see Weber 1973: 515; Weber 1949: 25; and Roth and Schluchter 1979: 55–59.

3. On the importance in ethical questions of the distinction between *to whom* and *for what* one is responsible, see above all Picht 1980: 202ff.; Huber 1983: 55ff.

4. Here, see Weber 1973: 504; Weber 1949: 15, a passage I will return to later.

5. Here, see Henrich 1952, part 2; and the discussion between Dieter Henrich, Claus Offe, and Wolfgang Schluchter in Henrich, Offe, and Schluchter 1988: 155ff.

6. Weber 1973: 508; Weber 1949: 18.

7. This holds for the typology of ethics as I developed it in Schluchter 1981: 39–69.

8. On the division of Weber's work into three phases, see Schluchter 1989, chapters 1, 12, 13, and appendix 1. The attempt has been made to trace this post-1910 change back to the influence of Georg Lukács, who started working in Heidelberg in the summer of 1912 and was involved in an intensive exchange of ideas with Max Weber. On this attempt, see the interesting book by Beiersdörfer 1986, esp. 88. For example, Beiersdörfer

claims that "Weber develops the conception of 'the ethics of conviction and responsibility,' inspired by an essay by Lukács, and in his confrontation with the 'Russian idea,' with the world of ideas of Tolstoy and Dostoyevsky as they are communicated to him in the specifically Lukácsian interpretation" (ibid., 91). The essay referred to here is entitled, "Von der Armut am Geiste. Ein Gespräch und ein Brief" (On the poverty of the spirit: A conversation and a letter); Lukács reflected here on his complicitous involvement in the suicide of his friend, Irma Seidler. The way in which he portrayed this process in its ethical significance clearly made an impression on Max Weber and even more of one on Marianne Weber. See Marianne Weber 1926: 474 and her letter to Lukács, July 31, 1912, thanking him for the manuscript given her to read (Lukács 1982, letter 168). In the text, which probably originated in August 1911, Lukács differentiated between an ethic of duty and an ethic of love, or more precisely, between a life lived according to (social) duties and one lived in accordance with goodness. It is a contrast of the outer and the inner life; it is a contrast of a life in adherence to (social) forms and of one that breaks with these forms for the sake of goodness, which he illustrated with figures from Dostoyevsky's novels (Sonia, Prince Myshkin, and Alexei Karamazov). The beatific lives of these "agnostics of the act," conducted unconditionally for the sake of the salvation of the Other, is fundamentally, of course, a life beyond any ethic, inasmuch as such goodness goes beyond all ethical categories.

Clearly, Weber did in fact give long and intensive thought to the "Russian idea." However, he did not owe his familiarity with it (or his perspective on it) to Lukács. Moreover, the distinction between the ethic of duty and that of love, or in Lukács's later formulation in correspondence with Paul Ernst, between the first and second ethic, between duty to the forms and duty to the imperatives of the soul, is not equatable with the distinction between the ethic of conviction and that of responsibility. Weber publicly developed his conception of the "Russian idea" long before Lukács entered his life: first, in his reports on the bourgeois revolution in Russia (1906), then in his addresses in the discussion of Ernst Troeltsch's speech on "Stoic-Christian Natural Right" ("Das stoisch-christliche Naturrecht und das moderne profane Naturrecht") at the First German Convention of Sociologists (Erster Soziologentag, 1910). The addresses made at the convention even provide the categories for coming to grips with Lukács's essay. The goodness described by Lukács as the unconditional surrender to the Other is in Weber the acosmic love of humanity, which rejects every forming of the world. Weber contrasts this to the unconditional surrender to an object, a cause, a work. This distinction, also found in Lukács's essay, is for Weber, however, one located *within* the realm of the (religious) ethic of conviction. It is the distinction between mysticism and asceticism reflected in the contrast between Russian and Calvinist religiosity. It is not by chance that Marianne Weber emphasized in her thank-you letter that it is the presentation of the irresolvable and thus tragic conflict between surrender to the Other and surrender to the work that so fascinated her—and probably Max Weber as well—in the essay on the "Poverty of Spirit." This fascination is fully in keeping with the perspective that Weber sketched out at the convention and then worked out in detail in his comparative sociology of religion.

9. On the nature of the general context of this controversy, see Schluchter 1989, chapter 1.

10. Weber 1971: 1.

11. Even some contemporaries in this surely not "unpatriotic" epoch were shocked by the speech, as Theodor Heuss reports (Weber 1971: xiii). An example: "The economic policy of a German state just as much as the evaluative standard (*Wertmaßstab*) of a German economic theoretician can thus only be German" (Weber 1971: 13). Incidentally, aside from its contents, only someone who has not yet distinguished between a theoretical value relation and a practical evaluation can make such a statement. On this, see Schluchter 1989: 10–16. On Weber's exaggerated nationalism and on the German national *Machtstaat* as a political ideal and the highest value, see Mommsen 1974, part 3, and Nolte 1963: 535ff.

Recently, one has been given the chance to witness a rather peculiar rehabilitation of this "immature" inaugural lecture that is supposed to serve as a key, as a kind of genetic code to Weber's overall work. On this, see Hennis 1987: 46ff, 161ff. (In the latter passage, the "early writings on economics" as a whole are given this role.) Hennis is fully aware that Weber later distanced himself from the inaugural lecture. Nevertheless, Hennis claims that this distancing does not affect the fact that Weber in this "famously infamous" speech first formulated his central question clearly, the question of the "development of humanity." (If this were the case, would it not have to be more accurately: the development of German humanity?) Be that as it may, this still should not obscure the qualitative changes that occurred between the inaugural lecture and Weber's dual project, "Economy and the Societal Orders and Powers" ("Die Wirtschaft und die gesellschaftlichen Ordnungen und Mächte") and "The Economic Ethics of the World Religions" ("Die Wirtschaftsethik der Weltreligionen"). They are also reflected in Weber's own reevaluation of his speech. In a passage of importance in this context, however, Weber first did repeat his early and never renunciated thesis that cultural life represents a conflict and that "peace" merely means a "change in the struggle's forms, opponents, or contested objects, or in the chances of being selected," but not the end of the conflict. Whether such changes are to be positively evaluated depends on one's evaluative standard. Moreover: "One thing cannot be doubted: every single given order of social relations, regardless of its form, has to be analyzed in terms of *which human type* it gives the optimal chances of becoming the ruling type, by means of its outer and inner (motivational) selection process. Otherwise, the empirical investigation is not actually exhaustive, nor is even the actual necessary basis given for an *evaluation*, be it a 'consciously' subjective one or one making a claim to 'objective' validity. This was what my academic inaugural lecture—in a form certainly immature in a host of ways—attempted to express, a speech I can no longer identify with in many important points." (Quoted from Baumgarten 1964: 127).

In my view this reevaluation has three consequences. First, with the exception of this one point, Weber no longer wanted to identify with most of the other points of importance in his inaugural lecture. Second, the point he still sought to maintain was expressed in the inaugural lecture: "in a form certainly immature in a host of ways." Third, in its mature formulation, it states that societal orders or configurations of order are also, but not only, to be analyzed in terms of which type of personality and conduct they favor. This is neither a statement that shows interest for "the development of humanity" nor one that claims that external, and above all, internal motivational processes of selection can be exclusively conceived in terms of societal orders. Nor does it claim that these latter are mere means to ends in this context. In other words, the way it is formulated here, this point is compatible with Weber's developed program for sociological research, a research program that goes beyond (national) economics. Here, see Schluchter 1989: 48–52.

12. Currently, however, the nationalistic and Nietzschean undertones of the young Weber that he largely discarded in the course of his maturation seem to be making Weber's early position attractive once again, especially among neo-conservatives.

13. Weber 1971: 14, 18.

14. Weber 1971: 16.

15. Weber 1971: 24.

16. Weber 1971: 16.

17. Weber 1971: 18. On this, see also Weber's speech at the Erfurt convention for the establishment of a National Social Party (National-Soziale Partei) in November 1896. Here, in the discussion of Friedrich Naumann's proposed party program, Weber made the following point: "But politics is a hard business, and he who wants to be helmsman of the fatherland's political development, must have steady nerves and must not be too sentimental to pursue down-to-earth politics. He must above all be free of illusion and recognize the one fundamental fact: the unavoidable, eternal struggle of man against man on this earth" (Weber 1971: 28–29).

18. The expression comes from Gustav Radbruch. Weber later took up Radbruch's *Einführung in die Rechtswissenschaft* [Introduction to jurisprudence] Radbruch 1913) in both versions of the essay "Der Sinn der 'Wertfreiheit' der soziologischen und ökonomischen Wissenschaften" (Ethical neutrality) (1913, 1917). This essay can be conceived as a "new version" of the inaugural lecture. It is not just corrected, however; it is fundamentally revised and extended. Just by comparing the 1895 lecture to the 1913 essay, one receives evidence of the maturation process that Weber himself commented upon. The Weber of 1913 is simply a different Weber from the one of 1895. On this, see Chapter 2, note 17.

In the judgment of Theodor Heuss, the inaugural lecture, despite its thoroughly political intention, had no political impact; it merely gave Friedrich Naumann's conception of Christian socialism a politically nationalist accent (see Weber 1971: xiii). Naumann later defined—in his letters on religion—the relationship of Christian ethics to the this-worldly orders of politics and economy under the conditions of modern capitalism and the modern state. And indeed, in my view, he did this in a way largely congruent with Weber's conception (on which Naumann's discussion of the two ethics is also based) while largely eliminating the moralistic rhetoric reminiscent of "Ethical Culture" found in his proposed party program of 1896 (Weber 1971: 27).

19. Schnädelbach 1983: 201. Cf. esp. all of chapter 6 in Schnädelbach 1983, especially with its distinctions (ibid., 206) and its three types of value philosophy: teleological, transcendental, and phenomenological. In terms of this typology, Weber adhered to the transcendental approach, both terminologically and methodologically, after the turn of the century. On the basis of Schnädelbach's differentiating criteria, another typology could also be delineated, characterizing positions never fully developed historically. In any case, Schnädelbach's typology itself already shows that value theory is not monolithic, and that the variant that Weber's position ultimately represents has never been satisfactorily analyzed.

20. Weber 1973: 148; Weber 1949: 52.

21. Though commonly referred to as such, this debate could be more accurately termed a controversy on *freedom from value judgment*. See Guenther Roth's informative footnote in Roth and Schluchter 1979: 65–66.

22. Weber 1973: 504; Weber 1949: 15. The contents of this passage are unchanged vis-à-vis Weber's 1913 discussion comments (Weber 1913), but they find more succinct expression.

23. On the different forms of eudæmonism, see Windelband 1914: 265ff.

24. On epistemology, see Weber 1973: 208–9; Weber 1949: 106. Pre-Kantian is meant here, of course, in a typological rather than in a temporal sense.

25. Here, see Marianne Weber 1926: 317–97, and Roth, who provides a brilliant characterization of the German feminist movement of the time and of Marianne Weber's position in it.

26. The reports characterized by Weber as a collection of notes ordered in a makeshift fashion, appeared in the *Archiv für Sozialwissenschaft und Sozialpolitik* (hereafter *Archiv*), vols. 22, 23 (distributed on February 8 and August 25, 1906; cf. Weber 1906a, 1906b). They were thus written very soon after the events. They make up over 350 pages with large passages set in small print. Only the selections reprinted in Weber 1971 (30–108) are generally known to the scholarly public. The texts are now available in full length in series 1, bk. 10 of the *Max-Weber-Gesamtausgabe* (*MWG*), 1989. The quote itself is from the first report, "Zur Lage der bür-

gerlichen Demokratie in Rußland" (Weber 1906a: 345–46; Weber 1971: 59; Weber 1978c: 281 [this report is in part translated as "The Prospects for Liberal Democracy in Tsarist Russia" in Weber 1978c: 269–84]). It is a report more of Weber's hopes than of the actual political prospects. In actual political terms, the meager results of the revolution were: Russia's transition to pseudoconstitutionalism, which did not even succeed in establishing enlightened bureaucratic rationalism, and the failure of Zemstvo liberalism, of which the Russians, in Weber's words, can nevertheless be just as proud as the Germans can be of the Frankfurt Parliament. In spite of this failure, Weber conveys to his readers the hope that liberalism might become an effective political force in the future. This hope naturally presupposes that liberalism does not accede to compromises with a czarist regime unwilling to allow authentic constitutional reform. Only in this way can it remain "a 'force' on the plane of ideas beyond the reach of any external power" and restore its unity with the proletarian intelligentsia (Weber 1978c: 280; Weber 1971: 59; Weber 1906a: 345–46). On the character of the reports, see Weber 1906a: 234–35. That Weber's entire approach can be seen in terms of the problem of human rights is impressively developed in Brugger 1980, esp. sections 9, 14, and 15.

27. Weber's discussion proceeds from a review of a proposed constitution for the Russian Empire presented by a group within the Constitutional Democratic Party (Konstitutionell-Demokratische Partei). This faction dealt especially softly with the position of the Czar. It proposed a four-tiered electoral law in the framework of a two-chamber system and parliamentary monarchism with a constitutional court. Weber's sympathies lay with this political perspective.

28. *Erfolgsethik*, translated here as "success-oriented ethic," is often translated as "instrumental ethic." Weber 1906a: 254–55; Weber 1971: 36–37.

29. Weber employs this formulation later in a variety of passages. See for example, Weber 1973: 505; Weber 1949: 16; Weber 1971: 539; Weber 1958a: 120; Weber 1921, 1: 553; Weber 1921, 1: 193. In some cases it is attributed to the early Christians. It probably refers to Abraham's relationship to God in the New Testament interpretation in Romans. Here see Gen. 15:6, 17:17, 18:18 in connection with Romans 3 and 4. Weber finds this formulation, however, most consistently realized, not in early Christianity, but in the religious movement arising from the *Bhagavad-Gita*. In Christianity, the context of this formulation is apparently found in the teaching of the justification by faith, which gained renewed relevance through Luther. And it is in fact in his lecture on Genesis that a formulation very close to Weber's is found. In reference to Gen. 32:6 and following, Luther states: "Fac tuum officium, et eventum Deo permitte" (Luther, 44, 78, 14). Thanks are due to my late colleague Albrecht Peters for this reference. Proof of Weber's acquaintance with the Latin writings of Luther is given in *The Protestant Ethic*.

30. The expression *panmoralism* is the equivalent of what Weber termed an absolute ethic, especially in his speech "Politics as a Vocation": the unconditionality and unequivocality of imperatives one has to obey for their own sake irrespective of opportunities given. See Weber 1971: 538; Weber 1958a: 119.

31. Cf. also in this context Weber's letter of August 4, 1908, to Robert Michels: "There are two possibilities . . . (1) 'my empire is not of this world' (Tolstoy) *or a fully consistent syndicalism*, which is *nothing more* than the translation of the principle that 'the final goal is nothing to me, the *movement* is everything' into the *revolutionarily ethical* or the *personal* . . . —*or* (2) culture—i.e., objective culture expressing itself in 'accomplishments,' technical and otherwise, *affirmation* through *adjustment* to the conditions of *all* techniques, whether they be ec[onomi]c, political or whatever else. In the case of point (2) , all talk of 'revolution' is a farce, *every* thought of doing away with the 'domination of man over man' by means of *some type* of societal system, no matter how 'socialist,' by means of 'democracy,' no matter *how* sophisticated in form, is a utopia." Quoted in Mommsen 1981: 60. (1) corresponds to the two positions of panmoralism; (2) corresponds to a success-oriented ethic, whereby the latter, as in the writings on Russia, still remains underdefined. Weber already made use of the expression "love transcending the orders of the world" (*Akosmismus der Liebe*) in the second phase of his writings. The letter is now available also in *MWG*, ser. 2, bk. 5, 1990.

32. Weber 1906b: 397; Weber 1971: 106–7. The context of the passage is an open attack upon reactionary German *Realpolitiker*. On the critique of purely power-oriented politicians—and their inner weakness and powerlessness—see above all Weber 1958a: 116–17; Weber 1971: 535.

33. This being the title of an address—with clear reference to the sexual revolution in her own circle of friends and acquaintances—that Marianne Weber delivered at the Evangelischer Sozialer Kongreß (Evangelical Social Congress) in Strasbourg on Pentecost 1907 on the invitation of Adolf Harnack. She advocated a very balanced position between old and new. Eduard Baumgarten and Guenther Roth, for example, suspect that Max Weber jointly wrote the text with his wife, thus making it at least indirectly one of his writings. This I consider exaggerated. Nevertheless, the address does at least provide background information on this aspect of Weber's development in this, the second phase of his writings. See Marianne Weber 1919: 38ff.

34. Here see Weber 1924b: 446. He is apparently referring to Otto Gross in this passage.

35. Weber's view of the essay can be found in his letter to his coeditor, Edgar Jaffé, in which he voted for the rejection of the essay. The letter is addressed to Else Jaffé, however, with whom Gross was involved and who had his child. The letter is reprinted in Marianne Weber 1926: 378–84, along with a good summary of the teachings and effects of Otto Gross (ibid., 376–78); it is also reprinted in Baumgarten 1964: 644–48. See now

the unabridged and annotated edition of this crucial letter in *MWG*, ser. 2, bk. 5, section 393–403.

36. Baumgarten 1964: 646. This letter is also important because it gives indications of Weber's relationship to Freud and Nietzsche. Weber states that he has now become acquainted with Freud's major writings and recognizes their possible significance for phenomena of religious and moral history, but that he failed to find a precise casuistry (*Kasuistik*) in these writings. He praises Nietzsche for his aristocratic ethic (*Moral der Vornehmheit*) but rejects Nietzsche's biological embellishments in moral theory. This is fully in keeping with the perspective developed in the present essay. The formulation "aristocratic ethic" points to Georg Simmel's book *Schopenhauer und Nietzsche* (Simmel 1907, a book dedicated to Gustav Schmoller), whose last chapter was so entitled. We still have Weber's personal copy. His marginal notes demonstrate his extremely critical stance toward Nietzsche. His sharpest remark is found on p. 230, where Simmel wrote, "Nietzsche should have at least clearly drawn the line between his will to power and the common will to possess by making clear that the value of the former is borne, not by domination and brute force as external reality, but by the make-up of the sovereign soul, whose appearance and expression represents that sociological relationship [i.e., the detachment of the aristocratic and strong from the multitude, the mediocre, and the weak]." Weber added here: "Exactly that is *not* Nietzsche's view. It was precisely on this point that he himself happened to be a German philistine." A similar comment can also be found in his published work (see Weber 1921, 2:174).

At this point I will save myself the trouble of taking on the increasing numbers of those searching for traces of Nietzsche in Weber's work. The easiest way of doing this, of course, is taken by those who declare Nietzsche to be a silent guest, who only speaks up at exactly the point where Weber puts forth an important idea (the assumption being that Weber has to have the idea from someone else, and not just from anyone else, but from a "genial winged spirit," inasmuch as disciplinary specialists can only do the sweeping up). Writers of this persuasion then go on to claim that Weber also hid this allegedly constitutive influence; for this reason, one has to first catch on to his ruse. Wilhelm Hennis argues in this way (Hennis 1987: 167ff., esp. 176, 177, 185, 190). Such premises afford a wonderful basis for speculation, enabling the pursuit of a truly gay science. Here I prefer Georg Stauth and Bryan S. Turner, who claim that Weber fully transformed Nietzsche's critical perspective. What I do not share is their regret over this fact. If this transformation were not the case, there would hardly be a need to interest oneself in Weber's research program. The fact that he does not agree with Nietzsche on crucial points concerning methodology, the reconstruction of the genealogy of Occidental rationalism, the estimation of the cultural significance of the modern science of reality (*Erfahrungswissenschaft*), and value theory, is precisely what keeps Weber relevant today. See Stauth and Turner 1986.

37. Here, see Kant's characterization of the human species in his *Anthropologie*, B 313–20, A 315–22 (Kant 1977). The technical, pragmatic and moral aptitudes (*Anlagen*) correspond to the three types of imperatives.

38. In *The Rise of Western Rationalism*, I distinguish between "naturality" and "sociality" in order to characterize the distinction between magic and religion. This distinction is misleading, in that "sociality" naturally includes both. Moreover, the problem is of a much more general nature than is indicated by the manner in which I treated it there, as the distinction between the heroic and average ethic, or, between the virtuosi and mass ethic demonstrates. Slipping into the naturalism of everyday life is not for Weber a problem specific to a particular culture or development. Whether and how this capacity to make the axiological turn is connected to Kant's "causality through freedom" will have to be discussed later.

39. As quoted in Baumgarten 1964: 398–99. Weber then argues that thinking is not bound by the limits of science, and he thus makes a (Kantian) distinction between thinking on the one hand and empirical and rational cognition on the other.

40. Here, see Marianne Weber 1926: 391–92, with its report on Weber's interest in "the effects of an erotics unbound by norms upon the overall personality." It cites the following notable passage from Weber's correspondence from this period: "The ethical values are not *alone* in the world. Demanding renunciation, they can make *small* those who have become caught up in guilt. And they can lead to irresolvable conflicts in those cases where action without guilt is *impossible*. Here, one has to act (ethically) in such a way that the persons involved incur the least possible losses of human dignity, of the ability to be good and to love, of the ability to fulfill obligation, and of the value of their personalities, and that is often a difficult calculation." Here a (new?) basis of action is suggested: the weighing of ethical goods as an alternative to ethical rigorism. According to Weber, not only a life of moral integrity but also moral failure in the face of irresolvable conflict can lay claim to full humanity. See ibid., 393.

41. See Schluchter 1989, chapter 1, part 9. The debate's most important forum is the periodical *Logos*.

42. Here, see Schluchter 1989, chapter 4.1.

43. Weber 1921, 1: 552–53 (except for the addition of italics, the text remained identical to the 1915 version found in the *Archiv* 41:402–3.) The passage reads: "For there does not appear to be a means of resolving even the very first of questions: On what basis in an individual case should the ethical value of an action be determined: whether from the *success* of this undertaking or from its *intrinsic* value, however this may be ethically defined? Thus, whether and to what extent the responsibility of the actor for the consequences justifies the means, or, on the other hand, the value of the conviction at the basis of the action should give the actor the right to deny responsibility for the consequences and to attrib-

ute them to God or the depravity and folly that God has allowed in the world. The sublimation of the religious ethic in the sense of an ethic of conviction will tend to favor the latter alternative: 'the Christian does right and leaves the consequences to God.' In this way, however, if one's own action is truly consistently carried out, it will be condemned to the irrationality of consequences vis-à-vis the autonomous logic of the world."

44. Weber 1973: 505; Weber 1949.

45. Weber 1973: 505; Weber 1949: 16. Weber is probably referring to the *Elementarlehre*, section 1, in Kant 1976.

46. Weber 1971: 539–40. Two texts have to be mentioned in this context. The first is a letter to the editor of the periodical *Die Frau* that Weber wrote in 1916. It appeared under the title, "Zwischen zwei Gesetzen" (Between two laws), a title probably supplied by the editors. In this letter, Weber intervened in a discussion in the periodical concerning the misuse of the Gospel: on the one hand, as a means of political justification, and on the other, as a political program. Here, he pointed to the difference in *historical* duties of a small state (*Kleinstaat*) versus a large state (*Großstaat*), between those of a *Kulturstaat* versus those of a *Machtstaat*. In this context, he also touched upon the conflict between the demands of the Gospel and the lawfulness of this-worldly culture, taking a position, which at the very least approached that of Naumann as described above. This letter's ideas were taken up again by Marianne Weber in her subsequently published contribution to this debate. See her essay, "Der Krieg als ethisches Problem" (War as an ethical problem) (Marianne Weber 1915–16). On Weber's letter to the editor, see Weber 1971: 139ff., as well as Weber 1984: 95ff. Marianne's thesis is that whoever makes himself subject to the "Sermon on the Mount" and to the this-worldly culture, subjects himself to a dual law, which leads him into irresolvable conflicts.

The second text is this: in a 1912 fragment, Weber contested the claim that conflicts of this kind could be resolved with the help of formal rules. It is perhaps the first time that he formulated the distinction between an ethic of conviction and an ethic of responsibility. Here we find the statement: "Just as little are there formal rules for the degree to which the individual should orient his action in terms of a responsibility for *its* result or should attribute it to God and should be satisfied or is permitted to be satisfied with the purity of his own *intention*." The fragment is reprinted in Baumgarten 1964: 399ff. The changes to the original clearly made by Marianne Weber are incorporated without being marked as such. The fragment is also of interest because of the usage in it of the expression *Entgegengelten*, a validity confronting us, which originates from Emil Lask.

47. In his notes to the address "Politics as a Vocation," Weber had replaced power politics with the politics of responsibility in the corresponding passage. He recognized three kinds of politics: the politics of conviction, the politics of responsibility, and power politics. Only the first two

are constituted in terms of an ethical value relation, whereas only the last two are constituted in terms of a relation to reality.

48. See Kant's famous formulation: "It is impossible to conceive anything at all in the world, or even out of it, which can be taken as good without qualification, except a *good will.*" And further: "A good will is not good because of what it effects or accomplishes—because of its fitness for attaining some proposed end: it is good through its willing alone—that is, good in itself. Considered in itself, it is to be esteemed beyond comparison as far higher than anything it could ever bring about merely in order to favour some inclination or, if you like, the sum total of inclinations." Kant, *Grundlegung zur Metaphysik der Sitten,* BA 1, BA 3 (Kant 1977; Kant 1948: 61, 62). On Fichte, see for example the formulations in *Die Bestimmung des Menschen. Drittes Buch.* "Glaube" 3 (Fichte 1962, 2: 284–85). Incidentally, Max Weber probably shared Marianne Weber's conceptualization of the relationship between Kant and Fichte as well as her critique of Fichte. See her work, *Fichte's Sozialismus und sein Verhältnis zur Marx'schen Doktrin* (Fichte's Socialism and Its Relationship to Marxian Doctrine) (Marianne Weber 1900: 23–24).

49. It is generally known that Weber categorized Confucianism as such an ethic even as late as his essay on "Ethical Neutrality." See Weber 1973: 514; Weber 1949: 24. That he thus did violence to historical reality has been sufficiently demonstrated. See Schluchter 1983; and Schluchter 1989, chapter 3.

50. See Weber 1921, 1: 259–60; Weber 1958a: 287–88, 450 n. 5. One should add: especially any Nietzschean connotations. This offers at the same time an excellent illustration of *how* Weber deals with the more interesting of Nietzsche's constructs: he strips them of their biological embellishments and their moralistic undertones. In this way they are opened up to historical and sociological research at the same time that their validity claim is limited in two ways: They are conceived as *empirical* statements and connected to *definite* historical phenomena. The moralism of *resentment,* for example, a concept closely related to the distinction between master and slave morals, has much less historical range than Nietzsche believed. According to Weber, it has no application, for example, to the case of Buddhism, and has but very limited application to the Judeo-Christian tradition. Above all, however, it is not a constitutive element in the distinction between heroic and everyday ethics, or in our case, between virtuosi and mass ethics. The argument for religious stratification on the basis of a differentiation of ethical demands and the division of humankind into the "geniuses of virtue" and normal men, in Fichte's words, exhibits but superficial similarities to Nietzsche's original construct. Here, see Fichte 1962, vol. 4, part 3, section 16 (esp. 4: 185, 203). Weber certainly did not value Nietzsche as a moralist, and if he valued him at all, it was as a moral *psychologist,* and only insofar as he belonged in the category of psychologist of the spirit. He explicitly regarded Jaspers and Klages in this way, implicitly Freud, perhaps Kierkegaard, and,

not to be forgotten, Kant. Karl Jaspers provided similar sources for his psychology of weltanschauung in a book that Weber apparently regarded favorably, *Psychologie der Weltanschauungen* (Jaspers 1919). Jaspers mentions Kant, Kierkegaard, Nietzsche, and then Max Weber himself, clearly setting Weber off from the rest. Jaspers recognized the difference between posing and solving a problem. His evaluation of Weber's place in the intellectual history of this context is still notable today: "Max Weber's writings on the sociology of religion and politics contain a kind of psychological analysis of worldviews [weltanschauungen] differing from all previous such analyses. For it combines what had previously appeared uncombinable: the most concrete historical research and systematic thought. Its systematically objectivizing power, ultimately expressed in fragments rather than frozen into a system, is linked to a vibrant vehemence the likes of which we only experience in writers such as Kierkegaard and Nietzsche" (Jaspers 1919: 14). Jaspers also provided one of the most brilliant analyses of Nietzsche's position in moral philosophy and moral psychology. He was guided by the thesis that Nietzsche's enmity toward Christianity as a reality was actually "indivisible from his actual *commitment to Christianity*" as an ideal (*Anspruch*). See Jaspers 1985: esp. 10. In my mind, only on this level does the comparison to Weber make sense, because Weber's research allows the comparative analysis of *paradigmatic* reactions to the problem of modernity. By merely speculatively seeking traces of Nietzsche in Weber, one can only gain confirmation of Weber's declaration that "almost all sciences owe something to dilettantes, often very fruitful view-points. But dilettantism as a leading principle would be the end of science" (Weber 1921, 1: 14; Weber 1958b: 29). Certainly Weber was also indebted to Nietzsche for fruitful viewpoints. But he ultimately counted Nietzsche among the dilettantes and among the preachers, as almost every remark in his work shows. What Nietzsche said about Christianity can—in Weber's view—be equally said about himself: into the convent with him! (See Weber 1921, 1: 14; Weber 1958b: 29). Weber's characterization, however, is probably directed not only at Nietzsche, but at Sombart as well, and his evaluative contrast of traders and heroes, of trading and heroic peoples. See Sombart 1915.

51. Here, see Weber's remarks on the relationship between classes and status groups in *Economy and Society* (Weber 1972: 177–80, 285–314, 531–40; Weber 1978b: 302–307, 468–518, 926–40). An interesting attempt at further developing Weber's theoretical approach and applying it empirically in this regard is found in Pierre Bourdieu's *Distinctions* (Bourdieu 1984: esp. in part 1: 1, section 4, and in the conclusion).

52. Here, see esp. Weber 1921, 1: 12; Weber 1958a: 27: "The magical and religious forces, and the ethical ideas of duty based upon them, have in the past always been among the most important formative influences on [life] conduct."

53. See Schluchter 1989: 29 in reference to Weber 1949: 83; Weber 1973: 183.

54. In order to avoid misunderstandings, let me add that this distinction is not identical with that between private and political morals. Ethical values possess significance for both personal and sociopolitical life. Weber discussed both aspects, the individual-ethical and the socioethical (see, e.g., Weber 1973: 505; Weber 1949: 15–16). One has to separate the value relation from the area of application. Ethical values are relevant for most areas of life, and they thus stand in a relation of tension to the autonomous rights and lawfulness of these areas. For this reason, as Weber emphasized, "the tensions with the ethical" are not limited to the sphere of political action.

55. See Weber 1971: 141–42, Weber 1984: 97–98. Weber actually speaks here of "the historical duties of one's own people imposed by fate." But even the collective fate—just as the individual one—is ultimately the consequence of a series of ultimate decisions and is thus self-chosen. This he said expressly here: "And this is just as clear: that *without disgrace* we could never and can never avoid the choice once we had made it—back then as we created the Reich. Nor could we nor can we avoid the duties that we thus took upon ourselves. Even if we wanted to." Note the choice of words: *without disgrace, not without guilt.* Guilt is an ethical concept, as are conscience and responsibility, and allows the attribution of individual responsibility or culpability. It belongs to individual life and to individual fate. Disgrace on the other hand, similar to honor and prestige, can also be related to collective life and collective fate. Thus, for Weber there can be no collective guilt, though there can be collective disgrace (and perhaps collective shame). This is also seen in his stance toward the discussion of guilt subsequent to the First World War. Insofar as the fate of formations wielding political force is concerned, one can speak of interest, honor, and perhaps of reparations, but not of guilt and atonement. The formulation, "our responsibility in the face of history," or even, "our responsibility in the face of the future," is directed toward this political context and thus serves at the same time as an expression of the acceptance of the autonomous lawfulness and autonomous rights of the political as opposed to the ethical sphere. For examples on the topic of "war guilt" see Weber 1971: 537; Weber 1958a: 118, and Weber 1971: 476ff.; on the problem of political and collective solidarity (in contrast to individual solidarity, to brotherliness) and its penetration into the sphere of value, see above all, Weber 1972: 528; Weber 1978b: 922.

56. See Weber 1971: 140. Roughly put, Weber saw a need to choose between the following alternatives: either the self-assertion of German culture or Russian or Anglo-American (cultural) imperialism. Here he considered the "Russian" danger as the greater one. It is also the case that the consideration of historical duties determined his political evaluation of antimilitarism and pacifism, an evaluation that varied according to political context.

57. See Weber 1972, chapter 1, section 4; Weber 1978b.

58. Here, see Chapter 3 of this volume.

59. On Kant's distinctions, with which he, in his words, corrected a mistake found in the *Grundlegung zur Metaphysik der Sitten*, see esp. Kant 1965a, H6. Weber's distinctions, analogous to those of Kant, can be found in the Stammler essay. See Weber 1973: 334ff.; Weber 1977: 112ff. It is of course clear that Weber took an empirical view in interpreting Kant's distinctions.

60. See the definitions of means-ends rational and value rational orientation in Weber 1972, chapter 1, section 2; Weber 1978b.

61. On Kant, see *Die Metaphysik der Sitten*, AB 1–AB 52, esp. AB 13ff. (Kant 1977). On Weber, see 1973: 338; Weber 1977: 117.

62. On this, see also the interesting comment in Weber 1924b: 443–44.

63. Put in formal terms: Weber's appropriation of Kant's ideas leads to a sociology based upon Kantian principles. It does not negate the crucial premises of Kant's philosophy as found in his epistemology, or in his practical philosophy for that matter. It simply reserves judgment. Durkheim's appropriation of Kant leads to a sociological Kantianism that replaces these premises with sociological ones. This also forces him to deny the possibility of metaphysical reflection, whether dogmatic or critical, the possibility of which Weber never denied. Thus, in Durkheim, the metaphysics of nature turn into a (social) physics of nature, and the metaphysics of morals and law turn into a (social) physics of the same. He distinguishes neither between a critical and doctrinal use of reason nor between pure and empirical levels (between noumenal and phenomenal spheres). These are translated into the contrast between the individual and collective world. Nevertheless, the Kantian architectonic is maintained. It is simply thoroughly sociologized and historicized.

In contrast, Weber never denies the difference between transcendental and empirical concepts of nature, between transcendental and empirical concepts of freedom. In this context, his critique of Stammler is instructive. In Weber's words, the latter wished to be recognized as Kant's truest disciple, yet he grossly misunderstood Kant's teachings. One reason for this was his continuous conflation of these two levels of analysis. In epistemology, this meant he had regressed to a pre-Kantian position, to a Humian or even a Scholastic one. Also instructive in this context is Weber's critique of Wundt, who twisted Kant's principle of causality through freedom, "the philosophical arch[e]type of all metaphysical 'culture' and 'personality' theories of this sort" (Weber 1973: 62; Weber 1975: 16). On Stammler, see Weber 1973: 293, 309, 317; Weber 1977: 61–62, 81, 90–91. Naturally, Weber did not simply adapt Kant's philosophy. Thus, for example, in connection with his critique of Wundt, he stated that upon closer examination, Kant's metaphysical theory of freedom is self-contradictory. However, this intention was not to replace Kant's transcendental reflections on the category of causality and on the idea of freedom by means of his reflections from the science of reality on causal attribution and on the concept of action. Moreover, he undertook these reflections from the science of reality in the critical spirit of Kant, thus at the very least allowing the logical possibility of metaphysical interpretations of a Kantian kind. On the character of Kantian metaphysics, see, for example, Picht 1985 (esp. 550 for the construction of Kant's system).

64. As far as I can see, Weber makes this distinction only in the essay on "Ethical Neutrality." Nevertheless, it would make sense to do so because, according to his theory of value, the cognitive sphere is also a value sphere.

65. In the words of Weber 1972, chapter 1, section 2; Weber 1978b.

66. On *Richtigkeitsrationalität*—in English it can probably best be rendered as "the rationality of objective correctness"—to which Weber redundantly added the adjective "objective," see the "Kategorien" essay ("Über einige Kategorien der verstehenden Soziologie"), esp. section 2, Weber 1973: 432–38. On the distinction between a concept of progress free of evaluation (*wertungsfrei*) and one that is evaluative (*wertend*), see Weber 1973: 518–30, esp. 526; Weber 1949: 27–39, esp. 34–35.

67. See the letter to Tönnies cited earlier in this chapter (footnote 39), where scientific cognition is distinguished from reasoning. See also Weber 1973: 156; Weber 1958a: 59: "We are furthermore completely free of the prejudice which asserts that reflections on culture that go beyond the analysis of empirical data in order to interpret the world metaphysically can, because of their metaphysical character, fulfill no useful cognitive tasks. Just what these cognitive tasks are is primarily an epistemological question, the answer to which we must and can, in view of our purpose, disregard at this point."

68. See Weber 1973: 611; Weber 1958a: 154. There is clearly a difference between the possession of a positively religious person that rests upon revelations as facts important for salvation and the possession of ideas chosen freely by a person. More on this follows.

69. As is generally known, this is the distinction at the basis of "Kantian ideas." In my view, in Weber values are the placeholders for Kantian ideas. This is the sense in which Jaspers's remark has to be taken: "Max Weber was hardly acquainted with Kantian ideas." Wilhelm Hennis, who cites this remark, appears to believe that Jaspers intended to characterize Weber's lack of knowledge of Kant with it. That, of course, would be absurd. Kant pervades Weber's entire work. One need not go about searching for clues as in the case of Nietzsche. See Hennis 1987: 208.

70. Weber 1973: 155; Weber 1958a: 58. See the formulation already found in "Die 'Objektivität' sozialwissenschaftlicher und sozialpolitischer Erkenntnis," the "Objectivity" essay, which employs Kant's basic distinctions as well.

71. See here, once again, Weber's remarks in Weber 1973: 155–56; Weber 1958a: 58–59.

72. On this distinction, see Kant, *Die Religion innerhalb der Grenzen der bloßen Vernunft* (Religion within the limits of reason alone) B xxi–xxvi (Kant 1977) and Weber's distinction between salvation religions and the charisma of reason.

73. On value rationalization see Weber's explanatory statement in

Weber 1972, chapter 1, sections 2, 3; Weber 1978b: 25: "Examples of pure value-rational orientation would be the actions of persons who, regardless of possible cost to themselves, act to put into practice their convictions of what seems to them to be required by duty, honor, the pursuit of beauty, religious call, personal loyalty, or the importance of some 'cause' no matter in what it consists. In our terminology, value-rational action always involves 'commands' or 'demands' which, in the actor's opinion, are binding on him. It is only in cases where human action is motivated by the fulfillment of such unconditional demands that it will be called value-rational. This is the case in widely varying degrees, but for the most part only to a relatively slight extent." This explanation shows that action in accordance with the ethic of conviction is value-oriented, but not all value-oriented action follows an ethic of conviction. It also shows that action in accordance with the ethic of conviction can approach pure, absolute value rationality to a greater or lesser extent, and thus there are degrees or levels of rationality of an ethic of conviction, that is, different degrees or levels to which an ethic of conviction can be rationalized.

74. On the distinction between theoretical and practical axioms and between axioms and postulates that Weber employs in his scattered remarks on value theory, esp. in his essay on "Ethical Neutrality," see Windelband 1914: 12–13.

75. This countercritique (*Antikritik*) is found largely in the footnotes that were added to the monograph. They make primary reference to Sombart 1913 and Brentano 1916, esp. 117ff. The fact that Weber did *not* integrate the critiques and countercritiques from the Fischer-Rachfahl controversy into the revised edition of *The Protestant Ethic* reflects unfavorably on Wilhelm Hennis's assertion that Weber first revealed his central question: viz. the "development of humanity" "in complete candor" in his second critique of Rachfahl in the "Anticritical Last Word" (cf. Weber 1978a). See Hennis 1987: 22. One has to ask who is actually revealing what in complete candor!

76. Weber made reference to *Necessary Hints to Those That Would Be Rich* and *Advice to a Young Tradesman*. See Weber 1921, 1: 32, Weber 1958a: 192 n. 2. He quoted Franklin from Kürnberger 1855.

77. See Weber 1921, 1: 33, Weber 1958a: 51–52, with reference to Sombart's *Der moderne Kapitalismus* (Sombart 1902a). The epigram quoting Fugger disappeared from the second edition of 1916, but the substantive thesis did not. There Sombart wrote, "Jacob Fugger's saying, 'he wanted to profit as long as he could' I used as an epigram in the first edition to preface my depiction of the genesis of modern capitalism. I found it characteristic for the fully developed capitalistic mentality (which it certainly was). He was certainly ahead of his time" (Sombart 1916, 2: 56).

78. All quotes are from Weber 1921, 1: 33; Weber 1958a: 51–52.

79. On the ethical theory of classical utilitarianism and on the contemporary discussion based upon it, see Höffe 1975. See esp. his introduction, with the demand for a critical utilitarianism that integrates the prin-

ciples of utility, individual perfection, and fairness by means of the idea of humanity. For a continuation of his approach, see Höffe 1987. On the origins of utilitarianism in the radical philosophy of the English Enlightenment, see above all Halévy 1972. In Weber's view, it is not the philosophical as opposed to religious basis that primarily distinguishes the utilitarian ethic from the ethic of ascetic Protestantism; the central difference lies in the use of the principle of utility as a principle for grounding ethical duties. For ascetic Protestantism as for Kant, utility is not an ethical principle; indeed, it is anti-ethical. In ascetic Protestantism, grounding ethics on the basis of utility would have to lead to the idolatry of the flesh; in Kant, it would have to lead to the corruption of the human heart because it would be an expression of the fact that "motivations from moral law can only be pursued subordinate to other (nonmoral) ones" (Kant, *Religion*, B22, A20, in Kant 1977). The decisive aspect of the ethical foundations of that type of action treated in *The Protestant Ethic* is precisely its anti-utilitarianism, the purging of all eudaemonistic or hedonistic aspects and all egocentric maxims connected to them. Only in this manner can one grasp (as Weber—in opposition to Sombart—had already put it in the first version) that "bourgeois motive with which we are here dealing. There the motto of asceticism is 'Entsagen sollst du, sollst entsagen' [Renounce, thou shalt renounce!] in the positive capitalistic sense of 'Erwerben sollst du, sollst erwerben' [Acquire, thou shalt acquire!]. In its pure and simple non-rationality it is a sort of categorical imperative" (Weber 1921, 1: 190 n. 1; Weber 1958a: 276 n. 79). Duty and self-control, not utility or one's own perfection and growth, are the key motives. A moral of imperatives is contrasted to a moral of utility and perfection. As has already been implied, this had validity for Weber not only in a historical and sociological perspective, but in a normative-axiological one as well.

80. See Weber 1921, 1: 204; Weber 1958a: 182; the conclusion to the *General Economic History* (Weber 1923: 314–15; Weber 1961: 270).

81. The distinction between lifestyle and conduct is not found in this sense in Weber. He used the concept of conduct rather freely. A lifestyle belongs to the realm of technically practical action and adheres to processes of cultivation. Conduct belongs to the realm of morally practical action and also includes processes of moralization. This is not to imply that only ethical conduct exists. Conduct can also be based primarily upon nonethical values. Nevertheless, a relation has to exist to ethical values. The *Kulturmensch* (cultured person) is always a moral being, too. The reduction of humanity to the technically practical leads to the "last of men." In *The Protestant Ethic*, in a way reminiscent of Nietzsche, Weber closed his study by declaring them: "specialists without spirit, sensualists without heart."

82. On Alberti, see the footnote inserted in 1920 (Weber 1921, 1: 38–41; Weber 1958a: 194 n. 12). On the two transformation processes, see above all the close of the study (Weber 1921, 1: 202–6; Weber 1958a: 180–

83). The construction of a doctrine of prudence for living one's life need not be based on economic theories, of course; it can start from any of the theories of the sciences of reality. However, a science of reality can only teach how one can conduct one's life, and perhaps, how one seeks to conduct it. It cannot, however, teach how one *should* conduct it.

83. See Jaspers 1949: 15ff. Shmuel N. Eisenstadt has revived this idea and made it relevant to current sociological concerns. See his "General Introduction" to Eisenstadt 1987b: 10ff.

84. Here, see esp. Weber 1978b; Weber 1972: 261ff. I have described this process in a variety of contexts as the transition from a monistic to a dualistic view of the world. The "two-sided world" of magic in which the demons and gods enjoy only a relative superiority over man is replaced by the dualistic world of religion in which this superiority is progressively absolutized. This, of course, does not exclude the possibility of mediating constructs that lessen or even "overcome" this dualism. See, for example, Roth and Schluchter 1979, chapter 1.

85. On the distinction between action and norm and its systematic significance for the treatment of magical "ethics" and religious "ethics," see Schluchter 1981, chapter 4.B.1. In the following, I take up the concepts and distinctions used there, developing them further and at the same time correcting them.

86. Weber 1978b: 577; Weber 1972: 348. Incidentally, this text is a preliminary version of the "Intermediate Reflections."

87. Weber 1972: 349; Weber 1978b: 578.

88. Cf. Weber 1973: 510; Weber 1949: 20.

89. Weber repeatedly pointed out that theology and dogma are in no sense universal phenomena of all religions with ethics. See, for example, Weber 1973: 610; Weber 1958a: 153.

90. This intellectual labor is not confined to the religious ethic of conviction, however. For example, it is also found in the "sacred books of the Hindus, Muslims, Parsees and Jews, and the classical books of the Chinese," all of whom Weber subsumed under the ideal type of a ritualistic or law ethic, or more generally, under the ideal type of an ethic of norms. See Weber 1972: 348; Weber 1978b: 576–77.

91. See Jaspers 1983: 105. Jaspers felt that what Kant had actually formulated in his ethics was an alternative beyond both a rigorist ethic of conviction and an ethic of success based on calculations of advantage. And he felt that this truly third path was best characterized by Max Weber's concept of the ethic of responsibility: "The ethic of responsibility is the true ethic of conviction that seeks its way in the world bound neither to the standard of success nor to the rational foundation of a conviction. Its way is instead in the open space of possibilities, bound to an unconditional that shows itself only in the form of thought in action, and not in terms of any specific contents." Undoubtedly, this holds for the Kantian ethic, which is just as fully misrepresented as a rigorist ethic of

conviction as Weber's ethic of responsibility would be as an advantage-calculating ethic of success. Moreover, the first sentence in Jaspers's formulation even holds for the religious ethic of conviction, as Weber's formulation shows. Nevertheless, there is still a difference between religious ethics of conviction, Kant's ethic, and Weber's ethic. The following will try to show this.

92. This serves to correct a classification I made connecting ethics and types of conscience in Schluchter 1981: 64, figure 6. Against the backdrop of these considerations and those that follow, the arguments made in ibid., especially 59–66, would have to be rewritten today.

93. Good analyses of this process in terms of the move from means of physical sanctions to means of psychic sanctions can be found in Durkheim, and then later in Foucault. See, e.g., Durkheim 1899: 65ff.; Foucault 1976.

94. It is common knowledge that the classical objection to Kant's contentless formalism in ethics is found in the young Hegel. Cf. his essay, "Über die wissenschaftlichen Behandlungsarten des Naturrechts" (On the scientific ways of treating natural law) (Hegel 1969, 2: 434ff., esp. 459ff.) Here Hegel took up Kant's famous example of the *depositum* (deposit) in order to demonstrate the tautological character of a Kantian type of legislation based on practical reason. Hegel claimed that this legislation was superfluous because it neither provides laws nor defines anything, instead being dependent in everything it does on a given definition. The fact that Weber expressly defended Kant's formalism in ethics and nowhere took Hegel's distinction between morality and *Sittlichkeit* (ethical life) is but another indication that on basic questions, Weber tended to adhere to—in Lask's terminology—Kant's critical rationalism rather than to Hegel's emanationist rationalism. See Schluchter 1989, chapter 1.3.

95. Cf. Weber 1973: 506; Weber 1949: 16. Weber reformulated only the first part and used this part in the following argument. In "The Groundwork of the Metaphysics of Morals," ("Grundlegung zur Metaphysik der Sitten"), the corresponding practical imperative reads: "Act in such a way that you always treat humanity, whether in your own person or in the person of any other, never simply as a means, but always at the same time as an end." (Kant 1948, 61).

96. Weber 1973: 506; Weber 1949: 17.

97. Cf. the formulation in Weber 1973: 504 (Weber 1949: 15) that introduces the debate with Schmoller on this point. The passage in Weber 1973, from the middle of p. 505 to the top of p. 508 (Weber 1949, from p. 16 top to p. 18 bottom), was inserted into the text of 1913. In my view, it is one of the most important explications of value theory in Weber's work.

98. As cited in Weber 1973: 506; Weber 1949: 16.

99. Weber cited this interpretation of Kant by Fichte in "Politics as a Vocation." Cf. Weber 1971: 545ff. Cf. also Fichte 1962, 4: 167.

100. As written as early as in the first part of the essay on objectivity, where the relationship between theory and praxis is treated. Cf. Weber 1973: 155; Weber 1949: 58.

101. Kant 1948: 69, BA 16–17.

102. According to Kant, moral feeling is an "unusual feeling," produced not by pathological sensuousness but by practical reason. Respect for the law is "not the incentive to morality, it is morality itself, regarded subjectively as an incentive" (Kant 1976: 183; A 134–35). From the very beginning, the question arose as to the source of the strength of this ideal feeling in limiting self-love in its claims, in breaking with the inclinations. The question remains even if one admits, as Kant did, that the distinction of the principle of happiness from morality does not mean that "we should renounce the claims to happiness; it requires only that we take no account of them whenever duty is in question" (Kant 1976, 199; A 166). In Kant, this problem stood at the center of his effort to destroy the basis of both empiricist and dogmatic-metaphysical moral theories. Nevertheless, in his alternative, one thing he failed to resolve (as even thinkers immediately following him noted) was the problem of the "mediation" between morality and happiness. Kant's solution consisted in expanding critical moral philosophy into a moral theology. The defense of reason's idea of freedom, of whose existence we know through our moral action, is expanded to include reason's idea of God and of the immortality of the soul; the lawfulness of nature and that of freedom are brought together by means of the concept of the highest good. In this context, Kant's early version has to be distinguished from his mature one. Cf. Henrich 1971: 48ff. On the mature version, see above all Kant 1982. Here, see *The Critique of Teleological Judgement* (*Kritik der Urteilskraft*), and esp. "Appendix: Theory of the Method of Applying the Teleological Judgment" and "General Remark on Teleology," (part 2: 75–163). Weber, arguing primarily on the level of the psychology and sociology of morals, immediately transforms the interest in the will to obey (*Gehorchenwollen*) into a motive for duty. However, he (and naturally Kant as well) lacked a psychodynamic theory of conscience formation. He made no use of Freud's contribution to this field.

103. Cf. Weber 1949: 57, Weber 1973: 154.

104. Here, cf. Dieter Henrich's Weber dissertation. The fact that the basis of the theoretical-deductive method of proof employed by natural theology is destroyed does not, however, mean that one would necessarily do without the deduction of the law of morality and of the categorical imperative. The latter, however, is a deduction that "is dependent upon the factual self-certainty of moral beings," and thus, is based ultimately on a theory of evidence. Cf. Henrich 1975: 86. In this theory of evidence in ethics, Henrich considers Weber very close to Kant: "For Weber's ethics are related to Kant's, in that they, too, seek to provide a theory of evidence." Cf. Henrich 1952: 116.

105. Kant 1976: 130, A 35.

106. Kant 1976, A 54. It is common knowledge that there are several formulations of this basic law that are in part different from one another.

107. Cf. Wellmer 1986: 20. Wellmer distinguishes between two generalizing principles that build on each other without its being possible to derive the latter from the former with the help of an additional premise. The principles are a generalizing principle analogous to the principle of induction in the case of descriptive sentences, and a second-level generalizing principle that does not involve the character of generality of normative judgments, but rather the universalistic conditions making intersubjective recognition possible. Kant's moral principle requires generalization in both the first and second sense. It is for this reason that it can be termed a "universalizing principle." Cf. p. 20.

108. Cf. Schluchter 1981: 45. Today I would make this argument somewhat differently.

109. Kant, *Religion*, BA xviii f.

110. It cannot be proven that the formulation originates in Tertullian. The passage in *De carne Christi* 5 is the closest that can be found. Weber usually made use of the following uncustomary, as well as linguistically questionable formulation: credo non quod, sed quia absurdum est. In Tertullian, the passage is directed against Stoic and Platonic Christianity, that is, against the hegemony of philosophy.

111. This is the interpretation of Windelband 1907: 187. This is the edition that Weber used.

112. Cf. esp. part 4 of "Der philosophischen Religionslehre" (The philosophical doctrine of religion) in *Religion* (Kant 1977).

113. Weber 1973: 611; Weber 1958a: 154; and, for interpretation, Chapter 3 of this volume. The formula: "sacrifice of the intellect" (as well as *sacrificium intellectus* or *sacrifizio dell'intelletto*) is found throughout the literature on religion of this period. Examples appear in Friedrich Nietzsche (directed against Pascal), but also in Albrecht Ritschl or in Gerhart Schulze-Gävernitz. The conflict between faith and reason to which the formula points involves the necessity of renouncing even one's own rational convictions for the sake of obedience to the church. The formula probably arose as a (Protestant) reaction to the First Vatican Council, and is thus a polemical concept. Weber used it in order to characterize the unbridgeable opposition between the religious value sphere and the value sphere of science or scholarship (*Wissenschaft*), that is, the sphere of rational and empirical cognition.

114. In order to prevent possible misunderstandings, I do not mean this in a historical sense, that is, Kant was not the first to formulate such an ethic. I am also not claiming to give a comprehensive characterization of Kant's ethics, nor, more generally speaking, to offer an interpretation of Kant in any strict sense of the term. Instead, attention is directed to a typology of ethics that can serve as a foundation of Weber's investigations in historical sociology.

115. This reverses in a certain sense the sequential order found in

Hegel's *Philosophy of Right*. What is termed "concrete morality" here, would probably be called *Sittlichkeit* there. Jürgen Habermas—in a similar sense—sees a connection between the transition to a universalistic (cognitivist) morality, on the one hand, and the detachment from the culturally taken-for-granted and the distinctions between moral and evaluative questions, between questions of justice and those of the good life, on the other. Cf. Habermas 1983: 117ff. In Weber's theory this transition would correspond to the increasingly strict differentiation between ethical and cultural values, virtually imposed by the transition to a formal ethic.

"Concrete morality" could be taken in the sense of Hegel's natural *Sittlichkeit*, the starting point for the chapter on *Sittlichkeit* in the *Philosophy of Right*. This, however, would contradict Weber's thesis that at least the religious ethic of conviction leads to the break with the primeval solidarity of family, sib, and neighborhood. The religious ethic of conviction is already (substantively) universalistic: it transcends the dualism of in-group and out-group morality. It nevertheless remains, compared to the formal universalism of a cognitivist ethic of conviction, tied to the "life-world," and—in Habermas's terms—its success in abstracting from context and motivation are not as radical. Thus, the religious ethic of conviction is not confronted to the same degree by the problem of the mediation between abstract and concrete morality (or *Sittlichkeit*), even though naturally already acquainted with clearly differentiated subcultures of experts possessing their own specialized languages and forms of life. (The differentiation between everyday and sacred language, characteristic of many cultures, already points in this direction.)

116. Wellmer rightly states that the categorical imperative could never "operate in a normative 'vacuum.'" Cf. Wellmer 1986, 39. In Rüdiger Bubner, one also finds interesting analyses of the embedded character of maxims in the life-world and of the conceptual sequence: action—maxim—norm. Cf. Bubner 1985, esp. B.3, and his previous book, Bubner 1982 (1976).

117. Habermas 1983: 53.

118. Kant 1948: 101, BA 75.

119. Kant 1948: 102 BA 78.

120. Kant 1948: 109, BA 89.

121. Wellmer speaks of "the problematic of 'concretization' or application" as well as the fact that judgment plays a much more fundamental role in the application of moral norms "than Kant was willing to admit." Cf. Wellmer 1986: 28, 30. We saw earlier that according to Weber the importance of practical judgment increases with the transition from ethics of norms to ethics of principles. In addition to the problem of application, which involves the relation between norm and situation of action, for Weber, the following further-ranging problems—as presented above—are given: (1) the positing problem, that is, how to infer postulates from value axioms, and (2) the double "bridging problem," namely, (2a) the

constraints on the means of action (*Mittelgebundenheit*): To what extent should the ethical end justify morally corrupting means? and (2b) conflicts among different norms: (2b/1) among different ethical norms, and (2b/2) between ethical and nonethical norms. In solving these problems, practical reason does not play the same role as it does in the problem of application, strictly conceived. Aside from this latter problem, Wellmer also treats the problem of the intra-ethical conflict of norms (2b/2).

122. Kant 1982: B 158–60, A 156–58.

123. Cf. Habermas 1983: 75, in reference to George Herbert Mead, 1962 [1934]: 379ff.; and especially the formulation (ibid., 379): "Man is a rational being because he is a social being. The universality of our judgments, upon which Kant places so much stress, is a universality that arises from the fact that we take the attitude of the entire community, of all rational beings. We are what we are through our relationship to others."

124. Weber made use of this formulation in "Politics as a Vocation" in reference to Fichte and his interpretation of Kant's thesis on the radically evil in man. Cf. Weber 1971: 540; Weber 1958a: 121; and in Fichte, *Das System der Sittenlehre* (The system of moral doctrine), part 3, section 16, appendix (Fichte 1962). On Weber's estimation of Kant's realistic view of man, see also the letter to Jaffé cited in note 35.

125. Kant repeatedly pointed to the difference between renouncing and abstracting from something. Abstracting from happiness does not imply renouncing it, with the same holding for success. Cf. e.g., Kant 1983: A 208–10.

126. Cf. Weber 1921, 1: 554; Weber 1958a: 341. The original clause: "For the religious ethic" was expanded in the 1920 edition into "For the religious ethic of brotherliness, just as for a priori ethical rigorism . . ."

127. Weber 1921, 1: 555; Weber 1958a: 341.

128. This is reminiscent of Simmel, who pointed this out and at least in part also reacted to it in an æsthetic manner.

129. Weber 1921, 1: 555; Weber 1958a: 342. Even when the æstheticization of life leads to an æsthetic humanism, such as in Goethe, Weber remained skeptical. This is important for his concept of personality (personal character). He rejected not only romanticism but every effort "to want to make one's 'life' into a work of art," something he attributes to Goethe. Cf. Weber 1973: 591; Weber 1958a: 137, and on the romantic conception of the personality, Weber 1973: 132; Weber 1975: 192.

130. Kant 1982: B 120, A 119.

131. Kant 1982: B 120, A 118.

132. Kant 1982: B 121, A 120. Kant distinguished between affects and passions. Though affects are blind, they refer, in contrast to the passions, only to feeling, and thus, unlike the passions, do not make it impossible to define discretion or arbitrariness (*Willkür*) in accordance with principles.

133. On this, see Durkheim 1967, esp. 94ff. Nonetheless, Durkheim did follow Kant insofar as he also distinguished between the manner in which we pursue moral and nonmoral objects of desire. The worthiness of being pursued that moral objects of desire possess is, namely, a worthiness of being pursued sui generis. Clearly, he explained the genesis of this moral feeling (similar, for example, to the way George Herbert Mead explained it) in a way different from Kant: the crux is attachment to a historical social group and not to the "eternal" realm of the ends of reason, to reason outside of time. Incidentally, Mead accused Kant of a false (psychological and sociological) understanding of human desires. In Mead's view, Kant considered (as did the utilitarians) these desires to be oriented toward one's own pleasure, and thus toward a subjective condition, rather than toward an object, and thus an objective condition. Happiness can however, for Mead, only be adequately understood in terms of the object orientation for our desires. In the case of morals, motives and objects mutually support and strengthen one another. The better the object, the better the motive. Cf. Mead 1962: 384–85.

134. In the Christian tradition according to Weber, different variations of both tendencies existed. Here, one of the most important causes for this differentiation concerned the (theological) interpretation of the relationship between God and man. Man could be viewed here either as a child or a servant of God, and thus involved in a relationship of love or duty. In ascetic Protestantism, the second variation was, intellectually at least, brought to its logical conclusion. This occurred so completely that even the expectation of reciprocity—common to all ethics of norms and ethics of principles in a more or less sublimated form—was annulled (in the teaching of predestination). This annulment is one of the most important causes for the *inner* elective affinity between the ethic of ascetic Protestantism and the Kantian ethic, whereby the latter possesses a more human(e) character. And, of course, Weber demonstrated in *The Protestant Ethic* why an ethic of duty that fully realizes its ultimate consequences intellectually has no chance of being consistently realized in actuality. At a certain point it comes into conflict with the inner, ideal interests of man. Here, see my interpretations in Chapter 3 and Schluchter 1989, chapter 4.

135. In order to work out the difference to Kant more precisely, one would have to develop his theory of the highest good. This I am omitting because it would not yield any new aspects in terms of my typological interests.

136. Strictly speaking, the rational idea of freedom (which theoretically can be neither proved nor disproved) suffices for the purposes of Kant's construct, as an idea whose objective reality we are acquainted with as moral actors. In Kant's view, an action based on an ethic of conviction performed in order to attain a salvational good is only a dutifully enacted action, and not an action performed out of a sense of duty. Thus, in this point, I do not follow the Kantian construct.

137. Parsons 1967: 362–63.

138. In terms of Parsons's theory, this application would have meant developing types of control and the media connected to them for the personality system also. He never managed to do this. After he had developed the media for the social system, he first moved to the general system of action. A fully worked-out media theory, however, would have to contain media for all subsystems of the general system of action. On this, see the contributions to the problem of media by Baum 1976, esp. 448ff.; and Jensen 1984, esp. 160ff.

139. See, for example, my efforts to systematize "Intermediate Reflections" in Schluchter 1989, chapter 4.1. On the long-term processes of increasing affective control and their sociogenetic conditions, although from a purely Eurocentric perspective, see above all Elias 1969, esp. vol. 1. That these processes of internal control had already found their start relatively early in the context of the institution of the confession in the medieval church, is shown by Hahn 1982. See also Hahn 1988.

140. See here, e.g., Weber 1972: 726. The fact that Kant attests only to human nature's tendency toward evil, but not to its naturally evil constitution, exempts him at the outset from a problem that has always controlled all religious ethics of conviction, at least in the Christian tradition: How can man develop at all toward good under his own powers? For Kant, evil character expresses itself in the self-incurred reversal in the hierarchy of motives: self-love is placed *ahead of* moral law. This false prioritization is correctable at any time, by means of a revolution in the way of thinking, even though it might then take a long time until this new order of priority becomes routine.

141. Kant 1960: B 134, A 126.

142. Cf. Kant 1960: B 133–40, A 125–32.

143. In this context, of course, one would have to investigate more precisely Kant's "characterology" and his considerations concerning the development of an intelligible and perceptive (*sensibel*) character.

144. Cf. Weber 1978b: 865–80; Weber 1972: 496–503. Two discussions in the sociology of law deal with the form-content problem: the discussion of the substantive principles of sacred (natural) law and their relation to formalism, and the discussion of the substantive principles of profane (natural) law and their relation to formalism. In the first case, variants of religious ethics of principles are treated. Here, comparison shows that Christianity represents that variant among cases of sacred law whose formal characteristics are most strongly developed. In Weber's judgment, that earns it at least a "relatively special position" among the cases of sacred law in the major cultures (Weber 1978b: 828; Weber 1972: 480). Nevertheless, it still remains but one variation within the framework of ethics of principle. It does not mark the transition to a reflexive principle. In the second case, it is different. Here, precisely this transition is the focus of discussion. The transition to a reflective principle of law in formal, rational, natural law was one of the developmental-historical conditions for the comprehensive positivization of law.

145. Naturally, this presupposes that one follows systematic interests

and does not exile Weber, for whatever reasons, into the nineteenth century or to Old Europe. Such unkindred spirits as Wilhelm Hennis and Niklas Luhmann appear to be in agreement in the effort to do just that.

146. On this, cf. Weber 1971: 541–42; Weber 1958a: 122, where Weber accused his colleague, Friedrich Wilhelm Foerster, one of the cofounders of "Ethical Culture" in Germany, of assuming just the opposite in his book (Weber was presumably referring to *Politische Ethik und Politische Pädagogik* [Foerster 1918], published in 1918). In fact, one can read there that "first one has to realize the basic truth that good can never come of evil, and evil can never come of good" (Foerster 1918: 202). Foerster later defended himself against this critique by commenting that Weber's view was based upon a quote of Foerster that Weber had heard in discussion and that was taken out of context.

147. Weber expressly emphasized that what is at stake here is the justification of moral action. Cf. Weber 1973: 505; Weber 1949: 16.

148. I am intentionally using the concept of relevance. On the distinction between "conditioned" and "relevant," see Weber 1973: 162; Weber 1958a: 65.

149. Fichte, *System der Sittenlehre*, part 2, section 13 (Fichte 1962, 4: 155–56).

150. One could consider them as special ethical bridging principles distinct from general bridging principles that hold for every ethic. An example of such a general bridging principle would be the axiom: "Obligation implies ability." Thus, according to this interpretation, bridging principles would still belong in the realm of practical reason and could not be equated with rules of judgment. This would hold whether these latter rules concern defining practical judgment, according to which existing norms are applied to situations of action, or whether these rules involve reflexive judgment, according to which norms are sought for situations of action.

151. Kant 1982: 153 (B 159, A 157). This is a characterization of an enlarged, instead of a narrow way of thinking. The latter is characterized by an inability to reflexively overcome a particularist standpoint.

152. Baumgarten 1964: 399.

153. Baumgarten 1964: 400. The fragment is dated around 1912. That it is a statement about a supposed "Hellmuth Kaiser," as cited by Baumgarten, is improbable, since a relevant work by an author of this name has not (yet) been shown to exist. As mentioned earlier, Baumgarten published the version presumably edited by Marianne Weber, and not the original. The attempt is made in the fragment to demonstrate that ethical formalism cannot provide a rule for making decisions, neither for conflicts within the ethical sphere, nor for conflicts between this and other value spheres.

154. These processes naturally include processes of interaction.

155. Wellmer 1986: 19.

156. Wellmer 1986: 18–19.

157. See the passage already cited, Weber 1973: 62; Weber 1975: 118.

158. Henrich 1952, esp. 120ff.

159. There is an intrinsic connection between calculability (*Berechenbarkeit*), the empirical concept of personality, the empirical concept of freedom, and the objectification of understanding (*Verstehen*). See Weber's dispute with Knies and the problem of irrationality in the sciences of action. *Because* human free will "projects itself" into the realm of action, because this will can "lawfully" define itself, and because constant motives can establish themselves in this process, the specific dignity of personal action is not irrationality in the sense of incalculability, but rather rationality in the sense of calculability. Weber resisted the false identifications corresponding to Roscher's romantic concept of personality: "In place of the distinction between purposeful human action, on the one hand, and the natural and historical conditions for this action, on the other, we therefore find an *entirely different* distinction. The 'free' *and therefore irrational-concrete*, action of persons, on the one hand, *nomological* determination of the naturally given conditions for action on the other" (Weber 1973: 45; Weber 1975: 96). One sees that Weber advocates a position in relation to the problem of freedom and necessity that leaves open the question whether Kant's philosophy is to be accepted or not. At any rate, only because (empirical) freedom is given, can calculable action exist. In other words, freedom is the condition that makes calculable and thus understandable human action possible!

160. It is general knowledge that the concept of individual law was developed by Georg Simmel in conjunction with a critique of Kant's ethics. I follow Simmel's argumentation, inspired as it is by vitalist philosophy, in only a very limited sense. Cf. Simmel 1913. Cf., further, Schluchter 1989, chapter 1.6.

161. Henrich 1952: 118.

162. Weber 1973: 510; Weber 1949: 20.

163. That Weber did develop an approach to a scientific philosophy of morality is emphasized by Dieter Henrich. Cf. Henrich 1952: 117. He further emphasizes that the claim that "Weber's theory is to be equated with a simple relativism [has to] be dropped completely" (ibid., 123).

164. Habermas 1983: 86ff.

165. In "Science as a Vocation" Weber says that a certain type of teacher "stands in the service of 'moral' forces; he fulfills the duty of bringing about self-clarification and a sense of responsibility" (Weber 1973: 608; Weber 1958a: 152). The value discussion fulfills a similar pedagogical function.

166. Cf. Weber 1973: 604–5; Weber 1958a: 148–49, and for interpretation, Schluchter 1989, chapter 8.

167. Cf. Weber 1973: 510–11; Weber 1949: 20.

168. Weber 1973: 505; Weber 1949: 16.

169. The statement reads: "However, it is immensely moving when a *mature* man—no matter whether old or young in years—is aware of

a responsibility for the consequences of his conduct and really feels such responsibility with heart and soul. He then acts by following an ethic of responsibility and somewhere he reaches the point where he says: 'Here I stand; I can do no other.' That is something genuinely human and moving. And every one of us who is not spiritually dead must realize the possibility of finding himself at some time in that position. In so far as this is true, an ethic of ultimate ends [conviction] and an ethic of responsibility are not absolute contrasts but rather supplements, which only in unison constitute a genuine man—a man who *can* have the 'calling for politics'" (Weber 1971: 547; Weber 1958a: 127).

170. One point that could speak in favor of such an option might be the distinction between a formal and substantive monotheism and polytheism of values. The famous formulation of Weber's would permit such an interpretation: "Many old gods ascend from their graves; they are disenchanted and hence take the form of impersonal forces. They strive to gain power over our lives and again they resume their eternal struggle with one another" (Weber 1958a: 149; Weber 1973: 605). The monotheism of values is the "metaphysical dogma" that as a type demonstrates an elective affinity to the ethic of conviction. And it has an affinity to the monological principle. On the other hand, the "metaphysical dogma" that as a type demonstrates an elective affinity to the ethic of responsibility is the polytheism of values. It, however, has an elective affinity to the dialogic principle. From this viewpoint, I would have to revise completely my earlier proposition. Cf. Schluchter 1981: 64, figure 6.

171. On this, cf. esp. Weber 1971: 533–34, 546.

172. Henrich 1952: 127–28 (italicized in original).

173. On this, cf. esp. Simmel 1957b: 127. Cf. further, his concept of fate, Simmel 1957a: 8ff.

174. Weber 1971: 533–34; Weber 1958a: 115.

175. Cf. Schelting, 1934: 53.

176. Cf. on this also, sharing the critical stance to Kant, Hans Jonas 1979, esp. 170–71.

177. Hans Jonas has classified ethics according to their position in the controversies between substantive and formal principles, and between objective and subjective principles. "Subject ethics" are without objects in the sense that their focus resides on how action is performed, on subjective conviction, not on what is performed in action. "Object ethics," in contrast, are related to objects in the sense that the binding power of action issues from the claim of the object. Jonas employs examples from Nietzsche, Sartre, and Heidegger as illustrations of subject ethics, but interestingly places Weber's distinction between the ethics of conviction and responsibility on the side of object ethics. Here, he views the ethic of conviction as a utopian variant of an object ethic, but the ethic of responsibility as a realistic variant of the same. He appears to be undecided about the status of Kant's ethic. He sees its subject-ethical elements but considers them absurd in their consequences, as well as factually refuted by

the object-ethical elements. Cf. Jonas 1979: 167ff., 398–99. That Weber's ethics are object ethics—a classification I agree with—does not contradict my claim that, in comparison to the ethic of conviction, the ethic of responsibility is marked by a stronger turn to the "objects," to what happens to the "cause" in question.

178. Kant 1960: B 134, 136, A 126, 128.

179. In this context, we find the following passage from Kant's work on religion: "In an already existing political community, all citizens certainly do find themselves, as such, in a *natural state of ethics*, and they are justified to stay that way. For a political community that wanted to force its citizens to enter into an ethical community would be a contradiction (in terms) since the latter already includes freedom from compulsion among its concepts. Certainly, every political community can hope that one finds within it the mastery of the emotions in accordance with the laws of virtue; for there where its coercive means cannot reach, because the human judge cannot see through another human, the virtuous convictions would bring into effect that which is demanded. Woe to the legislator who sought to bring into effect by force a constitution directed at ethical ends! For not only would he bring into effect precisely the opposite of the ethical constitution, he would also undermine and make insecure his political constitution" (Kant 1960: B 132, A 124).

180. On this volitive aspect of Weber's concept of truth, which I also consider applicable to the concept of *Richtigkeit* (rightness), cf. Weber 1973: 213; Weber 1958a: 110–11. Jürgen Habermas wants to do away with this last decisional residue. Cf. Habermas 1983: 109–10. Incidentally, in their sociological aspect, such preconditions have been the object of investigation since Durkheim and Parsons. They run under the rubric of the noncontractual elements of contract.

181. Habermas 1983: 102.

« *Chapter 3* »

1. These six *Kulturreligionen* (major religions) are Confucianism, Hinduism, Buddhism, Judaism, Islam, and Christianity. With the exception of Judaism, all were also regarded by Weber to be world religions because they had been capable of attracting an especially great number of followers. The concept of salvational religion calls forth yet another grouping. On the interrelation of these concepts, cf. Schluchter 1989, chapter 3. *Kulturreligion* is the broadest of the three concepts. Speaking of six religions is of course problematic insofar as each of them can be further subdivided, and Weber does precisely that, especially in the case of Christianity. This subdivision is related to his general interest in the distinctive development of the West and his special interest in the distinctive shape of ascetic Protestantism; thus, in many comparisons, the latter often appears on its own. One problem in the comparative studies in the sociology of religion is that, especially in the non-Western movements,

the units of analysis remain at too high a level of aggregation. This also holds for Islam. Here, cf. the essays by Ira Lapidus and Rudolph Peters in Schluchter 1987a.

2. Weber speaks of "cultural areas" (*Kulturkreise*) in several passages. He avoids the term "civilization" often used today (and used to translate *Kulturkreis* throughout this essay). It is well-known that "civilization" was used in turn-of-the-century Germany as a "counterterm" to the concept of culture, a connotation still alive in Weber's brother Alfred's proposal to distinguish processes of culture, civilization, and society. This contrast did not exist in Anglo-American linguistic usage. Here the concept of civilization was used in a "value-free" sense as, for example, in the contemporary works of S. N. Eisenstadt. I consider the distinction between *Kulturreligion* and *Kulturkreis* useful because it points to the fact that a given religion is not necessarily identical with any ethnic, political, or linguistic boundaries, and that a civilization can encompass several religions (as well as nonreligious symbolic universes).

3. Here cf. Marianne Weber 1926: 358.

4. Cf., for example, the two large-scale projects, Schiele and Zscharnack 1909–13 and Hinneberg 1906, esp. part 1, sections 2, 4. Weber used these works extensively.

5. This is comprehensively treated in Kuenzlen 1978.

6. The controversy began with H. Karl Fischer's 1907 critique. In 1909, Felix Rachfahl entered into the debate. Weber ended the controversy with an anticritical last word, the second part of which he used "to summarize once again in a few pages some of the features of my *real* 'thesis' that were stubbornly ignored by Rachfahl, solely for those who have not recently carefully re-read my essays" (cf. Weber 1978d: 283). At the same time he emphasized "that *everything* said in my countercritique was already just as clearly located in my essays" (Weber 1978d: 328). I can only agree with this, if one includes the sect essays of 1906 here. It is a riddle to me how Wilhelm Hennis can claim that Weber ultimately clarified his central question for the first time in these responses to critique. In Hennis's view, it is first here, especially in the "Anticritical Last Word" that we are "finally" (!) told "what was Weber's central concern." Hennis expresses his admiration for Rachfahl, "for keeping so much countenance in the face of so much 'hide and seek' and the intentional or unintentional covering-up of 'central' intentions" (cf. Hennis 1987: 16, 21–22). It was obviously a good idea in 1910 for Weber once again to summarize his thesis in the space of a few pages. It appears that even today those who read it carefully in its original version are a "tiny minority" (cf. Weber 1978d: 283).

7. Marianne Weber 1926: 346.

8. Cf. Weber 1976, esp. chapter 1, "Economic Theory and Ancient Society," 35–80. On this, see e.g., Roth, G., "Introduction," in Weber 1978b: 1–lvii. Further, see the essays by Jürgen Deininger and Stefan Breuer in Schluchter 1985b and Schluchter 1980: 134ff.

9. Weber 1978d: 321.

10. Cf. Weber 1978d: 322; Weber 1958b: 26; Weber 1921, 1: 12; as well as the outline to the older version of Weber 1972, reprinted in Schluchter 1989: 467.

11. Weber 1978d: 322.

12. Weber 1978d: 324, where Weber speaks of "objective political" and "objective economic" preconditions that he contrasts to the antitraditionalist "spirit." Here one sees that it is hardly "Weberian" to establish institutions and motives as opposing alternatives, as is often done, especially in Anglo-American literature on Weber. Cf., for example, Collins 1986, esp. chapter 2. Here, too, one finds Weber's supposedly last word on Protestantism (ibid., 34). Cf. also Turner 1974; more on this book later. Even Jeffrey Alexander's attempt to come to grips with the most important positions in sociological theory on the basis of the distinction between epistemological and sociological forms of materialism and idealism and to measure their "maturity" using the yardstick of multidimensionality does not do justice to Weber, as will be shown in the following. Cf. Alexander 1983, esp. vols. 1, 3.

13. Weber discusses these relationships in terms of three interactions: spirit—spirit, spirit—form, and form—form. Reflections of interest in this context can be found in Schmid 1981.

14. Weber 1978a: 1128–29; Weber 1978d: 323–24.

15. As Weber still puts it in his *General Economic History* (Weber 1923: 17). Here, too, I find no change between 1904 and 1920. The critique of historical materialism always has two sides to it, a methodological and a substantive one. Methodologically, it involves the rejection of every form of reductionism; substantively, it concerns the underestimation of the relatively autonomous significance of the political vis-à-vis the economic, and of the spirit vis-à-vis the form. More on this follows. Further, see Schluchter 1989, chapter 1.

16. On the degree of dissemination of the concept of developmental history at the turn of the century, cf. Roth 1987c. However, the methodological status of the concept in Weber's usage remains underdefined here. To overcome this, one has to draw upon Heinrich Rickert, for in this case too, Weber primarily follows Rickert. Cf. Rickert 1902, chap. 4.5 (436ff., esp. 472–73). Rickert distinguishes seven concepts of development and defines the logical structure of the fourth (the crucial one for both him and Weber) in the following manner: Here "an individual course of events (*Werdegang*) is formed into a teleological unity by having its uniqueness related to one value. In this way, the uniqueness is combined with the unity of a sequence of events to become a historical process of development" (ibid., 473). In this manner, Rickert moves the historical individual constituted by the theoretical value relation from the simultaneous into the successive and thus logically separates developmental history from mere change, but also from "progressive" development. It is easy to see that Weber adheres to this idea in the "Objectivity" essay in those passages where he discusses ideal-typical developmental constructions in

terms of their relationship to history and contrasts these constructions to Marxist laws of development. Cf. Weber 1973: 203ff., esp. 205. (I will not deal with Rickert's important distinction in this context between primary and secondary historical individuals that Weber also adopts.) The refusal to identify development with progress in no way implies that the historian would not be justified in speaking of developmental stages. On the contrary: "The historian must be able first to conceive of *processes* as necessary units, and secondly, be able not only to separate them from the outside, but also to subdivide them internally into a number of stages, that is, he always has to present an assessable series of different stages that make up the essential parts of the historical course of events [in question]" (Rickert 1902: 437; cf. also the somewhat changed formulation in the second edition, 389–90). Thus, one can speak of development and developmental stages without falling prey to the errors of classical evolutionism. Admittedly, this presupposes the possibility of distinguishing between evaluation and theoretical value relation, which is at the basis of Rickert's (and Weber's) theory of the conceptualization of historical reality. (Although the possibility of making this distinction presupposes a value theory, it does not presuppose any specific one.) Rickert dealt comprehensively with the logical problems that this concept of developmental history raises for the concept of universal history in Rickert 1907, esp. 3: 396ff. Weber wrote to Rickert about it: "*Everything* in part 3 is highly appealing to me" (letter of November 3, 1907). I myself have used the concept of developmental history in *The Rise of Western Rationalism* (Schluchter 1981) in order to distinguish Weber's approach from both classical evolutionism and neo-evolutionary approaches, whether they tend to be of developmental-logical (Habermas) or of functionalistic provenance (Parsons, Luhmann). Cf. esp. the introduction and conclusion. (In the English edition, I have replaced "societal or social history" [*Gesellschaftsgeschichte*] with "developmental history" [*Entwicklungsgeschichte*] throughout. Cf. "Translator's Note" in Schluchter 1981: x.) If Wilhelm Hennis finds it hard to understand that "such different spirits as Friedrich Tenbruck, Wolfgang Schluchter, and Jürgen Habermas cannot resist finding *evolution-theoretic* elements in Weber's work," when for Weber history occurred as a chain of circumstances (cf. Hennis 1987: 204), then he studiously overlooks not only the differences between these different spirits, but above all that Weber did in fact have a theory of development. That his theory is not identical with that of classical evolutionism ("an inner lawfulness and teleological determinateness of development," in Hennis's imprecise formulation) is something that I have demonstrated particularly in opposition to Friedrich Tenbruck.

Classical evolutionism, however, is not the only form a theory of development can take, despite what Hennis appears to assume. That history occurs as a chain of circumstances does not rule out its reconstruction teleologically (in Rickert's sense!). That development does not mean progress does not imply that one has to abstain from all theories of development. Hennis has here, as well as in other systematically difficult questions, little to offer outside of polemics. It is difficult for me to grasp how, with such explicit rejection of all theories of development, one can view Weber's central question as the "development [!] of humanity [in the singular!]" (cf. Hennis 1987: 8ff.). Incidentally, Rickert's concept of historical development allows one to speak of the universal history of a civilization. This history is universal if it encompasses all those developmental stages (or phases) that are essential from a given value standpoint. Weber constantly uses the concepts of developmental history, universal history, and developmental stage (or phase) in this manner. For him, too, developmental theory exists for the sake of working out the distinctive character of a historical individual and its explanation and not for the sake of constructing "general developmental schemata." Cf., inter alia, the remarks already found in Weber 1976: 288. This interconnection is not seen in Wolfgang J. Mommsen's most recent works on the concept of universal history in Weber, which results in misclassifying Weber's approach. In my view, these articles shed more darkness than light on the subject since they actively confuse such undefined terms as the "substantive theory of universal history" (in contrast to the formal theory thereof?), "evolutionism," "teleology," "neo-evolutionism," and "neo-idealism" (in contrast to neomaterialism?), only to sometimes speak then of world history. Cf. Mommsen 1985, 1986, 1989a.

17. My formulations are deliberately "equivocal" because one has to distinguish, as Weber's methodology shows throughout, between the logical-formal significance and the substantive significance (*Bedeutung*), just as this distinction is made explicitly in terms of the concept of culture, the concept of cultural significance, and the concept of development (between the creation of meaning and the social bearer of meaning!).

18. Cf. the formulation in Weber 1958b: 26–27 (Weber 1921: 12).

19. I have previously indicated that one can divide Weber's work into three phases. Cf. the chart in Schluchter 1989, as well as chapters 1, 12, and 13 there. Whereas the second qualitative transformation—taking place in 1910—is of a substantive nature, the first one, connected to the publication of Rickert's fourth and fifth chapters of the *Limits* (Rickert 1902) is methodological in character. Beginning with his essay on Roscher, Weber transforms Carl Menger's distinctions between economic history, realistic economic theory, and exact economic theory, with the help of Rickert, into an approach for the cultural sciences that requires concept construction and concept application.

20. On the significance of the sociology of music for an adequate understanding of the problematic of rationalization, cf. Schluchter 1989, chapter 4.1.

21. Marianne Weber 1926: 349.

22. Weber 1958b: 17; Weber 1921: 4. It remained "the most fateful force" among them, however.

23. Weber 1958b: 27; Weber 1921: 12.

24. Thus, beyond the discipline of economics, the discipline he belonged to beginning with his appointment to Freiburg. On this, cf. also Marianne Weber 1926: 349.

25. On this, cf. Schluchter 1989, chapter 8.

26. Marianne Weber 1926: 346.

27. For this reason Weber was very modest in his claims about his comparative studies. He never considered them comprehensive cultural analyses. His primary concern was the refinement of the issues raised, just as had already been the case in the "Agrarian Sociology" (cf. e.g., Weber 1924a: 280). Moreover, in such an approach, one can never completely avoid schematic analyses (cf. Weber 1976).

28. Here, cf. inter alia, Becker 1924, esp. chapters 1, 2, 4, 9, 13, 14; Goldziher 1910; Wellhausen 1897, 1902; Kohler 1905; and Hurgronje 1888. Studies by Goldziher and Wellhausen are still being translated into English.

29. Weber 1921, 1: 237. (Passage omitted in corresponding English version. Cf. Weber 1958a: 267.) This writing originally appeared as early as October 1915 in the *Archiv für Sozialwissenschaft und Sozialpolitik*. For exact publication dates, cf. Schluchter 1989: 471–72.

30. Now also cited in Winckelmann 1986: 36.

31. Cf. Winckelmann 1986: 42.

32. Weber 1921, 1: 237. It is interesting that Weber only brings this reference up to date in 1920 instead of omitting it, even though he had in the meantime revised the "Introduction" and above all the first parts of the study of Confucianism.

33. On this, Schluchter 1989, chapter 13; Tenbruck 1977.

34. References in this direction from the correspondence can now be found in Winckelmann 1986: 42ff. In this way, the conjectures I derived from the texts on the development of Weber's work can be made more precise. Cf. Schluchter 1989, chapter 4.5.

35. Cf. Weber 1958a: 267; Weber 1921, 1: 237–38, where Islam along with Confucianism, Hinduism, Buddhism, Christianity, and—set apart from these—Judaism, is named as a religious ethic to be treated.

36. This announcement has now also been reprinted in Winckelmann 1986: 45–46.

37. Cf. Weber 1952: 5; Weber 1921, 3: 7.

38. As does Randall Collins (1986, chapter 2), who apparently does not realize that the editors of the *Wirtschaftsgeschichte* (Weber 1923) filled in gaps in the text with the help of Weber's published and unpublished writings. This is why there is not a thought in this reconstruction that cannot be found elsewhere in his work.

39. Cf. Schluchter 1989, chapter 12.

40. Weber 1978b: 611; Weber 1972: 367; emphasis added. The English translation omits the reference to "third," the very point emphasized here.

41. This also follows from a formulation in the "Author's Introduction," where Weber speaks of a "systematic study of the Sociology of Religion" that has yet to be made (Weber 1958b: 30; Weber 1921, 1: 15).

42. Weber 1978b: 623; Weber 1972: 375; further, Weber 1952: 5; Weber 1921, 3: 7.

43. Weber 1958b: 13; Weber 1921, 1: 1.

44. Cf. Weber 1923: 16. Incidentally, the terminological introduction to the *General Economic History* was omitted in the English translation (cf. Weber 1961), which means that American Weber scholars who do not read German—and their numbers are legion—are not acquainted with it. Nevertheless, this formulation is unusual insofar as Weber mostly avoids the concept of society.

45. Especially Benjamin Nelson and Friedrich H. Tenbruck—in various essays—have drawn attention to the significance of Weber's scattered remarks on scientific development. On Weber's estimation of Chinese scientific development, see Sivin 1983.

46. See the attempt by Collins (1986), which, however, I do not hold to be completely successful. Cf. Chapter 4 of this volume.

47. Cf. Weber 1923: 239. Further, Weber 1978b: 161–62; Weber 1972: 94; and Weber 1958b: 17–23; Weber 1921, 1: 4–9.

48. Weber 1923: 239.

49. Weber 1978b: 240; Weber 1972: 139. Here are similarities to Marx. Under these conditions, the category of profit-oriented or acquisitive capital (*Erwerbskapital*) leads, so to speak, an "antediluvian existence." This of course does not imply that Weber's explanation of the rise of modern capitalism is identical with Marx's explanation of primitive accumulation.

50. Weber 1961: 232–33; Weber 1923: 270.

51. Cf. Weber 1958b: 26–27; Weber 1921, 1: 12, where the focus is primarily on inner resistance, inner obstructions. In *Economy and Society*, however, attention is also constantly given to sources of external resistance, above all those that one "structure" offers another. Cf., for example, the points defining the interaction between political domination and economy in the newer version of the sociology of domination.

52. There is still no analysis of different types of church organization in the *Protestant Ethic*. The sect essays of 1906 represent the first move in this direction. It is known that Weber revised and expanded them for vol. 1 of *The Collected Essays on the Sociology of Religion*; he linked them to the *Protestant Ethic* (also now revised) by inserting a passage ("Where, in spite of a different doctrinal basis, similar ascetic features have appeared, this has generally been the result of Church organization. Of this we shall come to speak in another connection" [Weber 1958b: 128; Weber 1921, 1: 128]. This statement is followed by the reference to the sect essay). Thus, the relationship between internal and external—a relationship incidentally that in my view has a Kantian background—has

first to be analyzed in terms of its field of application. On the relationship between motive and institution, see the instructive remarks in Weber 1973: 188–89.

53. The concept "precapitalist" is used above all in the *General Economic History*. The quote is from Weber 1958b: 26; Weber 1921, I: 12.

54. Weber gives the following definition in the essay on "Objectivity": "For *our* purposes, an end is the conception of a *success* that becomes the *cause* of an action" (cf. Weber 1973: 183). That is a definition completely in the spirit of Kant. Weber further distinguishes between teleological rules and normative rules (*Zweck-Maxime* and *Norm-Maxime*) in the *Critique of Stammler*, that is, in that text at the beginning of the development of his theory of action. In this way he lays the basis, completely in the sense of a historicization of Kant, for the later distinction between means-ends (instrumental) and value rationality. For an elaboration, cf. Chapter 2 of this volume. The significance of this Kantian background that allows Weber to overcome the utilitarianism of economic theory is, in my view, misjudged by both Jürgen Habermas and Gregor Schöllgen. They claim that Weber in his theory of action would prioritize instrumental (or success-related) orientation and labor, respectively, and accuse him of subsuming an orientation to reaching understanding under an orientation to success and praxis under production. This would be true if Weber had remained within the limits of the economic theory of action. However, in the transition to the second phase of his work at the very latest, he went beyond these limits. The *Protestant Ethic* in particular demonstrates, through the example of a *historical* analysis, the consequences this "breakthrough" has for research strategy. It represents one long plea for recognizing that the origin of attitudes, even economic attitudes, cannot be adequately understood in terms of a utilitarian theory of action. For a critique of Weber's supposedly too narrow concept of action, cf. Habermas 1984, esp. chapter 3, "Intermediate Reflections"; and Schöllgen 1985, e.g., 41, 108ff. On the early beginnings of Weber's nonutilitarian action theory, cf. Weber 1977: 105–15, esp. 112–15; Weber 1973: 328–37, esp. 334–37.

55. On this concept, closely connected to Weber's concept of personality, see Chapter 2 of this volume and Schluchter 1989, chapter 8.

56. Cf. Schluchter 1989, chapter 4.1.

57. Weber 1958b: 30; Weber 1921, I: 15.

58. Weber 1958a: 90; Weber 1921, I: 82.

59. *Archiv* 20, 1905: 53.

60. Weber 1958b: 55; Weber 1921, I: 37.

61. Weber 1958b: 56; Weber 1921, I: 38. This was something that Weber had already sought to show in his study of agricultural laborers from east of the Elbe.

62. Weber 1958b: 196; Weber 1921, I: 40n.; inserted in 1920, in order to clarify Weber's original position vis-à-vis the objections of Sombart and Brentano.

63. Weber 1958b: 232 n. 66; Weber 1921, 1: 111 n. (inserted in 1920). Weber apparently developed this concept in analogy to that of "entanglements of argument" (*Problemverschlingung*), which repeatedly appeared in neo-Kantian writings.

64. Weber 1958b: 233 n. 66; Weber 1921, 1: 111 n. 4 (in this passage the decisive points were unchanged from the early version of the text).

65. Weber 1958b: 125–26; Weber 1921, 1: 124–25.

66. Weber 1958b: 117; Weber 1921, 1: 114.

67. On this, see Weber 1978d: 317. This has interesting consequences for the selection of sources. First, one needs sources that make the dogmatic foundations visible. Then, one requires sources that throw light on the psychic problems of the faithful. Only in the *Protestant Ethic* does Weber use both types of sources. In contrast, in his studies of other cultural religions, he contents himself largely with the demonstration of their dogmatic foundations.

68. Weber 1958a: 280; Weber 1921, 1: 252.

69. Weber 1958b: 125–26; Weber 1921, 1: 125.

70. Weber 1978b: 575; Weber 1972: 348.

71. Weber 1958a: 115; Weber 1921, 1: 110 (inserted in 1920).

72. Weber 1958a: 112; Weber 1921, 1: 105.

73. Weber 1978b: 575; Weber 1972: 348.

74. Weber 1958a: 108–9; Weber 1921, 1: 101.

75. On these interests cf. Weber 1923: 16. There he distinguishes between economic, magic and religious, political, and status group interests. They can be developed out of the combination of material and ideal interests with interests from within and interests from without. Incidentally, this combination also yields the most important areas of culture: the economic order, the religious order, the politico-legal order, and the social order. Cf. my effort at systematization in Schluchter 1981: 34–35, which I would conceive of somewhat differently today. Modifications are already found in Schluchter 1989, chapter 2, a revised version of Schluchter 1988d, chapter 2.

76. This also goes to show how unreasonable it is to link the so-called Protestantism thesis exclusively to the theory of predestination, as for example, Collins does.

77. Weber 1978b: 572; Weber 1972: 346.

78. Weber 1978b: 518; Weber 1972: 314.

79. Weber 1978b: 518; Weber 1972: 315.

80. Weber 1978b: 447; Weber 1972: 273. In another context I have suggested classifying Mohammed more as an ethical savior than as an ethical prophet, which deviates from Weber's own classification. Cf. Schluchter 1989, chapter 4.2. The justification for my approach was that Islam, like Christianity, was originally a movement of personal charisma, which is even further strengthened in Islam due to its political character. More on this follows.

81. Weber 1958a: 104–5; Weber 1921, 1: 94.

82. Weber 1978b: 523; Weber 1972: 317.

83. Weber 1978b: 623–24; Weber 1972: 375.

84. Ulrich 1912. Referred to in Weber: Weber 1958b: 227 n. 36, 240 n. 106; Weber 1921, 1: 102 n. 2, 128 n. 1 (both passages inserted in 1920). It is not clear whether Weber had already been familiar with this dissertation while writing the first version of *Economy and Society*. The argumentation there (Weber 1978b: 572–76; Weber 1972: 346–48) in any case does not preclude this possibility. On the conception of predestination in Islam, cf. also Peters 1987.

85. Weber 1958b: 221 n. 12; Weber 1921, 2: 92 n. 1.

86. Ulrich 1912: 57.

87. Ulrich 1912: 67–68.

88. Weber 1978b: 623–24; Weber 1972: 375.

89. Ulrich 1912: 14.

90. Weber 1978b: 574; Weber 1972: 347.

91. Weber 1978b: 573; Weber 1972: 346.

92. Weber traces this back to the institution of confession in lay Catholicism and to the affectual turn of religion in Lutheranism.

93. Cf. Ulrich 1912: 126ff.

94. Weber 1978b: 573; Weber 1972: 347.

95. Weber 1978b: 574; Weber 1972: 347.

96. Cf. Ulrich 1912: 47. On the foundations of Islamic doctrine in general, see Tibi 1985, esp. chapters 1, 2.

97. Weber 1978b: 573; Weber 1972: 347.

98. Weber 1958b: 227 n. 36; Weber 1921, 2: 102 n. 2.

99. Weber 1978b: 575; Weber 1972: 347.

100. In this sense Weber in fact considered only ancient Judaism and ascetic Protestantism successfully antimagical religions. Obviously, Islamic reform movements are also inspired by the turn away from magical practices of the masses. Cf. Metcalf 1987.

101. Weber 1978b: 575; Weber 1972: 347.

102. Weber 1978b: 623–24; Weber 1972: 375. It is obvious from this quote that Weber does not pass judgment on Islam as such, but tries to point to a peculiar appropriation of the religious sources through a social stratum at a specific period of time. It is true, however, that he neglected contervailing tendencies strengthening the truly salvational elements in these sources.

103. Weber 1978b: 472; Weber 1972: 288.

104. Weber 1978b: 627; Weber 1972: 376.

105. Weber 1958a: 269; Weber 1921, 1: 240.

106. Naturally, even long-term world rejection need not necessarily lead to world mastery, as the analysis of the Indian religions demonstrates. Above all, the lack of the idea of proof and the nature of the first decisive bearer stratum of the religion drive Islam, in Weber's view, to active, innerworldly political action, making it into a "political" religion that tends toward world adjustment. On this, cf. Weber 1921, 2: 220–21,

where Islam, along with Confucianism, is contrasted to Buddhism, a radically world-rejecting salvation religion that leads to world flight. Weber's views are, however, too simple, even for early Islam; witness the contributions by Lapidus 1987 and Levtzion 1987.

107. Weber 1978b: 574; Weber 1972: 347.

108. Cf. e.g., Hall 1985: 85ff., esp. 96; further, see Gellner 1985.

109. Weber 1958b: 126; Weber 1921, I: 125.

110. Weber 1958b: 26–27; Weber 1921, I: 12.

111. I thus find it difficult to take seriously the problem that moves Wilhelm Hennis: Which comes first, personality or life order? Naturally, this question has to arise if one assumes a relation of priority. However, neither Weber nor modern sociology does so (insofar as one can even speak about the latter in the singular). It is much more a state of correlation. Thus, it is in principle unimportant whether the address Weber gave at Burg Lauenstein in 1917 was entitled "Personality and the Life Orders" ("Die Persönlichkeit und die Lebensordnungen") (as Marianne Weber reports), or conversely, "Life Orders and the Personality" ("Die Lebensordnungen und die Persönlichkeit") (as a participant, Ferdinand Tönnies, recorded in his notebook on September 29, 1917). It is indisputable that Weber's entire approach is based on a theory of personality that is not merely empirical but is linked to a theory of value. This has been known at least since Dieter Henrich's dissertation and was already implicit in Karl Löwith's essay on Marx and Weber. However, for Weber's "sociology," and especially for his sociology of religion, personality and life order stand in correlation to one another. Technically, this correlation can assume all values between $+1$ and -1 (a favorable, indifferent, or obstructive relationship). In his review of the first published volume of the *Max Weber-Gesamtausgabe* (Weber 1984), Hennis (1984) writes: "Whoever knows the weight the word 'personality' possessed in Weber's generation, whose language was so deeply marked by Goethe and Nietzsche, can simply not imagine that Weber could have strung them together the other way around. But a modern sociologist cannot only do so, he has to. It is almost something of an existential question for the predominant form of sociology to grant 'life orders' (vulgarly the 'society') precedence over the 'individual.' The decisive question for every Weber interpretation can only be whether that also holds for Weber's sociology." Naturally, it does not hold for it, but neither does the opposite. (Incidentally, is this a linguistic or a theoretical problem, and why is it insinuated that of all people the historian Mommsen had made manipulations in the manner of modern sociology?) On the philosophical side of the theory of personality, which, in my view, must be read against the backdrop of Kant, see Henrich 1952, esp. part 2, "Die Grundlagen der Ethik" (The foundations of ethics); on the "philosophical" idea of man in Weber (and Marx), see Löwith 1960, esp. 30ff.: 65–66. For a comprehensive account, see Chapter 2 and Schluchter 1989, chapter 8.

112. Weber wrote to Rickert on April 26, 1920, apparently after the

"Basic Sociological Terms" of the later version of *Economy and Society* were already in the press, that one could develop practically everything out of the basic concept of subjectively intended meaning (with its four orientations of meaning) and the basic concept of order (with the conception of its validity). In this way, he defines his sociology as a theory of action and order on the basis of the division between theoretical value relation and practical evaluation. As the published version of these basic terms shows, he in fact did hold fast to the concept of the theoretical value relation. Cf. Weber 1978b: 18; Weber 1972, 8.

113. This is something that especially in the Anglo-American discussion is often overlooked. Cf. Chapter 3, n. 12.

114. Weber 1978c: 172; Weber 1921, 1: 205–6.

115. Weber 1958b: 128; Weber 1921, 1: 128.

116. Weber 1958a: 302–22; Weber 1921, 1: 207–36.

117. Weber 1958b: 122; Weber 1921, 1: 121.

118. Weber 1958a: 320; Weber 1921, 1: 234.

119. Weber 1958b: 128; Weber 1921, 1: 128.

120. Weber 1978b: 439; Weber 1972: 268.

121. Weber 1978b: 1174; Weber 1972: 700.

122. Weber 1958a: 325; Weber 1921, 1: 538.

123. Crone 1980: 62.

124. Weber 1978b: 575; Weber 1972: 348. Weber points to the elective affinity between the structural principle of democracy and that of the sects; he also makes references to the contribution of the ascetic Protestant sects in the development of a concept of freedom of conscience that also includes the freedom of conscience of others. Weber 1978b: 1208–10; Weber 1972: 724–26.

125. Cf. Ignaz Goldziher 1910, especially "Vorlesung 1. Muhammed und der Islam" (Mohammed and Islam); further, Weber 1972: 375; Weber 1978b: 623–24.

126. See Crone 1980: 13ff.

127. Becker 1924: 353.

128. Crone 1980: 8.

129. Crone 1980: 10.

130. Crone 1980: 15.

131. Wellhausen 1902: 5.

132. Wellhausen 1897: 92ff.

133. Wellhausen 1902: 2.

134. Watt 1964: 96.

135. Wellhausen 1902: 9.

136. Weber 1978b: 1244; Weber 1972: 746.

137. Wellhausen 1902: 9.

138. Wellhausen 1902: 12; Becker 1924: 347.

139. Naturally, this should not be understood as a regression. On this, cf. Levtzion 1987; he shows that Islam was initially thoroughly particularistic, formulating as it did an *Arabic* monotheism. It was only under

the Abbasids that it developed toward universalism, an essential component in the successful dissemination of Islam.

140. Wellhausen 1897: 101ff.

141. His family was supposedly entrusted with ritual functions.

142. On this, Wellhausen 1897: 68ff.

143. I have created this term following Reinhard Bendix, who speaks of "reference societies." Cf. Bendix 1978, esp. part 2.

144. Becker 1924: 343, 347.

145. According to the construct, Islam is responsible for the restitution of this establishment of religion, at the same time ridding it of the aberrations it suffered under Judaism and Christianity.

146. Hall 1985: 85.

147. Weber 1978b: 1138; Weber 1972: 673.

148. Weber 1978b: 474; Weber 1972: 289.

149. Weber 1978b: 474, 1174; Weber 1972: 289, 708.

150. Weber 1978b: 474; Weber 1972: 289. Incidentally, this passage allows one to conclude that Weber did not consider Islam to be exclusively a religion of warriors. To the extent that other carrier strata move to the forefront, elements of a salvation religion can also assert themselves. In fact, Weber never unambivalently classified Islam. Cf. Schluchter 1989: 144 (figure 13).

151. On this, cf. Schluchter 1981: 82–138, esp. 118–38.

152. Weber 1978b: 1015; Weber 1972: 587. Weber apparently follows Becker here, who cited 833 as the turning point.

153. See the epigram prefacing the essay. Also the formulations in Weber (Weber 1978b: 229, 239, 259; Weber 1972: 131, 138, 151). On Islamic patrimonialism, see also Rodinson 1987, Hardy 1987, Eaton 1987, and Eisenstadt 1987b (all in Schluchter 1987).

154. Weber 1978b: 1020; Weber 1972: 590, 1072.

155. Weber 1978b: 1070; Weber 1972: 625.

156. Weber 1978b: 1082: Weber 1972: 634.

157. Weber 1978b: 232, 260; Weber 1972: 133–34, 151. This was the case because the lack of all binding traditions is practically a historical impossibility.

158. Weber 1978b: 1072–74; Weber 1972: 627–28.

159. Weber 1978b: 1104; Weber 1972: 650.

160. Weber 1978b: 1105; Weber 1972: 650.

161. Weber 1978b: 1105–6; Weber 1972: 650–51.

162. See Chapter 4; and Poggi 1988 and Breuer 1988 in Schluchter 1988. Previously, Schluchter 1981: 139–74, esp. 153–74. In Weber, cf. Weber 1978b: 1051–69, esp. 1055–56; Weber 1972: 611–24, esp. 613–14.

163. Weber 1978b: 828–30; Weber 1972: 480–81.

164. This is the title of the aforementioned book by Patricia Crone (Crone 1980).

165. Aside from Crone 1980, see Pipes 1981.

166. Cf. Pipes 1981: xxiii.

167. Weber 1978b: 1015; Weber 1972: 587.
168. Weber 1978b: 1053–54; Weber 1972: 613.
169. Cf. Becker 1924, esp. 243.
170. Weber 1978b: 1016; Weber 1972: 587.
171. Weber 1978b: 1096; Weber 1972: 644.
172. Weber 1924b: 323ff., esp. part 3, and my study, "Modes of Capitalism: Imperial Rome and Imperial Germany," in Schluchter 1989: 281–314, esp. 305–13. Weber even conjectures that this institution originates in Islam, reaching Europe via Spain.
173. Becker 1924: 240.
174. Weber 1978b: 1105; Weber 1972: 650.
175. Becker 1924: 236.
176. Weber points to the Ottoman Empire, with its institution of the conscription of boys. Cf. Weber 1978b: 1016; Weber 1972: 588. Here, see also Anderson 1980, chapter 7.
177. Weber 1978b: 1075; Weber 1972: 628–29.
178. Weber 1978b: 1095; Weber 1972: 643.
179. Weber 1961: 207; Weber 1923: 239.
180. On the distinction between the principles of household and market and on the basic concepts in the sociology of the economy connected to it, see my efforts in Schluchter 1980: 136–42, revised in Schluchter 1989, chapter 9.
181. Weber 1978b: 1104–9, esp. 1108–9; Weber 1972, 650–53, esp. 653.
182. Weber 1978b: 239, 260; Weber 1972: 138, 151.
183. Weber 1978b: 240; Weber 1972: 139.
184. Here, see also Hall 1985: 97.
185. Weber 1978b, 1231–33; Weber 1972, 739–40.
186. Readers should also see Chapter 4, and further, the outstanding dissertation by Song-U Chon (Chon 1985). See also Schreiner 1986 as well as the literature cited in that publication.
187. Weber 1978b: 1220; Weber 1972: 732.
188. Weber 1978b: 1352; Weber 1972: 804.
189. Weber 1978b: 1363; Weber 1972: 811. Weber mentions the Sicilian empire under Dionysius, the Attic confederacy, the Carthaginian empire, and the Roman-Italic empire.
190. Weber 1978b: 1239; Weber 1972: 742.
191. Here Weber is thinking of the Italian *popolo* and probably Cologne as well.
192. Here, see also Weber's Vienna address on the sociology of the state as reported in the *Neuen Freien Presse*, October 26, 1917, p. 10. The fourth concept of legitimation (in addition to the traditional, the rational-legal, and the charismatic) was here the democratic one, its "specific social carrier, however, the *sociological formation of the Occidental city*."
193. Weber 1978b: 1339–40; Weber 1972: 796.

194. Especially succinctly formulated in Weber 1958c: 37–38; Weber 1921, 2: 39–40.

195. Weber refers to the saying "Stadtluft macht frei" (town air makes one free). Here, see above all Mitteis 1976, who points in particular to the distinction in legal position between slaves in antiquity and the medieval unfree and explains that the conception of a slave without master was an incomprehensible conception in Germanic law (Mitteis 1976: 193–94). Thus, there are also degrees of freedom in the countryside.

196. Cf. Hurgronje 1888 and Weber 1978b: 1232; Weber 1972: 739.

197. Weber 1978b: 1231: Weber 1972: 739.

198. Weber 1978b: 1016; Weber 1972: 587.

199. Weber 1978b: 1352; Weber 1972: 804.

200. Weber 1978b: 1251; Weber 1972: 750.

201. Here cf. Weber 1958b: 16; Weber 1921, 1: 3; in connection with Weber 1978b; 1108; Weber 1972: 653.

202. Weber 1978b: 828; Weber 1972: 480.

203. Weber 1978b: 259; Weber 1972: 151; in combination with Weber 1978b: 240–41; Weber 1972: 139.

204. Weber 1958b: 15–16; Weber 1921, 1: 3.

205. One attempt to cull a sociology of education and cultivation out of Weber is found in Lenhart 1986.

206. Weber 1978b: 828; Weber 1972: 480.

207. Weber 1978b: 790; Weber 1972: 459.

208. Weber 1978b: 820; Weber 1972: 475.

209. Weber 1978b: 791; Weber 1972: 460.

210. Weber 1978b: 819, and more generally, 790; Weber 1972: 460, 474.

211. Weber 1978b: 821; Weber 1972: 475.

212. Weber 1978b: 821–22; Weber 1972: 475–76. On *hijal* literature and its importance in the mutual adjustment between the law of custom and the Sharia, see Schacht 1935, esp. 218. I use Schacht in part to correct Weber's presentation.

213. Weber 1978b: 819; Weber 1972: 474.

214. Here, see Hall 1985: 88, who generally places the opposition between the *ulemas* and political domination at the center of analysis. On this problem, see also Rodinson 1987 and Gellner 1987.

215. Here see Schacht 1935: 222 and Weber 1978b: 821; Weber 1972: 476. Schacht speaks of a combination of the principle of person (*Personalprinzip*) (Moslem) and that of territory (the land of Islam).

216. Weber 1978b: 822; Weber 1972: 476.

217. Weber 1978b: 823; Weber 1972: 477. The distinction between legally immanent and legally transcendent conditions as well as the demarcation between the spheres within legally immanent conditions are central to Weber's sociology of law, just as the German distinctions between *formal* and *formell* and between *material* and *materiell* are. If one does not see this, Weber's sociology of law does in fact become an "incompre-

hensible" text. This is seen in Crone 1987. I have made an attempt to analyze the sociology of law taking these distinctions into account in Schluchter 1981: 82–105. Of interest in this context is Breuer and Treiber 1984.

218. Here see Weber 1978b: 1116; Weber 1972: 657. He speaks only of theocratic kadi justice. Schacht points to the necessity of differentiation. As is well known, kadi justice for Weber is not a concept restricted in application to Islam.

219. Weber 1978b: 822; Weber 1972: 476.

220. Schacht 1935: 222.

221. Weber 1978b: 828; Weber 1972: 480.

222. Weber 1978b: 828; Weber 1972: 480.

223. Weber 1978b: 792; Weber 1972: 460–61.

224. Weber 1978b: 793; Weber 1972: 461.

225. Schacht 1935: 236.

226. Weber 1978b: 577–78; Weber 1972: 349. There are also parallels between Christianity and Islam in the treatment of the usurer. A religion's orientation on such a matter per se is unimportant in this context. It is only interesting as an indicator of the existence of a dualism between in-group and out-group morals, something that appears in some form in all traditional economic ethics.

227. Schacht 1935: 237–38.

228. Rodinson 1986 and Turner 1974. See also Rodinson's article (1987), which, however, follows a somewhat different line of argument in comparison to the book.

229. Rodinson 1986: 26ff., esp. 32.

230. Rodinson 1986: 146ff.

231. Rodinson 1986: 160–61.

232. Cf. Rodinson 1986: 17.

233. Rodinson 1986: 115.

234. Cf. Rodinson 1986: 140.

235. Rodinson appears not to be acquainted with the entire theory of objective possibility and adequate causation or with Weber's methodological writing in general.

236. Gerhard Wagner and Heinz Zipprian in particular have pointed out this question. Cf. Wagner and Zipprian 1986, where it is argued that the problem arises through adherence to Rickert.

237. Here see Schluchter 1989: 140–46.

238. Rodinson 1986: 181.

239. Marx 1971, 2: 55.

240. Rodinson 1986: xxx.

241. Turner 1974: 8–9.

242. Turner 1974: 20–21.

243. Schluchter 1989, chapters 3, 4.

244. Turner 1974: 75.

245. Turner 1974: 172.

246. Weber 1978d: 325.

247. Weber 1949: 106; Weber 1973: 208.

« *Chapter 4* »

1. Weber 1889b. Strictly speaking, Weber's first publication was Weber 1889a. It represents a partial publication of Weber 1889b, and its printing is evidently connected with the requirements for obtaining a doctorate at the University of Berlin. The faculty of law, however, in which Weber received his degree, had already been given the text of Weber 1889b. A misleading account is given in Winckelmann 1963, and my account in Schluchter 1978, 15 n. 2 follows it. I thus now correct this account.

2. Weber 1924a: 321.

3. Limited and unlimited partnership are the translations of *Kommanditgesellschaft* and *offene Handelsgesellschaft*, respectively.

4. Weber 1924a: 322. It is interesting that here Weber already puts forth the methodological theses that one has to keep legal and economic aspects separate from one another in the analysis, and one always has to keep in mind that authoritative legal principles for economic action can arise in areas far removed from the economy.

5. The investigation covers above all Pisa and Florence. On the "one-sidedness" of the sources used, seen in today's terms, see Reyerson 1988.

6. Weber 1924a, 440. The unlimited partnership (*offene Handelsgesellschaft*) is an association of persons that in questions of liability involves the "entire character of property rights of the socii," whereas the limited partnership (*Kommanditgesellschaft*) constitutes a participatory relationship in which the partner is not really liable, but rather participates in the profits and losses of the undertaking in proportion to his investment. This is in any case what Weber claims the medieval legal sources show.

7. Weber 1978c: 159; Weber 1921, 1: 189.

8. Here, see Weber 1924a: 317–18. In the first version of *Economy and Society*, Weber dealt with the separation of household and firm in a section entitled "Die Auflösung der Hausgemeinschaft: Änderungen ihrer funktionellen Stellung und zunehmende 'Rechenhaftigkeit.' Entstehung der modernen Handelsgesellschaften." In English, it has been translated as: "The Disintegration of the Household: The Rise of the Calculative Spirit and of the Modern Capitalist Enterprise." Cf. Weber 1978b: 375–80; Weber 1972: 226–30. The title, however, presumably is the creation of the editors Marianne Weber and Melchior Palyi. In his planned outline of 1914, it was simply termed "Household, Enterprise, and Oikos." On the cultural-historical significance of the division between the business and private realm, see also Weber 1924a: 268. In addition, of course, see Weber 1978b: 98–99, 379; Weber 1972: 53, 229; and Weber 1978c: 159; Weber 1958b: 21–22.

9. Weber 1978c: 159; Weber 1921, 1: 190.

10. Weber 1978c: 172; Weber 1921, 1: 206n; *Archiv für Sozialwissenschaft und Sozialpolitik* [hereafter *Archiv*] 21 (1905), 110.

11. Weber 1978c: 173; Weber 1921, 2: 206n.

12. Here, see Schluchter 1989: 469–71 (appendix 2b).

13. Here, see Weber 1921, 3: v. See also Schluchter (1989, chapter 6) and Chapter 3 of this volume, where this is shown to be the case for the planned depictions of early Christianity and Islam. Passages concerning talmudic Judaism, Eastern Christianity, or the Eastern churches are relatively few in number. The outlines of Weber's position on talmudic Judaism in its antique and medieval phases of development can be reconstructed by means of the fragment on the Pharisees and Weber's dispute with Werner Sombart (cf. Sombart 1911a, 1913). In contrast, it is more difficult to obtain a grasp of his position on Eastern Christianity and the developments of the Eastern churches. However, the effort could prove rewarding, especially if the writings on the bourgeois revolution in Russia are included in the attempt. It is fair to assume that this line of development tended to be of secondary importance for Weber's overall project. This does not hold for medieval and modern Judaism because it belongs to the "preliminary studies" for the planned monograph on Western Christianity. We will return to Weber's debate with Sombart later.

14. On the classification of Weber's work into three phases, see Schluchter 1989, chapter 1. The methodological and theoretical breakthroughs and expansions of thematic scope cited there naturally hold for our context as well. Weber expressly and publicly emphasized in the controversy ensuing upon his Protestantism studies that his viewpoints in the analysis of a constitutive condition of the modern capitalist spirit originated from studies that went back before the turn of the century and were above all not prompted by Werner Sombart's relevant investigations (cf. Sombart 1902a, 1902b, 1903; and Weber's remarks in Weber 1978d: 150, with reference to *Archiv* 20, 1904, 19 n. 1). In spite of this, there is much evidence for believing that Weber did not yet consider Western development as a singular development (*Sonderentwicklung*) that requires a separate analysis of its mentality in addition to an analysis of its institutions, an independent analysis of the history of its religion and domination in addition to one of its economic and legal history, a terminological classification system especially equipped for this task, and a reconstruction of its roots all the way back to the regulated anarchy of ancient Israel. Moreover, it was only the work on the third edition of "Agrarian Conditions of Antiquity" (see Weber 1976: 35–386) that convinced Weber of the legitimacy of talking of "ancient capitalism" without reservations (Weber 1978d: 186), just as one can talk of medieval, early modern, or modern capitalism. On this, more later. Above all, however, only the effort to develop the interconnection between economy and religion for all great religions of the world, not yet visible in 1910, but already far along by the end of 1913, necessarily presupposed a treatment of Christianity that went beyond the pre-Reformation phase. For more detail here, see Schluchter 1989, chapter 12.

15. Cf. Schluchter 1989, chapter 1.1. In the printed "outline" to these lectures distributed to the students, the part relevant to our context is found in "book three," which is entitled: "The Historical Foundations of the Economy." It is subdivided as follows:

Section 8. The typical early stages of the economy
Section 9. The economic development of ancient coastal civilization
Section 10. The agrarian foundations of medieval inland civilization
Section 11. The urban economy and the origin of the modern forms of enterprise
Section 12. The rise of the national economy

In my view, three things are indicated by this outline. First, Weber relatively closely follows Karl Bücher's theory of economic stages. Second, one gets the impression in looking at the subdivisions of paragraphs 9–13 (not reproduced here) that three important later works have already been anticipated here: "Der Streit um den Charakter der altgermanischen Sozialverfassung in der deutschen Literatur des letzten Jahrzehnts" (The dispute over the character of the ancient Germanic social structure in the German literature of the last decade) of 1904 (Weber 1924a: 508–56), "The Agrarian Sociology" (Weber 1976: 35–386), and at least parts of "The City" (Weber 1978b: 1212–1372), the exact date of origin of which is still unknown. Third, in comparing the "Outline" of 1898 with that of the *General Economic History* (Weber 1961), one finds many parallels, but at least two weighty differences: the *General Economic History* no longer adheres to the conventional model of economic stages, and in its chapter on the rise of modern capitalism (in the "Outline" entitled "The Rise of the National Economy"), there is a section on the development of capitalist mentality that is missing in the "Outline." Moreover, the factors of city, state, and bourgeoisie clearly play a much more significant role in the *General Economic History* than they do in the "Outline."

16. On the distinctions among these partial orders and their concomitant interests and orientations, see above all Weber 1923: 1–17 [omitted in the English; cf. Weber 1961]; Weber 1921, 1: 1–16, 536–73; Weber 1958b: 13–31; Weber 1958a: 323–59; and my attempt at systematization in Schluchter 1989, chapter 2.5.

17. See Troeltsch 1977 and Troeltsch 1981a, esp. parts 1–3.

18. Here see Weber 1958b: 188 n. 1, 284 n. 119; Weber 1921, 1: 18 n, 206 n.; and Weber 1978d: 322.

19. Here, cf. Weber's remarks in Weber 1978d: 322 and Weber 1958b: 188 n. 1; Weber 1921, 1: 18 n.

20. For a more detailed analysis, see Chapter 3.

21. In this context, see Winckelmann 1986, esp. 45–46. The passage reproduced here comes from a letter quoted there from September 11, 1919.

22. On the announcement, see Schluchter 1989: 425, and Winckelmann 1986: 45–46.

23. Weber 1958b: 27; Weber 1921, 1: 12.

24. Here see *Archiv* 44 (1917/1918): 52n.

25. Weber 1976: 356; Weber 1924a: 269. "Agrarian Conditions in Antiquity" appeared in 1909 (cf. Weber 1976, 35–385, where it makes up the first two chapters of a translation entitled *The Agrarian Sociology of Ancient Civilizations*. The misleading translation of the original title will be used throughout the present essay) and marked, along with the studies "On the Psychophysics of Industrial Labor," the end of the second phase of Weber's work. For more detail, see Chapter 3.

26. Weber 1976: 341; Weber 1924a: 257.

27. Weber 1976: 366; Weber 1924a: 278. Weber notes here that "sometimes phenomena of ancient culture have disappeared completely and then come to light again in an entirely new context. In other respects, however, the cities of Late Antiquity, especially of the Hellenistic Near East, were the precursors of the organization of medieval trade and industry, just as the manors of Late Antiquity were the precursors of the estates of medieval agriculture."

28. Cf. Weber 1958b: 13; Weber 1921, 1: 1; and the "Author's Introduction" as a whole (Weber 1958b: 13–31; Weber 1921, 1: 1–16).

29. Weber 1978c: 192; Weber 1921, 2: 363.

30. Weber 1978c: 199; Weber 1921, 2: 372.

31. Weber 1978c: 199; Weber 1921, 2: 372.

32. All quotes come from Weber 1952: 5; Weber 1921, 3: 7, first in the *Archiv* 44 [1917/1918]: 58.

33. Here, see, for example, Chapter 3.

34. See, for example, Weber 1978d: 323–25; Weber 1961: 255–56; Weber 1923: 296–97; Weber 1976: 336–58; Weber 1923: 254–71; and Weber 1978b: 727–814; Weber 1972: 735–822. The dating and placing of "The City" is one of the most difficult of editorial problems. Cf. Schluchter 1989, chapter 13. The conclusion to the "Agrarian Sociology" definitely represents a preliminary stage of this essay. But it lacks both the comparison with Asian cities and, in the context of the medieval city, the emphasis on the break with the old legitimate powers (i.e., usurpation). Moreover, Weber terms commercial towns "industrial towns" here, something that no longer occurs in "The City." All these points indicate that the text was produced in the context of the two major projects, and at a time when the division of labor in content and purpose between the two projects was still relatively imprecise, but in any case before the start of the First World War. Thus, it might actually have been written as chapter 8c, "Nonlegitimate Domination: Typology of Cities" of the manuscript "The Economy and the Societal Orders and Powers" of 1914. (Although Weber does cite literature from 1914, e.g., from a work by Max Strack on freedmen from that year [Weber 1978b, 1357], most of the publications quoted are relatively old. One possible explanation of this is that Weber summarized here preliminary works of his going as far back as before 1900, works pointed to by the "Outline.") However, even if Weber did intend to incorporate "The City" into the first version of *Economy and*

Society, it is highly improbable that he would have proceeded in the same sense in the second version. The sociology of domination had been completed for the new version, and it is true that it was to be followed by the treatment of specifically Western political associations, including urban ones (cf. Weber 1978b: 240–41; Weber 1972: 139). He hardly would have taken unchanged an already completed manuscript for this task, however, especially not one that, as Marianne Weber puts it, possesses a "largely descriptive form." I thus suspect that, after deciding to write a second version of *Economy and Society* and to have it published in conjunction with the *Collected Essays in the Sociology of Religion*, Weber would have incorporated "The City" into the latter collection of essays, in its present form or in a changed form based upon the original. Here, see Schluchter 1989, chapter 12. This conjecture is also supported by the position of the analysis of the city and citizenry in the *General Economic History*; Weber 1961: 233–49; Weber 1923: 270–89.

35. Here I am adopting Weber's own formulation, as he employed it in the second critique of Rachfahl, in the "Anticritical Last Word." Cf. Weber 1978d: 285. Weber did not enlarge the scope of the investigation, but he envisioned other studies to deal with unresolved issues; moreover, he did not integrate the study of Protestantism into the series on the economic ethics of the world religions, but only linked it to them by means of an "Author's Introduction." These purely formal indications are evidence in my view of something that Rachfahl questioned and that has been repeatedly put in question since, namely, that Weber did not change his original thesis because he still considered it correct in 1920. He desired only to place it in the overall context of cultural development, especially that of the West. For this reason, he planned the *Collected Essays in the Sociology of Religion* (which he also considered entitling "Collected Essays in the Sociology of the *Kulturreligionen*") to conclude with a volume on Western Christianity. This is implied in the references given in the revised passages of the text. We will return to this momentarily.

36. For more detail here, see Schluchter 1989, chapter 5.

37. Weber 1978c: 161 n. 2; Weber 1921, I: 192 n. 1; *Archiv* 21 (1905), 101 n. 69. In 1905, he stated with all the clarity that could be desired that he wanted "separately at a later date to consider the question of the class determinants of religious movements" (in 1920: "not consider here the question . . . [on this, see my essays on the 'Economic Ethics of the World Religions']"). In 1905 and 1920, he remarked that for those "whose conscience cannot be appeased without finding economic ('materialist,' as they are unfortunately still called) explanations . . . that I consider the influence of economic developments on the destiny of systems of religious ideas to be very important, and that I shall later attempt to examine the way in which, in this case, the processes of mutual adaptation and the general relationships between the two came to be what they were. But the contents of these religious ideas can by no means be deduced from the 'economic' influences: they are themselves—let us be quite firm about

this—the most powerful formative elements of 'national character,' they have their own compelling power" (in 1920: "they follow their own inner logic and have purely their own compelling power"). Just this passage alone and the fact that Weber adopts it practically unchanged in the revised version could have convinced anyone that he did not change his position on the so-called materialism-idealism dichotomy between 1904–5 and 1920, and in terms of this question, there was no difference between the studies of Protestantism and the studies of the economic ethics of the world religions. For more detail here, see Schluchter 1989, chapter 1, and Chapter 3.

38. However, Weber considered this task partially accomplished with the new version of the essay on the sects, which no longer adhered to the old drafts of this essay from 1906. Incidentally, the essay on the sects points back to the section of the sociology of domination in the first version of *Economy and Society* entitled "Political and Hierocratic Domination" ("Politische und hierokratische Herrschaft").

39. The new version of *Economy and Society* probably would have been organized in a similar fashion. See Schluchter 1989; on the "division of labor," see Chapter 3.

40. Weber 1958b: 24; Weber 1921, 1: 10. Weber expressly states that though this rise of the Western bourgeoisie is closely related to the rise of the capitalist organization of labor, it is not simply identical with the latter.

41. Here see Schluchter 1989, chapters 3.3, 4.2, and 12.

42. Moreover, the *General Economic History* is not limited to the West, but also includes the comparison between the West and Asia. Weber titled the lecture course that serves as the basis for the reconstructed text in the winter semester of 1919–20 "Outline of Universal Social and Economic History." Some view this text as Weber's last word on capitalism— even as his last work(!)—and at the same time as the most comprehensive general theory of the rise of capitalism available as of today, as Randall Collins puts it (Collins 1986: 19–21). This is a strong statement, which I would not like to contradict. I would, however, like to contradict the way in which Weber's "mature theory" is interpreted in this context. More on this later.

43. Weber 1958b: 258 n. 192; Weber 1921, 2: 162 n.

44. Cf. Sombart 1913: 303ff.

45. Weber 1958b: 202 n.; Weber 1921, 1: 58 n.

46. The quote is from Weber 1958b, 198 n. 12; Weber 1921, 1: 41 n.; the thought from Weber 1958b, 202–203 n.; Weber 1921, 1: 58 n. On this largely unrealized aspect, cf. the contributions of Lerner 1988 and Selge 1988 (both in Schluchter 1988).

47. Weber 1958b: 212 n. 10; Weber 1921, 1: 72 n.; Weber would have principally used a work of Paul Honigsheim here (Honigsheim 1969).

48. Cf. Weber 1978b: 611–23; Weber 1972: 367–74.

49. Cf. Weber 1951, chapter 30; Weber 1923, chapter 4, section 9.

50. In my view, unambiguous evidence of this is found in the relevant chapter of the *General Economic History*. It ends with the reference to the historical significance of the Reformation in eliminating the *consilia evangelica*, to the subsequent transformation of the concept of asceticism by ascetic Protestantism and the monitoring of the ethical adequacy of the individual through the establishment of a unique form of "church discipline." Cf. Weber 1961, 258–70, esp. 268–70; Weber 1923: 300–15, esp. 312–15. I cannot understand how Randall Collins can claim that in the *General Economic History* Weber reduces "the ideal factor to a relatively small place in his overall scheme"; this text represents, after all, a social and economic history, not a history of religion. Moreover, its novelty vis-à-vis standard economic histories lies precisely in the fact that it nevertheless grants this side of the causal chain its own chapter. In addition, Collins claims that Weber "greatly transformed" his original Protestantism thesis in now viewing ascetic Protestantism as merely an intensification of a motivational factor already found in Christianity; furthermore, Weber now only attributed to this factor negative significance "in the sense that it removes one of the last institutional obstacles diverting the motivational impetus of Christianity away from economic rationalization." This, however, is precisely the crucial point of the original Protestantism thesis—namely, the question, Under which conditions is the inner resistance overcome such that even the Catholic and Lutheran economic ethics still maintain a position against the objectification of economic relations? Thus, there is no trace of a "greatly transformed" thesis here. For the quotes, see Collins 1986: 20–21, 33.

The "Anticritiques" make it clear that, aside from the five topics named above, Weber was also interested in further differentiating the tendencies present within ascetic Protestantism. Not all ascetic Protestants were adherents of the doctrine of predestination, something Weber had already emphasized in the first version of the *Protestant Ethic*, illustrating this in terms of the Baptists. (For this reason, Collins is fully off target when he remarks that Weber's failure to mention the doctrine of predestination in the *General Economic History* shows that he had changed his original thesis. See Collins 1986, 33.) In this context, Weber apparently also intended to analyze the Huguenots. Cf. Weber 1978d: 320, 322. Indeed, as early as 1908, Weber had already expressed the intention of producing a separate edition of the studies of Protestantism for which he would revise and supplement. He announced that this edition would be published in the spring of 1909. Cf. Weber 1978d: 54.

51. See Weber 1958b: 191 n. 23; Weber 1921, 1: 28 n. 3. See also Reinhard Bendix's instructive remarks in Bendix 1967. Weber emphasized that what was new was not the claimed interconnection, but that it has recently come to be challenged. As evidence that contemporaries were already aware of the phenomenon, he inserted a quote by John Wesley into the second edition that "would be a very suitable motto to inscribe over all that has been said so far." Cf. Weber 1978c: 165; Weber 1921, 1: 196–

97. An established relation is not already a valid causal attribution, how-ever, or, put in today's terms, a correlation is not an explanation. This was also clear to Weber.

52. Weber 1958b: 26; Weber 1921, 1: 12.

53. In contrast to Marx, Weber considers the formal rationality of capi-tal accounting and its external and internal preconditions the distinguish-ing features (*das Spezifische*) of modern capitalism. (Although, as in Marx, these preconditions include formally free labor and the complete appropriation of all means of production by the owners, in Weber, these are by no means all of the preconditions.) In contrast to Brentano, Weber sees the specifically modern capitalist features in the opportunities for continual marketing and in the rational tempering of the acquisitive drive (politically oriented adventure capitalism versus economically oriented rational capitalism). In contrast to Simmel, with whom he shares the view of the objectification of social relations concomitant with modern capitalism, Weber strictly distinguishes between a monetary economy and capitalism. In contrast to Sombart, with whom he shares the view of the calculability concomitant with modern capitalism, the rationaliza-tion of economic management, and the comprehensive rationalization of the whole economy (Schumpeter), Weber more strongly emphasizes the rational organization of labor vis-à-vis other developmental aspects than Sombart does. It is clear to see that the definitions overlap (least in the case of Brentano), but they are not identical. On the disagreement with Brentano, Simmel, and Sombart, see esp. Weber 1958b: 185 n. 2; Weber 1921, 1: 4 n. 1. There, Weber relates his discussion to Simmel 1978 (in the second expanded German Leipzig edition of 1907) and to Sombart 1902a and 1902b (in the second revised Munich and Leipzig edition of 1916). The latter included the first two volumes on the precapitalist economy and on European economic life in the age of early capitalism (the third volume, on the age of advanced capitalism, first appeared in 1927, and thus after Weber's death). Interestingly, Weber was apparently closer to the first edi-tion of Sombart's "beautiful main work on capitalism" than to the second one in contents, but not in method, for in the revision of the studies of Protestantism, the second edition is not taken into account anywhere as far as I know. On Schumpeter's judgment, see Schumpeter 1987, esp. 205. The latter also contains an interesting comparison with Marx.

54. That Weber was fully aware of this problem is seen in a critical response to Brentano. The latter had not only rejected the conceptual dif-ferentiation that Weber had proposed, but even "made the claim, incom-prehensible to me, that the concept of the 'spirit' of (modern!) capitalism, created for the purposes of this analysis, already presupposes what it is supposed to prove." Cf. Weber 1958b: 198 n. 13; Weber 1921, 1: 42 n. 1. It still remains to be critically examined whether Weber was in fact able to make this required separation.

55. Weber 1958b: 21; Weber 1921, 1: 7.

56. Weber 1958b: 25; Weber 1921, 1: 11.

57. Cf. Schluchter 1981 and Schluchter 1980, esp. chapter 1 (in English, in Roth and Schluchter 1979, chapter 1). Further, cf. Schluchter 1989, chapters 3.2, 4.1.

58. Guenther Roth especially has repeatedly made the effort to draw attention to the mode of analysis Weber actually practiced. Cf. his writings in Bendix and Roth 1971, esp. chapters 6 and 13, and in Roth and Schluchter 1979, esp. "Epilogue." Further, cf. Roth 1987, esp. appendix. The distinction between methodology and method is not easy to make in Weber. Methodology, in Rickert's sense, refers primarily to a theory of concept formation in a science of reality (*Erfahrungswissenschaft*) (individualizing and generalizing), whereas method refers to the mode of analysis, such as that of interpretive sociology, for example. In the "Basic Sociological Terms" of the second version of *Economy and Society*, foundations of method are spoken of, not methodological foundations. For this reason, I have chosen to use the term "method" in the following.

59. Cf. for example Weber 1978d: 164, 170–71, 263–70.

60. On this, see for example, Weber 1978d: 324.

61. This is reminiscent of Rickert's distinction between relative-historical or absolute-historical terms. For more detail here, see Schluchter 1989, chapter 1.3.

62. On this, see Weber 1978d: 170. Weber expressly says that both cases involve ideal-typical constructs, thus confirming the interpretation suggested here.

63. Here cf. Weber 1958b: 17–19, esp. 19; Weber 1921, I: 4–6, esp. 6. This comparison can even be made by means of accounting in natural goods, even though the limits of rationality are narrowly drawn in this case. Cf. Weber 1978d: 55.

64. Weber 1958b: 19; Weber 1921, I: 6.

65. Weber 1978d: 171. In order to distinguish between these different cases, I speak, following later formulations, of one-sidedly and reciprocally favorable, indifferent, and obstructive relationships. Cf. Chapter 3.

66. Here see also Schluchter 1989, chapter 11.

67. Weber 1978d: 170.

68. Weber 1978d: 170.

69. Another is, for example, in Brentano's terms, the "pagan emancipation" from economic traditionalism, which in his view starts with Machiavelli and subverts the Christian ideas of the prohibition of usury and of the just price. Brentano criticizes Weber for supposedly neglecting this element of emancipation from traditionalism (cf. Brentano 1916, esp. 132–33). However, Weber left out this aspect not for reasons of substance, but of methods. Even in the first version of the studies of Protestantism, he had emphasized the independent significance of humanist rationalism for modern vocational culture. Cf. Weber 1978c: 171, 171 n. 2; Weber 1921, I: 205, 205 n. 1.

70. Weber 1978d: 285.

71. For this reason, Weber remarks in a letter that the series represents

the general realization of the method of the studies of Protestantism (cf. Chapter 3). M. Rainer Lepsius takes up the attribution problem involved both in the studies of Protestantism and more generally in Weber's approach as such. Cf. Lepsius 1986.

72. See here for example, Weber 1958b: 55; Weber 1921, 1: 37. The notion of historical legacies pervades the work of Reinhard Bendix. Cf. esp. Bendix 1978, 1982.

73. As formulated in Weber 1924a: 517, with regard to the dispute between the Knapp school and the Meitzen school on the status of the "manorial hypothesis" in explaining the earliest periods of German social history.

74. For more detail, see Schluchter 1989, chapter 1.4 and Chapter 3.

75. Weber 1924a: 517. At the same time, Weber attacks the use of the stage concept in Hildebrandt's book (Hildebrandt 1896) and its use by the Knapp school, especially by Werner Wittich.

76. Here, cf. Schluchter 1989, chapter 1.8.

77. Cf. Bücher 1914, esp. 10ff.

78. In a letter from which another passage is often quoted (December 30, 1913), we read, "Because Bücher and his 'Developmental Stages' are completely inadequate, I have worked out a complete theory and narrative exposition [*Darstellung*], which relates the major forms of association [*Gemeinschaftsformen*] to the economy." Cf. Schluchter 1989, chapter 13, and Winckelmann 1986: 36.

79. One way to assess the differences between the authors is to compare section 6a in Bücher 1914 with part 2, chapter 3 of *Economy and Society* (Weber 1978b: 356–69). Moreover, whereas Bücher divided his stages according to the relation between production and consumption, Weber focused on the relations of domination and appropriation connected to economic units of production and consumption and their legal forms. In addition, Bücher limited his developmental stages to those of European culture, whereas Weber also took non-European conditions into consideration. But one sees the extent to which Weber never stopped admiring Bücher's earlier works in the second version of *Economy and Society*. The sociology of the economy follows Bücher's authoritative discussions over large sections. See Bücher 1922. Weber had the greatly expanded second edition from 1898 (first edition, 1893) in his own library, also Bücher 1909. Weber himself terms them "basic works" (Weber 1978b: 114–15; Weber 1972: 63).

80. As Weber referred to the study in Weber 1958b: 188 n. 1; Weber 1921, 1: 18 n.

81. Troeltsch 1977: 186.

82. Here, see Schluchter 1981: 39–81.

83. Here, cf. for example, Sombart 1916, vol. 1, chapters 4–12. He defines craft as "that form of providing welfare in the organization of an exchange economy in which the economic subjects are technical workers who are legally and economically autonomous and governed by the idea

of sustenance, who act traditionally, and who stand in the service of the organization as a whole" (Sombart 1916, 1: 188). On the concept of economic epoch, he writes: "From the perspective of realist empiricism, the concept corresponding to that of economic system is that of the economic epoch. This I conceive as a historical span of time in which a certain economic system, or more precisely, in which a mode of economic activity concomitant with a certain economic system was predominant" (Sombart 1916, 1: 22). The mode of economic activity includes both form and mentality, following Sombart's general tendency to define economic epochs according to economic spirit. Although the latter cannot arise without certain external conditions, in Sombart's view, it ultimately produces the form of economic organization adequate to it. This holds for Sombart at least since his book *Der Bourgeois* (Sombart 1913), revealingly subtitled, "On the history of modern economic man." On its interpretation, see also Mitzman 1973, esp. 254ff., where the priority of the viewpoint of "intellectual history" in distinguishing between precapitalist, early capitalist, and advanced capitalist epochs is demonstrated (the relationship of entrepreneurial spirit to bourgeois spirit).

84. Weber 1961: 207; Weber 1923: 239.

85. Weber 1949: 75–76; Weber 1973: 174–75 (emphasis omitted).

86. Weber 1964: 62; Weber 1921, 1: 349.

87. Weber 1978b: 240–41; Weber 1972: 139.

88. Cf. here Schluchter 1989, chapter 6.8; further, Schluchter 1981: 154–56. Apparently, Weber followed Troeltsch here. Cf. Troeltsch 1977, esp. part 2, chapter 4.

89. Weber 1978d: 324.

90. Weber 1978d: 167.

91. Weber 1978d: 168.

92. Sombart 1927: 1010. Similarly in Weber 1978c: 70; Weber 1921, 1: 203.

93. Cf. Berman 1983, esp. the introduction and conclusion. Further, Stock 1985 and 1988. Stock finds that Weber underestimated the significance of the development from the eleventh to the thirteenth century for the formation of modern Western rationalism. I will seek to show in the following that this criticism is only in part justified. It is true, however, that the communication revolution brought about through the growth in the use of writing and its concomitant institutions, is not dealt with in Weber, in contrast to Stock.

94. Berman speaks of the "Papal Revolution" with which, in his view, the singular development of the West first actually begins. This pan-European revolution of the eleventh and twelfth centuries is then followed by the Reformation and the English, American, French, and Russian Revolutions. Berman sees a radical discontinuity between the period prior to, and the period following 1050–1150. One formulation in this context reads: "One of the purposes of this study is to show that in the West, modern times—not only modern legal institutions and modern le-

gal values but also the modern state, the modern church, modern philosophy, the modern university, modern literature, and much else that is modern—have their origin in the period 1050–1150 and not before" (Berman 1983: 4). Weber would have taken exception to this last point, however.

95. Collins 1986: 33 n. 11.

96. For the argument here, see Schluchter 1989, chapter 1.8.

97. On this, see Berman 1983: 542, who sarcastically remarks on Marxian periodization: "Unfortunately for this Marxian analysis, the 'feudal mode of production'—that is, the manorial system—had broken down by the end of the fourteenth century, all over Europe, and the 'capitalist' mode of production, as defined by Marx, only came into being in the eighteenth, or at the earliest the seventeenth century. This leaves a 'transition' period of some three or four centuries during which a central state power developed, namely, the absolute monarchies of Europe." Here see also Marc Bloch (Bloch 1961: 533): "From the middle of the thirteenth century onwards European societies diverged decisively from the feudal pattern." Bloch, however, then goes on to show its aftereffects.

A passage characteristic for Marx is found in one of his articles from the *Neue Rheinische Zeitung* at the end of 1848: "The revolutions of 1648 and 1789 were not English and French revolutions, they were revolutions of a European style. They were not the victory of a certain class of society over the old political order; they were the proclamation of political order for the new European society. The bourgeoisie was victorious in them; but the victory of the bourgeoisie was at that time the victory of a new social order, the victory of bourgeois property over feudal property, of nationality over provincialism, of competition over the guild, of partitioning over primogeniture of dominion, of the owner of the land over the rule of land over the owner, of enlightenment over superstition, of the family over family name, of industry over heroic idleness, of bourgeois law over medieval privileges." Cf. Marx 1971, vol. 3, bk. 1: 71–72. Hegel also has the modern age begin with the French Revolution. Tocqueville, however, had already seen "further." On the role of the French Revolution in Weber, see also the discussion between Dieter Henrich, Claus Offe, and Wolfgang Schluchter in Henrich, Offe, and Schluchter 1988.

98. Berman 1983: 550.

99. These are the main lines of development. The studies of Islam and Eastern Christianity presumably would have tended to follow what in developmental perspective are secondary or collateral lines of development.

100. Especially relevant in our context are the short section on canon law in the sociology of law, and the longer section on political and hierocratic domination in the sociology of domination. Interestingly, medieval Christianity is hardly cited in the sociology of religion. This could lead one to conjecture that Weber conceived of the plan to write a study of Western Christianity relatively late, perhaps after the publication of the first essays on the economic ethics of the world religions at the end of 1915, when this project increasingly "took on a life of its own."

101. This is the title of chapter 3 in Collins 1986: 45ff.

102. Weber 1978d: 170.

103. Weber 1978d: 171. In the studies of Protestantism, Benjamin Franklin's instructions were used as a provisional description of "what is here meant by the 'spirit' of capitalism." See Weber 1958b: 48; Weber 1921, 1: 31.

104. Cf. Marx 1971, 4: xxx–xxxi: "The mode of depiction, however, has to formally distinguish itself from the mode of research. Research has to appropriate the material in detail, analyze its different forms of development, and uncover their underlying connection. It is only after this task has been completed that the real movement can be suitably depicted. If this is successful, and there is a reproduction of the life of the material in ideas, it might take on the appearance of an a priori construct."

105. This incidentally holds not only for the *Collected Essays in the Sociology of Religion* (*Gesammelte Aufsätze zur Religionssoziologie*), but also for *Economy and Society*. The "Basic Sociological Terms" are followed by the "Sociological Categories of Economic Action" ("Basic Categories of Economic Action" would have been the literal translation of the German original), which in a certain sense culminate in sections 30 and 31, in which the various kinds, forms, and trajectories of capitalism are defined. At the same time it is stated there that the difference between Western capitalism and the other kinds, forms, and trajectories of capitalism "calls for an explanation, and this explanation cannot be given on economic grounds alone." See Weber 1978b: 166; Weber 1972: 96. Weber emphasizes that his sociology of the economy contains only generally held economic views in a somewhat more specific form. It is precisely here, in my view, where the value interest is reflected, that Weber's approach is separated from other, purely economic methods of explanation, which are both seductive and contestable. Here, cf. Weber 1978b: 115; Weber 1972: 63.

106. Here, cf. the discussions in Weber 1978b: 116–17; Weber 1972: 63–64. The antithesis of the technical concept of the enterprise (*Betrieb*), which "designates the continuity of the combination of certain types of services with each other and with material means of production" is intermittent or technically discontinuous economic activity, whereas the antithesis to the economic concept of the firm (*Unternehmung*) is the concept of the household.

107. The quote is from Weber 1978b: 166; Weber 1972: 97. On the listing of features, see Weber 1978b: 147–48, 162; Weber 1972: 85, 94; and esp. Weber 1978c: 336–40; Weber 1921, 1: 7–11.

108. Cf. Weber 1978b: 117; Weber 1972: 64.

109. Weber 1978b: 161; Weber 1972: 94.

110. Weber 1978b: 161; Weber 1972: 94.

111. For the quote see Weber 1978b: 122–23; Weber 1972: 68; and on the concept of the "formal-order-enforcing organization" (*Ordnungsverband*), for which the pure *Rechtsstaat* provides the prototype, see Weber

1978b: 74; Weber 1972: 38. Weber naturally recognized that not only the modern state, but also unions and employers' associations pursue an economic policy of substantive regulation, which, in his view, always restricts the autonomy of capitalist enterprises. The recent discussion of the modern interventionist state could take as its stating point the distinctions between an organization enforcing a formal order and an economically regulative organization, and between formal and substantive regulation of the economy. In addition, the tendency of the modern state toward interventionism, which Weber naturally saw, represented for him one of the principal limits to formal economic rationality. In the modern market economy, formal and substantive rationality unavoidably come to diverge, for the freedom and openness of the markets can never be absolute; if they were, severe social problems would be the result because the market mechanism on its own does not produce a balance between efficient commodity production and distributive justice!

112. Here see Weber's early analysis of the stock market and the stock market system in Weber 1924b: 265ff., esp. 285ff.

113. Weber 1978b: 109; Weber 1972: 59.

114. Cf. Weber 1961: 208; Weber 1923: 239.

115. See Weber 1978c: 338; Weber 1921, I: 10.

116. Naturally, peaceful does not mean without struggle. Quite the contrary, according to Weber, capital accounting in its formally most rational shape presupposes the struggle of man against man. Cf. Weber 1978b, 93; Weber 1972: 49. Market prices result from conflicting interests. Nevertheless, it does make a difference if this struggle is carried out by peaceful means and in the framework of a given order (regulated competition); or if, as in political capitalism, the exploited opportunities are of a "purely irrational-speculative character"; or further, if the pursuit of profit makes use of means of violence and thus collects booty, "either in an actual war or by the fiscal plunder of subject peoples over a long period." For the quotes, see Weber 1978c: 336; Weber 1921, I: 7. Further, cf. Weber 1978b: 38; Weber 1972: 20.

117. Weber 1978b: 165–66; Weber 1972: 96.

118. Weber 1978c: 338; Weber 1921, I: 9. Further, Weber 1961: 233–34; Weber 1923: 270–71; with the differentiation of the economic, political, and status-group aspects of the concept of the bourgeoisie (*Bürgertum*). On the problems involved with this concept and its historical semantics, cf. Kocka 1987, and esp. the essays by Jürgen Kocka, M. Rainer Lepsius, and Hans-Ulrich Wehler.

119. One passage of the "Conceptual Introduction" to the *General Economic History* reads: "For this reason, economic history also has to come to terms with elements of a noneconomic nature. These include: magical and religious aspects, that is, the pursuit of salvational goods; political ones, that is, the pursuit of power; status-group interests, that is, the pursuit of honor." Furthermore, "Finally, we must emphasize that economic history (and especially the history of 'class struggles') is not, as

the materialist conception of history would want us to believe, identical with the history of culture as a whole. The latter is not merely a function of the former; instead, economic history provides only a base, without knowledge of which, however, it is unimaginable to fruitfully research any of the other major areas of culture" (Weber 1923: 16–17) (unfortunately, the entire "Conceptual Introduction" was not translated in the English version of the *General Economic History*).

120. For the quotes see Weber 1958b: 26; Weber 1921, 1: 12. See also Weber 1961, chapter 30; Weber 1923, chapter 4, section 9). One could even say that this final chapter in the *General Economic History* proves above all else how consistently Weber maintained the basic position he formulated in 1904–5.

121. For more detail, see Schluchter 1989, chapter 9.

122. Weber 1976: 409; Weber 1924a: 309.

123. Weber 1978b: 1055; Weber 1972: 614.

124. Weber 1976: 411; Weber 1924a: 310–11.

125. Weber 1976: 410; Weber 1924a: 310.

126. This is, incidentally, just further evidence of how mistaken it is to oppose the *General Economic History* to the sociology of religion. The former does not leave out the aspect of religious history; instead, it makes it part of the analysis, connecting it, if only loosely, to the economic and social-historical aspects. The fact that Weber was able to write the studies of Protestantism, "Agrarian Conditions," and "Economic Ethics of the World Religions" one after the other naturally does not indicate, as some Marxist-inspired readers would have it, that Weber fluctuated back and forth between materialism and idealism, but only that he was aware of what a viewpoint is. Here, see the relevant passages in the "Objectivity" essay, esp. Weber 1949: 70–72; Weber 1973: 169–70.

127. Cf. Weber 1976: 258–59; Weber 1924a: 189–90; and for example, Weber 1978b: 1180; Weber 1972: 704.

128. Cf. my efforts in Schluchter 1989, chapter 6.7.

129. Troeltsch 1977: 195.

130. Cf. Weber 1978b: 597; Weber 1972: 360, where Weber compares the relationships between the early and medieval churches to the "state," and explicitly follows Troeltsch, whose analyses had "brilliantly illuminated" this state of affairs. For more on this subject, see the passage in Weber 1978b: 1055–56; Weber 1972: 614–15.

131. Troeltsch 1977: 194.

132. Troeltsch 1977: 195–96.

133. Weber 1978b: 1161; Weber 1972: 690.

134. Weber 1978b: 1056; Weber 1972: 622.

135. Weber 1978b: 1161; Weber 1972: 691.

136. Berman 1983: 91.

137. Here cf. Troeltsch 1977: 195: "By forcing German kingship from its religious ideas of a national church and guiding it to care for the welfare of all of Christendom, universal emperorship once again raised the

papal idea of the universal church into the saddle, and the latter retained in its hand the heritage that half a millennium of national-church interpenetration of church and state, of the spiritual and the social, provided it with." And, on the idea of the universal church, see Troeltsch 1977: 206–7: "[A]gainst this national church, which had its center in the strongest, best-organized, and best-provided-for German church, the idea of the universal church had once again arisen since the tenth century, closely connected to a new wave of the ascetic ideal and a resurgence of the Roman world against the predominance of the German church. Concomitant with this was the resurgence of canon law against national-church law, and of the canonic concept of church property against the autonomous church (*Eigenkirche*)."

138. Troeltsch 1977: 192–93.

139. Weber 1978b: 513; Weber 1972: 312.

140. Cf. Weber 1978b: 1193; Weber 1972: 714. In this passage, Weber expressly reiterates that the coalition reached its zenith twice "in the Carolingian empire and during certain periods in which the Holy Roman Empire attained the height of its power."

141. Weber 1978b: 1193; Weber 1972: 713.

142. Troeltsch 1977: 209. Troeltsch himself says that the first two were finally formulated only by the First Vatican Council (*Vaticanum*). Ludger Honnefelder points out that Troeltsch (and certainly Weber as well) viewed medieval Catholicism from the perspective of neo-Scholastic philosophy and, in the terminology of the First Vatican Council, of something making itself especially (negatively) noticeable in the interpretation of Thomas and in the concept of the corporation (*Anstaltsbegriff*). Cf. Honnefelder 1988.

143. Cf. Weber 1978b: 560; Weber 1972: 339. There are evidently connections between the consolidation of sacramentalism and moderate idolatry (with images as mediators between God and man equated with transitus). This is in any case implied by the analysis of Jean-Claude Schmitt, who follows the discussion of the question of images from the seventh until the thirteenth centuries. Cf. Schmitt 1988. The first consistent theological justification of the image as a mediator occurs in Scholasticism. The heretic movements were not only antisacramental, they were also iconoclastic.

144. Weber 1978b: 562; Weber 1972: 340.

145. Weber 1978b: 562; Weber 1972: 340. Weber formulates the specific standpoint of the Catholic Church since Gregory VII in the following way: "In this theory, all human beings are capable of finding salvation if they but obey God's requirements enough for the accession of grace distributed by the church to suffice for their attainment of salvation. The level of personal ethical accomplishment must therefore be made compatible with average human qualifications, and this in practice means that it will be set quite low. Whoever can achieve more in the ethical

sphere, that is, the religious virtuoso, may thereby, in addition to insuring his own salvation, accumulate good works for the credit of the institution, which will then distribute them to those in need of good works." Weber 1978b: 560; Weber 1972: 339.

146. Cf. here also Schluchter 1989, chapter 11.

147. Weber observes that in the institution of grace, regardless of whether it is conceived in magical or ethical-soteriological terms, the compulsion is lost "to attain the *certitudo salutis* (certainty to be saved) by one's own powers, and so this category, which has such significant ethical consequences, recedes in importance" (Weber 1978b: 561; Weber 1972: 339). Troeltsch writes: "The atmosphere of status-group stratification and the organic way of thought are completely unacquainted with the unity of the 'ideal of perfection,' as is required by Protestant or modern individualism" (Troeltsch 1977: 232).

148. Weber 1978b: 598; Weber 1972: 360.

149. Here see Schluchter 1981: 172–74. Weber formulates this in Weber 1978b: 1174; Weber 1972: 708, in the following way: "Ideally at least, Occidental Christianity was also a unified polity, and this had certain practical consequences." Here one sees that it is justified to speak of a unified culture in the sense discussed above.

150. Cf. Weber 1978b: 1166–67; Weber 1972: 694–95; and Schluchter 1989, chapter 6.7.

151. As a basic reference here, see Grundmann 1970, esp. chapter 1. See also Richter 1975 and Rosenwein 1988.

152. Cf. Troeltsch 1977: 230ff. He treats this in terms of the ecclesiastization of monasticism. Rosenwein 1988 emphasizes, however, that given the variety of monastic reform movements and given the fact that Cluny was ready to work with any power in order to further disseminate its movement, one cannot speak of the instrumentalization of monasticism for the purposes of hierocratic rule (*hierokratische Lebensbeherrschung*) in such a general manner.

153. Weber 1978b: 1168; Weber 1972: 695. On the linkage of priesthood and monasticism, cf. the schema in Berman 1983: 210–11.

154. Weber 1978b: 1167; Weber 1972: 694.

155. Weber 1978b: 1167; Weber 1972: 694.

156. Weber 1978b: 1170; Weber 1972: 697.

157. On this distinction, see Parsons 1967, chapter 13, esp. 429–30.

158. For a general background here, see Luhmann 1964; Schluchter 1985a: 163–76; and Schluchter 1987b. Interestingly, Weber views the procedure by inquisition, for example, as a rationalization of the trial procedure that pointed the way for secular criminal justice: "A theocratic administration of justice can no more leave the discovery of the truth to the arbitrary discretion of the litigants than it can the expiation of wrong. It has to operate ex officio and to create a system of evidence which appears to offer the optimal possibilities of establishing the facts. Canon law

thus developed in the Western world the procedure of inquisition, which was subsequently taken over by secular criminal justice" (Weber 1978b: 830; Weber 1972: 481).

159. Weber 1978b: 1204–05; Weber 1972: 722. Weber states that this generally holds for "every church during its vigorous periods" (Weber 1978b: 1204; Weber 1972: 722).

160. Troeltsch 1977: 219. He generally draws attention to the connection between the consolidation of sacramentalism and the process of legalization.

161. Weber 1978b: 116; Weber 1972: 693. This can be understood as a variation of that ambivalence between tolerance toward within and absolutist claims toward without, which Reinhard Bendix analyzes on the basis of the example of early Christianity. Cf. Bendix 1988.

162. According to Weber, one way Christianity is characterized in comparison to other religions is by the fact that as a consequence of "the increasing penetration of intellectualism and the growing dispute surrounding it, it produced an unexampled mass of official and binding rational dogmas, a theological faith" (Weber 1978b: 564; Weber 1972: 341).

163. Cf. Weber 1978b: 566–67; Weber 1972: 343.

164. Weber 1978b: 566; Weber 1972: 342.

165. Weber makes reference to Augustine, for whom the personal acceptance of intellectual propositions is at best the lowest stage of faith. Cf. Weber 1978b: 566; Weber 1972: 342. On the struggle between faith and knowledge in Christianity in general, see Schluchter 1989, chapter 6.2. The interpretation of the maxim of faith in the absurd is part of this context.

166. Grundmann 1970: 6.

167. Grundmann 1970: 23. This passage also cites the other reasons why the church fought against such movements.

168. Here, see also the critical essays by Selge 1988 and Bynum 1988. Further, see Lerner 1988.

169. It is generally known that Weber built his never completed sociology of music around this thesis. For an interpretation of the latter, see Schluchter 1989, chapter 4.1.

170. Weber 1978b: 1169; Weber 1972: 696. On parallels between discipline in the monastery and the factory, see Treiber and Steinert 1980. On parallels between monastic and military discipline, see Weber 1978b: 1153; Weber 1972: 684.

171. Weber 1978b: 1169; Weber 1972: 704.

172. Weber 1978b: 561; Weber 1972: 339.

173. Weber 1978b: 1170; Weber 1972: 705.

174. Weber 1978b: 561; Weber 1972: 339. The state of affairs that Weber observed was put by Troeltsch in the following way: "It is the infinitely important sacrament of penance, artfully linked to a portion of the other sacraments as their precondition, that is the support of the spiritual domination of the world. From it arises the entire Christian ethic of the

church in exploring and advising the conscience, wiping away sins, and directing the sinner toward making amends and giving service. It leads to the unification of all ethical problems and antagonisms by means of the authority of the church, which in this way removes the responsibility for this unity in the performance of life from the individual and takes it upon itself. By means of this in turn, the ethics of the church change from mere theory to a practical force, which advises, punishes, and frees of sin large and small, noble and petty consciences, and above all, leads the latter toward the realization of the true value of life, the saving of the soul from a sinful world" (Troeltsch 1977: 220; see also Weber 1958b: 116–25; Weber 1921, 1: 113–24). Thus, it is not as if Troeltsch, and in this regard Weber is in agreement with him, wanted to deny the constant monitoring of conduct connected with the practice of the confessional, especially not in those cases where it is linked to a "specialized method of the confession of sin" (Weber 1978b: 561: Weber 1972: 339). Weber in particular, however, advanced the thesis that an expiation of sin tied to a general, or even more, to a collective confession of sin annuls the disciplining power of continuous monitoring via confessional, and that generally, periodic expiation relieves the conscience, so that ultimately, only in the absence of all institutional and sacramental grace does the development of an ethically rational mode of conduct, an inner-directed unification, ever take place. In typological terms, the medieval monk finds himself, so to speak, midway between the Catholic laity and ascetic Protestants. Institutional grace remains open to him, but he subjects himself at the same time to the pressure of creating unity in his life that is tied to the idea of proving oneself. On the supervisory effect of the practice of the confessional, see also Hahn 1982. Further, see Hahn 1988. This assessment of (external) sacramental control and (internal) ethical control probably reflects an individualistic (Protestant) bias in Troeltsch and Weber.

175. Weber 1978b: 1170; Weber 1972: 697.

176. Weber 1978b: 714–15; Weber 1972: 429. On this entire complex, one can now see Berman 1983, esp. 215ff.

177. Here, cf. Breuer 1988, who points out that although Weber considers Western feudalism of special significance in the formation of Western culture, he incorrectly dates the "feudal revolution." Breuer, with Georges Duby, places the latter in the eleventh century, and the coming-of-age of this "new" form of domination, connected as it is with a comprehensive structural transformation of the nobility, in the twelfth century. This latter development follows upon the emergence of a strong local stratum of lords with the dissolution of the Carolingian empire in the ninth and tenth centuries. The place of the old economy of villas and corveé labor is now taken by a seigneurial mode of production; the old connection between the warrior nobility and the peasantry is replaced by the division between an economically increasingly indispensable peasantry and the army of knights. Whereas Weber already considered the Carolingian empire to be feudal in character, the results of more recent

research suggest that this empire was actually more of a patrimonial state with feudal elements, with fief-based feudalism first maturing after its dissolution. Cf. also Marc Bloch's suggestion of two phases of feudalism: a first phase following the demise of the Carolingian empire, in which population declines and trade and monetary circulation is weak, and a second phase, from ca. 1050–1230, during which the population grows, and "internal" colonization and the expansion of trade and monetary circulation takes place—in short, where an enormous intensification of commerce and the strong expansion of artisans and merchants in the cities occurs. Cf. Bloch 1961, esp. 69–71. Thus, the "papal revolution" is joined by a "feudal revolution" that has been slightly relocated in time. Together with the "urban revolution," which we will discuss shortly, they represent the decisive components of the first transformation. On Weber's analysis of feudalism, cf. also Poggi 1988 and Speer 1978.

178. Weber 1978b: 1070; Weber 1972: 625.

179. Weber 1978b: 255; Weber 1972: 148. Cf. also Weber 1978b: 1069; Weber 1972: 623, where the Western knight's conduct is defined "by the feudal concept of honor and this in turn by the notion of vassalic fealty; this was the only type of status honor conditioned on the one hand by a consistent, internalized ethos and on the other by an external relationship to the lord." Thus, for Weber, the mode of conduct of the Western knight is based upon a self-directed personality, even though this self-direction is without religious foundation.

180. Weber 1978b: 1074; Weber 1972: 628.

181. Weber 1978b: 1072; Weber 1972: 627.

182. Weber 1978b: 1081; Weber 1972: 633.

183. The fully developed feudal relationship encompasses the following elements: the (temporally limited) granting of the powers and rights in exchange for military and/or administrative services; the purely personal grant; the grant on the strength of a contract, and thus between free men, involving not an ordinary business contract but a fraternization of two parties with unequal rights but mutual obligations of loyalty; and the grant that is premised upon and at the same time supports a mode of conduct that is specifically knightly in character. Here, cf. Weber 1978b: 255; Weber 1972: 148. Variations result from the nature of the "object" of the rights granted: domains, slaves, and serfs; taxes and contributions; or judiciary and military powers, which as a rule are connected with rule over free men.

184. Weber believes that the first of these two forms of curtailment of the free right of contract "took place relatively early in the Middle Ages; the second, later on" (Weber 1978b: 256; Weber 1972: 149).

185. Weber 1978b: 1082; Weber 1972: 633–34.

186. Weber 1978b: 472; Weber 1972: 288.

187. On the characterization of the feudal ethic, see esp. Weber 1978b: 1104–9; Weber 1972: 650–53.

188. For this reason, Weber expressly states that neither the feudal as-

sociation nor the *Ständestaat* are "indispensable intermediate links in the development from patrimonialism to bureaucracy" (Weber 1978b: 1087; Weber 1972: 637).

189. Here, cf. the list Weber composes in Weber 1978b: 258; Weber 1972: 150.

190. Weber 1978c: 333; Weber 1921, 1: 3. Cf. also Weber 1978b: 259, 1086–87; Weber 1972: 151, 636–38.

191. The unique dynamics connected to a structural pluralism are also underscored by Shmuel N. Eisenstadt. See Eisenstadt 1988.

192. On the urban revolution, which she dates from the eleventh until the fourteenth century, cf. Reyerson 1988.

193. If one follows Brian Stock, there is yet a fourth revolution, that of communication, which is connected to the increasing use of writing. With the revival of the monetary and market economy, ever more institutions arise that are dependent upon written communication. Naturally, one has to ask to what extent this revolution is part of the others, for example, certain legal developments. Cf. Stock 1983, 1988.

194. Weber 1978b: 829; Weber 1972: 480.

195. Weber 1978b: 259; Weber 1972: 151. This is similarly found in Weber 1978b: 240–41; Weber 1972: 139.

196. Weber 1978b: 1323; Weber 1972: 788.

197. Weber 1978b: 1339; Weber 1972: 796.

198. Weber 1978b: 1239; Weber 1972: 742.

199. Here, cf. the discussion of the "overall situation of the medieval cities" at the zenith of urban autonomy in Weber 1978b: 1323–35; Weber 1972: 788–96. Weber expressly emphasizes that medieval cities demonstrate marked structural differences and are extraordinarily varied in form.

200. Weber 1978b: 1240; Weber 1972: 743.

201. Weber 1978b: 1353; Weber 1972: 805. Weber remarks that this is something unknown in the medieval city. The latter is primarily economically oriented, unlike the primarily politically oriented city of antiquity.

202. Weber 1978b: 1243; Weber 1972: 745.

203. Here, cf. also Chapter 3.

204. As is known, Weber subdivided medieval cities into the southern European coastal and inland cities on the one hand and the northern European cities on the other. Among the latter he then distinguished between continental coastal and inland cities on the one hand and English cities on the other. Here, cf. also Weber 1961, part 4, chapter 28; Weber 1923, chap. 4, section 7. Weber's classification reads: (1) the Oriental city (the example of Mecca) versus the Western, Mediterranean city; (2) within the latter, the contrast between the city of antiquity (with the examples of the Greek cities and Rome) and the medieval city; (3) within the latter, the southern European city (with the examples of Venice and Genoa as coastal cities and Milan as an inland city) versus the English cities. The

English cities were separated from the rest because they were lacking the "notion of the commune as a territorial corporate body." See Weber 1978b: 1279; Weber 1972: 764.

205. In Weber 1961: 260; Weber 1923: 302; it is put succinctly: "Capitalism in the West was born in the industrial towns of the interior, not in the cities which were centers of sea trade."

206. Weber 1978b: 1351; Weber 1972: 803–4.

207. Weber 1978b: 1351–52; Weber 1972: 804.

208. Cf. Weber 1978b: 1302; Weber 1972: 776; where Weber writes: "The Italian *popolo* was not only an economic category, but also a political one. It was a separate political community within the urban commune, with its own officials, its own finances, and its own military organization. In the truest sense of the word it was a 'state within the state' —the first deliberately nonlegitimate and revolutionary political association." Admittedly, according to Weber, the development of Italian medieval cities follows a cycle that contrasts somewhat to that of the North. See Weber 1978b: 1322; Weber 1972: 788 and the interesting study by Breuer (1984). The development of Cologne, which is relevant here, starts with the rebellion against the archbishop in 1074 and leads to an autonomous city government and city law (*Stadtrecht*) of 1106.

209. Weber 1978b: 1259; Weber 1972: 755.

210. Weber 1978b: 1352; Weber 1972: 804.

211. Weber 1978b: 1323; Weber 1972: 788.

212. Cf. Weber 1978b: 1350–51; Weber 1972: 803, where the urban democracies of antiquity and the Middle Ages are contrasted.

213. Weber 1978b: 1351; Weber 1972: 804.

214. Weber 1978b: 1108; Weber 1972: 653.

215. Cf. the second epigraph to this Chapter. Further, cf. Weber 1961: 238; Weber 1923: 277, and the misleading, or at the very least, abridged account in Weber 1978b: 1243; Weber 1972: 745. On the universalism connected to this process and on the redefining of the stranger (*Fremde*) as the person of a different faith in early Christian development, cf. Bendix 1988.

216. Weber 1978b: 1243–48; Weber 1972: 745–48.

217. Weber 1978b: 1244; Weber 1972: 746.

218. Weber 1978b: 1247; Weber 1972: 747.

219. On the problems of this construct, which is at the basis of Weber's concept of the pariah, cf. Schluchter 1989, chapter 5.5.

220. Apart from the Jews, Weber also mentions the Lombards (and southerners of every provenance) and Syrians. Cf. Weber 1961: 166; Weber 1923: 193, where the causes of the first wave of anti-Semitism are also discussed.

221. Weber 1961: 263–64; Weber 1923: 305–6.

222. Here, cf. also Little 1988. Cf. also his book on the rise of a specifically urban form of spirituality out of the crisis of medieval urban culture, Little 1978, esp. part 4.

223. Weber 1978b: 1347; Weber 1972: 801.

224. Weber 1978b: 1362; Weber 1972: 811.

225. Weber emphasizes early the role of free domestic industry and of the free putting-out system in the genesis of the modern capitalist business establishment. As early as in "Agrarian Sociology" (Weber 1976: 44; Weber 1924a: 8), Weber disputed Eduard Meyer's thesis that one could simply not imagine how modern economic life in antiquity was. One part of Weber's argument is that there is no evidence for "the existence in antiquity even of 'cottage industry,' such as appeared in Europe as early as the thirteenth century, based on letting out production on contract. This system represents an advance on the simple exploitation of the producer by an experienced merchant, a phenomenon of course known even in antiquity." In his view, apparently, this form of production is of major developmental importance. Cf. also Weber 1978a: 1128; Weber 1978d: 323–24; and further, Weber 1978b: 1321, 148; Weber 1972: 73, 85. On the relationship between the guild system and the free putting-out system, cf. Weber 1961, chapter 11; Weber 1923, chapter 2, section 5. What is important is that Weber sees neither the putting-out system nor manufacturing nor the factory system (a distinction he considers artificial) arising on the basis of or at the cost of the crafts. Cf. Weber 1961: 136; Weber 1923: 157–58. The establishment of factories presupposed the mechanization of the production process, which was given its impetus neither by the free urban crafts nor by free urban domestic industry. Mining was its real forerunner. Incidentally, nowhere in his discussions of the history of production does Weber follow the Marxian logic of development: simple cooperation, manufacture, the factory. On this aspect of Weber's approach, cf. also the important study by Jakob Strieder (Strieder 1914), which includes a detailed investigation of the role of mining. Cf. also Strieder 1904, with its attack on Sombart's thesis of ground-rent-based accumulation. Strieder's motif reads: At the beginning there was trade!

226. Here, cf. the *Neue Freie Presse*, October 26, 1917, 10. This expansion of the typology is corroborated in the second version of *Economy and Society*. Cf. Weber 1978b: 266–67; Weber 1972: 155–56, "The Antiauthoritarian Reinterpretation of Charisma" ("Die herrschaftsfremde Umdeutung des Charisma"). Cf. further Schluchter 1989, chapters 6.6, 12.

227. Cf. Weber 1961: 252; Weber 1923: 292.

228. Here, cf. Weber 1961, chapter 17; Weber 1923, chapter 3, section 4; the quotation is from Weber 1961: 171; Weber 1923: 199. Weber still bases his analysis in part on his dissertation.

229. Cf. Weber 1961: 249–58; Weber 1923: 293–300.

230. Here, cf. Weber 1961: 229–33; Weber 1923: 265–70. Weber, however, disputes Sombart's thesis that the uniform mass requirements of war belong to the crucial historical preconditions of capitalism. He does this for the simple reason that war requirements were increasingly satisfied under the state's own direction. Neither population growth nor the

importation of precious metals played crucial roles (Weber 1961: 258–59; Weber 1923: 300–301). The degree of exploitation certainly did, however, since it decisively influences the purchasing power of the masses. The development from the feudal association to the modern patrimonial state via the *Ständestaat* was naturally linked to a structural transformation of the nobility. Here, see esp. Elias 1969, which describes the transformation of a knightly nobility into a court nobility, above all in terms of the French example. On the history of mentalities, which Elias in part depicts in terms of the sequence of concepts of courtesy, civility, and civilization, see also Becker 1988.

231. Weber 1961: 260; Weber 1923: 302.

232. Weber 1978d: 166.

233. Weber 1978c: 170; Weber 1921, 1: 203.

234. Weber often uses the concept of "ethos" in place of the concept of "ethic" in the second version of the *Protestant Ethic*, inasmuch as what is involved is practiced ethics, moral conduct.

235. It is true that Weber had terminological reservations against the expression "psychology" when used to describe the analysis of those components that can be understood according to the means-ends schema and thus in a pragmatic way. These reservations do not imply, however, that he lacked a "psychology" of his own, although of course it differed from both experimental psychology and the "psychology of drives." Karl Jaspers termed it a psychology of worldviews (*Weltanschauungspsychologie*). As yet, no thorough investigation has been made of Weber's view on psychology. On his terminological reservations, cf. Weber 1978d: 184–86.

236. A careful examination of the productiveness of experimental psychology such as that advocated by Ernest Kraepelin and his school in clarifying questions of cultural science played an important role in this context. Weber, however, ultimately assessed this school as involving no more than a fashionable "characterology." The decisive works of Weber usually overlooked in this context are those concerning the selection and adjustment of the labor force of private industry and the psychophysics of industrial labor. See Weber 1924b: 1–60, and 61–255, respectively. These are passages central to Weber's effort to make his distinctions precise between pragmatic and psychological understanding and between observational and interpretive explanation, which, in the third phase of his work, turned into primary elements of the method of interpretive sociology. Karl Jaspers's study of psychopathology was also of significance for Weber; it arose out of intimate intellectual exchange with Weber, and its conclusions were "sanctioned" by the latter. On the fashionable term "characterological" see Weber 1924b: 395.

237. Weber 1958b: 65; Weber 1921, 1: 49.

238. Weber 1978d: 165.

239. Weber 1978d: 165. Weber's critique of both the psychology of classical economics and the older historical school of economics is found in the essay on Roscher and Knies (Weber 1975). It can at the same time

be interpreted as a critique of utilitarian social theories (see Weber 1973: 30ff.). The case against deductive and inductive psychological reductionism in the cultural sciences is presented above all in the essay on objectivity (e.g., Weber 1949: 87–89; Weber 1973: 187–89). This passage also includes Weber's definition of the relationship of institution and motive (Weber 1949: 88–89; Weber 1973: 189).

240. Cf. e.g., Weber 1978d: 165.

241. This may appear to sound cynical, at least for the case of workers. Did they have any choice other than adjusting to external necessity? Nonetheless, Weber expressly says, "Capitalism in the period of its emergence needed workers who would be available for economic use on grounds of conscience. Today capitalism is in the saddle and can compel their labor without rewards in the next world" (Weber 1978c: 168 n. 2; Weber 1921, 1: 201 n.). External compulsion is certainly a powerful educational tool. It only forms a person "from without," however, as does any form of compulsion. According to Weber, the masses also had to be trained to produce surpluses, and in a traditional milieu, external necessity and external compulsion alone do not suffice for this! On the distinction of the two types of action and their theoretical background, see Chapter 2.

242. Weber 1958a: 280; Weber 1921, 1: 252.

243. Weber 1958b: 73–75; Weber 1921, 1: 56–60. Weber supplemented the original version in this passage with a reference to *turpitudo* in Thomas Aquinas. In the first version, there was already a reference to Anthony of Florence and to the fact that even this monastic ethic, which went the furthest within the Catholic economic ethic in recognizing the capitalist pursuit of profit, ultimately did not get beyond tolerating acquisition as an end in itself.

244. Weber 1958b: 53; Weber 1921, 1: 35–36.

245. *Corpus Iuris Canonici, Decretum Gratiani,* Pars I c. ii. Dist. lxxxviii. In Weber 1961: 262; Weber 1923: 305, the complete maxim is reproduced: Homo mercator vix aut numquam potest Deo placere (The merchant can hardly or never please God).

246. Weber 1978b: 1190–91; Weber 1972: 720.

247. Here cf. Weber 1978b: 1188–91; Weber 1972: 710–12; the quote is found in Weber 1978b: 1190; Weber 1972: 712. On the ban on taking interest, see also Nelson 1969. On the controversial discussion involving the prohibition of usury, the differing positions of orthodox and heterodox tendencies on it, and a critique of the positions of Weber and Nelson, see Reyerson 1988. Of course, what is usually overlooked in the discussion is that the prohibition of usury per se played a completely peripheral role in Weber's argument. On the problematic as a whole, see also Little 1978, esp. part 3.

248. Weber 1978d: 168; Weber 1958b: 71–72; Weber 1921, 1: 55.

249. Weber 1958b: 73; Weber 1921, 1: 56.

250. On this, cf. also Weber 1958b: 72–73; Weber 1921: 1: 55–56.

251. It is striking that Durkheim also saw a connection between utilitarianism and pragmatism. Cf. esp. his lecture on pragmatism and sociology in Durkheim 1987, esp. 121ff.

252. Here, cf. Weber 1958b, 232 n. 66; Weber 1921, 1: 112 n., which also includes the critique of William James. For more detail, see Chapter 2.

253. Weber 1978c: 162 n. 1; Weber 1921, 1: 193 n.

254. Weber 1958b: 68–69; Weber 1921, 1: 53.

255. Cf. Weber 1978b: 611–23; Weber 1972: 367–74, where Jews, Catholics, and Puritans are compared against the backdrop of Sombart's theses. Julius Guttmann's critique of Sombart (Guttmann 1913) contributed to Weber's argument.

256. Brentano 1916: 153.

257. For example, Brentano sees capitalism penetrating the feudal system by means of the war of aggression. The Crusades are for him a case of the amalgamation of capitalism and the system of war, and the Fourth Crusade he regarded as a "true orgy of modern capitalism." Cf. Brentano 1916: 42.

258. Incidentally, Weber in no way disputed that the pagan mentality Brentano cites had been of importance for the psychic side of modern economic development; it simply did not belong in an analysis of the influence of religious ethics on conduct. Moreover, the former had different effects from the latter: "It was not the mode of conduct (of the rising bourgeoisie) that was influenced by this other mentality, but the policy of statesmen and princes; and these two partly, but by no means always, convergent lines of development should, for purposes of analysis, be kept perfectly distinct" (Weber 1958b: 198 n. 12; Weber 1921, 1: 41 n.). In the original plan for building upon the results of the Protestantism studies, Weber had also planned to treat these interrelationships. Cf. Weber 1958b: 183; Weber 1921, 1: 205.

259. Cf. Sombart 1911a: 293. "Renewed" reflections because the first edition of his *Modern Capitalism* (cf. Sombart 1902a, 1902b) had already contained thoughts on this. The most important "intermediate results" are contained in Sombart 1911a and 1913. These works were stimulated not least of all by Weber's studies.

260. Cf. Sombart 1913: 136ff., 153ff. and chapters 17–22. In his depiction of the Catholic ethic, Sombart bases his work on that of Troeltsch and on the small book (dissertation) by Franz Keller (Keller 1912), an apologetic writing from a Catholic viewpoint, upon which Weber passed stern judgment. Cf. Weber 1958b: 191 n. 19, 200 n. 29; Weber 1921, 1: 27 n. 2, 56 n. 1.

261. Sombart 1913: 338: "Just as little as Puritanism did Judaism teach anything different from Thomism in the points essential to us."

262. Sombart 1913: 333.

263. This is not to say that Weber did not approach Sombart's work with great sympathy. Weber viewed Sombart, like Ernst Troeltsch, as a

comrade fighting for a common cause, in spite of their many substantive differences. For example, about Sombart's essay on the capitalist entrepreneur (Sombart 1909), with which Sombart began to revise the presentation he made in Sombart 1902a, 1902b (Sombart 1909: 752) of the genesis of the capitalist spirit, Weber states that "the great agreement, especially in methods, in all essential points, releases [me] from the duty to comment at length" (Weber 1978d: 170). In the second version of the *Protestant Ethic*, Weber sought to defend Sombart against Brentano's criticisms. Although Weber considered the latter well founded in many points, he found Brentano very unfair in his general presentation (cf. Weber 1958b: 187 n.; Weber 1921, 1: 18 n.).

264. Weber 1978c: 334 n. 1; Weber 1921, 1: 5 n.

265. Weber 1958b: 57; Weber 1921, 1: 42–43.

266. Cf. Sombart 1913: 355. Sombart claims that in their treatment of aliens the Jews were the first to break with morally based restraint and thus paved the way for the ruthless acquisitiveness characterizing advanced capitalism (cf. Sombart 340ff.). He distinguishes between the early-capitalist and the advanced-capitalist type of entrepreneur, between the old-style and the new-style bourgeois. Guttmann contests the correctness of Sombart's interpretation of the rights of aliens in Jewish law; he claims that whereas substantive law and economic solidarity holds for relations among Jews, relations with outsiders were governed by formal law and formal legality. In no way were these latter relations predominated by ruthless acquisitiveness. See Guttmann 1913: 197. Weber's distinction between in-group and out-group morals among Jews is closer to Guttmann's than to Sombart's view. Moreover, "double standards in business" are not limited to Jews, in Weber's view, but are instead a component of all traditional economic life.

267. For example, by pointing to the dissemination of individual writings.

268. Weber 1958b: 196; Weber 1921, 1: 39 n.

269. Weber 1958b: 197 n.; Weber 1921, 1: 40 n.

270. For more detail, see Schluchter 1989, chapter 4.1.

271. It is an interesting question whether Weber's thesis applies only to doctrines of prudence or whether it also holds for nonreligious ethics. Without a doubt he considers the psychological levers of nonreligious ethics to be less effective than those of religious ethics because in the former case, the "desire for and promise of salvation" is, so to speak, cognitively weakened. Here, see Chapter 2.

272. The manner in which Clifford Geertz defines religion and depicts the components of this definition comes relatively close to this concept of religious practice: "(1) a system of symbols which act to (2) establish powerful, pervasive, and long-lasting moods and motivations in men by (3) formulating conceptions of a general order of existence and (4) clothing these conceptions with such an aura of factuality that (5) the moods and motivations seem uniquely realistic" (Geertz 1973: 90).

273. Weber 1958b: 201; Weber 1921, 1: 57 n.

274. Weber 1978b: 614; Weber 1972: 369.

275. Weber 1978c: 152; Weber 1921, 1: 181.

276. Weber 1952: 4; Weber 1921, 3: 6.

277. Weber 1978c: 169; Weber 1921, 1: 202.

278. On this, cf. Weber 1961: 261–67; Weber 1923: 303–10. Here, too, this text merely reiterates something that can be found in other parts of Weber's work.

279. Weber 1978b: 613; Weber 1972: 369. Weber cited the following specifically economic achievements of Jewry in the Middle Ages and the modern age: "[M]oneylending, from pawnbroking to the financing of great states; certain types of commodity business, particularly retailing, peddling, and produce trade of a distinctively rural type; certain branches of wholesale business; and trading in securities, above all the brokerage of stocks. . . . [Furthermore], money-changing; money-forwarding or check-cashing, which normally accompanies money-changing; the financing of state agencies, wars, and the establishment of colonial enterprises; tax-farming; banking; credit; and the floating of bond issues" (Weber 1978b: 612–13; Weber 1972: 368).

280. Weber 1978b: 613; Weber 1972: 369.

281. These are Julius Guttmann's words (Guttmann 1913: 197).

282. Weber 1978b: 616; Weber 1972: 370.

283. Guttmann 1913: 189–90.

284. Cf. Weber 1958b: 118–20, 235 n. 79; Weber 1921: 1: 116–18, 117 n. 2; the latter reference is his reply to Brentano.

285. Weber 1958b: 203n; Weber 1921: 1: 58 n.

286. Weber 1958b: 116; Weber 1921, 1: 113–14.

287. As Ernst Troeltsch puts it (Troeltsch 1977: 615). This is similar in substance to Weber. Here cf. Chapter 3, where the Islamic and Calvinist conceptions of predestination are compared. Weber had already emphasized in the first version of the *Protestant Ethic* that the concept of the proof of one's salvation is more important than that of predestination (indeed, radicalization to practically the same extent can occur even without the latter).

288. Out of the long series of reconstruction efforts, let us mention two of the most recent: Poggi 1983 and Marshall 1982; out of the even longer series of historically oriented examinations, let us mention Marshall 1980, and above all, Otsuka 1982 and Lehmann and Roth 1993. Cf. also Lehmann 1988. An interesting effort at explaining the English Revolution by combining Weber's theory of patrimonialism with a Marx-inspired theory of manufacturing for a social formation in transition is found in Gould 1987.

289. Cf. Weber 1958b: 104; Weber 1921, 1: 93.

290. Weber 1958b: 106; Weber 1921, 1: 97; this passage was added to the second version.

291. Weber 1958a: 320; Weber 1921, 1: 234.

292. Weber 1958b: 149; Weber 1921, 1: 158; this passage was added to the second version.

293. Weber 1958b: 104; Weber 1921, 1: 93.

294. Weber 1958b: 105; Weber 1921, 1: 95. The context makes it unambiguously clear that Weber envisions a new historical form of individualism, in spite of his skepticism vis-à-vis such a conception. Here cf. also the analysis of Louis Dumont (Dumont 1985), which closely follows Troeltsch.

295. This concept also forms the basis of the two lectures on "Science as a Vocation" and "Politics as a Vocation" (see Weber 1958a: 77–156; and Chapter 1).

296. Weber 1978c: 170; Weber 1921, 1: 203.

297. Weber 1978d: 171.

298. Weber 1958b: 166; Weber 1921, 1: 183.

299. Weber 1961: 270; Weber 1923: 315.

300. Sombart 1913: 236.

301. Sombart 1913: 250.

302. Weber 1978c: 170; Weber 1921, 1: 203.

303. For greater detail, see Schluchter 1985a, introduction.

304. Weber 1958a: 116; Weber 1971: 546.

305. Cf. Weber 1958b: 174; Weber 1921, 1: 195–96.

306. Weber 1958b: 170; Weber 1921, 1: 189.

307. Weber 1958a: 117; Weber 1971: 548. Weber says this of politicians who are not serving a cause they believe in.

308. Weber's contemporary diagnosis is of course more complex and includes an institutional aspect as well as this psychic one. The key to the analysis of mechanized petrifaction is the process of bureaucratization that prefaces all suborders of the overall configuration of order in the age of advanced capitalism. For more detail here, cf. Schluchter 1975, esp. the introduction and conclusion; and Schluchter 1989, chapters 9, 10. On the normative foundations of Weber's reaction to the danger of the loss of meaning and freedom under the conditions of advanced capitalism, see chapter 2 above and Schluchter 1989, chapter 8. See also Henrich, Offe and Schluchter 1988.

309. Cf. Collins 1986: 28. The *General Economic History* was not Weber's last word on capitalism. He did not downgrade the importance of so-called ideal factors vis-à-vis institutional ones in his late work, and he did not overlook the importance of the Middle Ages for the rise of modern capitalism.

« *Epilogue* »

1. This will be done in my forthcoming book *Handlung, Ordnung und Kultur. Studien zur Grundlegung der verstehenden Soziologie* (Action, order, and culture: Studies in the foundation of interpretive sociology).

Bibliography

Albert, Hans. 1978. *Traktat über rationale Praxis*. Tübingen: J. C. B. Mohr (Paul Siebeck).

Alexander, Jeffrey. 1982/83. *Theoretical Logic in Sociology*. 4 vols. Berkeley: University of California Press.

Anderson, Perry. 1980 [1974]. *Lineages of the Absolutist State*. London: Verso Editions.

Arendt, Hannah, and Karl Jaspers. 1985. *Briefwechsel 1926–1969*. L. Köhler and H. Saner, eds. Munich: Piper.

Baum, Rainer C. 1976. "Part IV: Generalized Media in Action." Introduction. In Jan J. Loubser, R. C. Baum, A. Effrat, and V. Meyer Lidz, eds., *Explorations in General Theory in Social Science: Essays in Honor of Talcott Parsons*, 1: 448–69. New York: The Free Press.

Baumgarten, Eduard. 1964. *Max Weber. Werk und Person*. Tübingen: J. C. B. Mohr (Paul Siebeck).

Becker, Carl Heinrich. 1924. *Islamstudien*. Vol. 1. Leipzig: Quelle & Meyer.

Becker, Marvin B. 1988. "Der Umschwung zur Zivilität in Westeuropa vom späten 13. bis zum 16. Jahrhundert. Eine Untersuchung ausgewählter Regionen." In Schluchter 1988b: 498–528.

Behrend, F., ed. 1907. *Der freistudentische Ideenkreis. Programmatische Erklärung*. Munich: Bavaria Verlag.

Beiersdörfer, Kurt. 1986. *Max Weber und Georg Lukács. Über die Beziehung von verstehender Soziologie und Westlichem Marxismus*. Frankfurt: Campus.

Bendix, Reinhard. 1967. "The Protestant Ethic—Revisited." *Comparative Studies in Society and History* 9: 266–73.

———. 1978. *Kings or People*. Berkeley: University of California Press.

———. 1982. *Freiheit und historisches Schicksal. Heidelberger Max Weber-Vorlesungen 1981*. Frankfurt: Suhrkamp.

———. 1984. *Force, Fate, and Freedom: On Historical Sociology.* Berkeley: University of California Press.

———. 1988. "Der Anspruch auf absolute Wahrheit im frühen Christentum." In Schluchter 1988b: 129–64.

———. 1989. "Sociological Reflections on the Early Christian Claim to Absolute Truth." In R. Bendix, *Embattled Reason: Essays on Social Knowledge,* 2: 241–87. New Brunswick, N.J.: Transaction.

Bendix, Reinhard, and Guenther Roth. 1971. *Scholarship and Partisanship: Essays on Max Weber.* Berkeley: University of California Press.

Benjamin, Walter. 1921. "Zur Kritik der Gewalt." *Archiv für Sozialwissenschaft und Sozialpolitik* 47 (3): 809–32.

———. 1977. *Gesammelte Schriften.* R. Tiedemann and H. Schweppenhäuser, eds. Frankfurt: Suhrkamp.

Berman, Harold J. 1983. *Law and Revolution: The Formation of the Western Legal Tradition.* Cambridge, Mass.: Harvard University Press.

Birnbaum, Immanuel. 1963. "Erinnerungen an Max Weber." In König and Winckelmann 1963: 19–21.

———. 1974. *Achtzig Jahre dabei gewesen. Erinnerungen eines Journalisten.* Munich: Süddeutscher Verlag.

———. 1982. "Transcript of an interview with Horst J. Helle." Max-Weber-Archiv, Munich.

Blake, Stephen P. 1979. "The Patrimonial-Bureaucratic Empire of the Mughals." *Journal of Asian Studies* 39 (1): 77–94.

Bloch, Marc. 1961. *Feudal Society.* 2 vols. L. A. Manyon, trans. Chicago: University of Chicago Press.

Bourdieu, Pierre. 1984. *Distinction: A Social Critique of the Judgement of Taste.* R. Nice, trans. Cambridge, Mass.: Harvard University Press.

Brentano, Lujo. 1916. *Die Anfänge des modernen Kapitalismus.* Munich: Verlag der K. B. Akademie der Wissenschaften.

Breuer, Stefan. 1984. "Blockierte Rationalisierung. Max Weber und die italienische Stadt des Mittelalters." *Archiv für Kulturgeschichte* 66: 47–85.

———. 1988. "Der okzidentale Feudalismus in Max Webers Gesellschaftsgeschichte." In Schluchter 1988b: 437–75.

Breuer, Stefan, and Hubert Treiber, eds. 1984. *Zur Rechtssoziologie Max Webers. Interpretation, Kritik, Weiterentwicklung.* Opladen: Westdeutscher Verlag.

Brubaker, Rogers. 1984. *The Limits of Rationality: An Essay on the Social and Moral Thought of Max Weber.* London: Allen & Unwin.

Brugger, Winfried. 1980. *Menschenrechtsethos und Verantwortungspolitik. Max Webers Beitrag zur Analyse und Begründung der Menschenrechte.* Freiburg: Albers.

Bubner, Rüdiger. 1982. *Handlung, Sprache und Vernunft. Grundbegriffe praktischer Philosophie.* Frankfurt: Suhrkamp.

———. 1984. *Geschichtsprozesse und Handlungsnormen. Untersuchungen zur praktischen Philosophie.* Frankfurt: Suhrkamp.

Bücher, Karl. 1909. "Gewerbe." In J. Conrad, L. Elster, W. Lexis, E. Loening, eds., *Handwörterbuch der Staatswissenschaften* 4: 847–80. Jena: G. Fischer.

———. 1914. "Volkswirtschaftliche Entwicklungsstufen." In *Grundriss der Sozialökonomik*. Part 1: Wirtschaft und Wirtschaftswissenschaft, 1–18. Tübingen: J. C. B. Mohr (Paul Siebeck).

———. 1922. *Die Entstehung der Volkswirtschaft*. 16th ed. Vol. 1. Tübingen: J. C. B. Mohr (Paul Siebeck).

Bynum, Caroline Walker. 1987. *Holy Feast and Holy Fast: The Religious Significance of Food to Medieval Women*. Berkeley: University of California Press.

———. 1988. "Mystik und Askese im Leben mittelalterlicher Frauen. Einige Bemerkungen zu den Typologien von Max Weber und Ernst Troeltsch." In Schluchter 1988b: 355–82.

Chon, Song-U. 1985. *Max Webers Stadtkonzeption. Eine Studie zur Entwicklung des okzidentalen Bürgertums*. Göttingen: Edition Herodot.

Collins, Randall. 1986. *Weberian Sociological Theory*. Cambridge, Eng.: Cambridge University Press.

Crone, Patricia. 1980. *Slaves on Horses: The Evolution of the Islamic Polity*. Cambridge, Eng.: Cambridge University Press.

Curtius, Ernst Robert. 1919. "Max Weber über 'Wissenschaft als Beruf.'" *Die Arbeitsgemeinschaft* 1 (2): 197–203.

Deutsche Akademische Freischar. 1913. *Freideutsche Jugend. Zur Jahrhundertfeier auf dem Hohen Meißner*. Jena: Eugen Diederichs.

Diederichs, Eugen. N.d. *Leben und Werk. Ausgewählte Briefe und Aufzeichnungen*. Lulu von Strauss und Torney-Diederichs, ed. Jena: Eugen Diederichs.

Duchrow, Ulrich. 1983. *Christenheit und Weltverantwortung. Traditionsgeschichte und systematische Struktur der Zweireichelehre*. 2nd ed. Stuttgart: Klett.

Dumont, Louis. 1985. "A Modified View of Our Origins: The Christian Beginnings of Modern Individualism." In M. Carrithers, S. Collins, and S. Lukes, eds., *The Category of the Person: Anthropology, Philosophy, History*, pp. 93–122. Cambridge, Eng.: Cambridge University Press.

Durkheim, Emile. 1899. "Deux lois de l'évolution pénale." *L'Année sociologique* 4 (1899–1900): 65–95.

———. 1967. *Soziologie und Philosophie*. Frankfurt: Suhrkamp.

———. 1987. *Schriften zur Soziologie der Erkenntnis*. H. Joas, ed. Frankfurt: Suhrkamp.

Eaton, Richard M. 1987. "Islamisierung im spätmittelalterlichen Bengalen." In Schluchter 1987a: 156–79.

Ebbinghaus, Julius. 1968. *Gesammelte Aufsätze, Vorträge, Reden*. Hildesheim: Olms.

Eisenstadt, Shmuel N., ed. 1987a. *Kulturen der Achsenzeit*. Frankfurt: Suhrkamp.

————. 1987b. "Webers Analyse des Islams und die Gestalt der islamischen Zivilisation." In Schluchter 1987a: 342–59.

————. 1988. "Max Webers Überlegungen zum westlichen Christentum." In Schluchter 1988b: 554–80.

Elias, Norbert. 1969. *Über den Prozeß der Zivilisation. Soziogenetische und psychogenetische Untersuchungen.* 2nd ed. 2 vols. Bern: Franke.

Fichte, Johann Gottlieb. 1962. *Ausgewählte Werke.* 6 vols. I. H. Fichte, ed. Darmstadt: Wissenschaftliche Buchgesellschaft.

Foerster, Friedrich Wilhelm. 1918. *Politische Ethik und Politische Pädagogik. Mit besonderer Berücksichtigung der kommenden deutschen Aufgaben.* Munich: Ernst Reinhard.

Foucault, Michel. 1976. *Überwachen und Strafen. Die Geburt des Gefängnisses.* Frankfurt: Suhrkamp.

Frank, Manfred. 1986. *Die Unhintergehbarkeit von Individualität. Reflexionen über Subjekt, Person und Individuum aus Anlaß ihrer 'postmodernen' Toterklärung.* Frankfurt: Suhrkamp.

Geertz, Clifford. 1973. *The Interpretation of Cultures: Selected Essays.* New York: Basic Books.

Gellner, Ernest. 1985. *Leben im Islam. Religion als Gesellschaftsordnung.* Stuttgart: Klett.

————. 1987. "Warten auf den Imam." In Schluchter 1987a: 272–93.

Giddens, Anthony. 1976. *New Rules of Sociological Method.* London: Hutchinson.

Goldziher, Ignaz. 1910. *Vorlesungen über den Islam.* Heidelberg: Winter.

Götz von Ohlenhusen, Irmtraut and Albrecht. 1981. "Walter Benjamin, Gustav Wyneken und die Freistudenten vor dem Ersten Weltkrieg." *Jahrbuch des Archivs der deutschen Jugendbewegung* 13: 99–128.

Gould, Mark. 1987. *Revolution in the Development of Capitalism: The Coming of the English Revolution.* Berkeley: University of California Press.

Grundmann, Herbert. 1970. *Religiöse Bewegungen im Mittelalter.* Darmstadt: Wissenschaftliche Buchgesellschaft.

Gundolf, Friedrich. 1916. *Goethe.* Berlin: Georg Bondi.

Guttmann, Julius. 1913. "Die Juden und das Wirtschaftsleben." *Archiv für Sozialwissenschaft und Sozialpolitik* 36: 149–212.

Habermas, Jürgen. 1973. "Wahrheitstheorien." In H. Fahrenbach, ed., *Wirklichkeit und Reflexion. Walter Schulz zum 60. Geburtstag,* pp. 211–66. Pfullingen: Neske.

————. 1983. *Moralbewußtsein und kommunikatives Handeln.* Frankfurt: Suhrkamp.

————. 1984. *Vorstudien und Ergänzungen zur Theorie des kommunikativen Handelns.* Frankfurt: Suhrkamp.

————. 1984/87. *The Theory of Communicative Action.* 2 vols. T. McCarthy, trans. Boston: Beacon Press.

————. 1986a. "Entgegnung." In Honneth and Joas 1986: 327–405.

————. 1986b. "Moralität und Sittlichkeit. Treffen Hegels Einwände gegen Kant auch auf die Diskursethik zu?" In W. Kuhlmann, ed., *Moralität und Sittlichkeit. Das Problem Hegels und die Diskursethik*, pp. 16–37. Frankfurt: Suhrkamp.

Hahn, Alois. 1982. "Zur Soziologie der Beichte und anderer Formen institutionalisierter Bekenntnisse: Selbstthematisierung und Zivilisationsprozeß." *Kölner Zeitschrift für Soziologie und Sozialpsychologie* 34: 407–34.

———. 1988. "Sakramentale Kontrolle." In Schluchter 1988b: 229–53.

Halevy, Elie. 1972. *The Growth of Philosophic Radicalism*. London: Faber and Faber.

Hall, John A. 1985. *Powers and Liberties: The Causes and Consequences of the Rise of the West*. Berkeley: University of California Press.

Hamilton, Gary G. 1984. "Patriarchalism in Imperial China and Western Europe: A Revision of Weber's Sociology of Domination." *Theory and Society* 13: 393–425.

Hardy, Peter. 1987. "Islamischer Fundamentalismus. Glaube, Handeln, Führung." In Schluchter 1987a: 190–216.

Hegel, G. W. F. 1969. *Werkausgabe in 20 Bänden*. Frankfurt: Suhrkamp.

Heidegger, Martin. 1984. *Sein und Zeit*. 15th ed. Tübingen: Max Niemeyer Verlag.

Hennis, Wilhelm. 1984. "Im 'langen Schatten' einer Edition. Zum ersten Band der Max Weber-Gesamtausgabe." In *Frankfurter Allgemeine Zeitung*, no. 207: 10.

———. 1987. *Max Webers Fragestellung. Studien zur Biographie des Werks*. Tübingen: J. C. B. Mohr (Paul Siebeck).

———. 1988. *Max Weber. Essays in Reconstruction*. Keith Tribe, trans. London: Allen & Unwin.

Henrich, Dieter. 1952. *Die Einheit der Wissenschaftslehre Max Webers*. Tübingen: J. C. B. Mohr (Paul Siebeck).

———. 1971. *Hegel im Kontext*. Frankfurt: Suhrkamp.

———. 1975. "Die Deduktion des Sittengesetzes." In A. Schwan, ed., *Denken im Schatten des Nihilismus*, pp. 55–112. Darmstadt: Wissenschaftliche Buchgesellschaft.

———. 1982. *Fluchtlinien. Philosophische Essays*. Frankfurt: Suhrkamp.

———. 1987. "Karl Jaspers: Thinking with Max Weber in Mind." In W. J. Mommsen and J. Osterhammel, eds., *Max Weber and His Contemporaries*, pp. 528–40. London: Allen & Unwin.

———. 1990. *Eine Republik Deutschland. Reflexionen auf dem Weg aus der deutschen Teilung*. Frankfurt: Suhrkamp.

Henrich, Dieter, Claus Offe, and Wolfgang Schluchter. 1988. "Max Weber und das Projekt der Moderne. Eine Diskussion mit Dieter Henrich, Claus Offe und Wolfgang Schluchter." In C. Gneuss and J. Kocka, eds., *Max Weber. Ein Symposion*, pp. 155–83. Munich: Deutscher Taschenbuchverlag.

Heuss, Theodor. 1963. *Erinnerungen 1905–1933*. Tübingen: Rainer Wunderlich Verlag.

Hildebrandt, Richard. 1896. *Recht und Sitte auf den verschiedenen wirtschaftlichen Kulturstufen.* Vol. 1. Jena: G. Fischer.

Hinneberg, Paul, ed. 1906. *Kultur der Gegenwart. Ihre Entwicklung und ihre Ziele.* Berlin: B. G. Teubner.

Hinske, Norbert, ed. 1981. *Was ist Aufklärung? Beiträge aus der Berlinischen Monatsschrift.* 3rd ed. Darmstadt: Wissenschaftliche Buchgesellschaft.

Höffe, Otfried, ed. 1975. *Einführung in die utilitaristische Ethik. Klassische und zeitgenössische Texte.* Munich: C. H. Beck.

———. 1987. *Politische Gerechtigkeit. Grundlegung einer kritischen Philosophie von Recht und Staat.* Frankfurt: Suhrkamp.

Honigsheim, Paul. 1969 [1914]. *Die Staats- und Sozial-Lehren der französischen Jansenisten im 17. Jahrhundert.* Darmstadt: Wissenschaftliche Buchgesellschaft.

Honnefelder, Ludger. 1988. "Die ethische Rationalität des mittelalterlichen Naturrechts. Max Webers und Ernst Troeltschs Deutung des mittelalterlichen Naturrechts und die Bedeutung der Lehre vom natürlichen Gesetz bei Thomas von Aquin." In Schluchter 1988b: 254–75.

Honneth, Axel, and Hans Joas, eds. 1986. *Kommunikatives Handeln. Beiträge zu Jürgen Habermas' "Theorie des kommunikativen Handelns."* Frankfurt: Suhrkamp.

Huber, Wolfgang. 1983. "Sozialethik als Verantwortungsethik." In A. Bondolfi, W. Heierle, and D. Mieth, eds., *Ethos des Alltags: Festgabe für Stephan H. Pfürtner zum 60. Geburtstag,* pp. 55–76. Zurich: Benziger.

Hübinger, Gangolf. 1987. "Kulturkritik und Kulturpolitik des Eugen Diederichs-Verlags im Wilhelminismus. Auswege aus der Krise der Moderne?" In H. Renz and F. W. Graf, eds., *Troeltsch Studien.* Vol. 4: *Umstrittene Moderne. Die Zukunft der Neuzeit im Urteil der Epoche Ernst Troeltschs,* pp. 92–114. Gütersloh: Gerd Mohn.

Hughes, H. Stuart. 1977. *Consciousness and Society: The Reorientation of European Thought, 1890–1930.* Rev. ed. New York: Vintage Books.

Hurgronje, Christian Snouck. 1888. *Mekka.* Vol. 1: *Die Stadt und ihre Herren.* The Hague: Nijhoff.

Husserl, Edmund. 1911. "Philosophie als strenge Wissenschaft." *Logos* 1: 289–341.

Jaffé, Edgar. 1917. "Lauenstein." *Europäische Staats- und Wirtschaftszeitung* 2, 42 (20 Oct.): 995.

Jaspers, Karl. 1913. *Allgemeine Psychopathologie. Ein Leitfaden für Studierende, Ärzte und Psychologen.* Berlin: Springer.

———. 1919. *Psychologie der Weltanschauungen.* Berlin: Springer.

———. 1949. *Vom Ursprung und Ziel der Geschichte.* Munich: Piper.

———. 1983. *Kant. Leben, Werk, Wirkung.* 2nd ed. Munich: Piper.

———. 1985. *Nietzsche und das Christentum.* 3rd ed. Munich: Piper.

———. 1988. *Max Weber.* Munich: Piper.

Jensen, Stefan. 1984. "Aspekte der Medien-Theorie. Welche Funktion haben die Medien in Handlungssystemen?" *Zeitschrift für Soziologie* 13: 145–64.

Jonas, Hans. 1979. *Das Prinzip Verantwortung. Versuch einer Ethik für die technologische Zivilisation.* Frankfurt: Suhrkamp.

Kahler, Erich von. 1920. *Der Beruf der Wissenschaft.* Berlin: Georg Bondi.

Kalberg, Stephen. 1980. "Max Weber's Types of Rationality: Cornerstones for the Analysis of Rationalization Processes in History." *American Journal of Sociology* 85: 1145–79.

Kant, Immanuel. 1948. *The Moral Law.* H. J. Paton, trans. London: Hutchinson's University Library.

———. 1960. *Religion Within the Limits of Reason Alone.* T. M. Greene and H. H. Hudson, trans. New York: Harper & Row.

———. 1965a. *First Introduction to the Critique of Judgment.* J. Haden, trans. Indianapolis: Bobbs-Merrill.

———. 1965b. *The Metaphysical Elements of Justice.* J. Ladd, trans. Indianapolis: Bobbs-Merrill.

———. 1971. *The Doctrine of Virtue.* M. J. Gregor, trans. Philadelphia: University of Pennsylvania Press.

———. 1976. *The Critique of Practical Reason.* Lewis White Beck, trans. New York: Garland.

———. 1977. *Werke in zwölf Bänden.* W. Weischedel, ed. Darmstadt: Wissenschaftliche Buchgesellschaft.

———. 1982. *The Critique of Judgement.* J. C. Meredith, trans. New York: Oxford University Press.

———. 1983. "On the Proverb: That May Be True in Theory But Is of No Practical Use." In Immanuel Kant, *Perpetual Peace and Other Essays on Politics, History, and Morals.* T. Humphrey, trans. Indianapolis: Hackett.

Keller, Franz. 1912. *Unternehmung und Mehrwert.* Paderborn: Schriften der Görres-Gesellschaft, Heft 12.

Kocka, Jürgen, ed. 1986. *Max Weber, der Historiker.* Göttingen: Vandenhoeck & Ruprecht.

———. 1987. *Bürger und Bürgerlichkeit im 19. Jahrhundert.* Göttingen: Vandenhoeck & Ruprecht.

Kohler, Joseph. 1905. "Zum Islamrecht." *Zeitschrift für vergleichende Rechtswissenschaft* 17: 194–216.

König, René, and Johannes Winckelmann, eds. 1963. *Max Weber zum Gedächtnis.* Opladen: Westdeutscher Verlag.

Kuenzlen, Gottfried. 1978. "Unbekannte Quellen der Religionssoziologie Max Webers." *Zeitschrift für Soziologie* 7: 215–27.

Kürnberger, Ferdinand. 1855. *Der Amerikamüde.* Frankfurt: Meidinger.

Lapidus, Ira M. 1987. "Die Institutionalisierung der frühislamischen Gesellschaften." In Schluchter 1987a: 125–41.

Lehmann, Hartmut. 1988. "Asketischer Protestantismus und ökonomischer Rationalismus. Die Weber-These nach zwei Generationen." In Schluchter, 1988b: 529–53.

Lehmann, Hartmut, and Guenther Roth, eds. 1993. *Weber's Protestant Ethic: Origins, Evidence, Context.* New York: Cambridge University Press.

Leichter, Käthe. 1963. "Weber als Lehrer und Politiker." In König and Winckelmann 1963: 125–42.

Lenhart, Volker. 1986. "Allgemeine und fachliche Bildung bei Max Weber." *Zeitschrift für Pädagogik* 32: 529–41.

Leo, Johannes. 1963. "Erinnerungen an Max Weber." In König and Winckelmann 1963: 17–18.

Lepsius, M. Rainer. 1977. "Max Weber in München. Rede anläßlich der Enthüllung einer Gedenktafel." *Zeitschrift für Soziologie* 6 (1977): 103–18.

———. 1986. "Ideen und Interessen. Die Zurechnungsproblematik bei Max Weber." In F. Neidhardt, M. R. Lepsius, and J. Weiss, eds., *Kultur und Gesellschaft,* pp. 20–31. Opladen: Westdeutscher Verlag.

———. 1989. "Die Bewohner des Hauses Ziegelhäuser Landstraße 17 in Heidelberg." Manuscript.

Lerner, Robert E. 1988. "Waldenser, Lollarden und Taboriten. Zum Sektenbegriff bei Weber und Troeltsch." In Schluchter 1988b: 312–25.

Levine, Donald N. 1981. "Rationality and Freedom: Weber and Beyond." *Sociological Inquiry* 51: 5–25.

Levtzion, Nehemia. 1987. "Aspekte der Islamisierung. Eine kritische Würdigung der Beobachtungen Max Webers." In Schluchter 1987a: 142–55.

Little, Lester K. 1978. *Religious Poverty and the Profit Economy in Medieval Europe.* London: Paul Elek.

———. 1988. "Laienbruderschaften in norditalienischen Städten." In Schluchter 1988b: 383–409.

Löwith, Karl. 1960. "Max Weber und Karl Marx." In Löwith, *Gesammelte Abhandlungen. Zur Kritik der geschichtlichen Existenz,* pp. 1–67. Stuttgart: Klett.

———. 1986. *Mein Leben in Deutschland vor und nach 1933. Ein Bericht.* Stuttgart: J. B. Metzler.

Luhmann, Niklas. 1964. *Funktion und Folgen formaler Organisation.* Berlin: Duncker & Humblot.

Lukács, Georg. 1912. "Von der Armut am Geiste. Ein Gespräch und ein Brief." *Neue Blätter* 2: 67–92.

———. 1916. "Theorie des Romans. Ein geschichtsphilosophischer Versuch über die Formen der großen Epik." *Zeitschrift für Ästhetik und allgemeine Kunstwissenschaft* 11: 225–71, 390–431.

———. 1953. *Goethe und seine Zeit.* 2nd ed. Berlin: Aufbau Verlag.

———. 1967. *Geschichte und Klassenbewußtsein. Studien über marxistische Dialektik.* Amsterdam: Thomas de Munter.

———. 1982. *Briefwechsel 1902–1917.* Stuttgart: J. B. Metzler.

Mahrholz, Werner. 1919. "Die Lage der Studentenschaft." *Die Hochschule* 3: 8.

Marshall, Gordon. 1980. *Presbyteries and Profits: Calvinism and the Development of Capitalism in Scotland, 1560–1707.* Oxford, Eng.: Clarendon Press.

———. 1982. *In Search of the Spirit of Capitalism: An Essay on Max Weber's Protestant Ethic Thesis.* New York: Columbia University Press.

Marx, Karl. 1971. *Werke—Schriften—Briefe.* 6 vols. H. J. Lieber, ed. Darmstadt: Wissenschaftliche Buchgesellschaft.

Maurenbrecher, Max. 1917. "Der Krieg als Ausgangspunkt einer deutschen Kultur." *Die Tat* 9: 97–107.

Mead, George Herbert. 1962 [1934]. *Mind, Self and Society: From the Standpoint of a Social Behaviorist.* Chicago: University of Chicago Press.

Metcalf, Barbara. 1987. "Islamische Reformbewegungen." In Schluchter 1987a: 242–55.

Meyer-Frank, Julie. 1982. "Erinnerungen an meine Studienzeit." In H. Lamm, ed., *Vergangene Tage. Jüdische Kultur in München,* pp. 212–16. Munich: Langen-Müller.

Mill, John Stuart. 1874. *Three Essays on Religion.* London: Longmans, Green, Reader, and Dyer.

———. 1885. *Über Religion—Natur. Die Nützlichkeit der Religion. Theismus. Drei nachgelassene Essays.* Berlin: Duncker.

Mitteis, Heinrich. 1976. "Über den Rechtsgrund des Satzes 'Stadtluft macht frei'." In C. Haase, ed., *Die Stadt des Mittelalters,* 2: 182–202. Darmstadt: Wissenschaftliche Buchgesellschaft.

Mitzman, Arthur. 1973. *Sociology and Estrangement: Three Sociologies of Imperial Germany.* New York: Alfred A. Knopf.

Mommsen, Wolfgang J. 1974. *Max Weber und die deutsche Politik 1890–1920.* 2nd ed. Tübingen: J. C. B. Mohr (Paul Siebeck).

———. 1981. "Die antinomische Struktur des politischen Denkens Max Webers." *Historische Zeitschrift* 233: 35–64.

———. 1984. *Max Weber and German Politics, 1890–1920.* Chicago: University of Chicago Press.

———. 1985. "Max Weber. Persönliche Lebensführung und gesellschaftlicher Wandel in der Geschichte." In P. Alter, W. J. Mommsen, and T. Nipperdey, eds., *Geschichte und politisches Handeln. Theodor Schieder zum Gedächtnis,* pp. 261–81. Stuttgart: Klett.

———. 1986. "Max Webers Begriff der Universalgeschichte." In Kocka 1986: 51–72.

———. 1989a. "The Antinomical Structure of Max Weber's Political Thought." In Mommsen, *The Political and Social Theory of Max Weber,* pp. 24–43. Chicago: University of Chicago Press.

———. 1989b. "The Two Dimensions of Social Change in Max Weber's Sociological Theory." In Mommsen, *The Political and Social Theory of Max Weber,* pp. 145–65. Chicago: University of Chicago Press.

Münch, Richard. 1982. *Theorie des Handelns. Zur Rekonstruktion der Beiträge von Talcott Parsons, Emile Durkheim und Max Weber.* Frankfurt: Suhrkamp.

Naumann, Friedrich. 1904. *Briefe über Religion*. Berlin-Schöneberg: Buchverlag Die Hilfe.

Nelson, Benjamin. 1969. *The Idea of Usury: From Tribal Brotherhood to Universal Otherhood*. 2nd ed. Chicago: University of Chicago Press.

Nietzsche, Friedrich. 1960. *Werke in drei Bänden*. K. Schlechta, ed. 2nd ed. Munich: Carl Hanser.

Nolte, Ernst. 1963. *Der Faschismus in seiner Epoche. Die Action française. Der italienische Faschismus. Der Nationalsozialismus*. Munich: Piper.

Oakes, Guy. 1988. *Weber and Rickert: Concept Formation in the Cultural Sciences*. Cambridge, Mass.: MIT Press.

———. 1989. *Die Grenzen der kulturwissenschaftlichen Begriffsbildung. Methodologie und Werttheorie bei Weber und Rickert. Heidelberger Max Weber-Vorlesungen 1982*. Frankfurt: Suhrkamp.

Ollig, Hans-Ludwig, ed. 1987a. *Materialien zur Neukantianismus-Diskussion*. Darmstadt: Wissenschaftliche Buchgesellschaft.

———. 1987b. "Die Religionsphilosophie der Südwestdeutschen Schule." In Ollig 1987a: 428–57.

Otsuka, Hisao. 1982. *The Spirit of Capitalism: The Max Weber Thesis in an Economic Historical Perspective*. Tokyo: Iwanami Shoten.

Parsons, Talcott. 1967. *Sociological Theory and Modern Society*. New York: The Free Press.

Perpeet, Wilhelm. 1987. "Formale Kulturphilosophie." In Ollig 1987a: 362–77.

Peters, Rudolph. 1987. "Islamischer Fundamentalismus. Glaube, Handeln, Führung." In Schluchter 1987a: 217–41.

Picht, Georg. 1980. "Rechtfertigung und Gerechtigkeit. Zum Begriff der Verantwortung." In Picht, *Hier und Jetzt. Philosophieren nach Auschwitz und Hiroschima*. Vol. 1: 202–17. Stuttgart: Klett.

———. 1985. *Kants Religionsphilosophie*. Stuttgart: Klett.

Pipes, Daniel. 1981. *Slave Soldiers and Islam: The Genesis of a Military System*. New Haven, Conn.: Yale University Press.

Plessner, Helmuth. 1963. "In Heidelberg 1913." In König and Winckelmann 1963: 30–34.

Poggi, Gianfranco. 1983. *Calvinism and the Capitalist Spirit: Max Weber's Protestant Ethic*. London: Macmillan.

———. 1988. "Max Webers Begriff des okzidentalen Feudalismus." In Schluchter 1988b: 476–97.

Popper, Karl. 1965. *Das Elend des Historizismus*. Tübingen: J. C. B. Mohr (Paul Siebeck).

Radbruch, Gustav. 1950 [1913]. *Einführung in die Rechtswissenschaft*. 2nd ed. Stuttgart: K. F. Koehler.

Rawls, John. 1972. *A Theory of Justice*. London: Oxford University Press.

Reyerson, Kathryn L. 1988. "Der Aufstieg des Bürgertums und die religiöse Vergemeinschaftung im mittelalterlichen Europa. Neues zur Weber-These." In Schluchter 1988b: 410–36.

Richter, Helmut, ed. 1975. *Cluny. Beiträge zu Gestalt und Wirkung der cluniazensischen Reform.* Darmstadt: Wissenschaftliche Buchgesellschaft.

Rickert, Heinrich. 1902. *Die Grenzen der naturwissenschaftlichen Begriffsbildung. Eine logische Einleitung in die historischen Wissenschaften.* Tübingen: J. C. B. Mohr (Paul Siebeck).

———. 1907."Geschichtsphilosophie." In W. Windelband, ed., *Die Philosophie im Beginn des 20. Jahrhunderts. Festschrift für Kuno Fischer,* pp. 321–422. 2nd ed. Heidelberg: C. Winter.

———. 1911. "Lebenswerte und Kulturwerte." *Logos* 2: 131–66.

———. 1913. "Vom System der Werte." *Logos* 4: 295–327.

———. 1926. "Max Weber und seine Stellung zur Wissenschaft." *Logos* 15: 222–37.

———. 1929. *Die Grenzen der naturwissenschaftlichen Begriffsbildung.* 5th ed. Tübingen: J. C. B. Mohr (Paul Siebeck).

———. 1986. *The Limits of Concept Formation in Natural Science.* Guy Oakes, ed. and trans. New York: Cambridge University Press.

Robinson, Francis. 1987. "Säkularisierung im Islam." In Schluchter 1987a: 256–71.

Rodinson, Maxime. 1986. *Islam und Kapitalismus.* Frankfurt: Suhrkamp.

———. 1987. "Islamischer Patrimonialismus. Ein Hindernis für die Entstehung des modernen Kapitalismus?" In Schluchter 1987a: 180–89.

Rosenwein, Barbara. 1988. "Reformmönchtum und der Aufstieg Clunys. Webers Bedeutung für die Forschung heute." In Schluchter 1988b: 276–311.

Roth, Guenther. 1978. Introduction to Max Weber, *Economy and Society.* G. Roth and C. Wittich, eds. Berkeley: University of California Press.

———. 1987a. "Max Webers zwei Ethiken und die Friedensbewegung damals und heute." In Roth 1987b: 201–30.

———. 1987b. *Politische Herrschaft und persönliche Freiheit. Heidelberger Max Weber-Vorlesungen 1983.* Frankfurt: Suhrkamp.

———. 1987c. "Rationalization in Max Weber's Developmental History." In S. Whimster and S. Lash, eds., *Max Weber, Rationality, and Modernity,* pp. 75–91. London: Allen & Unwin.

———. 1988. "Marianne Weber and Her Circle." Introduction to Marianne Weber, *Max Weber: A Biography.* 2nd ed. New Brunswick: Transaction Books.

———. 1989. "Weber's Political Failure." *Telos* 78 (Winter 1988/89): 136–49.

Roth, Guenther, and Wolfgang Schluchter. 1979. *Max Weber's Vision of History: Ethics and Methods.* Berkeley: University of California Press.

Salz, Arthur. 1921. *Für die Wissenschaft gegen die Gebildeten unter ihren Verächtern.* Munich: Drei Masken Verlag.

Schacht, Joseph. 1935. "Zur soziologischen Betrachtung des islamischen Rechts." *Der Islam* 22: 207–38.

Scheler, Max. 1922. "Weltanschauungslehre, Soziologie und Weltanschauungssetzung." *Kölner Vierteljahreshefte für Sozialwissenschaften* 2 (1): 18–33.

Schelting, Alexander von. 1934. *Max Webers Wissenschaftslehre. Das logische Problem der historischen Kulturerkenntnis. Die Grenzen der Soziologie des Wissens.* Tübingen: J. C. B. Mohr (Paul Siebeck).

Schiele, Friedrich Michael, and Leopold Zscharnack, eds. 1909–13. *Die Religion in Geschichte und Gegenwart. Handwörterbuch in gemeinverständlicher Darstellung.* 5 vols. Tübingen: J. C. B. Mohr (Paul Siebeck).

Schluchter, Wolfgang. 1971. *Wertfreiheit und Verantwortungsethik. Zum Verhältnis von Wissenschaft und Politik bei Max Weber.* Tübingen: J. C. B. Mohr (Paul Siebeck).

———. 1979. *Die Entwicklung des okzidentalen Rationalismus. Eine Analyse von Max Webers Gesellschaftsgeschichte.* Tübingen: J. C. B. Mohr (Paul Siebeck).

———. 1980. *Rationalismus der Weltbeherrschung.* Frankfurt: Suhrkamp.

———. 1981. *The Rise of Western Rationalism.* G. Roth, trans. Berkeley: University of California Press.

———, ed. 1983. *Max Webers Studie über Konfuzianismus und Taoismus. Interpretation und Kritik.* Frankfurt: Suhrkamp.

———. 1984 [1979]. "Value-Neutrality and the Ethic of Responsibility." In Roth and Schluchter 1979: 195–206.

———. 1985a. *Aspekte bürokratischer Herrschaft. Studien zur Interpretation der fortschreitenden Industriegesellschaft.* Frankfurt: Suhrkamp.

———, ed. 1985b. *Max Webers Sicht des antiken Christentums. Interpretation und Kritik.* Frankfurt: Suhrkamp.

———, ed. 1987a. *Max Webers Sicht des Islams. Interpretation und Kritik.* Frankfurt: Suhrkamp.

———. 1987b. "Modes of Authority and Democratic Control." In V. Meja, D. Misgeld, and N. Stehr, eds., *Modern German Sociology,* pp. 291–323. New York: Columbia University Press.

———. 1988a. "Gesinnungsethik und Verantwortungsethik. Probleme einer Unterscheidung." In Schluchter 1988d, 1: 165–338.

———, ed. 1988b. *Max Webers Sicht des okzidentalen Christentums. Interpretation und Kritik.* Frankfurt: Suhrkamp.

———. 1988c. "Religion, politische Herrschaft, Wirtschaft und bürgerliche Lebensführung. Die okzidentale Sonderentwicklung." In Schluchter 1988d, 2: 382–505.

———. 1988d. *Religion und Lebensführung.* 2 vols. Frankfurt: Suhrkamp.

———. 1989. *Rationalism, Religion, and Domination.* N. Solomon, trans. Berkeley: University of California Press.

Schmid, Michael. 1981. "Struktur und Selektion. Emile Durkheim und

Max Weber als Theoretiker struktureller Evolution." *Zeitschrift für Soziologie* 10: 17–37.

Schmitt, Jean-Claude. 1988. "Vom Nutzen Max Webers für den Historiker und die Bilderfrage." In Schluchter 1988b: 184–228.

Schnädelbach, Herbert. 1983. *Philosophie in Deutschland 1831–1933.* Frankfurt: Suhrkamp.

Schöllgen, Gregor. 1985. *Handlungsfreiheit und Zweckrationalität. Max Weber und die Tradition der praktischen Philosophie.* Tübingen: J. C. B. Mohr (Paul Siebeck).

Schreiner, Klaus. 1986. "Die mittelalterliche Stadt in Webers Analyse und die Deutung des okzidentalen Rationalismus." In Kocka 1986: 119–50.

Schulze, Friedrich, and Paul Ssymank. 1932 [1931]. *Das deutsche Studententum von den ältesten Zeiten bis zur Gegenwart.* Munich: Verlag für Hochschulkunde.

Schumpeter, Joseph A. 1987. "Sombarts Dritter Band." In B. vom Brocke, ed., *Sombarts 'Moderner Kapitalismus.' Materialien zur Kritik und Rezeption,* pp. 196–219. Munich: Deutscher Taschenbuch Verlag.

Schwab, Alexander. 1914. "Die Richtung in der Meissner Bewegung." In Vorort der Deutschen Freien Studenterschaft, ed., *Studenterschaft und Jugendbewegung,* pp. 34–46. Munich: Max Steinbach.

Schwab, Franz Xaver. 1917. "Beruf und Jugend." *Die weissen Blätter. Eine Monatsschrift* 4: 97–113.

Seel, Martin. 1986. "Die zwei Bedeutungen 'kommunikativer' Rationalität. Bemerkungen zu Habermas' Kritik der pluralen Vernunft." In Honneth and Joas 1986: 53–72.

Selge, Kurt-Victor. 1988. "Max Weber, Ernst Troeltsch und die Sekten und neuen Orden des Spätmittelalters (Waldenser, Humiliaten, Franziskaner)." In Schluchter 1988b: 326–54.

Simmel, Georg. 1907. *Schopenhauer und Nietzsche. Ein Vortragszyklus.* Leipzig: Duncker & Humblot.

———. 1913. "Das individuelle Gesetz. Ein Versuch über das Prinzip der Ethik." *Logos* 4: 117–60.

———. 1957a. *Brücke und Tür. Essays des Philosophen zur Geschichte, Religion, Kunst und Gesellschaft.* M. Landmann and M. Susman, eds. Stuttgart: Köhler.

———. 1957b. "Vom Heil der Seele." In Simmel 1957a: 122–35.

———. 1978. *The Philosophy of Money.* T. Bottomore and D. Frisby, trans. London: Routledge & Kegan Paul.

Sivin, Nathan. 1983. "Chinesische Wissenschaft. Ein Vergleich der Ansätze von Max Weber und Joseph Needham." In Schluchter 1983: 342–62.

Sombart, Werner. 1902a. *Der moderne Kapitalismus.* Vol. 1. *Die Genesis des Kapitalismus.* Leipzig: Duncker & Humblot. (A 2nd, rev. ed. appeared in 1916.)

———. 1902b. *Der moderne Kapitalismus*. Vol. 2. *Die Theorie der kapitalistischen Entwicklung*. Leipzig: Duncker & Humblot.

———. 1903. *Die deutsche Volkswirtschaft im 19. Jahrhundert*. Berlin: Bondi.

———. 1909. "Der kapitalistische Unternehmer." *Archiv für Sozialwissenschaft und Sozialpolitik* 29: 689–758.

———. 1911a. *Die Juden und das Wirtschaftsleben*. Munich: Duncker & Humblot.

———. 1911b. "Verlagssystem (Hausindustrie)." In J. Conrad, L. Elster, W. Lexis, E. Loening, eds., *Handwörterbuch der Staatswissenschaften*. 8: 233–61. Jena: G. Fischer.

———. 1913. *Der Bourgeois. Zur Geistesgeschichte des modernen Wirtschaftsmenschen*. Munich: Duncker & Humblot.

———. 1915. *Händler und Helden. Patriotische Besinnungen*. Munich: Duncker & Humblot.

———. 1916. *Der moderne Kapitalismus*. 2nd, rev. ed. 2 vols. Munich: Duncker & Humblot.

———. 1927. *Der moderne Kapitalismus*. 3 vols. Munich: Duncker & Humblot.

Speer, Heino. 1978. *Herrschaft und Legitimität. Zeitgebundene Aspekte in Max Webers Herrschaftssoziologie*. Berlin: Duncker & Humblot.

Spranger, Eduard. 1929. *Der Sinn der Voraussetzungslosigkeit in den Geisteswissenschaften*. Darmstadt: Wissenschaftliche Buchgesellschaft.

Stauth, Georg, and Bryan S. Turner. 1986. "Nietzsche in Weber oder die Geburt des modernen Genius' im professionellen Menschen." *Zeitschrift für Soziologie* 15: 81–94.

Stock, Brian. 1983. *The Implications of Literacy: Written Language and Models of Interpretation in the Eleventh and Twelfth Centuries*. Princeton: Princeton University Press.

———. 1985. "Rationality, Tradition, and the Scientific Outlook: Reflections on Max Weber and the Middle Ages." In P. O. Long, ed., *Science and Technology in Medieval Society*: *Annals of the New York Academy of Sciences* 441: 7–19.

———. 1988. "Schriftgebrauch und Rationalität im Mittelalter." In Schluchter 1988b: 165–83.

Strieder, Jacob. 1904. *Zur Genesis des modernen Kapitalismus. Forschungen zur Entstehung der großen bürgerlichen Kapitalvermögen am Ausgang des Mittelalters und zu Beginn der Neuzeit, zunächst in Augsburg*. Leipzig: Duncker & Humblot.

———. 1914. *Studien zur Geschichte kapitalistischer Organisationsformen. Monopole, Kartelle und Aktiengesellschaften im Mittelalter und zu Beginn der Neuzeit*. Munich: Duncker & Humblot.

Taylor, Charles. 1986. "Sprache und Gesellschaft." In Honneth and Joas 1986: 35–52.

Tenbruck, Friedrich H. 1977. "Abschied von *Wirtschaft und Gesellschaft*." *Zeitschrift für die gesamte Staatswissenschaft* 133: 703–36.

Theunissen, Michael. 1977. *Der Andere. Studien zur Sozialontologie der Gegenwart*. Berlin: Walter de Gruyter.

Tibi, Bassam. 1985. *Der Islam und das Problem der kulturellen Bewältigung des sozialen Wandels*. Frankfurt: Suhrkamp.

Treiber, Hubert, and Heinz Steinert. 1980. *Die Fabrikation des zuverlässigen Menschen. Über die 'Wahlverwandtschaft' von Kloster- und Fabrikdisziplin*. Munich: Heinz Moos Verlag.

Troeltsch, Ernst. 1922. *Der Historismus und seine Probleme. Das logische Problem der Geschichtsphilosophie*. Tübingen: J. C. B. Mohr (Paul Siebeck).

———. 1977 [1912]. *Die Soziallehren der christlichen Kirchen und Gruppen*. Aalen: Scientia Verlag.

———. 1981a [1925]. *Aufsätze zur Geistesgeschichte und Religionssoziologie*. Aalen: Scientia Verlag.

———. 1981b. "Die Revolution in der Wissenschaft. Eine Besprechung von Erich von Kahlers Schrift gegen Max Weber: 'Der Beruf der Wissenschaft' und der Gegenschrift von Arthur Salz: 'Für die Wissenschaft gegen die Gebildeten unter ihren Verächtern'." In Troeltsch 1981a: 653–77. (Originally 1921 in *Jahrbuch für Gesetzgebung, Verwaltung und Volkswirthschaft im Deutschen Reich* 45 [4]: 65–94.)

Turner, Bryan S. 1974. *Weber and Islam: A Critical Study*. London: Routledge & Kegan Paul.

Ulrich, F. 1912. *Die Vorherbestimmungslehre im Islam und Christentum. Eine religionsgeschichtliche Parallele*. Gütersloh: C. Bertelsmann.

Wagner, Gerhard. 1987. *Geltung und normativer Zwang. Eine Untersuchung zu den neukantianischen Grundlagen der Wissenschaftslehre Max Webers*. Freiburg: Alber.

Wagner, Gerhard, and Heinz Zipprian. 1986. "The Problem of Reference in Max Weber's Theory of Causal Explanation." *Human Studies* 9: 21–42.

Watt, W. Montgomery. 1964. *Muhammad: Prophet and Statesman*. Oxford: Oxford University Press.

Weber, Marianne. 1900. *Fichte's Sozialismus und sein Verhältnis zur Marx'schen Doktrin*. Tübingen: J. C. B. Mohr (Paul Siebeck).

———. 1915–16. "Der Krieg als ethisches Problem." *Die Frau* 23: 705–20.

———. 1919. *Frauenfragen und Frauengedanken. Gesammelte Aufsätze*. Tübingen: J. C. B. Mohr (Paul Siebeck).

———. 1926. *Max Weber. Ein Lebensbild*. Tübingen: J. C. B. Mohr (Paul Siebeck).

———. 1975. *Max Weber*. Harry Zohn, trans. New York: Wiley.

Weber, Max. 1889a. *Entwickelung des Solidarhaftprinzips und des Sondervermögens der offenen Handelsgesellschaft aus den Haushalts- und Gewerbegemeinschaften in den italienischen Städten*. Stuttgart: Gebrüder Kröner.

————. 1889b. *Die Geschichte der Handelsgesellschaften im Mittelalter. Nach südeuropäischen Quellen.* Stuttgart: F. Enke.

————. 1906a. "Zur Lage der bürgerlichen Demokratie in Rußland." *Archiv für Sozialwissenschaft und Sozialpolitik* 22 (1): 234–353.

————. 1906b. "Rußlands Übergang zum Scheinkonstitutionalismus." *Archiv für Sozialwissenschaft und Sozialpolitik* 23 (1): 165–401.

————. 1913. "Gutachten zur Werturteilsdiskussion im Ausschuß des Vereins für Sozialpolitik." Printed for conference use only. Reprinted in Baumgarten 1964: 102–39.

————. 1917. "Der Sinn der 'Wertfreiheit' der soziologischen und ökonomischen Wissenschaften." *Logos* 7 (1): 40–88.

————. 1920–21. *Gesammelte Aufsätze zur Religionssoziologie.* 3 vols. Tübingen: J. C. B. Mohr (Paul Siebeck).

————. 1923. *Wirtschaftsgeschichte. Abriß der universalen Sozial- und Wirtschaftsgeschichte.* S. Hellman and M. Palyi, eds. Munich: Duncker & Humblot.

————. 1924a. *Gesammelte Aufsätze zur Sozial- und Wirtschaftsgeschichte.* Tübingen: J. C. B. Mohr (Paul Siebeck).

————. 1924b. *Gesammelte Aufsätze zur Soziologie und Sozialpolitik.* Tübingen: J. C. B. Mohr (Paul Siebeck).

————. 1949. *The Methodology of the Social Sciences.* E. A. Shils and H. A. Finch, eds. and trans. New York: The Free Press.

————. 1951. *Gesammelte Aufsätze zur Wissenschaftslehre.* 2nd ed. Tübingen: J. C. B. Mohr (Paul Siebeck).

————. 1952. *Ancient Judaism.* H. H. Gerth and D. Martindale, eds. and trans. Glencoe, Ill.: The Free Press.

————. 1958a [1946]. *From Max Weber.* H. H. Gerth and C. W. Mills, eds. and trans. New York: Oxford University Press.

————. 1958b. *The Protestant Ethic and the Spirit of Capitalism.* T. Parsons, trans. New York: Charles Scribner's Sons.

————. 1958c. *The Religion of India.* H. H. Gerth and D. Martindale, eds. and trans. New York: The Free Press.

————. 1961 [1927]. *General Economic History.* New York: Collier.

————. 1964. *The Religion of China: Confucianism and Taoism.* H. H. Gerth, ed. and trans. New York: Free Press, 1951. Reprint, New York: Macmillan.

————. 1971. *Gesammelte politische Schriften.* 3rd ed. Tübingen: J. C. B. Mohr (Paul Siebeck).

————. 1972 [1921–22]. *Wirtschaft und Gesellschaft.* J. Winckelmann, ed. 5th ed. Tübingen: J. C. B. Mohr (Paul Siebeck).

————. 1973 [1922]. *Gesammelte Aufsätze zur Wissenschaftslehre.* 4th ed. Tübingen: J. C. B. Mohr (Paul Siebeck).

————. 1975. *Roscher and Knies: The Logical Problem of Historical Economics.* Guy Oakes, trans. New York: The Free Press.

————. 1976. *The Agrarian Sociology of Ancient Civilizations.* R. I. Frank, trans. London: New Left Books. Includes a translation of

"Agrarverhältnisse im Altertum," first published in *Handwörterbuch der Staatswissenschaften*, 1909, and later reprinted in the *Gesammelte Aufsätze zur Sozial- und Wirtschaftsgeschichte* (see Weber 1924a).

————. 1977. *Critique of Stammler*. G. Oakes, trans. New York: The Free Press.

————. 1978a. "Anticritical Last Word on *The Spirit of Capitalism*." W. M. Davis, trans. *American Journal of Sociology* 83: 1105–31.

————. 1978b. *Economy and Society*. G. Roth and C. Wittich, eds. Berkeley: University of California Press.

————. 1978c. *Max Weber: Selections in Translation*. W. G. Runciman, ed. E. Mathews, trans. Cambridge, Eng.: Cambridge University Press.

————. 1978d. *Die protestantische Ethik II. Kritiken und Antikritiken*. J. Winckelmann, ed. Gütersloh: Siebenstern.

————. 1984. *Zur Politik im Weltkrieg*. Ser. 1, vol. 15 of *Max Weber-Gesamtausgabe*. W. J. Mommsen in cooperation with G. Hübinger, ed. Tübingen: J. C. B. Mohr (Paul Siebeck).

————. 1988. *Zur Neuordnung Deutschlands*. Ser. 1, vol. 16 of *Max Weber-Gesamtausgabe*. W. J. Mommsen in cooperation with W. Schwentker, ed. Tübingen: J. C. B. Mohr (Paul Siebeck).

————. 1989. *Die Wirtschaftsethik der Weltreligionen. Konfuzianismus und Taoismus*. Ser. 1, vol. 19 of *Max Weber-Gesamtausgabe*. H. Schmidt-Glintzer in cooperation with P. Kolonko, ed. Tübingen: J. C. B. Mohr (Paul Siebeck).

————. 1992. *Wissenschaft als Beruf/Politik als Beruf*. Ser. 1, vol. 17 of *Max Weber-Gesamtausgabe*. W. J. Mommsen and W. Schluchter in cooperation with B. Morgenbrod, eds. Tübingen: J. C. B. Mohr (Paul Siebeck).

————. 1995. *Zur Psychophysik der industriellen Arbeit*. Ser. 1, vol. 11 of *Max Weber-Gesamtausgabe*. W. Schluchter in cooperation with S. Frommer, ed. Tübingen: J. C. B. Mohr (Paul Siebeck).

————. 1996. *Wirtschaft, Staat und Sozialpolitik*. Ser. 1, vol. 8 of *Max Weber-Gesamtausgabe*. W. Schluchter in cooperation with B. Morgenbrod, ed. Tübingen: J. C. B. Mohr (Paul Siebeck).

Wellhausen, Julius. 1902. *Das arabische Reich und sein Sturz*. Berlin: Reimer.

————. 1927 [1897]. *Reste arabischen Heidentums, gesammelt und erläutert*. 2nd ed. Berlin: De Gruyter.

Wellmer, Albrecht. 1986. *Ethik und Dialog. Elemente des moralischen Urteils bei Kant und in der Diskursethik*. Frankfurt: Suhrkamp.

Winckelmann, Johannes. 1963. "Max Webers Dissertation." In König and Winckelmann 1963: 10–12.

————. 1986. *Max Webers hinterlassenes Hauptwerk. Die Wirtschaft und die gesellschaftlichen Ordnungen und Mächte*. Tübingen: J. C. B. Mohr (Paul Siebeck).

Windelband, Wilhelm. 1907. *Lehrbuch der Geschichte der Philosophie.* Tübingen: J. C. B. Mohr (Paul Siebeck).

———. 1914. *Einleitung in die Philosophie.* Tübingen: J. C. B. Mohr (Paul Siebeck).

Wolandt, Gerd. 1987. "Überlegungen zu Kants Erfahrungsbegriff." In Ollig 1987a: 378–95.

Index

In this index an "f" after a number indicates a separate reference on the next page, and an "ff" indicates separate references on the next two pages. A continuous discussion over two or more pages is indicated by a span of page numbers, e.g., "57–59." *Passim* is used for a cluster of references in close but not consecutive sequence.

Library of Congress Cataloging-in-Publication Data

Schluchter, Wolfgang.
Paradoxes of modernity : culture and conduct in the theory of Max
Weber / Wolfgang Schluchter ; translated by Neil Solomon.
p.   cm.
Translation of an unpublished German manuscript.
Includes bibliographical references and index.
ISBN 0-8047-2455-5
1. Weber, Max, 1864–1920.   I. Title.
B3361.Z7S336   1996
301'.092—dc20   95-16141   CIP

Original printing 1996

Last figure below indicates year of this printing:

05   04   03   02   01   00   99   98   97   96